AN INTRODUCTION TO POETRY

106
184
187 - Def of
        Treason
250 - Blake
309 - Frost
320 - Drink to
326 * coy Mistress
353
356 - Rose, Go
    Intamations
        to Immortily

AN
INTRODUCTION TO
POETRY

X. J. KENNEDY

Tufts University

LITTLE, BROWN AND COMPANY

Boston · Toronto

Library of Congress Catalog Card No. 66–14352

Fourth Printing

*Published simultaneously in Canada
by Little, Brown & Company (Canada) Limited*

Printed in the United States of America

ACKNOWLEDGMENTS

*Selections from works by the following poets were made possible by the kind
permission of their respective publishers:*

Auden, W. H. "Musée des Beaux Arts," "The Unknown Citizen" (copyright 1940 by W. H. Auden), and "The Quarry" (copyright 1937, renewed 1964 by W. H. Auden) are reprinted from *The Collected Poetry of W. H. Auden.* 'James Watt' from "Academic Graffiti" (© 1960 by W. H. Auden) is reprinted from *Homage to Clio* by W. H. Auden. These selections are reprinted by permission of Random House, Inc. and Faber and Faber Ltd. (London).

Bacheller, Irving. Fragment of the poem "To a Dead Classmate" from *In Various Moods* by Irving Bacheller (Harper & Brothers, 1910) is reprinted with the permission of Harper & Row, Publishers.

Belloc, Hilaire. "The Hippopotamus" and "Henry King" from *Cautionary Verses* by Hilaire Belloc are reprinted by permission of Alfred A. Knopf, Inc. and A. D. Peters & Co. (London).

Bentley, Edmund Clerihew. 'Sir Christopher Wren' is reprinted from *Biography for Beginners* (or *Clerihews Complete*) by Edmund Clerihew Bentley, by permission of A. P. Watt & Son (London) for Nicholas Bentley and Werner Laurie Ltd.

Berryman, John. "Dream Song No. 14" ('Life, friends, is boring') is reprinted from *77 Dream Songs* by John Berryman, by permission of Farrar, Straus & Giroux, Inc.; copyright © 1964 by John Berryman.

Betjeman, John. "In Westminster Abbey" from John Betjeman's *Collected Poems* (Houghton Mifflin, 1959) is reprinted by permission of John Murray (London).

Bishop, Elizabeth. "The Fish" from *Poems* by Elizabeth Bishop is reprinted by permission of Houghton Mifflin Company.

Bly, Robert. "Inward Conversation," (a translation of "Recueillement" by Baudelaire) is reprinted by permission of Robert Bly.

Brinnin, John Malcolm. "Song for Strangers in Wales" from *The Selected Poems of John Malcolm Brinnin* is reprinted by permission of Little, Brown and Co. — Atlantic Monthly Press; copyright © 1958 by John Malcolm Brinnin. This poem originally appeared in *The New Yorker.*

Brown, T. E. "My Garden" from *The Collected Poems of T. E. Brown* is reprinted with the permission of Macmillan & Company Ltd. and The Macmillan Co. of Canada, Ltd. (St. Martin's Press, Inc.)

Campbell, Roy. "On Some South African Novelists" is reprinted from *Adamaster* by Roy Campbell, published by The Dial Press, Inc. (New York), by permission of Curtis Brown Ltd. (London).

Causley, Charles. "Recruiting Drive" from *Union Street* by Charles Causley is reprinted by permission of Rupert Hart-Davis Limited (London).

Chaucer, Geoffrey. F. N. Robinson's text of "The Complaint of Chaucer to His Purse" is reprinted from *The Poetical Works of Chaucer* (F. N. Robinson, Ed.) by permission of Houghton Mifflin Company.

Crane, Hart. "Voyages (II)" is reprinted from *The Collected Poems of Hart Crane* by permission of Liveright, Publishers, N.Y.; copyright © renewed, 1961 by Liveright Publishing Corp.

Creeley, Robert. "Oh No" (copyright 1959 by Robert Creeley) is reprinted from *For Love* by Robert Creeley, with the permission of Charles Scribner's Sons.

vi

CONTENTS

TO THE STUDENT

What is poetry? Pressed for an answer, Robert Frost made a classic reply: "Poetry is the kind of thing poets write." In all likelihood, Frost was not trying merely to evade the question but to chide his questioner into thinking for himself. A trouble with definitions is that they may arrest thought. Perhaps Frost was afraid that had he said, for instance, "Poetry is a playful, rhythmical composition of words expressing an attitude, designed to surprise and delight, and to arouse an emotional response in its reader or hearer," the questioner would have settled back in his chair, content to have learned an important truth about poetry. He would have learned nothing: or not nearly so much as he might learn by continuing to wonder. And Frost recognized — for he says so in a poem — that there can be truth that sets the logical mind going vainly in a circle in pursuit of it.

ROBERT FROST (1874–1963)

The Secret Sits

> We dance round in a ring and suppose,
> But the Secret sits in the middle and knows.

Though not necessarily a Secret, the nature of poetry does elude simple definitions; in this respect it is rather like jazz. Asked by an auditor at one of his concerts, "What is jazz?" Louis Armstrong replied, "If you don't know now, you never will." If poetry is to be deeply known and powerfully experienced, definitions of its essence will be of little help. We must go to it, willing to see and hear. For this reason, you are asked in reading this book to delay concluding what poetry is and, instead, to examine some poems. At the end of the book, the problem of definition will be taken up again (for those who may wish to pursue it).

Confronted with *An Introduction to Poetry* you may be wondering, "Who needs it?" and you may well be right. You can hardly have avoided meeting poetry before — in nursery rimes and popular songs — and perhaps you already have a friendship, or at least a fair acquaintance, with some of the master poets of the English-speaking world. What this book will offer is an introduction to the *study* of poetry. It will aim toward helping you look at a poem closely and perceptively, toward giving you a wider vocabulary of critical terms with which to express your understanding more accurately. It will suggest ways to form your own judgments of the poetry you read and, along the way, will offer some poems that may be new to you.

A common objection to such a book as this is that poetry ought not to be studied at all. In this view, a poem is usually either (1) a series of beautiful noises to be funneled through one ear and out the other without being allowed to trouble the mind; or (2) an experience so sacrosanct that to analyze it in a classroom is as mechanical and unfeeling as dissecting a hummingbird. To the first view it might be countered that a good poem has something to say to every literate reader — something not necessarily a moral or a message, but something that appeals to one's mind *together with* his feelings. Against the second view, it might be argued that there are perfectly good reasons for which, on occasion, even a hummingbird may be dissected. Seeing its structure, we may derive a more intelligent pleasure from seeing it stay in the air, knowing how and why it does so. But poems are far less perishable than hummingbirds; and luckily we do not need to murder to dissect. The risk of a poem's dying while being analyzed is not nearly so great as the risk of our not deeply seeing it or of misinterpreting it. It is doubtful that any excellent poem has ever vanished from human memory as a result of close reading and analysis. As a rule, poems that vanish are poems no one reads and no one analyzes, for no one sufficiently cares.

Poetry is something to care about. In fact, a persuasion of long standing among mankind is that the hearing of a poem, as well as the making of a poem, is nothing less than a religious act. Poetry, in speech and song, was inseparable from classic Greek drama, which — for playwright, actor, and spectator alike — was a holy-day ceremony. The Greeks' belief that a poet writes a poem only by supernatural assistance is clear from the invocations to the Muse that begin the *Iliad* and the *Odyssey*, and from the opinion of Socrates (in Plato's *Ion*) that a poet has no powers of invention until divinely possessed. Among the ancient Celts, poets were regarded as magicians and priests; and whoever insulted one of them might expect to receive a curse in rime, potent enough to afflict him with boils and to curdle the milk of his cows. Such identifications between the poet and the magician are less common these days; although we know that poetry is involved in the primitive white-magic of children, who bring themselves good luck in a game with the charm "Roll, roll, Tootsie-roll! / Roll the marble in the hole!" and who warn against a hex while jumping a sidewalk: "Step on a crack, / Break your mother's back." But in this age when we pride ourselves that a computer may solve the riddle of all creation as soon as it is programmed, magic may seem to have an infinitesimal place, and so too, poetry. It is dangerous, however, to dismiss what we do not logically understand. To read a poem at all, we have to be willing to offer it responses *besides* a logical understanding. Whether we attribute the effect of a poem to a divine spirit or to the reactions of our glands and cortexes, we have to take the reading of poetry seriously (not solemnly), if only because — as some of the poems in this book may demonstrate — few other efforts can repay us so generously, both in wisdom and in joy.

TO THE INSTRUCTOR

1. AIMS AND ASSUMPTIONS

The publishers tell me that, while textbooks in calculus do not usually inspire controversy, nothing can be more likely to draw fire than an introduction to poetry, a matter about which most of us have our own persuasions. I would expect that, while most of the explanations will be found conventional, the instructor will find some useful occasions for dissent along the way. (Such may be the chapter on bad poetry and the section on archetypes.) I would not usurp the instructor's right to teach poetry in a different fashion but would offer short discussions of its elements, which (if we both agree) students may read by themselves, freeing class time for the study of poems. Written on the assumption that poetry is best approached through close reading, this book is offered as a basic guide, anthology, and handbook of terms for first or second year college courses.

2. PLAN OF THE BOOK

There is one, but it obliges no one to follow it. The instructor who wishes to do so can omit chapters or take them up in a different sequence. The student may meet a few words unknown to him, whose definitions he can find by using the index of terms. Besides the overall order of the book, which will appear from its contents pages, each chapter has an interior order. Poems placed last may be taken to review the chapter as a whole, also some notions introduced in any previous chapters. Some chapters, to make them manageable, have been divided into parts. Most questions and exercises at the end of each part are designed to point the student toward what has just been dealt with. To fit hundreds of poems into such an arrangement is to feel like a man urging a flock of doves to light upon a scaffolding. Some doves have refused to light, or have lit askew. I have tried not to pose them, nor pressure them.

3. SELECTION OF POEMS

Twelve poets are represented with seven or more poems each — Shakespeare, Donne, Herrick, Blake, Wordsworth, Keats, Emily Dickinson, Hopkins, Hardy, Yeats, Stevens, and Frost — for those who may wish to study a poet in more depth than isolated poems permit. Otherwise, the only criteria of selection have been quality (or illustrative inferiority), usefulness for teaching, and the wish to offer variety and some historical distribution. In general, more complicated poems have been chosen over very simple ones; there are few hey-nonny-nonny songs and only a sampling of light verse. The assumption was that difficult poems are sometimes easier and more rewarding to teach than poems about which one may have little to say but "Look at this." Extracts have been admitted four times (besides short illustrative quotations).

4. ANTHOLOGY

With limited space, it has not seemed practicable to try to represent the history of English poetry without giving the student a distorted oversimplification. Nevertheless, the instructor can find in the Anthology poems to illustrate, for instance, neoclassical poetry both elder and contemporary (Dryden and Yvor Winters). To make them easy to find, poems are given alphabetically by names of poets. Many poems will suggest similarities of subject and theme, and can be paired for comparison: Melville's "The Berg" and Hardy's "Convergence of the Twain"; Frost's "Stopping by Woods" and "The Draft Horse"; Whitman's "City Dead-House" and Wilde's "Harlot's House"; Marlowe's "Passionate Shepherd" and Donne's "The Bait"; Shakespeare's "Spring" and "Winter"; the ballad of Edward and W. H. Auden's "The Quarry" — to name a few.

5. TEXTS

Spellings in earlier poems have been modernized (*rose-lipped* for *ros-lip'd*) and made American, unless the sound of a word would be changed. But I have left the *y* in Blake's strange "Tyger" and let Whitman keep his *bloom'd* on the conviction that *bloomed* would no more resemble Whitman than a portrait of him in a starched collar. Untitled poems, except for those that have titles assigned by custom ("The Twa Corbies," "Carrion Comfort"), are identified by all or part of their first lines. Chaucer's "Complaint" is given as edited by F. N. Robinson; the poems of Emily Dickinson, as edited by Thomas H. Johnson.

6. GLOSSES

It would have been simpler to gloss no word a student could find in a desk dictionary, on the grounds that the rummaging of dictionaries is good moral discipline; but it seemed best not to require the student to exchange poem for dictionary as many as ten times in reading a single lyric. Glosses have been provided for whatever seemed likely to stand in the way of pleasure and understanding.

7. ORTHOGRAPHY

The spelling *rime* has been preferred to *rhyme* on the theory that *rime* is easier to distinguish from *rhythm*.

8. ACKNOWLEDGMENTS

I regret that an ethic of anonymity keeps me from thanking by name twelve scholars and critics who, by the publisher's arrangement, subjected a first draft of this book to a cross fire from which it emerged shaken but hardier. My deepest thanks are due to Sylvan Barnet, of Tufts University, for reading the book in both versions and for throwing open his personal storehouse of learning, illustration, definition, and succinct ways of putting things. Many times he has written into the manuscript things I should have said. I have usually included them without change. Despite his kindness, there are probably errors, all of them my own idea. Thanks are owed to Dorothy Mintzlaff Kennedy; Martin B. Friedman, John Oliver Perry, and Celia L. Towne of Tufts University; Bernard Waldrop, Dainis Bisenieks, and J. B. Wolgamot; Donald Hammonds, Warren Stone, Eileen Mason and Judith J. Kehs of Little, Brown and Company, who have been patient and helpful beyond the call of any publisher's duty; and to students at Tufts, Wellesley, the University of North Carolina at Greensboro, and the University of Michigan, who have caused some poems to make better sense to me.

TO THE MUSE

Give me leave, Muse, in plain view to array
Your shift and bodice by the light of day.
I would have brought an epic. Be not vexed
Instead to grace a niggling schoolroom text;
Let down your sanction, help me to oblige
Him who would lead fresh devots to your liege,
And at your altar, grant that in a flash
They, he and I know incense from dead ash.

X. J. K.

AN INTRODUCTION TO POETRY

ONE

ENTRANCES

How do we go about reading a poem? A literal-minded answer might be, "Just let your eye light on a page," but evidently there is more to the process than that, judging by how often an intelligent reader of prose finds poetry evading his understanding. First, let us make explicit a few assumptions. Poetry differs from most prose in that it is to be read slowly, carefully, and attentively. A poem is not to be galloped over like the daily news: at first look, it may only begin to give promise of some future pleasure. Not all poems are difficult, of course, and some can even be understood and enjoyed on first seeing. But all poems yield more if read twice; and the very best poems — after ten, twenty, fifty, or a hundred readings — can still go on yielding.

Approaching a thing written in lines and surrounded with white space, we need not expect it to be a poem just because it is **verse** (any composition in lines of more or less regular rhythm, usually ending in rimes). Here, for instance, is a specimen of verse that few will call poetry:

> Thirty days hath September,
> April, June, and November;
> All the rest have thirty-one
> Excepting February alone,
> To which we twenty-eight assign
> Till leap year makes it twenty-nine.

The functions of a poem are other than to serve as a memory-aid. To a higher degree than "Thirty days hath September," poetry appeals to the mind and arouses feelings. Poetry may be in verse and it may contain facts; but, more important, it makes some memorable imaginative statement that we treasure in itself, even if its verifiable facts are wrong. Coleridge's famous error of placing a star within the horns of the crescent moon, in "The Rime of the Ancient Mariner," does not stop the passage from being good poetry, though it is faulty astronomy.

Some people hold that the **meaning** of a poem consists in every element that can be perceived: the poem's sound, its rhythms, even the pattern it makes on the page. But this book will use the word in a narrower way, and will call *meaning* that element of a poem which "makes sense" and which will submit to **paraphrase.** In paraphrase, we put into our own words what we understand the poem to say, restating all ideas that seem essential, coming out and saying what the poem may only suggest. A paraphrase, of course, is not a poem. It may be longer or shorter, and nearly always is couched in language easier to forget than the original. To compare a poem to its paraphrase is, in fact, an excellent way to see the distance that separates poetry from prose.

A. E. HOUSMAN (1859–1936)

'Loveliest of trees'

> Loveliest of trees, the cherry now
> Is hung with bloom along the bough,
> And stands about the woodland ride
> Wearing white for Eastertide.   4
>
> Now, of my threescore years and ten,
> Twenty will not come again,
> And take from seventy springs a score,
> It only leaves me fifty more.   8
>
> And since to look at things in bloom
> Fifty springs are little room,
> About the woodlands I will go
> To see the cherry hung with snow.   12

A paraphrase of Housman's poem might say something like this: "The cherry is the most beautiful tree of all. Now it is Easter time, the cherry tree in the woods has white blossoms. I am twenty, my life is passing. I expect to live the average life-span of seventy years. I'm going to see only fifty more springs, so I had better go out into the woods and look at the cherry tree." And the paraphrase might include, to catch the deeper implication: "I believe that in his lifetime a man should enjoy all the beauty he can find, because death is The End — period." These dull remarks, roughly faithful to what Housman is saying, are about as far from being poetry as a cherry pit is from being a cherry. Nevertheless, they do have the usefulness of helping whoever makes the paraphrase to understand both the argument of Housman's poem and its basic attitude.

To make a successful paraphrase, weigh each word of the original with care. A classic failure is that of the student (quoted by Matthew Arnold) who took the line in *Macbeth*, "Can'st thou not minister to a mind diseased?" and paraphrased it, "Can you not wait upon the lunatic?" Admittedly, a paraphrase never tells *all* that a poem contains; for when we think we have paraphrased a poem in full, it may be that we have just begun to understand it. This is a fact not easily grasped by anyone who regards a poem as a kind of puzzle or a document written in secret code with a message slyly concealed. The effect of a poem — one's whole mental and emotional response to it — consists in much more than simply a moral or message, or the dictionary definitions of its words. By its sound, rhythms, associations and suggestions, it works upon the reader's unconscious. T. S. Eliot put it well when he said in *The Use of Poetry and the Use of Criticism* that the prose sense of a poem is chiefly useful in keeping the reader's mind "diverted and quiet, while the poem does its work upon him." (Eliot went on to liken the meaning of a poem to the bit of meat a burglar brings along to his job, to throw to the family dog.) But making a paraphrase can have value. It allows us to see a poem in detail and as a whole; to define what the poem states, and also what it suggests. And we may even find that, in taking the words of the poet and replacing them with our own, we receive a pleasurable shock, though at first the poem had no effect on us.

When we tell (as we do in classrooms) what we understand a poem to mean, it is common to proceed as if there existed one ideal interpretation, fixed and not subject to change. This procedure sometimes makes a student feel that his instructor is being arbitrary. No paraphrase will be accepted by every perceptive reader in the world, and it is doubtful that any paraphrase can express what the poet originally had in mind. Even to the poet himself, this meaning may be irretrievable. Asked to explain his difficult *Sordello*, Robert Browning replied that when he had written the poem only God and he knew

3

what it meant; "Now, only God knows." Still, to analyze a poem *as if* we could be certain of its meaning is, in general, a more fruitful approach than to proceed as if no certainty could ever be had. The latter method is likely to end in complete subjectivity: the attitude of the reader who says, "Housman's 'Loveliest of trees' is really about a walk in the snow; it is, because I think it is; how can you prove me wrong?"

All of us bring to our readings of poems certain personal associations, as Housman's 'Loveliest of trees' might convey a particular pleasure to a reader who had climbed cherry trees when he was small. To some extent, these associations are inevitable, even to be welcomed. But we need to distinguish between irrelevant, tangential responses and those the poem calls for. The reader who can't stand 'Loveliest of trees' because cherries remind him of blood, is reading a poem of his own, not Housman's. It is hardly possible for all readers to reduce their differing responses to a poem to an exact conformity, and it would be unthinkable to try. But we all can read the same text and compare our understandings of it. We may then see that some paraphrases tell us more about a poem than others do, being more faithful, more discriminating, and more precise.

How, then, does one set about reading an unfamiliar poem, especially a poem with apparent difficulties? Here are some suggestions:

1. On first look, try reading the poem once straight through, pushing on despite all sorts of obstacles. Do not dwell needlessly on a particular troublesome word, at least not until the poem is seen as a whole; for on reading the poem for a second time, some of its difficulties may be resolved by seeing them as parts of a larger design.

2. On second reading, pick out for particular consideration whatever words, phrases, lines, or passages are still troublesome.

3. Look up in a dictionary unfamiliar words. In a dictionary or encyclopedia look up names of places and persons, foreign words, references to mythology and special areas of learning.

4. Try to paraphrase the poem as a whole or perhaps the more difficult lines.

5. Read the poem aloud. Often the meaning of poetry will be discovered from speaking it or from hearing it spoken. Even if you are no actor, deciding how to speak a poem can be a means of understanding. Some poems, like bells, seem heavy things till heard. Listen while reading the following lines from Alexander Pope's *Dunciad*. Berating the minor poet James Ralph, who had sung praise to a mistress named Cynthia, Pope makes the goddess of Dullness exclaim:

> "Silence, ye wolves! while Ralph to Cynthia howls,
> And makes night hideous — answer him, ye owls!"

When *ye owls* slide together and become *yowls*, poor Ralph's serenade is turned into the nightly outcry of a cat.

We have taken it for granted, thus far, that poetry differs from prose; yet all these strategies — reading straight through and then going back, isolating difficulties, trying to paraphrase, reading aloud, using a dictionary — might be employed in unraveling a complicated piece of prose. Poetry, after all, is similar in most respects; at the very least, it is written in the same language. And like prose, poetry imparts knowledge. It tells us, for instance, something about the season and habitat of cherry trees, and how one can feel toward them. The knowledge to be gained from Housman's poem is knowledge of a different order from that in a textbook of botany. Maybe a poet knows no more of cherry trees than a writer of seed-catalog descriptions, if as much. But Housman's perception of cherry blossoms as snow, with the implication of their brevity, indicates a kind of knowledge that seed catalogs do not ordinarily reveal.

JOHN KEATS (1795–1821)

'Where's the Poet?'

> Where's the Poet? show him! show him,
> Muses nine! that I may know him.
> 'Tis the man who with a man
>   Is an equal, be he King,
> Or poorest of the beggar-clan,   5
>   Or any other wondrous thing
> A man may be 'twixt ape and Plato;
>   'Tis the man who with a bird,
> Wren or Eagle, finds his way to
>   All its instincts; he hath heard   10
> The Lion's roaring, and can tell
>   What his horny throat expresseth,
> And to him the Tiger's yell
>   Comes articulate and presseth
> On his ear like mother-tongue.   15

———

ANONYMOUS (Scottish; traditional folk ballad)

Bonny Barbara Allan

It was in and about the Martinmas time,
　　When the green leaves were afalling,
That Sir John Graeme, in the West Country,
　　Fell in love with Barbara Allan.　　　　　　　　　　　　　　4

He sent his men down through the town,
　　To the place where she was dwelling:
"O haste and come to my master dear,
　　Gin° ye be Barbara Allan."　　　　　　　　　　*if*　　8

O hooly°, hooly rose she up,　　　　　　　　　　*slowly*
　　To the place where he was lying,
And when she drew the curtain by:
　　"Young man, I think you're dying."　　　　　　　　12

"O it's I'm sick, and very, very sick,
　　And 'tis a' for Barbara Allan." —
"O the better for me ye's never be,
　　Tho your heart's blood were aspilling.　　　　　　　16

"O dinna ye mind°, young man," said she,　　　　*don't you*
　　"When ye was in the tavern adrinking,　　　　　*remember*
That ye made the healths° gae round and round,　　*toasts*
　　And slighted Barbara Allan?"　　　　　　　　　　20

He turned his face unto the wall,
　　And death was with him dealing:
"Adieu, adieu, my dear friends all,
　　And be kind to Barbara Allan."　　　　　　　　　　24

And slowly, slowly raise she up,
　　And slowly, slowly left him,
And sighing said she could not stay,
　　Since death of life had reft him.　　　　　　　　　28

She had not gane a mile but twa,
　　When she heard the dead-bell ringing,
And every jow° that the dead-bell geid,　　　　　　*stroke*
　　It cried, "Woe to Barbara Allan!"　　　　　　　　32

"O mother, mother, make my bed!
　　O make it saft and narrow!
Since my love died for me today,
　　I'll die for him tomorrow."　　　　　　　　　　　36

Bonny Barbara Allan. 1. *Martinmas:* Saint Martin's day, November 11.

6

1. In any line does the Scottish dialect cause difficulty? If so, try reading the line aloud.

2. Without ever coming out and explicitly calling Barbara hard-hearted, this ballad reveals that she is. In which stanza, and by what means, is her cruelty demonstrated?

3. At what point does Barbara evidently have a change of heart? Again, how does the poem dramatize this change rather than talk about it?

4. In many American versions of this ballad, noble knight John Graeme becomes an ordinary citizen. The gist of the story is the same, but at the end are these further stanzas, incorporated from a different ballad:

> They buried Willie in the old churchyard
>   And Barbara in the choir;
> And out of his grave grew a red, red rose,
>   And out of hers a briar.
>
> They grew and grew to the steeple top
>   Till they could grow no higher;
> And there they locked in a true love's knot,
>   The red rose round the briar.

Do you think this appendage heightens or weakens the final impact of the story? Can the American ending be defended as an integral part of a new poem? Explain.

5. Paraphrase lines 9, 15–16, 22, 25–28. By putting these lines into prose, what has been lost?

A. E. HOUSMAN (1859–1936)

'In the morning'

In the morning, in the morning,
  In the happy field of hay,
Oh they looked at one another
  By the light of day.   4

In the blue and silver morning
  On the haycock as they lay,
Oh they looked at one another
  And they looked away.   8

1. Who are *they*? How do you know?
2. Sum up their story.
3. In your summary, what did you find necessary to say that Housman leaves unsaid?
4. From your answer to Question 3, what inferences can be drawn about the nature of certain poetry?
5. Read the poem aloud. In what respects is its sound more memorable than that of the same story told in prose?

EMILY DICKINSON (1830–1886)

'It was not Death'

It was not Death, for I stood up,   *a*
And all the Dead, lie down—
It was not Night, for all the Bells
Put out their Tongues, for Noon.

It was not Frost, for on my Flesh   *b*
I felt Siroccos—crawl—
Nor Fire—for just my Marble feet
Could keep a Chancel, cool—

And yet, it tasted, like them all,   *c*
The Figures I have seen
Set orderly, for Burial,
Reminded me, of mine—

As if my life were shaven,   *d*
And fitted to a frame,
And could not breathe without a key,
And 'twas like Midnight, some—

When everything that ticked—has stopped—   *e*
And Space stares all around—
Or Grisly frosts—first Autumn morns,
Repeal the Beating Ground—

But, most, like Chaos—Stopless—cool—   *f*
Without a Chance, or Spar—
Or even a Report of Land—
To justify—Despair.

Questions

1. Here, in paraphrase, are the first three stanzas of this poem:
   a. I was sure I wasn't dead, as I might have thought I was. I knew I was alive from the fact that I found myself standing up, and I know that the dead always lie down. It wasn't night; instead, all the bells were ringing the noon hour.
   b. I didn't feel cold, for I felt warm winds blowing across my skin. I didn't feel hot, for my feet were like marble, so cold that all by themselves they could have cooled the space in back of a church altar.
   c. And yet somehow I felt as if I really were dead, and in the dark, and simultaneously hot and cold. I have seen corpses laid out for burial, and the sight of my own body made me think of them.

So far, how faithful to the meaning of the poem do you find this paraphrase? What, besides coldness, do the words *Frost* and *Marble* (stanza

8

b) also suggest? What other interpretations might be given to any of these lines, or indeed, to the speaker's situation?

2. In other respects besides meaning, how do paraphrase and poem compare?

3. Paraphrase the rest of the poem.

4. In this book, those poems by Emily Dickinson, for which the poet's own manuscripts survive, are given capital letters and punctuation as she wrote them. (This text follows the edition of Thomas H. Johnson.) Can you see any justification for her practice?

Exercise

Write a paraphrase of the following poem or another poem suggested by your instructor. To do so, you may have to look up in a dictionary any words that need defining. Try to include all points you think essential and to explain important suggestions and comparisons.

JOHN DONNE (1572–1631)

'Batter my heart, three-personed God'

Batter my heart, three-personed God, for you
As yet but knock, breathe, shine, and seek to mend;
That I may rise and stand, o'erthrow me, and bend
Your force to break, blow, burn, and make me new.   4
I, like an usurped town to another due,
Labor to admit to you, but oh, to no end;
Reason, your viceroy in me, me should defend,
But is captived, and proves weak or untrue.   8
Yet dearly I love you, and would be lovèd fain
But am betrothed unto your enemy;
Divorce me, untie or break that knot again;
Take me to you, imprison me, for I,   12
Except you enthrall me, never shall be free,
Nor ever chaste, except you ravish me.

TWO

THE PERSON IN THE POEM

1. THE POET'S "I"

"I wandered lonely as a cloud," said William Wordsworth in the opening line of a famous poem. Most of us probably will accept this statement at face value. Evidently it is the poet's way of telling us that he, William Wordsworth, British subject, age thirty-seven, of Dove Cottage, Grasmere, took a walk by himself. And yet, despite the first person pronoun, a moment's thought will reveal that, for all we know, the truth may be otherwise. For a poem is not *necessarily* autobiographical, and the fact that a poet says "I" gives us no guarantee that he is not creating a fictitious person to speak through, as Samuel L. Clemens, in a familiar novel, puts words into the mouth of a first-person speaker named Huckleberry Finn. In poetry, too, some distinction needs to be made between the living writer and his words on the printed page.

Most of us find it easy to tell the difference between an experience in life and an experience conveyed to us in a work of art — unlike a man in the Philippines who, watching a movie of a villain sneaking up on a cowboy hero, pulled out a revolver and peppered the screen. Reading a poem or story about the death of someone, our emotions are different from those we might feel if we were actually present to witness the final agonies. It is even possible to derive a kind of pleasure from such a poem, not because we are hard-hearted or sadistic, but because — as has recently been said — "pleasure is inherent even in the act of understanding." [1] The following poem is not grim, though it speaks of the most horrific event imaginable.

[1] Karl Shapiro and Robert Beum, A *Prosody Handbook* (New York, 1965), p. 100.

ARCHIBALD MACLEISH (b. 1892)

The End of the World

> Quite unexpectedly as Vasserot
> The armless ambidextrian was lighting
> A match between his great and second toe,
> And Ralph the lion was engaged in biting   4
> The neck of Madame Sossman while the drum
> Pointed, and Teeny was about to cough
> In waltz-time swinging Jocko by the thumb —
> Quite unexpectedly the top blew off: 8
>
> And there, there overhead, there, there hung over
> Those thousands of white faces, those dazed eyes,
> There in the starless dark the poise, the hover,
> There with vast wings across the canceled skies,   12
> There in the sudden blackness the black pall
> Of nothing, nothing, nothing — nothing at all.

We can take pleasure from this poem, not because of the nature of its subject, but from other elements: its sound, its entertaining portrait of a circus frozen in a split-second, and the colossal pun in "the top blew off" (*top* being also the "big top" or circus tent, and perhaps the lid of the enormous pot of all creation). The very fact that MacLeish's poem employs rime and lines of uniform length sets it apart from prose and indicates that it is something other than description of experience. Such artifice, as Richard Wilbur has suggested, serves to declare that the poem "is not the world, but a pattern imposed upon the world or found in it." [2]

We need not deny that a poet's experience can contribute to his poem nor that the emotion in the poem can belong to him. Still, to write a good poem one has to do more than live and feel. It seems a pity that, as Randall Jarrell has said of bad poets in *Poetry and the Age*, a cardinal should write verses worse than his youngest choirboy's and that after ten years in the army of the Czar, an aging Ukrainian should still be unable to write a decent poem. But the writing of poetry, more than the keeping of a diary, requires skill and imagination — qualities that travel and breadth of experience do not necessarily give. For much of her mature life, Emily Dickinson seldom strayed far from her father's house and grounds in Amherst, Massachusetts; yet her rimed descriptions of a snake, a bee, and a hum-

[2] "The Genie in the Bottle," in *Mid-Century American Poets*, John Ciardi, ed. (New York, 1950), p. 7.

ming bird contain more poetry than some attempts at epics by men who have traveled as widely as an epic hero.

This is to suggest, then, that poetry is more than a record of personal experience and of emotions felt in ordinary life. But isn't poetry often thought to be "self-expression"? Surely it is, but what a poem expresses is not necessarily a statement of the poet's thoughts and emotions. It is something further: a statement that the poet's thoughts and emotions have led him to make. As W. H. Auden has observed:

> "Why do you want to write poetry?" If the young man answers: "I have important things I want to say," then he is not a poet. If he answers: "I like hanging around words listening to what they say," then maybe he is going to be a poet.[3]

A poem is not a polemic. Neither is it a color-slide photograph of what the poet has seen, projected upon a page. Here is the poem by Wordsworth quoted earlier: it contains an abundance of personal experience, but it also contains something more.

WILLIAM WORDSWORTH (1770–1850)

I Wandered Lonely as a Cloud

> I wandered lonely as a cloud
>   That floats on high o'er vales and hills,
> When all at once I saw a crowd,
>   A host, of golden daffodils,
> Beside the lake, beneath the trees,
> Fluttering and dancing in the breeze.   6
>
> Continuous as the stars that shine
>   And twinkle on the milky way,
> They stretched in never-ending line
>   Along the margin of a bay:
> Ten thousand saw I at a glance,
> Tossing their heads in sprightly dance.   12
>
> The waves beside them danced; but they
>   Out-did the sparkling waves in glee;
> A poet could not but be gay,
>   In such a jocund company;
> I gazed — and gazed — but little thought
> What wealth the show to me had brought: 18

[3] "Squares and Oblongs," in *Poets at Work* (essays by Rudolf Arnheim, W. H. Auden, Karl Shapiro, and Donald A. Stauffer; New York, 1948), p. 171.

For oft, when on my couch I lie
In vacant or in pensive mood,
They flash upon that inward eye
Which is the bliss of solitude;
And then my heart with pleasure fills,
And dances with the daffodils. 24

In a celebrated definition, Wordsworth called poetry "the spon-
taneous overflow of powerful feelings . . . recollected in tranquility."
Although in this poem Wordsworth's emotions may have overflowed
spontaneously, they were captured on paper only by an expense of effort over a period of years. Between the first printing of the poem in
1807 and the version of 1815 given here, Wordsworth made several
deliberate improvements. He changed *dancing* to *golden* in line 4,
Along to *Beside* in line 5, *Ten thousand* to *Fluttering and* in line 6,
laughing to *jocund* in line 16, and added a whole stanza (the second).
In fact, the writing of the poem was unspontaneous enough for
Wordsworth, at a loss for lines 21–22, to take them from his wife
Mary. It is likely that the experience of daffodil-watching was not
entirely his to begin with, but was derived in part from the recollec-
tions his sister Dorothy Wordsworth had set down in her journal of
April 15, 1802, two years earlier:

It was a threatening, misty morning, but mild. We set off after
dinner from Eusemere. Mrs. Clarkson went a short way with us,
but turned back. The wind was furious, and we thought we must
have returned. We first rested in the large boat-house, then under
a furze bush opposite Mr. Clarkson's. Saw the plough going in the
field. The wind seized our breath. The Lake was rough. . . . When
we were in the woods beyond Gowbarrow Park we saw a few daffodils close to the water-side. We fancied that the lake had floated
the seeds ashore, and that the little colony had so sprung up. But
as we went along there were more and yet more; and at last, under
the boughs of the trees, we saw that there was a long belt of them
along the shore, about the breadth of a country turnpike road. I
never saw daffodils so beautiful. They grew among the mossy
stones about and about them; some rested their heads upon these
stones as on a pillow for weariness; and the rest tossed and reeled
and danced, and seemed as if they verily laughed with the wind,
that flew upon them over the Lake; they looked so gay, ever
glancing, ever changing. This wind blew directly over the Lake to
them. There was here and there a little knot, and a few stragglers
a few yards higher up; but they were so few as not to disturb the
simplicity, unity, and life of that one busy highway.

13

Notice that Wordsworth's poem echoes a few of his sister's very words. Weaving poetry out of their mutual memories, Wordsworth has offered the experience as if altogether his own, made himself lonely, and left Dorothy out. The point is not that Wordsworth is a liar or a plagiarist but that, like any other good poet, he has transformed ordinary life into art. A necessary process of interpreting, shaping, and ordering had to intervene between the experience of looking at daffodils and the finished poem.

2. SUBJECT, THEME AND TONE

Poems, like Wordsworth's on daffodils, make statements. But because these are not the direct statements we expect from letters and diary-entries, often what a poet *states* tells us less about his attitudes than does whatever he *implies*. Like any other work of art, a poem is likely to reflect the moral and political views of its craftsman; but it does not have to be a declaration of personal belief. To read poetry, we do not have to know the poet's personal creed. That Andrew Marvell belonged to the religious and political party of the Puritans is a fact that few readers have found necessary to recall in reading "To His Coy Mistress." More often, in reading poetry, we are concerned not with the poet's private commitments but with the attitude he expresses in his poem.

In looking for this attitude, it may be helpful to try to state the **theme** of a poem: that central thought which the poem as a whole conveys. Theme is not the same as "subject matter." For instance:

ANNE STEVENSON (b. 1933)

The Television

> Hug me, mother of noise,
> Find me a hiding place.
> I am afraid of my voice.
> I do not like my face.

In this brief poem the **subject** — the topic dealt with — is television-viewing. The *theme* might be summed up in one of several ways: Television offers the unhappy viewer an illusion of maternal love and comfort. Or perhaps: A person who cannot stand his own company seeks in television a means of escape. We have no certain means of knowing the poet's personal attitude toward television. There is no need for us to know, but it is probably safe to infer that she distrusts it.

WILLIAM SHAKESPEARE (1564–1616)

'Not marble nor the gilded monuments'

> Not marble nor the gilded monuments
> Of princes shall outlive this pow'rful rime;
> But you shall shine more bright in these contènts
> Than unswept stone, besmeared with sluttish time.   4
> When wasteful war shall statues overturn,
> And broils° root out the work of masonry,   *brawls, battles*
> Nor Mars his sword nor war's quick fire shall burn
> The living record of your memory.   8
> 'Gainst death and all oblivious enmity
> Shall you pace forth; your praise shall still find room
> Even in the eyes of all posterity
> That wear this world out to the ending doom.   12
>   So, till the Judgment that° yourself arise,   *when*
>   You live in this, and dwell in lovers' eyes.

The subject of this famous sonnet is poetry or certain poetry. Probably the poem is addressed to a man and is a statement of deep friendship. (*Lovers* in line 14 may, in Elizabethan English, mean "admirers.") Attempts to summarize Shakespeare's works are usually rough indeed, but one way to state his theme here might be: The ability of poetry to last until the end of time makes its mortal subject immortal.

To work out a statement of a poet's theme is useful mainly as a way to help oneself understand a poem. The strategy will work more successfully on some poems than on others, with best results to be had from poems that clearly assert some proposition (as Shakespeare's does). Theme may be centrally important to a poem by Robert Frost, who liked his poems to say something. "Theme alone can steady us down," wrote Frost of himself and his fellow poets: it can prevent poets from "giving way to undirected associations and kicking ourselves from one chance suggestion to another in all directions as of a hot afternoon in the life of a grasshopper." [4]

EXERCISE ONE

Read a few poems from the Anthology and try to state their subjects and their themes. Make each statement of theme a complete sentence.

---

[4] "The Figure a Poem Makes," preface to *Complete Poems* (New York, 1949).

In wild Westerns, when one tough hombre taunts another, it is customary for the second to drawl, "Smile when you say that, pardner" or "Mister, I don't like your tone of voice." In reading a poem, since we can neither see the poet's face nor hear his voice, we have to infer his attitude from other evidence. Mainly, we have to read his words as closely as possible.

Like tone of voice, **tone** in literature is whatever conveys an attitude toward the person being addressed. Like the manner of a person, the manner of a poem may be friendly or belligerent toward its reader; condescending or respectful. And again, like tone of voice, tone in a poem may tell us how the speaker feels about *himself*; for example, his manner may be cocksure or humble. But most of the time when we ask, "What is the tone of a poem?" we mean, "What attitude does the poet take toward his theme or subject?" Is he affectionate, hostile, earnest, playful, sentimental, sarcastic, or what? We may never be able to know, of course, the poet's "true feelings." All we need see are the feelings we are supposed to share while reading the poem on the page. Tone, strictly speaking, is not an attitude but whatever in the poem makes an attitude clear.

In some poems the poet's attitude toward theme or subject, reader, or himself may be so simple that we can describe it in one word. But in other poems his attitudes may be so mingled that it becomes impossible to describe them in a single word without doing the poem an injustice. In "To His Coy Mistress" (pp. 326–327), for instance, does Marvell take a serious or a playful attitude toward the fact that he and his lady are destined to become food for worms? There is no one-word answer. Such a mingled tone may be seen in the following poem. Wife of a governor of the Massachusetts Bay Colony and the earliest American poet of note, Anne Bradstreet saw her first book, *The Tenth Muse Lately Sprung Up in America* (1650), published in England without her consent. She wrote these lines to preface a second edition:

ANNE BRADSTREET (1612?–1672)

The Author to Her Book

> Thou ill-formed offspring of my feeble brain,
> Who after birth did'st by my side remain,
> Till snatched from thence by friends, less wise than true,
> Who thee abroad exposed to public view;
> Made thee in rags, halting, to the press to trudge,   5
> Where errors were not lessened, all may judge.

16

At thy return my blushing was not small,
My rambling brat (in print) should mother call;
I cast thee by as one unfit for light,
Thy visage was so irksome in my sight;   10
Yet being mine own, at length affection would
Thy blemishes amend, if so I could:
I washed thy face, but more defects I saw,
And rubbing off a spot, still made a flaw.
I stretched thy joints to make thee even feet,   15
Yet still thou run'st more hobbling than is meet;
In better dress to trim thee was my mind,
But nought save homespun cloth in the house I find.
In this array, 'mongst vulgars may'st thou roam;
In critics' hands beware thou dost not come;   20
And take thy way where yet thou are not known.
If for thy Father asked, say thou had'st none;
And for thy Mother, she alas is poor,
Which caused her thus to send thee out of door.

In the author's comparison of her book to an illegitimate ragamuffin, we may be struck by the details of scrubbing and dressing a child: real details that might well occur to a mother who had scrubbed and dressed many. As she might feel toward such a child, so she feels toward her book. She starts by deploring it but, as the poem goes on, cannot refrain from a bit of affection. Humor enters (as in the pun in line 15, *feet* suggesting metrical feet), and *homespun cloth* suggests something both homely and serviceable. By the end of the poem, Mrs. Bradstreet seems to regard her book-child with tender sympathy, amusement, and a certain indulgent awareness of all its faults.

Poems like this, that have humor, are sometimes confounded with so-called **light verse**. This term seems to imply an inferiority to what we call poetry, and a lack of what Matthew Arnold expected of the greatest poets: "high seriousness." A distinguished anthologist once put Auden's "The Unknown Citizen" (p. 32) and Fearing's "Dirge" (p. 307) into the light verse section of his anthology, where in their depth and complexity they loomed over the trivia with which he surrounded them. And what of T. S. Eliot's excellent "The Love Song of J. Alfred Prufrock" (pp. 302–306)? In his attitudes toward his redemption-seeking hero, who wades with rolled-up trousers so as not to get them wet, Eliot is seriously humorous. To read his poem with understanding is to sense its mingling of several — even conflicting — attitudes. Simultaneously, a poet may be merry and in earnest.

17

ANONYMOUS (Irish popular ballad; eighteenth century)

Johnny, I Hardly Knew Ye

While going the road to sweet Athy,
  Hurroo! Hurroo!
While going the road to sweet Athy,
  Hurroo! Hurroo!
While going the road to sweet Athy,   5
A stick in my hand and a drop in my eye,
A doleful damsel I heard cry:
  "Och, Johnny, I hardly knew ye!"

(*Chorus:*)

"With drums and guns, and guns and drums
  The enemy near slew ye;   10
My darling dear, you look so queer,
  Och, Johnny, I hardly knew ye!

"Where are your eyes that looked so mild?
  Hurroo! Hurroo!
Where are your eyes that looked so mild   15
When my poor heart you first beguiled?
Why did you run from me and the child?
  Och, Johnny, I hardly knew ye!

"Where are the legs with which you run?
  Hurroo! Hurroo!   20
Where are the legs with which you run
When you went off to carry a gun? —
Indeed your dancing days are done!
  Och, Johnny, I hardly knew ye!

"It grieved my heart to see you sail,   25
  Hurroo! Hurroo!
It grieved my heart to see you sail
Though from my heart you took leg bail°   *escaped from*
Like a cod you're doubled up head and tail,   *custody*
  Och, Johnny, I hardly knew ye!   30

"You haven't an arm and you haven't a leg,
  Hurroo! Hurroo!
You haven't an arm and you haven't a leg,
You're an eyeless, noseless, chickenless egg,
You'll have to be put in a bowl to beg,   35
  Och, Johnny, I hardly knew ye!

"It's happy I am for to see you home,
  Hurroo! Hurroo!

18

It's happy I am for to see you home,
All from the island of Sulloon,   40
So low in flesh, so high in bone,
 Och, Johnny, I hardly knew ye!

"But sad as it is to see you so,
 Hurroo! Hurroo!
But sad as it is to see you so,   45
And to think of you now as an object of woe,
Your Peggy'll still keep ye on as her beau —
 Och, Johnny, I hardly knew ye!"

Johnny, I Hardly Knew Ye. A forerunner of the song "When Johnny Comes Marching Home Again (Hurrah! Hurrah!)." Each stanza, like the first, repeats the opening two lines and concludes with the chorus.

QUESTIONS

 1. What attitude or attitudes does Peggy take toward Johnny?
 2. What does the poem lead us to feel toward her?
 3. What does the poet gain by placing Peggy's words within a dramatic frame (by having her lament overheard by another speaker)?
 4. Taking the poem as a whole, how would you describe its tone?
 5. Would you call this light verse or poetry? Explain.

TED HUGHES (b. 1930)

Secretary

If I should touch her she would shriek and weeping
Crawl off to nurse the terrible wound: all
Day like a starling under the bellies of bulls
She hurries among men, ducking, peeping,   4

Off in a whirl at the first move of a horn.
At dusk she scuttles down the gauntlet of lust
Like a clockwork mouse. Safe home at last
She mends her socks with holes, shirts that are torn   8

For father and brother, and a delicate supper cooks:
Goes to bed early, shuts out with the light
Her thirty years, and lies with buttocks tight,
Hiding her lovely eyes until day break.   12

QUESTIONS

 1. Comment on the phrase in line 2, *the terrible wound*. Would the speaker himself regard the offense as "terrible"?
 2. What traits has the secretary in common with *a starling* (line 3) and *a clockwork mouse* (7)?
 3. Does the poet express one attitude toward his subject or is the tone of his poem a mingling of more than one? Explain, referring to particulars in the poem.

19

WALT WHITMAN (1819–1892)

To a Locomotive in Winter

Thee for my recitative,
Thee in the driving storm even as now, the snow, the winter-
day declining,
Thee in thy panoply°, thy measur'd dual throbbing   *suit*
and thy beat convulsive,   *of armor*
Thy black cylindric body, golden brass and silvery steel,
Thy ponderous side-bars, parallel and connecting rods, gyrat-   5
ing, shuttling at thy sides,
Thy metrical, now swelling pant and roar, now tapering in
the distance,
Thy great protruding head-light fix'd in front,
Thy long, pale, floating vapor-pennants, tinged with delicate
purple,
The dense and murky clouds out-belching from thy smoke-
stack,
Thy knitted frame, thy springs and valves, the tremulous   10
twinkle of thy wheels,
Thy train of cars behind, obedient, merrily following,
Through gale or calm, now swift, now slack, yet steadily
careering;
Type of the modern — emblem of motion and power —
pulse of the continent,
For once come serve the Muse and merge in verse, even as
here I see thee,
With storm and buffeting gusts of wind and falling snow,   15
By day thy warning ringing bell to sound its notes,
By night thy silent signal lamps to swing.

Fierce-throated beauty!
Roll through my chant with all thy lawless music, thy swing-
ing lamps at night,
Thy madly-whistled laughter, echoing, rumbling like an   20
earthquake, rousing all,
Law of thyself complete, thine own track firmly holding,
(No sweetness debonair of tearful harp or glib piano thine,)
Thy trills of shrieks by rocks and hills return'd,
Launch'd o'er the prairies wide, across the lakes,
To the free skies unpent and glad and strong.   25

20

EMILY DICKINSON (1830–1886)

'I like to see it lap the Miles'

> I like to see it lap the Miles—
> And lick the Valleys up—
> And stop to feed itself at Tanks—
> And then—prodigious step
>
> Around a Pile of Mountains—   5
> And supercilious peer
> In Shanties—by the sides of Roads—
> And then a Quarry pare
>
> To fit its Ribs
> And crawl between   10
> Complaining all the while
> In horrid—hooting stanza—
> Then chase itself down Hill—
>
> And neigh like Boanerges—
> Then—punctual as a Star   15
> Stop—docile and omnipotent
> At its own stable door—

QUESTIONS

1. What differences in tone do you find between these two poems? Point out in each poem whatever contributes to these differences.

2. *Boanerges* in Emily Dickinson's last stanza means "sons of thunder," a name given by Christ to the disciples John and James (see Mark 3:17). How far should the reader work out the particulars of this comparison? Does it make the tone of the poem serious?

3. In Whitman's opening line, what is a *recitative*? What other specialized terms from the vocabulary of music and poetry does each poem contain? How do they help underscore Whitman's theme?

4. Poets and songwriters probably have regarded the locomotive with more affection than they have shown most other machines. Can you think of any other poems or songs for example? Why do you suppose this to be?

5. What do these two poems tell you about locomotives that you would not be likely to find in a technical book on railroading?

6. Discuss: Are the subjects of both poems identical?

21

3. LYRIC AND DIDACTIC POETRY

In ancient Greece a lyric, as its name suggests, was a poem sung to the music of a lyre. Today, **lyric** denotes a short poem expressing the thoughts, feelings, and attitudes of a single speaker: "The Television" and 'Not marble nor the gilded monuments.' Partly because we now prefer our narratives in prose (short stories and novels having virtually replaced the narrative poem), lyrics at present are more plentiful than any other kind of poetry in English. Although most lyrics of the past two centuries have been read on printed pages, some lyrics still are sung. If you know "Auld Lang Syne," you know one such poem.

A lyric is often written in the first person ("I wandered lonely as a cloud . . ."), but not always. It may be a description of, say, a landscape, in which the poet does not mention himself at all; for instance, Hopkins' "Inversnaid" (p. 160). Though a lyric may relate an incident or episode, we tend to think of it as a reflective poem in which little physical action takes place, unlike a narrative poem such as "The Rime of the Ancient Mariner." Lyric poetry includes such varieties as the **ode**, usually longer than other lyrics, and characterized by a tone of seriousness and elevation (Wordsworth's "Ode: Intimations of Immortality," Shelley's "Ode to the West Wind," Keats's "Ode to a Nightingale," and "Ode on a Grecian Urn"); and the **elegy**, whose tone is melancholy or sadly contemplative, often on the subject of a death (Milton's "Lycidas" and Whitman's "When Lilacs Last in the Dooryard Bloom'd").

In **didactic poetry** — poetry apparently written to teach or convey a message — themes are more evident. In a lyric, the speaker may express sadness; in a didactic poem, he may explain that sadness is inherent in life. Usually a didactic poem clearly states or implies a moral, or sets forth a critical comment on society. The name can also refer to a long poem that imparts a body of knowledge: Lucretius' *On the Nature of Things*, Ovid's *Art of Love*, Karl Shapiro's *Essay on Rime*. Such poetry was favored especially by classical Latin poets and by English poets of the eighteenth century. In *The Fleece* (1757), John Dyer celebrated the British woolen industry and included practical advice on raising sheep:

> In cold stiff soils the bleaters oft complain
> Of gouty ails, by shepherds termed the halt:
> Those let the neighboring fold or ready crook
> Detain, and pour into their cloven feet
> Corrosive drugs, deep-searching arsenic,
> Dry alum, verdegris, or vitriol keen.

22

But if the doubtful mischief scarce appears,
'Twill serve to shift them to a dryer turf,
And salt again: the utility of salt
Teach thy slow swains; redundant humors cold
Are the diseases of the bleating kind.

One might agree with Dr. Johnson's comment on Dyer's effort: "The subject, Sir, cannot be made poetical." But it may be argued that didactic poetry — to quote a recent view — "is not intrinsically any less poetic because of its subject-matter than lines about a rose fluttering in the breeze are intrinsically more poetic because of their subject-matter." [5] John Milton also described the sick sheep in "Lycidas," a poem few readers have thought unpoetic:

The hungry sheep look up, and are not fed,
But, swoll'n with wind and the rank mist they draw,
Rot inwardly, and foul contagion spread . . .

What makes Milton's lines better poetry than Dyer's is, among other things, a difference in tone. Sick sheep to Dyer mean the loss of a few shillings and pence; to Milton, whose sheep stand for English Christendom, they mean a moral catastrophe.

A tone of detached amusement, withering contempt, and implied superiority is characteristic of **satiric poetry,** a kind of didactic poetry. In a satiric poem, the poet ridicules some person or persons, or some aspect of human behavior, examining his victim by the light of his own principles and implying that the reader ought to share his view. (For an example see "A Paraphrase from the French," p. 301.) Subspecies are the **epistle,** a poem written as a letter addressed to someone (Pope's "Epistle to Dr. Arbuthnot"), and the **mock epic** (Dryden's "MacFlecknoe," Pope's "The Rape of the Lock"). A mock epic, though it imitates the exalted tone and the conventions of a classical epic poem, takes to task not epics but some person or some kind of human conduct, for failing to be worthy of the epic style.

As Wordsworth demonstrated in "I Wandered Lonely as a Cloud," a poet can write a lyric stating more than his own personal experience. It is sometimes said that a lyric expresses the thoughts of the poet himself; however, such a view is of little help in distinguishing lyric poetry from didactic, since both kinds of poetry can express a poet's thoughts. And reading either kind, we may expect to hear a voice not necessarily the poet's own.

[5] Sylvan Barnet, Morton Berman, and William Burto, A *Dictionary of Literary Terms* (Boston, 1960).

AMBROSE BIERCE (1842–1914?)

Art

One day a wag — what would the wretch be at? —
Shifted a letter of the cipher RAT,
And said it was a god's name! Straight arose
Fantastic priests and postulants (with shows,
And mysteries, and mummeries, and hymns,   5
And disputations dire that lamed their limbs)
To serve his temple and maintain the fires,
Expound the law, manipulate the wires.
Amazed, the populace the rites attend,
Believe whate'er they cannot comprehend,   10
And, inly edified to learn that two
Half-hairs joined so and so (as Art can do)
Have sweeter values and a grace more fit
Than Nature's hairs that never have been split,
Bring cates° and wines for sacrificial feasts,   *delicacies* 15
And sell their garments to support the priests.

QUESTIONS

1. What is the tone of this poem? By what various means is it communicated?
2. What is Bierce against? Is it art?

RICHARD LOVELACE (1618–1658)

To Lucasta

ON GOING TO THE WARS

Tell me not, Sweet, I am unkind
   That from the nunnery
Of thy chaste breast and quiet mind,
   To war and arms I fly.   4

True, a new mistress now I chase,
   The first foe in the field;
And with a stronger faith embrace
   A sword, a horse, a shield.   8

Yet this inconstancy is such
   As you too shall adore;
I could not love thee, Dear, so much,
   Loved I not Honor more.   12

24

WILFRED OWEN (1893–1918)

Greater Love

> Red lips are not so red
> As the stained stones kissed by the English dead.
> Kindness of wooed and wooer
> Seems shame to their love pure.
> O Love, your eyes lose lure
> When I behold eyes blinded in my stead!   6
>
> Your slender attitude
> Trembles not exquisite like limbs knife-skewed,
> Rolling and rolling there
> Where God seems not to care;
> Till the fierce love they bear
> Cramps them in death's extreme decrepitude.   12
>
> Your voice sings not so soft, —
> Though even as wind murmuring through raftered loft, —
> Your dear voice is not dear,
> Gentle, and evening clear,
> As theirs whom none now hear,
> Now earth has stopped their piteous mouths that   18
>   coughed.
>
> Heart, you were never hot,
> Nor large, nor full like hearts made great with shot;
> And though your hand be pale,
> Paler are all which trail
> Your cross through flame and hail:
> Weep, you may weep, for you may touch them not.   24

QUESTIONS

1. To whom is Owen's poem addressed? (If your answer is "to a lady," reread the last stanza. If still in doubt, see John 20:17.)

2. What is Lovelace's theme? What is Owen's?

3. What is the tone of Lovelace's poem? What does his punning (on *embrace*, perhaps also on *arms*) contribute to it?

4. What is the tone of Owen's poem? How does he make it clear?

5. Does Owen mention aspects of war that would have been unknown in Lovelace's time? What does Owen observe that Lovelace chooses to omit?

6. How well can we apply to each of these poems the labels *lyric* or *didactic*?

25

4. MASK AND IRONY

In classic Greek drama, actors wore *personae*: the Latin term for masks through which sound came. From this term is derived our word *person*. In the works of great playwrights, whether classical or modern, those speaking masks we call the persons of a drama are such persuasive imitations of life that we may forget we are watching a performance in a theater. We do not think, when Romeo plights his tragic love or when King Oedipus at last perceives the trick of the Fates against him, that what we hear is the voice of one man representing a fictive man, speaking words that still another man made.

And so, reading many a poem, we overhear words spoken to us through a **mask** (or fictitious person); and if the poem succeeds, we accept a convincing imitation of life. The mask and the poet's face may not be similar: a young male poet may write a lyric spoken by an elderly female. William Blake was white but he wrote a poem uttered by a black child; he was an eighteenth-century engraver, but he wrote a poem spoken by the ancient magician Merlin. The speaker in a poem need not even be human: there are good poems spoken by clouds, pebbles, and cats. An evident mask-making occurs in a **dramatic monologue**: a poem cast as a speech by a single person, made at a decisive or revealing moment, addressed to some other character, who does not speak. Robert Browning, who perfected the form, was fond of putting words into the mouths of characters only remotely like himself (see "My Last Duchess," pp. 289–290); Browning himself, from all reports, was more ingratiating.

We need not expect that in every poem the poet will wear a mask unlike his face. When Wordsworth tells us, "I wandered lonely as a cloud/ . . . When all at once I saw a crowd," we may recognize some distinction between the voice of the living poet and the voice of the riming speaker. Still, the feelings expressed in the poem might well closely resemble those actually felt by Wordsworth himself. All poets, we might suppose, choose masks that, to some extent, fit their features. T. S. Eliot was not J. Alfred Prufrock, but he may have felt similar uncertainties. William Butler Yeats, whose poems are uttered through many masks, contrived characters to express conflicting aspects of his own personality: contemplative man versus man of action, priest versus reprobate. Setting his masks to debate with one another in a poem, Yeats dramatized his quarrel with himself. "Crazy Jane Talks with the Bishop" (p. 377) may be an instance. Neither an aging slut nor a man of the cloth, Yeats was attracted to both "bodily lowliness" and "heavenly mansion."

26

There are moments when a poet is content to let himself and the person in the poem be identified. In declaring, "I wandered lonely," Wordsworth makes no effort to detach himself. There are other moments when the effect of a poem depends upon a discrepancy between the mask a poet speaks through and his own view of things. Evidently Robert Browning wishes us to see that, unlike his speaker the Duke, he would not put away lovely young duchesses.

To see such a discrepancy between the poet and his mask is to be aware of **irony.** In itself, irony is neither a tone nor an attitude, but a manner of speaking that implies a discrepancy. Often, a writer who speaks ironically holds one attitude, while stating another (but, as we will see, the term *irony* has various uses). If the mask says one thing and we sense that the writer is in fact saying something else, the writer is using an **ironic point of view.** No finer illustration exists in English than Jonathan Swift's essay "A Modest Proposal," in which Swift creates a very earnest, humorless citizen who sets forth a reasonable plan to aid the Irish poor. The plan is so monstrous no sane reader can assent to it: the poor are to sell their children as meat for the tables of their landlords. From behind his falseface, Swift — whose true voice is meant to be heard — recommends not cannibalism but love and Christian charity. An ironic point of view need not imply bitter humor, as it does in Swift's essay. Here is a poem in which an innocent child speaks. Behind the mask of the child, though, we sense a compassionate and knowing poet.

ROBERT HERRICK (1591–1674)

Another Grace for a Child

> Here a little child I stand,
> Heaving up my either hand;
> Cold as paddocks° though they be,   *toads*
> Here I lift them up to Thee
> For a benison° to fall   *benediction*
> On our meat, and on us all. *Amen.*

A poem is often made complicated and more interesting by the poet's use of another kind of irony. **Verbal irony** occurs whenever words say one thing but mean another, most commonly the contrary: "Oh, I just *love* to write term papers on a Saturday night!" Verbal irony is easily confused with **sarcasm,** a peculiar sort of verbal irony, bitter or mocking in tone, designed to hurt someone: "Oh, she's the most lovable person in the world!" (This statement, if spoken, would be given exaggerated emphasis by tone of voice.) A famous instance of sarcasm is Mark Antony's line in his oration over the body of slain Julius Caesar: "Brutus is an honorable man." Antony repeats this line until the enraged populace begins shouting exactly what he means to call Brutus and the other conspirators: traitors, villains, murderers. But verbal irony is gentler. We had best be alert for it on the printed page, for if we miss it, our interpretations of a poem will go wild.

J. V. CUNNINGHAM (b. 1911)

On a Nice Book

Your book affords
The peace of art,
Within whose boards
The passive heart   4

Impassive sleeps,
And like pressed flowers,
Though scentless, keeps
The scented hours.   8

What is the tone of this poem? Warm gratitude? A closer look is necessary. First the title, in which we are struck by a verbal irony. Surely *nice* is a dull and colorless adjective to be so prominently displayed. It suggests what some mother means when she wishes her son would settle down and marry a "nice girl" (some unattractive but harmless sort, very good at darning socks, walking dogs, and making apple pie just like grandma's). And is the peacefully sleeping heart that of the book's author or its reader? We are not sure. We are sure, however, that synonyms for *passive* and *impassive* are "submissive" and "unfeeling"; and we do know that this is not the way one responds to a good book, by which one is likely to be engrossed and stimulated. If it is the reader's heart, the idea of keeping it asleep in a book suggests the discouraging prospect that the book will make of it an object of sentiment, like an old valentine or a lock of baby's hair. Or if the passive heart is the author's, then a paraphrase of what Cunningham is saying in the last three lines might be: "Your heart, as seen in your poems, is no live and beating thing; it is old-fashioned and dried up. It has lost any perfume it once had." In either reading, it seems likely that the "nice" book is inoffensive, mawkish, and full of sentimental conventions.

Another illustration of verbal irony may be useful:

ROBERT CREELEY (b. 1926)

Oh No

> If you wander far enough
> you will come to it
> and when you get there
> they will give you a place to sit   4
>
> for yourself only, in a nice chair,
> and all your friends will be there
> with smiles on their faces
> and they will likewise all have places.   8

The title of Creeley's poem helps point out that between the speaker's words and his attitude lie deep differences. In line 2, what is *it*? Old age? The wandering suggests a conventional metaphor: the journey of life. Is *it* a literal rest home for "senior citizens," or perhaps some naïve popular concept of Heaven (such as we meet in comic strips: harps, angels with hoops for haloes, etc.) in which the saved all sit around in a ring, smugly congratulating one another? We cannot be sure, but the speaker's attitude toward this final sitting-place is definite. It is a place for the selfish, as we infer from the phrase *for yourself only*. And *smiles on their faces* may hint that the smiles are unchanging and forced. There is a difference between saying "They had smiles on their faces" and "They smiled": the latter suggests that the smiles came from within. Throughout the poem, the speaker is talking down to us. His word *nice*, like Cunningham's, is to be regarded with distrust. If we see through him, as Creeley implies that we can do, we realize that, while pretending to be sweet-talking us into a seat, he is actually revealing the horror of a little Hell. And the title is the poet's reaction to it (or the speaker's unironic, straightforward one): "Oh no! Not *that!*"

Dramatic irony usually refers to a situation in a play wherein a character, whose knowledge is limited, says, does, or encounters something of greater significance than he knows. We, the spectators, realize the meaning of this speech or action, for the playwright has afforded us superior knowledge. In Sophocles' *King Oedipus*, when Oedipus vows to punish whoever has brought down a plague upon the city of Thebes, we know — as he does not — that the man he would punish is himself. (Some critics speak of **tragic irony** instead

29

of dramatic irony.) Superior knowledge can be enjoyed, not only by spectators in a theater, but by readers of poetry as well. In *Paradise Lost*, we know in advance that Adam will fall into temptation, and we recognize his blithe overconfidence when he neglects a warning. The situation of Oedipus contains also **cosmic irony**, or **irony of fate**: some Fate with a grim sense of humor seems cruelly to trick a man. Cosmic irony clearly exists in poems in which Fate or the Fates are personified and seen as hostile, as in Thomas Hardy's "The Convergence of the Twain" (pp. 312–313); and it may be said to occur too in such a poem as Robinson's "Richard Cory" (p. 336) or in Mac-Leish's "The End of the World" (p. 11). Evidently it is a twist of Fate for the most envied man in town to kill himself and another twist of Fate for spectators at a circus to find themselves suddenly beholding a greater and more horrific show than they had paid for.

To sum up: the effect of irony depends upon the reader's noticing some incongruity or discrepancy between two things. In *verbal irony*, there is a contrast between the speaker's words and his meaning; in an *ironic point of view*, between the writer's attitudes and those spoken by a fictitious character; in *dramatic irony*, between the limited knowledge of a character and the fuller knowledge of the reader or spectator; in *cosmic irony*, between a character's aspirations and the treatment he receives at the hands of Fate. Although in the work of an inept poet, irony can sometimes be crude and obvious, it is invaluable to a poet of more complicated mind, who can imagine more than one perspective.

EXERCISE TWO

Point out the kinds of irony that occur in the following poem.

THOMAS HARDY (1840–1928)

The Workbox

> "See, here's the workbox, little wife,
> That I made of polished oak."
> He was a joiner°, of village life;   *carpenter*
> She came of borough folk.   4
>
> He holds the present up to her
> As with a smile she nears
> And answers to the profferer,
> " 'Twill last all my sewing years!"   8

30

"I warrant it will. And longer too.
    'Tis a scantling that I got
Off poor John Wayward's coffin, who
    Died of they knew not what.   12

"The shingled pattern that seems to cease
    Against your box's rim
Continues right on in the piece
    That's underground with him.   16

"And while I worked it made me think
    Of timber's varied doom:
One inch where people eat and drink,
    The next inch in a tomb.   20

"But why do you look so white, my dear,
    And turn aside your face?
You knew not that good lad, I fear,
    Though he came from your native place?"   24

"How could I know that good young man,
    Though he came from my native town,
When he must have left far earlier than
    I was a woman grown?"   28

"Ah, no. I should have understood!
    It shocked you that I gave
To you one end of a piece of wood
    Whose other is in a grave?"   32

"Don't, dear, despise my intellect,
    Mere accidental things
Of that sort never have effect
    On my imaginings."   36

Yet still her lips were limp and wan,
    Her face still held aside,
As if she had known not only John,
    But known of what he died.   40

———

W. H. AUDEN (b. 1907)

The Unknown Citizen

(TO JS/07/M/378

THIS MARBLE MONUMENT

IS ERECTED BY THE STATE)

He was found by the Bureau of Statistics to be
One against whom there was no official complaint,
And all the reports on his conduct agree
That, in the modern sense of an old-fashioned word, he was
    a saint,
For in everything he did he served the Greater Community.   5
Except for the War till the day he retired
He worked in a factory and never got fired,
But satisfied his employers, Fudge Motors Inc.
Yet he wasn't a scab or odd in his views,
For his Union reports that he paid his dues,   10
(Our report on his Union shows it was sound)
And our Social Psychology workers found
That he was popular with his mates and liked a drink.
The Press are convinced that he bought a paper every day
And that his reactions to advertisements were normal in   15
    every way.
Policies taken out in his name prove that he was fully in-
    sured,
And his Health-card shows he was once in hospital but left
    it cured.
Both Producers Research and High-Grade Living declare
He was fully sensible to the advantages of the Installment
    Plan
And had everything necessary to the Modern Man,   20
A phonograph, a radio, a car and a frigidaire.
Our researchers into Public Opinion are content
That he held the proper opinions for the time of year;
When there was peace, he was for peace; when there was
    war, he went.
He was married and added five children to the population,   25
Which our Eugenist says was the right number for a parent
    of his generation,
And our teachers report that he never interfered with their
    education.
Was he free? Was he happy? The question is absurd:
Had anything been wrong, we should certainly have heard.

32

1. Read the three-line epitaph at the beginning of the poem as carefully as you read what follows. How does the epitaph help establish the mask through which the rest of the poem is spoken?
2. Who is speaking?
3. What discrepancies do you find between the speaker's attitude toward his subject and that of the poet himself? By what is the poet's attitude made clear?
4. What does the word *unknown* mean in the name Auden echoes, The Unknown Soldier? What does it mean in the title of this poem?
5. What tendencies in present-day society does Auden satirize?
6. How would you expect the speaker to define a "Modern Man," if to such a man, a phonograph, a radio, a car, and a refrigerator are "everything necessary"?

JOHN BERRYMAN (b. 1914)

'Life, friends, is boring'

Life, friends, is boring. We must not say so.
After all, the sky flashes, the great sea yearns,
we ourselves flash and yearn,
and moreover my mother told me as a boy
(repeatedly) "Ever to confess you're bored
means you have no   6

Inner Resources." I conclude now I have no
inner resources, because I am heavy bored.
Peoples bore me,
literature bores me, especially great literature,
Henry bores me, with his plights & gripes
as bad as achilles,   12

who loves people and valiant art, which bores me.
And the tranquil hills, & gin, look like a drag
and somehow a dog
has taken itself & its tail considerably away
into mountains or sea or sky, leaving
behind: me, wag.   18

QUESTIONS

1. Henry (line 11) is the central figure of Berryman's *77 Dream Songs.* Achilles (12), Greek hero of the Trojan war, was portrayed by Shakespeare as a sulking malcontent. Is a comparison of Henry, a rather ordinary American citizen, to Achilles likely to result in a heightening of Henry's importance or in a sense of ironic discrepancy? Discuss.
2. What is confused or self-contradictory in the precept "Ever to confess you're bored means you have no Inner Resources"?

3. What could the poet be trying to indicate by capitalizing *Inner Resources* in line 7 but not in line 8? By writing *achilles* with a small letter?

4. In line 14, what discrepancy do you find between the phrases *the tranquil hills* and *a drag*?

5. In the last line, what double meaning is there in the word *wag*?

6. True or false? "In comparing 'ourselves' to the sky and to the 'great sea,' the speaker takes the attitude that he and his readers have dignity and grandeur, their emotions being as powerful as lightningbolts and tides." Why do you find this paraphrase consistent with the tone of the poem, or inconsistent?

7. Are the speaker's attitudes toward life, his readers, and himself completely negative? Or is there any reason to infer otherwise?

EXERCISE THREE

In each of the following poems, consider:

1. What is the poet's subject?
2. What is his theme?
3. Does he speak through the mask of any particular character?
4. What is the speaker's attitude toward his subject?
5. Whom does the speaker address? What attitude does he take toward this hearer?
6. Is there any ironic discrepancy between attitudes expressed by the speaker and those we are supposed to feel?
7. Is this poem a lyric? A didactic poem? Or does neither label apply?

WILLIAM BLAKE (1757–1827)

The Chimney Sweeper

When my mother died I was very young,
And my father sold me while yet my tongue
Could scarcely cry " 'weep! 'weep! 'weep! 'weep!"
So your chimneys I sweep, and in soot I sleep.   4

There's little Tom Dacre, who cried when his head,
That curled like a lamb's back, was shaved: so I said
"Hush, Tom! never mind it, for when your head's bare
You know that the soot cannot spoil your white hair."   8

And so he was quiet, and that very night,
As Tom was a-sleeping, he had such a sight!
That thousands of sweepers, Dick, Joe, Ned, and Jack,
Were all of them locked up in coffins of black.   12

And by came an Angel who had a bright key,
And he opened the coffins and set them all free;
Then down a green plain leaping, laughing, they run,
And wash in a river, and shine in the sun.   16

Then naked and white, all their bags left behind,
They rise upon clouds and sport in the wind;
And the Angel told Tom, if he'd be a good boy,
He'd have God for his father, and never want joy.   20

And so Tom awoke; and we rose in the dark,
And got with our bags and our brushes to work.
Though the morning was cold, Tom was happy and warm;
So if all do their duty they need not fear harm.   24

JOHN MILTON (1608–1674)

On the Late Massacre in Piemont

Avenge, O Lord, thy slaughtered saints, whose bones
   Lie scattered on the Alpine mountains cold;
   Even them who kept thy truth so pure of old,
   When all our fathers worshiped stocks and stones,   4
Forget not: in thy book record their groans
   Who were thy sheep, and in their ancient fold
   Slain by the bloody Piemontese, that rolled
   Mother with infant down the rocks. Their moans   8
The vales redoubled to the hills, and they
   To heaven. Their martyred blood and ashes sow
   O'er all the Italian fields, where still doth sway
The triple Tyrant; that from these may grow   12
   A hundredfold, who, having learnt thy way,
   Early may fly the Babylonian woe.

On the Late Massacre in Piemont. Despite hostility between Catholics
and Protestants, the Waldenses, members of a Puritan sect, had been
living in the Piemont, that region in Northwest Italy bounded by the
crests of the Alps. In 1655, ignoring a promise to observe religious liberty,
troops of the Roman Catholic ruler of the Piemont put to death several
members of the sect. 4. *When . . . stones:* Englishmen had been Catholics, worshiping stone and wooden statues (so Milton charges) when the
Waldensian sect was founded in the twelfth century. 12. *The triple
Tyrant:* the Pope, to whom is attributed authority over earth, Heaven,
and Hell. 14. *Babylonian woe:* destruction expected to befall the city of
Babylon at the world's end as punishment for her luxury and other
wickedness (see Revelation 18:1–24). Protestants took Babylon to mean
the Church of Rome.

ROBERT BROWNING (1812–1889)

Soliloquy of the Spanish Cloister

Gr-r-r — there go, my heart's abhorrence!
    Water your damned flower-pots, do!
If hate killed men, Brother Lawrence,
    God's blood, would not mine kill you!   4
What? your myrtle-bush wants trimming?
    Oh, that rose has prior claims —
Needs its leaden vase filled brimming?
    Hell dry you up with its flames!   8

At the meal we sit together;
    Salve tibi!° I must hear   *Hail to thee!*
Wise talk of the kind of weather,
    Sort of season, time of year: 12
Not a plenteous cork-crop: scarcely
    Dare we hope oak-galls, I doubt;
What's the Latin name for "parsley"?
    What's the Greek name for "swine's snout"?   16

Whew! We'll have our platter burnished,
    Laid with care on our own shelf!
With a fire-new spoon we're furnished,
    And a goblet for ourself,   20
Rinsed like something sacrificial
    Ere 'tis fit to touch our chaps —
Marked with L. for our initial!
    (He-he! There his lily snaps!)   24

Saint, forsooth! While brown Dolores
    Squats outside the Convent bank
With Sanchicha, telling stories,
    Steeping tresses in the tank,   28
Blue-black, lustrous, thick like horsehairs,
    — Can't I see his dead eye glow,
Bright as 'twere a Barbary corsair's?
    (That is, if he'd let it show!)   32

When he finishes refection,
    Knife and fork he never lays
Cross-wise, to my recollection,
    As do I, in Jesu's praise.   36
I, the Trinity illustrate,
    Drinking watered orange-pulp —
In three sips the Arian frustrate;
    While he drains his at one gulp!   40

Oh, those melons! if he's able
   We're to have a feast; so nice!
One goes to the Abbot's table,
   All of us get each a slice.   44
How go on your flowers? None double?
   Not one fruit-sort can you spy?
Strange! — And I, too, at such trouble,
   Keep them close-nipped on the sly!   48

There's a great text in Galatians,
   Once you trip on it, entails
Twenty-nine distinct damnations,
   One sure, if another fails;   52
If I trip him just a-dying,
   Sure of heaven as sure can be,
Spin him round and send him flying
   Off to hell, a Manichee?   56

Or, my scrofulous French novel
   On grey paper with blunt type!
Simply glance at it, you grovel
   Hand and foot in Belial's gripe;   60
If I double down its pages
   At the woeful sixteenth print,
When he gathers his greengages,
   Ope a sieve and slip it in't?   64

Or, there's Satan! — one might venture
   Pledge one's soul to him, yet leave
Such a flaw in the indenture
   As he'd miss till, past retrieve,   68
Blasted lay that rose-acacia
   We're so proud of! *Hy, Zy, Hine.* . . .
'St, there's Vespers! *Plena gratia*
   Ave, Virgo!° Gr-r-r — you swine!   *Hail, Virgin,*
                                                   full of grace!

Soliloquy of the Spanish Cloister. 3. *Brother Lawrence*: one of the speaker's fellow monks. 31. *Barbary corsair*: a pirate operating off the Barbary coast of Africa. 39. *Arian*: a follower of Arius, heretic who denied the doctrine of the Trinity. 49. *a great text in Galatians*: a difficult verse in this book of the Bible; Brother Lawrence will be damned as a heretic if he wrongly interprets it. 56. *Manichee*: another kind of heretic, one who (after the Persian philosopher Mani) sees in the world a constant struggle between good and evil, neither able to win. 60. *Belial*: here, not specifically Satan but (as used in the Old Testament) a name for wickedness. 70. *Hy, Zy, Hine*: possibly the sound of a bell to announce evening devotions, possibly the beginning of a formula to summon the Devil.

JONATHAN SWIFT (1667–1745)

On Stella's Birthday

> Stella this day is thirty-four
> (We shan't dispute a year or more) —
> However, Stella, be not troubled,
> Although thy size and years are doubled,   4
> Since first I saw thee at sixteen,
> The brightest virgin on the green,
> So little is thy form declined,
> Made up so largely in thy mind.   8
>   Oh, would it please the gods, to split
> Thy beauty, size, and years, and wit,
> No age could furnish out a pair
> Of nymphs so graceful, wise, and fair,   12
> With half the luster of your eyes,
> With half your wit, your years, and size.
> And then, before it grew too late,
> How should I beg of gentle Fate   16
> (That either nymph might have her swain)
> To split my worship too in twain.

On Stella's Birthday. 18. *my worship:* as Dean of St. Patrick's in Dublin, Swift was addressed as "Your Worship."

WORDS AND THEIR ORDER

Whether the poet wears a mask or speaks to us person-to-person, a poem (as we have seen) confronts us with some kind of face. We have now to consider what comes through this face: words.

1. THE EXACT WORD

Like a good writer of prose, a poet often seeks what the French call *le mot juste*: the one word that will succeed better in its place than any other word. Unable to fill a two-syllable gap in an unfinished line that went "The seal's wide — — gaze toward Paradise," the American poet Hart Crane began paging through an unabridged dictionary. When he had reached S, he found the object of his quest in *spindrift*: sea spray driven by a strong wind. (This poem will be found on p. 63.) A word, however, does not have to be so unusual to be *le mot juste*, nor so hard to find. Any word can be the right word, if used in the right place. It may be a word as ordinary and everyday as *from*. Consider the difference between "The sedge is withered *on* the lake" (a misquotation of a line by Keats) and "The sedge is withered *from* the lake" (what Keats in fact wrote). Keats's line suggests, as the altered line does not, that, because the sedge (a growth of grasslike plants) has withered *from* the lake, it seems to have withdrawn mysteriously. Though apparently slight, the misquotation creates a new poem, one not nearly so interesting.

It is a great temptation for some poets, especially novices, to invent new words, ignoring the existing resources of the English language. Such a poet will never say "Her eyes shine like a chipmunk's" or "Her chipmunk eyes shine" if he can say "Her chipmunkeyeshine" or

"Her chipmunkily-shiny eyes." But a veteran poet — even experiment-loving E. E. Cummings — seems to regard an invented word as a thing for special occasions. When Gerard Manley Hopkins calls a falcon "dapple-dawn-drawn," the coined word startles, but startles us into the realization that the poet really *is* looking at bird and dawn through fresh eyes, seeing qualities that could hardly be expressed in language more conventional. Memorable, too, is the coined word in the opening of a poem by Emily Dickinson: "The *overtakelessness* of those / Who have accomplished Death . . ." Most words in poetry, however, are the common property of all of us; and often *le mot juste* is what novelist Joseph Conrad called "the fresh usual word." Each word is both fresh and usual in the following poem:

WALTER SAVAGE LANDOR (1775–1864)

Mother, I Cannot Mind My Wheel

> Mother, I cannot mind my wheel;
> > My fingers ache, my lips are dry:
> Oh! if you felt the pain I feel!
> > But oh, who ever felt as I!   4
>
> No longer could I doubt him true,
> > All other men may use deceit;
> He always said my eyes were blue,
> > And often swore my lips were sweet.   8

Familiar as all these words are, their freshness comes from the illusion that we hear an actual girl expressing actual grief. The words are those we might expect to break from her lips. How well Landor has chosen them and set them in place may be seen by rewriting the poem, substituting a few different words:

> Mom, I can't tend my spinningwheel;
> > I have chapped lips, my fingers hurt:
> Ouch! you should feel the pain I feel!
> > No girl was ever done such dirt!

The superiority of Landor's version should be evident. It inheres not in any unusual qualities of Landor's words, but in his ability to persuade us that his words correspond to the girl's feelings.

If a poet troubles to seek out the best words available, the least we can do is to find out what his words mean. This is to suggest that the dictionary is a firm ally in reading poems and, if the poems are more than a century old, is indispensable. Meanings change. As T. S. Eliot reminds us in "Burnt Norton," words "strain, / Crack and sometimes break, under the burden, / Under the tension, slip, slide, perish, / Decay with imprecision, will not stay in place, / Will not stay still." When the Elizabethan poet George Gascoigne wrote, "O Abraham's brats, O brood of blessed seed," the word *brats* implied neither irritation nor contempt. When in the seventeenth century Andrew Marvell imagined two lovers' "vegetable love," he referred to a vegetative or growing love, not one resembling a lettuce. And when King George III called a building an "awful artificial spectacle," he was not condemning it, but praising it as an awe-inspiring work of art. There is nothing to be done about this inevitable tendency of language, although in reading poetry we can watch out for it. If you suspect that a word has shifted in meaning over the years, most standard desk dictionaries will be helpful; an unabridged dictionary, more helpful yet; and most helpful of all, the *Oxford English Dictionary* (OED), which gives, for each definition, successive examples of the word's written use down through the past thousand years. (No reader need feel a grim obligation to keep interrupting the poem in order to rummage his dictionary; but if a poem is worth reading very closely, he may wish any aid he can find.)

When is a word the "right" word? No ironbound rules exist. And yet, because precise observation — whether of something real or something imaginary — is a quality we expect of good poetry, we do find poets, more often than not, selecting words that point to concrete details and tangible objects. A poet may do so even when dealing with an abstract idea: "brightness" is a general name for light, but in Thomas Nashe's line, "Brightness falls from the air," the abstraction is given the weight of a falling body. If a poem reads *daffodils* instead of *flowers*, *ten thousand* instead of *numerous*, *diaper years* instead of *infancy*, we call its **diction** — its choice of words — relatively particular and concrete, rather than general and abstract. By the concreteness and particularity of his words, the poet shows himself to be aware of the physical world.

The nature of this experience was aptly defined by William Butler Yeats, who criticized W. E. Henley for not showing awareness of the physical world in his poetry. Obsessed by theories of what a poet ought to do, Henley's poetry (says Yeats) is "abstract, as even an actor's movement can be when the thought of doing is plainer to his mind than the doing itself: the straight line from cup to lip, let us say, more plain than the hand's own sensation weighed down by that heavy spillable cup." [1] To find words to convey the sense of that heavy spillable cup was to Yeats a goal, one that surely he attained in "Among School Children" by describing a woman's stark face: "Hollow of cheek as though it drank the wind / And took a mess of shadows for its meat." A more abstract-minded poet might have written, "Her hollow cheek and wasted, hungry look." Ezra Pound gave a famous piece of advice to his fellow poets: "Go in fear of abstractions." This is *not* to say that a poet cannot employ abstract words, nor that all poems have to be about physical things. The abstractness of much of T. S. Eliot's *Four Quartets* — a poem concerned with time, eternity, history, language, reality and other things that cannot be handled — is evidence to the contrary. But although poets need not always write in concrete, physical terms, they must sometimes be able to.

One of the valuable services of poetry is to recall for us the concrete, physical sense that certain words once had, but have since lost. "Most of the words we use today to express intellectual, emotional, spiritual concepts had originally physical significance," said John Livingston Lowes in an essay, "The Noblest Monument of English Prose." " 'Wrong,' for instance, originally implied something twisted; 'implied' itself involves the idea of something folded within another thing — as 'involve' rests on the concept of something rolled or wrapped about. 'Concept' itself goes back to the notion of seizing or grasping." As the English critic H. Coombes has suggested, in his book *Literature and Criticism*,

> We use a word like *powerful* without feeling that it is really 'power-full.' We do not seem today to taste the full flavor of words as we feel that Falstaff (and Shakespeare, and probably his audience) tasted them when he was applauding the virtues of 'good sherris-sack,' which makes the brain 'apprehensive, quick, forgetive, full of nimble, fiery, and delectable shapes.' And being less aware of the life and substantiality of words, we are probably less aware of the things . . . that these words stand for.

Good poets, like Yeats, make us aware of "that heavy spillable cup." In so doing, they recall us to the substance of things and perhaps enlarge our joy in being alive.

[1] *The Trembling of the Veil* (1922), reprinted in *The Autobiography of William Butler Yeats* (New York, 1953), p. 177.

A startling illustration of how language can lose its vigor and concreteness is the version of a Bible text (Ephesians 5:15–16) on a subway poster issued by a Bible society:

> Be careful how you live,
> Not thoughtlessly but thoughtfully,
> Make the most of your opportunities
> For the times are evil.

"Make the most of your opportunities" might mean "Buy stock in Consolidated Soup" or some such practical advice. Queried where the poster's text had come from, a spokesman for the society said it was no official version, but one intended to "make better sense to the average man today." [2] The society may be right, but it is hard not to think that the average seventeenth-century man had a more exact and colorful diction available to him. The same text, in the King James Version, reads:

> See then that ye walk circumspectly, not as fools, but as wise,
> Redeeming the time, because the days are evil.

Why is the King James Version vivid and the society's translation drab? Unlike the line "Be careful how you live," "See that ye walk circumspectly" carries a sense of physical movement. To be *circumspect* (a word made of two Latin roots meaning "to look" and "around") is to be watchful on all sides. To *redeem* (literally "to buy back") is to do something more specific than *make the most of*; and *days* are more definite than *the times*. Call a man *thoughtless*, as the modern version would do, and he might not feel particularly affected; but call him a *fool* and you use a fighting term. The language of the Bible society's poster is about as memorable as that of a laundry ticket. But because King James's translators chose words with physical, tactile senses, their language has stuck in men's minds for three centuries. The modern version, then, does not say the same thing as the King James Version; indeed, it does not say much of anything at all.

[2] This inquiry was reported in *Esquire*, April 1958.

Much of the effect of the following poem depends upon our awareness of the precision with which the poet selects his words. We can better see this by knowing their derivations. For instance, *potpourri* comes from French: *pot* plus *pourri*. What do these words mean? (If you do not know French, look up the etymology of the word in a dictionary.) Look up the definitions and etymologies of *revenance, circumstance, inspiration, conceptual, commotion, cordial,* and *azure;* and try to state the meanings these words have in the poem.

RICHARD WILBUR (b. 1921)

In the Elegy Season

Haze, char, and the weather of All Souls':
A giant absence mopes upon the trees:
Leaves cast in casual potpourris
Whisper their scents from pits and cellar-holes.   4

Or brewed in gulleys, steeped in wells, they spend
In chilly steam their last aromas, yield
From shallow hells a revenance of field
And orchard air. And now the envious mind   8

Which could not hold the summer in my head
While bounded by that blazing circumstance
Parades these barrens in a golden trance,
Remembering the wealthy season dead,   12

And by an autumn inspiration makes
A summer all its own. Green boughs arise
Through all the boundless backward of the eyes,
And the soul bathes in warm conceptual lakes.   16

Less proud than this, my body leans an ear
Past cold and colder weather after wings'
Soft commotion, the sudden race of springs,
The goddess' tread heard on the dayward stair,   20

Longs for the brush of the freighted air, for smells
Of grass and cordial lilac, for the sight
Of green leaves building into the light
And azure water hoisting out of wells.   24

JOHN CLARE (1793–1864)

Mouse's Nest

I found a ball of grass among the hay
And progged it as I passed and went away;
And when I looked I fancied something stirred,
And turned again and hoped to catch the bird —   4
When out an old mouse bolted in the wheats
With all her young ones hanging at her teats;
She looked so odd and so grotesque to me,
I ran and wondered what the thing could be,   8
And pushed the knapweed bunches where I stood;
Then the mouse hurried from the craking° brood.   *crying*
The young ones squeaked, and as I went away
She found her nest again among the hay.   12
The water o'er the pebbles scarce could run
And broad old cesspools glittered in the sun.

Questions

1. What connections do you find between the last couplet and the rest of the poem?
2. "To prog" (line 2) means "to poke about for food; to forage." In what ways does this word fit more exactly here than *prodded, touched,* or *searched?*
3. Why is *craking* (10) better than *crying?*

2. SPEECH AND POETIC DICTION

Even if Samuel Johnson's famous *Dictionary* of 1755 had been as thick as Webster's unabridged, an eighteenth-century poet searching through it for words to use would have had a narrower choice. For in English literature of the **neoclassical period** or **Augustan age** — that period extending from about 1660 into the middle eighteenth century — many poets subscribed to a belief in **poetic diction**: "A system of words," said Dr. Johnson, "refined from the grossness of domestic use." The system admitted into a serious poem only certain words and subjects, excluding others as violations of **decorum** (propriety). Accordingly such common words as *rat, cheese, big, sneeze,* and *elbow,* although admissible to satire, were thought inconsistent with the loftiness of tragedy, epic, ode, or elegy. Dr. Johnson's biographer, Boswell, tells how a poet writing an epic on the sugar industry in the British West Indies reconsidered the word "rats" and instead wrote that "the whiskered vermin race, / A countless clan, despoil

45

the lowland cane." Johnson himself objected to Lady Macbeth's allusion to her "keen knife," saying that "we do not immediately conceive that any crime of importance is to be committed with a knife; or who does not, at last, from the long habit of connecting a knife with sordid offices, feel aversion rather than terror?" Probably Johnson was here the victim of his age, and Shakespeare was right, but Johnson's idea is right too: there are inappropriate words as well as appropriate ones.

Neoclassical poets chose their classical models more often from Roman writers than from Greek, as their diction suggests by its frequency of Latin derivatives. For example, a *net*, according to Dr. Johnson's dictionary, is "any thing reticulated or decussated, at equal distances, with interstices between the intersections." In company with Latinate words often appeared fixed combinations of adjective and noun ("finny prey" for "fish"), poetic names (a song to a lady named Molly might rechristen her Parthenia), and allusions to classical mythology.

It would be a mistake to regard all poetic diction, of which neoclassical is only one variety, as excess baggage and needless artifice. To a reader who knew at firsthand both living sheep and the pastoral poems of Virgil — as most readers nowadays do not — such a fixed phrase as "the fleecy care," which may seem stilted to us, could convey pleasurable associations. But "fleecy care" was more than a hifalutin way of saying "sheep"; as one scholar has pointed out, "when they wished, our poets could say 'sheep' as clearly and as often as anybody else. In the first place, 'fleecy' drew attention to wool, and demanded the appropriate visual image of sheep; for aural imagery the poets would refer to 'the bleating kind'; it all depended upon what was happening in the poem." [3]

Others besides neoclassicists have found some sort of poetic diction valuable: Anglo-Saxon poets, with their standard figures of speech, or **kennings** ("whale-road" for the sea, "ring-giver" for a ruler); authors of medieval folk ballads who, no less than neoclassicists, loved fixed epithet-noun combinations ("milk-white steed," "blood-red wine"); and Edmund Spenser, whose example made popular the adjective ending in -*y* (*fleecy, grassy, milky*).

Neoclassical poetic diction was evidently being abused when, instead of saying "uncork the bottle," a poet could write,

> Apply thine engine to the spongy door,
> Set *Bacchus* from his glassy prison free,

[3] Bonamy Dobrée, *English Literature in the Early Eighteenth Century, 1700–1740* (Oxford University Press, 1959), p. 161.

46

in some bad lines ridiculed by Alexander Pope in *Peri Bathous, or, Of the Art of Sinking in Poetry*. Too strictly applied, standards of decorum can lead a poet into such circumlocution and absurdity. An American neo-neoclassicist, E. J. Runk, in his justly forgotten *Washington: A National Epic* (1897), struggled manfully to preserve epic decorum though obliged to mention such New York place-names as Bear Mountain and Anthony's Nose:

> Where Bear Hill rears its gloomy flank,
> Confronting the Antonian Nose . . .

When Wordsworth, in his Preface to the *Lyrical Ballads*, expressed his celebrated reaction against eighteenth-century poetic diction and called for a poetry whose words were to be chosen according to different principles, he was, in effect, advocating a poetic diction of his own. In brief, Wordsworth denied the need to keep the language of poetry separate from that of speech; and asserted that "the language really spoken by men," especially by humble rustics, is plainer, more emphatic, and conveys "elementary feelings . . . in a state of greater simplicity." Wordsworth's practice had the effect of inviting much freshness into English poetry and, by admitting words that neoclassical poets would have called "low" ("His poor old *ankles* swell"), helped rid poets of the fear of being thought foolish for mentioning a commonplace.

This theory of the superiority of rural diction was, as Coleridge pointed out, difficult to adhere to; and, in practice, Wordsworth was occasionally to write a language as Latinate and citified as these lines on yew trees:

> Huge trunks! — and each particular trunk a growth
> Of intertwisted fibers serpentine
> Up-coiling, and inveterately convolved . . .

This sounds pedantic to us, especially the phrase *inveterately convolved*. In fact, some poets, notably Gerard Manley Hopkins, have subscribed to the view that English words derived from Anglo-Saxon (Old English) have more force and flavor than their Latin equivalents. *Kingly*, one may feel, has more power than *regal*. One argument for this view is that so many words of Old English origin, such as *man, wife, child, house, eat, drink,* and *sleep,* are basic to our living language. It may be true, too, that a language closer to Old English is particularly fit for rendering abstract notions concretely — as does the memorable title of a medieval work of piety, the *Ayenbite of Inwit* ("again-bite of inner wit" or "remorse of conscience"). And

47

yet this view, if accepted at all, must be accepted with heavy reservations. Words of Latin derivation can, if chosen well, convey a sense as precise and physical as that of any other words: an instance is *circumspectly* in the passage previously quoted from the King James Bible.

In this age of disappearing censorship, when books once smuggled into the country now appear in every drugstore, it might seem as though decorum were dead. Nevertheless, it is still with us; and we continue to suspect certain words if met in poetry, especially if their most obvious value is shock. A failure in point is a recent ode by a "beat" poet in which a four-letter word of Anglo-Saxon origin is intoned a meaningless number of times, quickly losing what little shock value it ever had. More carefully observed, standards of decorum can be valuable; for one thing, they provide the poet with something to shatter for special effect. In John Crowe Ransom's "Philomela," a poem detailing its speaker's search for the beauty of a nightingale's song, we are startled by the sudden line "I rose, and venomously spat." The effect of *spat* is electrifying, more so than that of the beat poet's four-letter word.

In a broad sense, poetic diction is something every poet employs, in that he selects certain words for a poem and excludes others. At present, poetry in English seems to be shunning fixed expressions, such as "fleecy care," and using, instead, a permissive medley of slang, plain speech, bookish or "inkhorn" words, even **dialect** (a variety of a spoken language peculiar to a social group or to a locality). When E. E. Cummings begins a poem, "mr youse needn't be so spry / concernin questions arty," we recognize another kind of diction: **vulgate** (speech not much affected by schooling). Handbooks of grammar sometimes distinguish various **levels of usage.** A sort of ladder is imagined, on whose rungs words, phrases, and sentences may be ranked in an ascending order of formality, from the curses of an illiterate thug to the Commencement Day address of a doctor of divinity. These levels range from *vulgate* through **colloquial** (the casual conversation or informal writing of literate people) and **general English** (most literate speech and writing, more studied than colloquial but not pretentious), up to **formal English** (the impersonal language of educated persons, usually only written, possibly spoken on dignified occasions). Recently, however, lexicographers have been shunning such labels. The designation "colloquial" has been expelled (*bounced* would be colloquial; *trun out*, vulgate) from Webster's Third New International Dictionary on the grounds that "it is impossible to know whether a word out of context is colloquial or not" and that the diction of Americans nowadays is more fluid than the labels suggest. Aware that we are being unscientific and even old-fashioned, we may find the labels useful, applied to words in the context of a poem. They may help roughly to describe what happens when, as in the following poem, a poet shifts from one level of usage to another. This poem employs, incidentally, a colloquial device throughout: omitting the subjects of sentences. In keeping the characters straight, it may be helpful to fill in the speaker for each *said* and for the verbs *saw* and *ducked* (lines 9 and 10).

JOSEPHINE MILES (b. 1911)

Reason

> Said, Pull her up a bit will you, Mac, I want to unload there.
> Said, Pull her up my rear end, first come first serve.
> Said, Give her the gun, Bud, he needs a taste of his own
>   bumper.
>
> Then the usher came out and got into the act: 4
> Said, Pull her up, pull her up a bit, we need this space, sir.
> Said, For God's sake, is this still a free country or what?
> You go back and take care of Gary Cooper's horse
> And leave me handle my own car. 8
>
> Saw them unloading the lame old lady,
> Ducked out under the wheel and gave her an elbow,
> Said, All you needed to do was just explain;
> *Reason, Reason* is my middle name. 12

Words on at least three levels of usage make up this miniature comedy: the vulgate of the old lady's driver ("leave me handle my own car"); the colloquial of the truck driver ("Give her the gun"); and the general English of the poet, who observes. There is also the suggestion of a contrast in formality between the truck-driver, who says "Mac," and the usher, who says "sir." Diction in this poem is a means of distinguishing the speakers from one another, of separating points of view.

"Reason" is a poem closer to ordinary speech than most, but poetry need not closely resemble ordinary speech. The language of Coleridge's "Kubla Khan" (p. 293) is more bookish, but it might be uttered by a literate person at a high pitch of excitement: it is an excellently speakable poem, as we can discover by reading it aloud. Few poets have found it necessary to limit the diction of poetry strictly to the speech of rustics. Perhaps the only general principle we can be sure about is that poems, whether rustic or researched, must persuade us that the speaker has used appropriate words.

ROBERT FITZGERALD (b. 1910)

Cobb Would Have Caught It

In sunburnt parks where Sundays lie,
Or the wide wastes beyond the cities,
Teams in grey deploy through sunlight.

Talk it up, boys, a little practice.

Coming in stubby and fast, the baseman   5
Gathers a grounder in fat green grass,
Picks it stinging and clipped as wit
Into the leather: a swinging step
Wings it deadeye down to first.
Smack. Oh, attaboy, attyoldboy.   10

Catcher reverses his cap, pulls down
Sweaty casque, and squats in the dust:
Pitcher rubs new ball on his pants,
Chewing, puts a jet behind him;
Nods past batter, taking his time.   15
Batter settles, tugs at his cap:
A spinning ball: step and swing to it,
Caught like a cheek before it ducks
By shivery hickory: socko, baby:
Cleats dig into dust. Outfielder,   20
On his way, looking over shoulder,
Makes it a triple. A long peg home.

Innings and afternoons. Fly lost in sunset.
Throwing arm gone bad. There's your old ball game.
Cool reek of the field. Reek of companions.   25

QUESTIONS

1. Who was Ty Cobb? The height of his career was from 1907 to 1919. Why does the title refer to Cobb rather than to a more recent player?

2. What levels of usage do you find in the diction of this poem? At what points does the diction shift from one level to another? What difference do these shifts mark?

3. Comment on the poet's use of the words and phrases *deploy* (line 3), *clipped as wit* (7), *casque* (12), *Caught like a cheek* (18). In each instance, what two things are being compared?

4. "Going home after a ball game, you are overpowered with disgust at the athletic aromas of your friends." Why is this paraphrase unfaithful to the tone of the last line?

50

THOMAS HARDY (1840–1928)

The Ruined Maid

"O 'Melia, my dear, this does everything crown!
Who could have supposed I should meet you in Town?
And whence such fair garments, such prosperi-ty?" —
"O didn't you know I'd been ruined?" said she.   4

— "You left us in tatters, without shoes or socks,
Tired of digging potatoes, and spudding up docks°;   *spading up*
And now you've gay bracelets and bright feathers   *dockweed*
   three!" —
"Yes: that's how we dress when we're ruined," said she.   8

— "At home in the barton° you said 'thee' and 'thou,'   *farmyard*
And 'thik oon,' and 'theäs oon,' and 't'other'; but now
Your talking quite fits 'ee for high compa-ny!" —
"Some polish is gained with one's ruin," said she.   12

— "Your hands were like paws then, your face blue and bleak
But now I'm bewitched by your delicate cheek,
And your little gloves fit as on any la-dy!" —
"We never do work when we're ruined," said she.   16

— "You used to call home-life a hag-ridden dream,
And you'd sigh, and you'd sock°; but at present you   *groan*
   seem
To know not of megrims° or melancho-ly!" —   *blues*
"True. One's pretty lively when ruined," said she.   20

— "I wish I had feathers, a fine sweeping gown,
And a delicate face, and could strut about Town!" —
"My dear — a raw country girl, such as you be,
Cannot quite expect that. You ain't ruined," said she.   24

QUESTIONS

1. Where does this dialogue take place? Who are the two speakers?

2. Comment on Hardy's use of the word *ruined*. What is the conventional meaning of the word, applied to a girl? As 'Melia applies it to herself what is its meaning?

3. Sum up the attitude of each speaker toward the other. What details of the new 'Melia does the first speaker most dwell upon? Would you expect Hardy to be so impressed by all these details, or is there, between his view of the characters and their view of themselves, any hint of an ironic discrepancy?

4. In losing her country dialect (*thik oon* and *theäs oon* for *this one* and *that one*), 'Melia is presumed to have gained in sophistication. What does Hardy suggest by her *ain't* in the last line?

Reword the following poem from Scottish dialect into general English prose, using the closest possible equivalents. Then try to assess what the poem has gained or lost. (In line 4, a *ploy*, as defined by Webster's Third New International Dictionary, is a pursuit or activity, "especially one that requires eagerness or finesse.")

HUGH MACDIARMID [CHRISTOPHER MURRAY GRIEVE] (b. 1892)

Wheesht, Wheesht

Wheesht°, wheesht, my foolish hert,	*hush*
For weel ye ken°	*know*
I widna ha'e ye stert	
Auld ploys again.	4
It's guid to see her lie	
Sae snod° an' cool,	*smooth*
A' lust o' lovin' by —	
Wheesht, wheesht, ye fule!	8

3. WORD ORDER

Among the languages of mankind, English is by no means the most fluid and flexible. It requires words to be placed in fairly definite and inviolable patterns, and whoever tries to depart too far from them will not be understood. The meaning is utterly changed by the word order in these two sentences, containing the same words but in different arrangements: "Zeus struck Sophocles dead," "Sophocles struck Zeus dead." This inflexibility was not true of Latin, in which a poet could lay down his words in whatever order he wished and, because their endings (inflections) showed what parts of speech they were, could trust that no reader would mistake his subject for his object. (E. E. Cummings has striven, in certain poems, for the freedom of Latin syntax; one such poem will be found at the end of this chapter.)

An arrangement of words in a sequence that indicates their relationships, we call **syntax**. Usually we take the term to refer not merely to the order of *words* in a sentence but to the organization of words, phrases, subjects and predicates, sentences, and larger units into the design of a whole. At present, though, we are concerned with word order, reserving other kinds of syntax for a later discussion (sec. 5, "Structure," in chap. 10).

52

Evidently, one of the prime advantages of English word order to poetry is that a poet can give a word greater or lesser prominence by setting it in a certain place. One place of considerable emphasis is the beginning of a sentence. Yeats, for instance, begins "The Scholars" with a direct look at his subject: *"Bald heads,* forgetful of their sins, / Old, learned, respectable bald heads . . ."; and Poe commences "To Helen" with direct address: *"Helen,* thy beauty is to me / Like those Nicean barks of yore . . ." A place of even greater emphasis is the very end of a sentence, especially when the last word is given further impact by a rime-sound, as in Browning's lines,

> We loved, sir — used to meet:
> How sad and bad and mad it was —
> But then, how it was sweet!

English word order, being rigid, challenges the poet to defy it, and by doing so, to achieve special effects. In this attempt, one device is **inverted word order:** a switching about of the positions of two or more words, contrary to a customary and expected pattern (as that of subject first, then predicate; or that of verb first, then its object or complement). This device is nothing bizarre: ordinary speech is continually inverting such patterns, to ask a question ("How much money have you?") or to exclaim ("A total wreck, the car was!" or "How warm it is!"). In poetry, this switch may be made by an incompetent poet unable to do anything else to get his rime to come out right, in which case it is usually awkward and obvious:

> He looked — she breathed — his heart beat wild with hope:
> Then all of a sudden she her eyes did ope.

But an unusual emphasis takes place when such an inversion is made in a statement, as when Milton concludes "Lycidas":

> At last he rose, and twitched his mantle blue:
> Tomorrow to fresh woods, and pastures new.

Perhaps the inversion in "mantle blue" gives desirable prominence to the color associated with heaven (and heaven is in part what the poem is about); certainly the inversion in "pastures new" heightens the note of rebirth. The last word of Milton's "On the Morning of

Christ's Nativity" also receives the attention due a word in its position, thanks to an inverted word order:

> And all about the courtly stable
> Bright-harnessed angels sit in order serviceable.

An inversion of syntax also may be used to emphasize a word in a *succeeding* line, as in Dryden's couplet,

> But Shakespeare's magic could not copied be;
> Within that circle none durst walk but he.

But if a poet inverts his syntax too far, the result may be ludicrous. In Robert Browning's "Rabbi Ben Ezra," a sage is remarking that man, because he is a creature higher than the animals, must be subject to doubts and torments:

> Poor vaunt of life indeed,
> Were man but formed to feed
> On joy, to solely seek and find and feast:
> Such feasting ended, then
> As sure an end to men;
> Irks care the crop-full bird? Frets doubt the maw-crammed beast?

Paraphrased and turned around into a more readily comprehensible word order, the last line might read: "Does any care irk the bird whose crop is full? Does any doubt fret the beast whose maw is crammed?" (Such paraphrase into general English is sometimes an excellent method for unlocking difficult poems.)

Clearly there can be some difference of formality in syntax, as well as in diction and tone. Compare the lines from the well-known nursery rime —

> Jack and Jill went up the hill
> To fetch a pail of water.
> Jack fell down and broke his crown
> And Jill came tumbling after . . .

with something more exalted, Milton's description of the descent of Satan: "Him the Almighty Power / Hurled headlong flaming from th' etheral sky." The out-of-the-ordinary syntax — object plus subject, instead of the usual subject plus object — seems fitting to the

54

extraordinary nature of the event described and possibly even imitates Satan's upside-down descent. To take another example from Milton, consider his exalted description of the fall of man:

> Earth trembled from her entrails, as again
> In pangs, and Nature gave a second groan;
> Sky loured, and, muttering thunder, some sad drops
> Wept at completing of the mortal sin
> Original; while Adam took no thought
> Eating his fill, nor Eve to iterate
> Her former trespass feared, the more to soothe
> Him with her loved society, that now
> As with new wine intoxicated both
> They swim in mirth, and fancy that they feel
> Divinity within them breeding wings
> Wherewith to scorn the Earth.

It is not that all the words in Milton's passage are bookish ones; indeed, many could be found in a nursery rime. What distinguishes the passage from "Jack and Jill" is that in sentence length (83 words) and complexity (use of subordinate clauses), Milton's lines seem far removed from ordinary speech, in which sentences tend to be shorter and simpler, and more like "Jack and Jill." For this fact in itself, Milton is neither to be blamed nor praised. Tone and occasion determine appropriateness of diction and word order. If all go well together, the poet will fasten the right word into the right place, and the result may be — as T. S. Eliot said in "Little Gidding" — a poem

>   . . . where every word is at home,
> Taking its place to support the others,
> The word neither diffident nor ostentatious,
> An easy commerce of the old and the new,
> The common word exact without vulgarity,
> The formal word precise but not pedantic,
> The complete consort dancing together . . .

E. E. CUMMINGS (1894–1962)

'anyone lived in a pretty how town'

anyone lived in a pretty how town
(with up so floating many bells down)
spring summer autumn winter
he sang his didn't he danced his did.   4

Women and men(both little and small)
cared for anyone not at all
they sowed their isn't they reaped their same
sun moon stars rain   8

children guessed(but only a few
and down they forgot as up they grew
autumn winter spring summer)
that noone loved him more by more   12

when by now and tree by leaf
she laughed his joy she cried his grief
bird by snow and stir by still
anyone's any was all to her   16

someones married their everyones
laughed their cryings and did their dance
(sleep wake hope and then)they
said their nevers they slept their dream   20

stars rain sun moon
(and only the snow can begin to explain
how children are apt to forget to remember
with up so floating many bells down)   24

one day anyone died i guess
(and noone stooped to kiss his face)
busy folk buried them side by side
little by little and was by was   28

all by all and deep by deep
and more by more they dream their sleep
noone and anyone earth by april
wish by spirit and if by yes.   32

Women and men(both dong and ding)
summer autumn winter spring
reaped their sowing and went their came
sun moon stars rain   36

56

1. Summarize the story told in this poem. Who are the main characters?
2. Rearrange the words in the two opening lines into the order you would expect them usually to follow. What effect does Cummings obtain by his unconventional syntax?
3. Another of Cummings' strategies is to use one part of speech as if it were another; for instance, in line 4, *didn't* and *did* are ordinarily verbs, but here are used as nouns. What other words in the poem perform functions other than their expected ones?

GERARD MANLEY HOPKINS (1844–1889)

Carrion Comfort

Not, I'll not, carrion comfort, Despair, not feast on thee;
Not untwist — slack they may be — these last strands of man
In me ór, most weary, cry *I can no more.* I can;
Can something, hope, wish day come, not choose not to be.   4
But ah, but O thou terrible, why wouldst thou rude on me
Thy wring-world right foot rock? lay a lionlimb against me? scan
With darksome devouring eyes my bruisèd bones? and fan,
O in turns of tempest, me heaped there; me frantic to avoid   8
    thee and flee?

  Why? That my chaff might fly; my grain lie, sheer and
    clear.
Nay in all that toil, that coil, since (seems) I kissed the rod,
Hand rather, my heart lo! lapped strength, stole joy, would
    laugh, chéer.
Cheer whom though? the hero° whose heaven-   *Christ*   12
    handling flung me, fóot tród
Me? or me that fought him? O which one? is it each one?
    That night, that year
Of now done darkness I wretch lay wrestling with (my God!)
    my God.

1. Robert Bridges, Hopkins' first editor, gave this poem its title. What does it mean?
2. In what places is the word order difficult to follow? Try to paraphrase, adding any words that Hopkins has left out.
3. How would you describe the syntax of the poem? What is the effect of all the questions, of the lines interrupted by asides, qualifications, parenthetical elements?
4. What words has Hopkins apparently made up? Try to define them from the context of the poem.

WALTER SAVAGE LANDOR (1775–1864)

Age

Death, though I see him not, is near
And grudges me my eightieth year.
Now, I would give him all those last
For one that fifty have run past.
Ah! he strikes all things, all alike,   5
But bargains: those he will not strike.

QUESTIONS

1. On what two meanings of the word *strike* does Landor's closing line depend?

2. What advantage is it to this epigram that the play on the word *strike* dawns on us only with the last word of the last line? Suppose the poem had ended in a different syntactical order:

Ah! all alike he strikes all things,
But he will not strike bargainings.

What would be lost?

EXERCISE THREE

In each of the following pairs of quotations, one is an original passage by a poet; the other, an inferior rewording of it. In each case which is the original? What alterations are inconsistent in level of usage? In which places does the word-order become awkward?

1. Sir Philip Sidney:

A.   Leave me, O Love, which reachest but to dust,
And thou, my mind, aspire to higher things;
Grow rich in that which never taketh rust:
Whatever fades, but fading pleasure brings.

B.   Go away, Love, which but to dust doth reach,
O mind of mine, fly up to better things;
Grow wealthy in what rust doth not impeach:
Whatever fades, a lot less pleasure brings.

2. Alexander Pope:

A.   The hungry judges soon the sentence sign,
And wretches hang that jurymen may dine.

B.   To pass the sentence fast is judges' feat,
And hang men so the jury lunch may eat.

3. John Donne:

A.   O angels, blow upon your trumpets now
And all you souls that wait the call, arise!
Go look around and find your bodies, thou
May come from all the corners of the skies . . .

B.   At the round earth's imagined corners, blow
Your trumpets, angels, and arise, arise
From death, you numberless infinities
Of souls, and to your scattered bodies go . . .

LEWIS CARROLL [CHARLES LUTWIDGE DODGSON] (1832–1898)

Jabberwocky

'Twas brillig, and the slithy toves
   Did gyre and gimble in the wabe:
All mimsy were the borogoves,
   And the mome raths outgrabe.   4

"Beware the Jabberwock, my son!
   The jaws that bite, the claws that catch!
Beware the Jubjub bird, and shun
   The frumious Bandersnatch!"   8

He took his vorpal sword in hand;
   Long time the manxome foe he sought —
So rested he by the Tumtum tree,
   And stood awhile in thought.   12

And, as in uffish thought he stood,
   The Jabberwock, with eyes of flame,
Came whiffling through the tulgey wood,
   And burbled as it came!   16

One, two! One, two! And through and through
   The vorpal blade went snicker-snack!
He left it dead, and with its head
   He went galumphing back.   20

"And hast thou slain the Jabberwock?
   Come to my arms, my beamish boy!
O frabjous day! Callooh, Callay!"
   He chortled in his joy.   24

'Twas brillig, and the slithy toves
   Did gyre and gimble in the wabe:
All mimsy were the borogoves,
   And the mome raths outgrabe.   28

QUESTIONS

1. Look up *chortled* (line 24) in your dictionary and find out its definition and origin.
2. In *Through the Looking-Glass*, Alice seeks the aid of Humpty Dumpty to decipher the meaning of this nonsense poem. "*Brillig*," he explains, "means four o'clock in the afternoon — the time when you begin *broiling* things for dinner." Does *brillig* sound like any other familiar word?
3. "*Slithy*," the explanation goes on, "means 'lithe and slimy.' 'Lithe' is the same as 'active.' You see it's like a portmanteau — there are two meanings packed up into one word." *Mimsy* is supposed to pack together both "flimsy" and "miserable." In the rest of the poem, what other portmanteau — or packed suitcase — words can you find?

59

WALLACE STEVENS (1879–1955)

Metamorphosis

Yillow, yillow, yillow,
Old worm, my pretty quirk,
How the wind spells out
Sep - tem - ber. . . .   4

Summer is in bones.
Cock-robin's at Caracas.
Make o, make o, make o,
Oto - otu - bre.   8

And the rude leaves fall.
The rain falls. The sky
Falls and lies with the worms.
The street lamps   12

Are those that have been hanged,
Dangling in an illogical
To and to and fro
Fro Niz - nil - imbo.   16

QUESTIONS

1. Explain the title. Of the several meanings of *metamorphosis* given in a dictionary, which best applies to the process that Stevens sees in the natural world?

2. What metamorphosis is also taking place in the *language* of the poem? How does it continue from line 4 to line 8 to line 16?

3. In the last line, which may recall the thickening drone of a speaker lapsing into sleep, *Niz - nil - imbo* seems not only a pun on the name of a month, but also a portmanteau word into which at least two familiar words are packed. Say it aloud. What are they?

4. What dictionary definitions of the word *quirk* seem relevant to line 2? How can a worm be a quirk? What else in this poem seems quirky?

RICHARD EBERHART (b. 1904)

The Fury of Aerial Bombardment

You would think the fury of aerial bombardment
Would rouse God to relent; the infinite spaces
Are still silent. He looks on shock-pried faces.
History, even, does not know what is meant.   4

You would feel that after so many centuries
God would give man to repent; yet he can kill
As Cain could, but with multitudinous will,
No farther advanced than in his ancient furies.   8

60

Was man made stupid to see his own stupidity?
Is God by definition indifferent, beyond us all?
Is the eternal truth man's fighting soul
Wherein the Beast ravens in its own avidity?   12

Of Van Wettering I speak, and Averill,
Names on a list, whose faces I do not recall
But they are gone to early death, who late in school
Distinguished the belt feed lever from the belt holding pawl.   16

QUESTIONS

1. As a Naval officer during World War II, Richard Eberhart was
assigned for a time as an instructor in a gunnery school. How has this experience apparently contributed to the diction of his poem?

2. In his *Life of John Dryden*, complaining about a description of a
sea fight Dryden had filled with nautical language, Samuel Johnson argued
that technical terms should be excluded from poetry. Is this criticism applicable to Eberhart's last line? Can a word succeed for us in a poem, even
though we may not be able to define it? (For more evidence, see also the
technical terms in Henry Reed's "Naming of Parts," p. 335).

3. Critics have found a contrast in tone between the first three stanzas of this poem and the last stanza. How would you describe this contrast? What does diction contribute to it?

EXERCISE FOUR

In the following six poems, what sorts of diction and syntax do you
find? In each poem, what could not be achieved by words and word order
of a different level of usage?

CATHERINE DAVIS (b. 1924)

'Your kindness is no kindness now'

Your kindness is no kindness now:
It is unkindness to allow
My unkind heart so to reveal
The differences it would conceal.
If I were, as I used to be,   5
As kind to you as you to me,
Or if I could but teach you how
To be unkind, as I am now,
That would be kindness of a kind,
To be again of a like mind.   10

SAMUEL JOHNSON (1709–1784)

On the Death of Mr. Robert Levet

Condemned to Hope's delusive mine,
  As on we toil from day to day,
By sudden blasts, or slow decline,
  Our social comforts drop away.   4

Well tried through many a varying year,
  See Levet to the grave descend,
Officious°, innocent, sincere,   *dutiful, full of kindly offices*
  Of every friendless name the friend.   8

Yet still he fills Affection's eye,
  Obscurely wise and coarsely kind;
Nor, lettered Arrogance, deny
  Thy praise to merit unrefined.   12

When fainting Nature called for aid,
  And hovering Death prepared the blow,
His vigorous remedy displayed
  The power of art without the show.   16

In Misery's darkest caverns known,
  His useful care was ever nigh,
Where hopeless Anguish poured his groan,
  And lonely Want retired to die.   20

No summons mocked by chill delay,
  No petty gain disdained by pride;
The modest wants of every day
  The toil of every day supplied.   24

His virtues walked their narrow round,
  Nor made a pause, nor left a void;
And sure the Eternal Master found
  The single talent well employed.   28

The busy day, the peaceful night,
  Unfelt, uncounted, glided by;
His frame was firm, his powers were bright,
  Though now his eightieth year was nigh.   32

Then with no throbbing, fiery pain,
  No cold gradations of decay,
Death broke at once the vital chain,
  And freed his soul the nearest way.   36

On the Death of Mr. Robert Levet. Dr. Johnson's friend Levet was a physician who generously tended the poor. 27–28: See Christ's parable of the talents, Matthew 25:13–30.

HART CRANE (1899–1932)

Voyages (II)

And yet this great wink of eternity,
Of rimless floods, unfettered leewardings,
Samite sheeted and processioned where
Her undinal vast belly moonward bends,
Laughing the wrapt inflections of our love;   5

Take this Sea, whose diapason knells
On scrolls of silver snowy sentences,
The sceptred terror of whose sessions rends
As her demeanors motion well or ill,
All but the pieties of lovers' hands.   10

And onward, as bells off San Salvador
Salute the crocus lusters of the stars,
In these poinsettia meadows of her tides, —
Adagios of islands, O my Prodigal,
Complete the dark confessions her veins spell.   15

Mark how her turning shoulders wind the hours,
And hasten while her penniless rich palms
Pass superscription of bent foam and wave, —
Hasten, while they are true, — sleep, death, desire,
Close round one instant in one floating flower.   20

Bind us in time, O Seasons clear, and awe.
O minstrel galleons of Carib fire,
Bequeath us to no earthly shore until
Is answered in the vortex of our grave
The seal's wide spindrift gaze toward paradise.   25

Voyages (II). In the first section of the poem, the speaker has contemplated the sea as dangerous, and concluded: "The bottom of the sea is cruel." With the transition "And yet . . . ," he begins a contrasting view.

WILLIAM WORDSWORTH (1770–1850)

'My heart leaps up'

My heart leaps up when I behold
   A rainbow in the sky;
So was it when my life began;
So is it now I am a man;
So be it when I shall grow old.   5
   Or let me die!
The Child is father of the Man;
And I could wish my days to be
Bound each to each by natural piety.

ANONYMOUS (American; nineteenth century?)

'As I was laying on the green'

As I was laying on the green,
A small English book I seen.
Carlyle's *Essay on Burns* was the edition,
So I left it laying in the same position.

ANONYMOUS (American Negro; collected 1936)

Scottsboro

Paper come out — done strewed de news
Seven po' chillun moan deat' house blues,
Seven po' chillun moanin' deat' house blues.
Seven nappy° heads wit' big shiny eye   *kinky*
All boun' in jail and framed to die,
All boun' in jail and framed to die.   6

Messin' white woman — snake lyin' tale
Hang and burn and jail wit' no bail.
Dat hang and burn and jail wit' no bail.
Worse ol' crime in white folks' lan'
Black skin coverin' po' workin' man,
Black skin coverin' po' workin' man.   12

Judge and jury — all in de stan'
Lawd, biggety name for same lynchin' ban',
Lawd, biggety name for same lynchin' ban'.
White folks and nigger in great co't house
Like cat down cellar wit' nohole mouse.
Like cat down cellar wit' nohole mouse.   18

Scottsboro. This folk blues, collected by Lawrence Gellert in *Negro Songs of Protest* (New York, 1936), is a comment on the Scottsboro case. In 1931 nine Negro youths, of Scottsboro, Alabama, were arrested and charged with the rape of two white women. Though eventually, after several trials, they were found not guilty, some of them at the time this song was composed had been convicted and sentenced to death.

FOUR

CONNOTATION AND ALLUSION

1. DENOTATION, CONNOTATION

In the late seventeenth century, Bishop Thomas Sprat declared that the members of the Royal Society sought in their writing to bring "all things as near the mathematical plainness" as they could. Such an effort would seem bound to fail, since words, unlike numbers, are ambiguous indicators. Although it may have troubled Bishop Sprat, the tendency of a word to have an elaborate multiplicity of meaning rather than a mathematical plainness, opens broad avenues to poetry.

Every word has at least one **denotation**: a meaning as defined by the dictionary. But the English language abounds in common words with so many denotations that a reader encountering such a word in a certain context may need to think twice to see what it means. The noun *field*, for instance, can denote a piece of ground, a sports arena, the scene of a battle, part of a flag, an occupation, and a number system in mathematics. Further, to add to its possible meanings, the word can be used as a verb ("Mantle fielded a grounder") or an adjective ("field trip," "field glasses").

A word can also have **connotations**: overtones or hints of additional meaning that it gains from all the contexts in which we have met it in the past. The word *tomahawk*, according to a dictionary, denotes "a light ax, having a head of stone or bone, employed as a tool and weapon by North American Indians." But by all its familiar associations, the word can rouse in us thoughts of warriors in paint and feathers — of scalps, blood-curdling yells, and Custer's Last Stand. Its connotations include "violence," "bloodshed," "sudden death," and "combat." The terms *druggist*, *pharmacist*, and *apothecary* denote a single occupation, but apothecaries seem to believe the connotations different. Think, too, of the difference between "Doc Jones" and "Abner P. Jones, M. D." In the mind's eye, the former appears in shirtsleeves.

Few people care more about this property of language than do advertisers, who know that connotations mean money. Recently a Boston automobile dealer advertised his secondhand cars not as "used" but as "pre-owned," as if fearing that "used car" would connote an old heap with soiled upholstery and mysterious engine troubles that somebody couldn't put up with. "Pre-owned," however, suggests that the previous owner has taken the trouble of breaking it in for you. Not long ago prune-packers, alarmed by a slump in sales, took a survey to determine the connotations of prunes in the public consciousness. Asked, "What do you think of when you hear the word *prunes?*" most people replied, "dried up," "wrinkled," or "constipated." Dismayed, the packers set out to create new contexts for prunes, in hopes of inducing new connotations. Soon, advertisements began to show prunes in gay, brightly colored settings, in the company of glamorous figure skaters.[1]

In imaginative writing, connotations are no less crucial. Consider this sentence: "A new brand of journalism is being born, or spawned" (Dwight Macdonald writing in *The New York Review of Books*). The last word, by its associations with fish and crustaceans, suggests that this new journalism is scarcely the product of human beings. And what do we make of Romeo's assertion that Juliet "is the sun"? Surely even a lovesick boy cannot mean that his sweetheart is "the incandescent body of gases about which the earth and other planets revolve" (to give a dictionary definition). He means, of course, that he thrives in her sight, that he feels warm in her presence or even at the thought of her, that she illuminates his world and is the center of his universe. Because in the mind of the hearer these and other suggestions are brought into play, Romeo's statement, literally absurd, makes excellent sense. In a famous poem of Blake, we see that both denotation and connotation are indispensable.

WILLIAM BLAKE (1757–1827)

London

> I wander through each chartered street,
> Near where the chartered Thames does flow,
> And mark in every face I meet
> Marks of weakness, marks of woe.

4

[1] For this and other instances of connotation-engineering, see Vance Packard's *The Hidden Persuaders* (New York, 1958), chap. 13.

In every cry of every man,
In every infant's cry of fear,
In every voice, in every ban,
The mind-forged manacles I hear.   8

How the chimney-sweeper's cry
Every black'ning church appalls;
And the hapless soldier's sigh
Runs in blood down palace walls.   12

But most through midnight streets I hear
How the youthful harlot's curse
Blasts the new-born infant's tear,
And blights with plagues the marriage hearse.   16

We list here only a few of the possible meanings of four of Blake's words:

Chartered (lines 1, 2)

> DENOTATIONS: (1) established by a charter (a written grant or a certificate of incorporation); (2) leased or hired.

> CONNOTATIONS: defined, limited, restricted, channeled, mapped, bound by law; bought and sold (like a slave or an inanimate object); Magna Charta; charters given crown colonies by the King; etc.

> OTHER THINGS IN THE POEM WITH SIMILAR CONNOTATIONS: *ban*; *manacles*; *chimney-sweeper*, *soldier*, *harlot* (all hirelings).

> INTERPRETATION OF THE LINES: The street has had mapped out for it the direction in which it must go; the Thames has had laid down to it the course it must follow. Street and river are channeled, imprisoned, enslaved (like every inhabitant of London).

Black'ning (line 10)

> DENOTATION: becoming black.

> CONNOTATIONS: the darkening of something once light, the defilement of something once clean, the deepening of guilt, the gathering of darkness at the approach of night, etc.

> OTHER THINGS WITH SIMILAR CONNOTATIONS: objects becoming marked or smudged (*marks of weakness, marks of woe* in the faces of passers-by; bloodied walls of a palace; marriage blighted with plagues); the word *appalls* (suggesting not only "to overcome with horror" but "to cast a pall or shroud over something"); *midnight streets*.

67

INTERPRETATION OF THE LINE: Literally, every London church grows black from soot, and hires a chimney-sweeper (a small boy) to help clean it. But Blake suggests too that by profiting from the suffering of the child laborer, the church is soiling its original purity.

Blasts, blights (lines 15–16)

DENOTATIONS: (1) Both *blast* and *blight* mean "to cause to wither"; or "to ruin and destroy." (2) Both are terms from horticulture. Frost *blasts* a bud and kills it; disease *blights* a growing plant.

CONNOTATIONS: sickness and death; gardens shriveled and dying; gusts of wind and the ravages of insects; things blown to pieces or rotted and warped; etc.

OTHER THINGS WITH SIMILAR CONNOTATIONS: faces marked with weakness and woe; the child become a chimney-sweep; the soldier killed by war; blackening church and bloodied palace; young girl turned harlot; the wedding carriage transformed into a hearse.

INTERPRETATION OF THE LINES: Literally, the harlot spreads the plague of syphillis, which, carried into marriage, can cause a baby to be born blind. In a larger and more meaningful sense, Blake sees the prostitution of even one young girl corrupting the entire institution of matrimony and endangering every child.

Some of the connotations listed above are more to the point than others; the reader of a poem nearly always has the problem of distinguishing relevant associations from irrelevant ones. This is why it may help to recall that a word derives at least part of its meaning from its context, that is, from the words around it. We need to read a poem in its entirety, and when a word leaves us in doubt, look for other things in the poem to corroborate (or refute) what we think it means. Relatively simple and direct in its statement, Blake's account of his stroll through the city at night becomes an indictment of a whole social and religious order. The indictment could hardly be this effective if it were "mathematically plain," its every word restricted to one denotation clearly spelled out for us.

SAMUEL JOHNSON (1709–1784)

A Short Song of Congratulation

Long-expected one and twenty
  Ling'ring year at last is flown,
Pomp and pleasure, pride and plenty,
  Great Sir John, are all your own.   4

Loosened from the minor's tether;
  Free to mortgage or to sell,
Wild as wind, and light as feather
  Bid the slaves of thrift farewell.   8

Call the Bettys, Kates, and Jennys
  Every name that laughs at care,
Lavish of your grandsire's guineas,
  Show the spirit of an heir.   12

All that prey on vice and folly
  Joy to see their quarry fly,
Here the gamester light and jolly
  There the lender grave and sly.   16

Wealth, Sir John, was made to wander,
  Let it wander as it will;
See the jockey, see the pander,
  Bid them come, and take their fill.   20

When the bonny blade carouses,
  Pockets full, and spirits high,
What are acres? What are houses?
  Only dirt, or° wet or dry.   *either*   24

If the guardian or the mother
  Tell the woes of willful waste,
Scorn their counsel and their pother,
  You can hang or drown at last.   28

QUESTIONS

1. Johnson states in line 24 the connotations that *acres* and *houses* have for the young heir. What connotations might we imagine these terms have for Johnson himself?

2. Why are Bettys, Kates, and Jennys more meaningful names as Johnson uses them than Elizabeths, Katherines, and Genevieves?

WALLACE STEVENS (1879–1955)

Disillusionment of Ten O'Clock

The houses are haunted
By white night-gowns.
None are green,
Or purple with green rings,
Or green with yellow rings,   5
Or yellow with blue rings.
None of them are strange,
With socks of lace
And beaded ceintures.
People are not going   10
To dream of baboons and periwinkles.
Only, here and there, an old sailor,
Drunk and asleep in his boots,
Catches tigers
In red weather.   15

QUESTIONS

1. What is lacking in the people who live in these houses? Why
should the poet's view of them be a "disillusionment"?
2. What contrast is drawn between the people and the old sailor?
What connotations (of *white night-gowns* and *sailor*) contribute to this
contrast?
3. What are *beaded ceintures?* What does the phrase suggest to you?
4. What do the colors suggest?

ROBERT HERRICK (1591–1674)

Upon Julia's Voice

So smooth, so sweet, so silv'ry is thy voice,
As, could they hear, the damned would make no noise,
But listen to thee (walking in thy chamber)
Melting melodious words, to lutes of amber.

QUESTION

Two denotations of the word *amber* are possible: (1) the fossilized
resin from which pipestems are sometimes made today, and which might
have been used to inlay the body of a lute; or (2) an alloy of four parts
of silver and one part of gold. In this poem, which denotation makes more
sense? Explain Herrick's comparison.

70

EXERCISE ONE

Here is a translation from Li Po, a Chinese poet of the eighth century:

EZRA POUND (b. 1885)

The Jewel Stairs' Grievance

> The jeweled steps are already quite white with dew,
> It is so late that the dew soaks my gauze stockings,
> And I let down the crystal curtain
> And watch the moon through the clear autumn.

Pound supplies these notes on connotations in the poem: "Jewel stairs, therefore a palace. Grievance, therefore there is something to complain of. Gauze stockings, therefore a court lady, not a servant who complains. Clear autumn, therefore she has no excuse on account of weather. Also she has come early, for the dew has not merely whitened the stairs, but has soaked her stockings. The poem is especially prized because she utters no direct reproach."

Try rewriting "The Jewel Stairs' Grievance," either into prose or a new poem, making explicit to an American reader every idea that, according to Pound, is suggested in the original by connotation. Then compare your noteless and connotationless poem with Pound's poem in its brevity. What, if anything, does this comparison show you about denotation and connotation?

2. ALLUSION

By an **allusion** — a reference to anyone or anything fictitious, historical, or actual — the poet expects us to bring to the poem some item of public knowledge and some usual responses. If this seems high-handed on his part, reflect that literature would be impossible if author and readers had no common supply of knowledge and associations. When A. E. Housman refers to a cherry tree, he has a right to assume that we have seen such a tree or a picture of one, or have heard a description of it. Similarly, T. S. Eliot said he wrote for the reader who knows at least Shakespeare and the Bible. (However, in his highly allusive long poem *The Waste Land*, Eliot apparently expected his readers to know a great deal more than that.)

Allusions have the value of saving space. By giving a brief introductory quotation from the speech of a damned soul in Dante's *Inferno*, Eliot can suggest that similarly "The Love Song of J. Alfred Prufrock" is to be the confession of a soul in torment, who sees no chance of escape.

If you said to someone, "Those neighbors across the street make more noise than the Beatles," and he replied, "More noise than what?" he might be said to be "out of it," which would be to call him an outsider to the mainstream of our current popular culture. In much the same way, someone bewildered by an allusion to a famous passage from the Bible or from Shakespeare or T. S. Eliot is in one respect "out of" the traditions of his civilization. "The study of history and of literature," as S. I. Hayakawa has said, "is not merely the idle acquisition of social polish, as practical men are fond of believing, but a necessary means both of increasing the efficiency of our communications and of increasing our understanding of what others are trying to communicate to us." [2] To the poet, then, allusion can be a subtle means of effecting such communication.

EXERCISE TWO

From your knowledge, supplemented by an encyclopedia if need be, explain the allusions in the following three poems.

J. V. CUNNINGHAM (b. 1911)

'Friend, on this scaffold'

Friend, on this scaffold Thomas More lies dead
Who would not cut the Body from the Head.

JOHN KEATS (1795–1821)

On First Looking into Chapman's Homer

Much have I traveled in the realms of gold,
And many goodly states and kingdoms seen;
Round many western islands have I been
Which bards in fealty to Apollo hold.   4
Oft of one wide expanse had I been told
That deep-browed Homer ruled as his demesne;
Yet did I never breathe its pure serene
Till I heard Chapman speak out loud and bold: 8
Then felt I like some watcher of the skies
When a new planet swims into his ken;
Or like stout Cortez when with eagle eyes
He stared at the Pacific — and all his men   12
Looked at each other with a wild surmise —
Silent, upon a peak in Darien.

[2] The argument of this paragraph comes from Hayakawa's *Language in Thought and Action* (New York, 1949).

72

JOHN DRYDEN (1631–1700)

Lines Printed under the Engraved Portrait of Milton

Three poets, in three distant ages born,
Greece, Italy, and England did adorn.
The first in loftiness of thought surpassed,
The next in majesty, in both the last:
The force of Nature could no farther go;
To make a third she joined the former two.

Lines Printed under the Engraved Portrait of Milton. These lines appeared in Tonson's folio edition of *Paradise Lost* (1668).

E. E. CUMMINGS (1894–1962)

'the Cambridge ladies'

the Cambridge ladies who live in furnished souls
are unbeautiful and have comfortable minds
(also, with the church's protestant blessings
daughters, unscented shapeless spirited)
they believe in Christ and Longfellow, both dead,   5
are invariably interested in so many things —
at the present writing one still finds
delighted fingers knitting for the is it Poles?
perhaps. While permanent faces coyly bandy
scandal of Mrs. N and Professor D   10
. . . . the Cambridge ladies do not care, above
Cambridge if sometimes in its box of
sky lavender and cornerless, the
moon rattles like a fragment of angry candy

QUESTIONS

1. To which city named Cambridge does Cummings allude? How do you know?
2. What is meant by the double allusion to Christ and Longfellow?
3. In line 3, why does *protestant* lack a capital letter? What is the denotative meaning of the word?
4. What do you understand by the interrupted syntax of *knitting for the is it Poles?*
5. What connotations are we to draw from the words *furnished* (line 1), *comfortable* (2), *permanent, coyly* (9), *lavender* and *cornerless* (13)?
6. What do the last four lines tell us about the Cambridge ladies? How can candy be "angry"?
7. How would you describe the tone of the poem? To what extent have allusion and connotation helped to communicate it?

73

MATTHEW PRIOR (1664–1721)

The Lady Who Offers Her Looking Glass to Venus

Venus, take my votive glass,
Since I am not what I was;
What from this day I shall be,
Venus, let me never see.

QUESTIONS

1. Explain the allusion to Venus.
2. What does *votive* mean? The phrase *my votive glass* could work in two ways: either in the sense of "my mirror, which is a votary" or of "mirror belonging to me, who am a votary." Can both these meanings function in this poem? In each case, who would be the object of adoration?
3. Which is the more nearly adequate statement of Prior's attitude toward the lady? "The silly old hag, she's only trying to fool herself!" or "Poor lady, she's lost her dearest possession." How do you know? What do you see in the poem to justify your answer?

JOHN LYLY (1554?–1606)

'Cupid and my Campaspe'

Cupid and my Campaspe played
At cards for kisses; Cupid paid.
He stakes his quiver, bow, and arrows,
His mother's doves and team of sparrows,   4
Loses them too; then down he throws
The coral of his lip, the rose
Growing on's cheek (but none knows how),
With these the crystal of his brow,   8
And then the dimple of his chin:
All these did my Campaspe win.
At last he set her both his eyes;
She won, and Cupid blind did rise.   12
    O Love! has she done this to thee?
    What shall, alas, become of me?

QUESTIONS

1. Lyly is usually given credit for this song from his play *Alexander and Campaspe*, but it may be the work of another. To what extent has its language deteriorated over the past three centuries? How many archaisms do you find in it?
2. According to mythology, who were Cupid and his mother?
3. What connotations do *coral, rose,* and *crystal* have in common?
4. Try moving the *alas* to any other position in the last line. What is the effect of this change in syntax?
5. What is the tone of the poem? How do you know?

74

ROBERT HERRICK (1591–1674)

To Daisies, Not to Shut So Soon

Shut not so soon; the dull-eyed night
   Has not as yet begun
To make a seizure on the light,
   Or to seal up the sun.   4

No marigolds yet closèd are;
   No shadows great appear;
Nor doth the early shepherd's star
   Shine like a spangle here.   8

Stay but till my Julia close
   Her life-begetting eye;
And let the whole world then dispose
   Itself to live or die.   12

QUESTIONS

1. Why is Julia's eye called "life-begetting"?
2. How would you answer the quibble that the poet is at fault in not mentioning her other eye?
3. What meanings do you find in "dull-eyed"? What connotations?
4. "To make a seizure" can be a legal term, meaning to claim land or property, as for instance a government might attach land that a citizen thought he had freely inherited. What would this denotation add to the meaning of the poem?
5 Look up *daisy* in your dictionary and see where the word comes from. How does awareness of this derivation help you in reading Herrick's poem?

ROBERT FROST (1874–1963)

Fire and Ice

Some say the world will end in fire,
Some say in ice.
From what I've tasted of desire
I hold with those who favor fire.
But if it had to perish twice,   5
I think I know enough of hate
To say that for destruction ice
Is also great
And would suffice.

QUESTIONS

1. What connotations of *fire* and *ice* contribute to the richness of Frost's comparison?
2. To whom does Frost allude in line 1? In line 2?

FIVE

IMAGERY

EZRA POUND (b. 1885)

In a Station of the Metro

> The apparition of these faces in the crowd;
> Petals on a wet, black bough.

Pound has said he wrote this poem to convey an experience: emerging one day from a train in the Paris subway (*Métro*), he beheld "suddenly a beautiful face, and then another and another." Originally he had described his impression in a poem thirty lines long. In this final version, each line contains an **image**, which, like a picture, may take the place of a thousand words.

Though the term *image* suggests a thing to be seen, we generally take it to mean *a word or sequence of words that refers to any sensory experience*. More often than not, this experience is a sight (**visual imagery,** as in Pound's poem); but it may be a sound (**auditory imagery**) or a touch (**tactile imagery,** as a perception of roughness or smoothness). It may be an odor or a taste; or perhaps such a bodily sensation as pain, the prickling of gooseflesh, or the pleasure of quenching one's thirst. Here is a non-visual image in another brief poem, a translation from the Japanese by Harold G. Henderson:

TANIGUCHI BUSON (1715–1783)

'The piercing chill'

> The piercing chill I feel:
>   my dead wife's comb, in our bedroom,
>   under my heel . . .

76

As in this **haiku** (in Japanese, a poem of seventeen syllables), an image can do more than start a sympathetic tingling of the nerve ends: it can convey — in a flash — understanding. Had he wished, the poet might have spoken of the dead woman, of the contrast between her death and his memory of her, of his feelings toward death in general. But how much less forceful such a discussion probably would be. Striking his bare foot against the comb, now cold and motionless but associated with the living wife (perhaps worn in her hair), the widower feels a shock as if he had touched the woman's corpse. A literal, physical sense of death is conveyed; the abstraction "death" is understood through the senses. To speak of the abstract in concrete terms is what poets frequently do; in this task, an image can be valuable.

An image may occur in a single word, a phrase, a sentence, or, as in this case, an entire short poem. To speak of the **imagery** of a poem — all its images taken collectively — is often more useful than to speak of separate images. To divide Buson's haiku into five images — *chill, wife, comb, bedroom, heel* — is possible, since any noun that refers to a visible object or a sensation is an image, but this is to draw distinctions that in themselves mean little and to disassemble a single experience.

It is misleading to say that an image causes the reader to experience a sense impression for himself. Reading the word "petals," no one literally sees petals; but one is given the occasion to imagine them. The image asks to be seen with the mind's eye. And although "In a Station of the Metro" records what Ezra Pound saw personally, it is of course not necessary for a poet actually to have lived through a sensory experience in order to write of it. Despite the image in his sonnet on Chapman's Homer (p. 72), Keats may never have beheld an unfamiliar planet through a telescope.

It is tempting to think of imagery as so much decoration, particularly when reading Keats, who fills his work with more sights, odors, and tastes than most poets do. But further scrutiny will show that a successful image is no mere paint, perfume, or artificial flavoring that the poet handily applies, but an accurate and effective means of communication. When Keats opens "The Eve of St. Agnes" with what have been called the coldest lines in literature, he evokes by a series of images a setting and a mood:

> St. Agnes' eve — Ah, bitter chill it was!
> The owl, for all his feathers, was a-cold;
> The hare limped trembling through the frozen grass,
> And silent was the flock in woolly fold:

Numb were the Beadsman's fingers, while he told
His rosary, and while his frosted breath,
Like pious incense from a censer old,
Seemed taking flight for heaven, without a death, . . .

Indeed, some literary critics would look for the meaning of a poem first of all in its imagery, in which they expect to see the mind of the poet more truly revealed than in whatever he explicitly *tells* us he believes. In his investigation of Wordsworth's "Ode: Intimations of Immortality," a poem that seems explicit, the critic Cleanth Brooks devotes his attention to the imagery of light and darkness, which he finds carries on and develops Wordsworth's thought.[1] A critic may speak of a poem's **image structure** or **pattern of imagery,** referring to the images in a poem taken all together or in related groups.

"The greatest poverty," wrote Wallace Stevens, "is not to live / In a physical world." In his own poems, surely, Stevens made us aware of our world's richness. He could take even a common object sold by the pound in supermarkets and, with precise imagery, recall to us what we have forgotten we have ever seen.

WALLACE STEVENS (1879–1955)

Study of Two Pears

I

Opusculum paedagogum°.   *a little work that teaches*
The pears are not viols,
Nudes or bottles.
They resemble nothing else.   4

II

They are yellow forms
Composed of curves
Bulging toward the base.
They are touched red.   8

III

They are not flat surfaces
Having curved outlines.
They are round
Tapering toward the top.   12

---

[1] "Wordsworth and the Paradox of the Imagination," in *The Well Wrought Urn: Studies in the Structure of Poetry* (New York, 1947).

78

IV

In the way they are modeled
There are bits of blue.
A hard dry leaf hangs
From the stem.   16

V

The yellow glistens.
It glistens with various yellows,
Citrons, oranges and greens
Flowering over the skin.   20

VI

The shadows of the pears
Are blobs on the green cloth.
The pears are not seen
As the observer wills.   24

Though Shakespeare's Theseus (in A *Midsummer Night's Dream*)
accused the poet of being concerned with "airy nothings," the poet
is usually very much concerned with what is really in front of him.
This concern is of use to us. Perhaps it may be, as Alan Watts has
remarked, that Americans are not the materialists they are sometimes
accused of being: for how could anyone, taking a look at an American
city, think that its inhabitants deeply cherish material things?
Involved in our personal hopes and apprehensions, anticipating the
future so hard that much of the time we see the present through a
film of thought across our eyes, perhaps we need a poet occasionally
to remind us that even the coffee we absentmindedly sip comes in
(as Yeats put it) a "heavy spillable cup."

JOHN KEATS (1795–1821)

Ode to a Nightingale

My heart aches, and a drowsy numbness pains
   My sense, as though of hemlock I had drunk,
Or emptied some dull opiate to the drains
   One minute past, and Lethe-wards had sunk:
'Tis not through envy of thy happy lot,   5
   But being too happy in thy happiness —
      That thou, light-wingèd Dryad° of the trees,   *nymph or*
      In some melodious plot   *spirit*
   Of beechen green, and shadows numberless,
      Singest of summer in full-throated ease.   10

O for a draught of vintage! that hath been
  Cooled a long age in the deep-delvèd earth,
Tasting of Flora and the country green,
  Dance, and Provençal song, and sunburnt mirth!
O for a beaker full of the warm South,   15
  Full of the true, the blushful Hippocrene,
    With beaded bubbles winking at the brim,
      And purple-stainèd mouth;
  That I might drink, and leave the world unseen,
    And with thee fade away into the forest dim: 20

Fade far away, dissolve, and quite forget
  What thou among the leaves has never known,
The weariness, the fever, and the fret
  Here, where men sit and hear each other groan;
Where palsy shakes a few, sad, last grey hairs,   25
  Where youth grows pale, and specter-thin, and dies;
    Where but to think is to be full of sorrow
      And leaden-eyed despairs,
  Where Beauty cannot keep her lustrous eyes,
    Or new Love pine at them beyond to-morrow.   30

Away! away! for I will fly to thee,
  Not charioted by Bacchus and his pards,
But on the viewless wings of Poesy,
  Though the dull brain perplexes and retards:
Already with thee! tender is the night,   35
  And haply the Queen-Moon is on her throne,
    Clustered around by all her starry Fays°;   *Fairies*
      But here there is no light,
  Save what from heaven is with the breezes blown
    Through verdurous glooms and winding mossy ways.   40

I cannot see what flowers are at my feet,
  Nor what soft incense hangs upon the boughs,
But, in embalmèd darkness, guess each sweet
  Wherewith the seasonable month endows
The grass, the thicket, and the fruit tree wild;   45
  White hawthorn, and the pastoral eglantine;
    Fast fading violets covered up in leaves;
      And mid-May's eldest child,
  The coming musk rose, full of dewy wine,
    The murmurous haunt of flies on summer eves.   50

Darkling° I listen; and, for many a time   *in darkness*
  I have been half in love with easeful Death,
Called him soft names in many a musèd rhyme,

To take into the air my quiet breath;
Now more than ever seems it rich to die,   55
    To cease upon the midnight with no pain,
        While thou art pouring forth thy soul abroad
            In such an ecstasy!
    Still wouldst thou sing, and I have ears in vain —
        To thy high requiem become a sod.   60

Thou wast not born for death, immortal Bird!
    No hungry generations tread thee down;
The voice I hear this passing night was heard
    In ancient days by emperor and clown:
Perhaps the self-same song that found a path   65
    Through the sad heart of Ruth, when, sick for home,
        She stood in tears amid the alien corn;
            The same that oft-times hath
    Charmed magic casements, opening on the foam
        Of perilous seas, in faery lands forlorn.   70

Forlorn! the very word is like a bell
    To toll me back from thee to my sole self!
Adieu! the fancy cannot cheat so well
    As she is famed to do, deceiving elf.
Adieu! adieu! thy plaintive anthem fades   75
    Past the near meadows, over the still stream,
        Up the hillside; and now 'tis buried deep
            In the next valley glades:
    Was it a vision, or a waking dream?
        Fled is that music: — Do I wake or sleep?   80

Ode to a Nightingale. 4. *Lethe:* river in Hades, a taste of whose waters
caused forgetfulness. 16. *Hippocrene:* fountain sacred to the Muses, on Mt.
Helicon, whose waters gave poetic inspiration. 32. *Bacchus . . . pards:*
The god of wine was sometimes depicted riding in a leopard-drawn
chariot. 66. *Ruth:* See the Book of Ruth in the Bible, chap. 2.

QUESTIONS

1. To what extent does Keats employ visual imagery in this poem?
2. What images appeal to senses other than sight?
3. Paraphrase, stanza by stanza, what Keats is saying. Is it possible to
divorce the meaning of the poem from its imagery? Explain.

ELIZABETH BISHOP (b. 1911)

The Fish

I caught a tremendous fish
and held him beside the boat
half out of water, with my hook
fast in a corner of his mouth.
He didn't fight. 5
He hadn't fought at all.
He hung a grunting weight,
battered and venerable
and homely. Here and there
his brown skin hung in strips 10
like ancient wall-paper,
and its pattern of darker brown
was like wall-paper:
shapes like full-blown roses
stained and lost through age. 15
He was speckled with barnacles,
fine rosettes of lime,
and infested
with tiny white sea-lice,
and underneath two or three 20
rags of green weed hung down.
While his gills were breathing in
the terrible oxygen
— the frightening gills,
fresh and crisp with blood, 25
that can cut so badly —
I thought of the coarse white flesh
packed in like feathers,
the big bones and the little bones,
the dramatic reds and blacks 30
of his shiny entrails,
and the pink swim-bladder
like a big peony.
I looked into his eyes
which were far larger than mine 35
but shallower, and yellowed,
the irises backed and packed
with tarnished tinfoil
seen through the lenses
of old scratched isinglass. 40
They shifted a little, but not
to return my stare.

82

— It was more like the tipping
of an object toward the light.
I admired his sullen face,   45
the mechanism of his jaw,
and then I saw
that from his lower lip
— if you could call it a lip —
grim, wet, and weapon-like,   50
hung five old pieces of fish-line,
or four and a wire leader
with the swivel still attached,
with all their five big hooks
grown firmly in his mouth.   55
A green line, frayed at the end
where he broke it, two heavier lines,
and a fine black thread
still crimped from the strain and snap
when it broke and he got away.   60
Like medals with their ribbons
frayed and wavering,
a five-haired beard of wisdom
trailing from his aching jaw.
I stared and stared   65
and victory filled up
the little rented boat,
from the pool of bilge
where oil had spread a rainbow
around the rusted engine   70
to the bailer rusted orange,
the sun-cracked thwarts,
the oarlocks on their strings,
the gunnels — until everything
was rainbow, rainbow, rainbow!   75
And I let the fish go.

QUESTIONS

1. Approximately what proportion of abstract, general language does
this poem contain? What proportion of imagery?

2. What is the speaker's attitude toward the fish? Comment in particular on the imagery of lines 61–64.

3. What attitude do the images of the rainbow of oil (line 69), the
orange bailer (or bailing bucket, 71), the sun-cracked thwarts (72) convey? Does the poet expect us to feel mournful because the boat is in such
sorry condition? What is meant by *rainbow, rainbow, rainbow?*

4. How do these images prepare us for the conclusion? Why does the
speaker let the fish go?

83

Taking the following poems as examples from which to start rather than as models to be slavishly copied, try composing a brief poem that consists largely of imagery.

WALT WHITMAN (1819–1892)

Cavalry Crossing a Ford

A line in long array where they wind betwixt green islands,
They take a serpentine course, their arms flash in the sun —
    hark to the musical clank,
Behold the silvery river, in it the splashing horses loitering
    stop to drink,
Behold the brown-faced men, each group, each person a
    picture, the negligent rest on the saddles,
Some emerge on the opposite bank, others are just entering   5
    the ford — while,
Scarlet and blue and snowy white,
The guidon flags flutter gayly in the wind.

WILLIAM CARLOS WILLIAMS (1883–1963)

Poem

As the cat
climbed over
the top of

the jamcloset
first the right
forefoot
    6

carefully
then the hind
stepped down

into the pit of
the empty
flowerpot
    12

ROBERT HERRICK (1591–1674)

God's Hands

God's Hands are round and smooth, that gifts may fall
Freely from them, and hold none back at all.

84

H. D. [HILDA DOOLITTLE] (1886–1961)

Heat

O wind, rend open the heat,
cut apart the heat,
rend it to tatters.

Fruit cannot drop
through this thick air —   5
fruit cannot fall into heat
that presses up and blunts
the points of pears
and rounds the grapes.

Cut the heat —   10
plough through it,
turning it on either side
of your path.

SIX

FIGURES OF SPEECH

1. WHY SPEAK FIGURATIVELY?

"I will speak daggers to her, but use none," says Hamlet, preparing to confront his mother. His statement makes sense only because we realize that the term *daggers* is to be taken two ways: literally (denoting sharp, pointed weapons) and non-literally (referring to something that can be used *like* weapons, namely, words). Reading poetry, we often meet comparisons between two things whose similarity we have never noticed before. When Marianne Moore observes that a fir tree has "an emerald turkey-foot at the top," her poem makes us conscious of resemblances in the natural world that, without the aid of the poem, almost certainly would have eluded us. The result is a pleasure that poetry richly affords: the sudden recognition of likenesses.

A treetop like a turkey-foot, words like daggers — such comparisons are called **figures of speech.** In its broadest definition, a figure of speech may be said to occur whenever a speaker or writer, for the sake of freshness or emphasis, departs from the usual denotations of his words. Certainly, when Hamlet says he will speak daggers, no one expects him to release pointed weapons from his lips; for *daggers* is not to be read solely for its denotation. Its connotations — sharp, stabbing, piercing, wounding — also come to mind, and we see ways in which words and daggers work alike. (Words too can hurt: by striking through pretenses, possibly, or by wounding their hearer's self-esteem.) In the statement "A razor is sharper than an ax," there is no departure from the usual denotations of *razor* and *ax*, and no figure of speech results. Both objects are of the same class; the comparison is not offensive to logic. But in "How sharper than a serpent's tooth it is to have a thankless child," the objects — snake's tooth (fang) and ungrateful offspring — are so disparate that no reasonable comparison may be made between them. To find similarity, we attend to the connotations of *serpent's tooth* — biting, piercing, pain — rather than to its denotations.

Figures of speech, then, are much more than ways of stating what is demonstrably untrue. They do, indeed, state a truth that more literal language cannot. Nor is a figure of speech to be regarded as a kind of wordplay or fantasy that has nothing to do with any reality we can perceive. Skillfully used, a figure of speech can help the mind's eye to see more clearly, to focus upon particulars.

ALFRED, LORD TENNYSON (1809–1892)

The Eagle

> He clasps the crag with crooked hands;
> Close to the sun in lonely lands,
> Ringed with the azure world, he stands.
>
> The wrinkled sea beneath him crawls;
> He watches from his mountain walls,
> And like a thunderbolt he falls.

This brief poem is rich in figurative language. In the first line, we are stopped short by the phrase *crooked hands*. An eagle does not have hands, we might protest; but the objection would be a quibble, for evidently Tennyson is indicating exactly how an eagle clasps a crag, in the way that human fingers clasp a thing. By implication, too, the eagle is a person. *Close to the sun*, if taken literally, is an absurd exaggeration, the sun being a mean distance of 93,000,000 miles from the earth. For the eagle to be closer to it by the altitude of a mountain is an approach so small as to be insignificant. But figuratively, Tennyson conveys that the eagle stands above the clouds, perhaps silhouetted against the sun, and for the moment belongs to the heavens rather than to the land and sea. The word *ringed* makes a circle of the whole world's horizons and suggests that we see the world from the eagle's height; the sea becomes an aged, sluggish animal; *mountain walls*, possibly literal, also suggest a fort or castle; and finally the eagle himself is likened to a thunderbolt in speed and in power, perhaps also in that his beak is — like our abstract conception of a lightningbolt — pointed. How much of the poem can be taken literally? Only *he clasps the crag, he stands, he watches, he falls*; the rest is made of figures of speech. The result is that, reading Tennyson's poem, we gain a bird's-eye view of sun, sea, and land — and even of bird. Like imagery, figurative language refers us to the physical world.

2. METAPHOR AND SIMILE

In poetry, among the most common figures of speech are metaphor and simile. Both may be seen in Shelley's lines from "Adonais":

> Life, like a dome of many-colored glass,
> Stains the white radiance of Eternity.

The first of these lines is a **simile**: a comparison of two things, indicated by some connective, usually *like, as, than,* or a verb such as *resembles*. The things compared have to be dissimilar in kind for a simile to exist: it is no simile to say "Your fingers are like mine"; it is a literal observation. But to say "Your fingers are like sausages" is to use a simile. Omit the connective — say "Your fingers are sausages" — and the result is a **metaphor**, a statement that one thing *is* something else, which, in a literal sense, it is not. In the second of Shelley's lines, it is *assumed* that Eternity is light or radiance, and we have an **implied metaphor**, one that uses neither a connective nor the verb *to be*. Here are examples:

O, my love is like a red, red rose.	(*Simile*)
O, my love resembles a red, red rose.	(*Simile*)
O, my love is redder than a rose.	(*Simile*)
O, my love is a red, red rose.	(*Metaphor*)
O, my love has red petals and sharp thorns.	(*Implied metaphor*)
O, I placed my love into a long-stem vase And I bandaged my bleeding thumb.	(*Implied metaphor*)

Often, a metaphor and a simile may be distinguished by much more than the superficial fact that they do or do not use some connective. In general, a simile refers to only one characteristic that two things have in common, while a metaphor is not plainly limited in how many resemblances it may indicate. To use the simile "He eats like a pig" is to compare man and animal in one respect: eating habits. But to say "What a pig he is!" is to use a metaphor that might also involve comparisons of appearance and morality. One might — if he prefers to classify figures of speech according to what they mean instead of which words they use — throw over the traditional usage, and call the line "My love is like a red, red rose" a metaphor rather than a simile because it conveys not just a single resemblance but many resemblances — of freshness, color (red cheeks and lips), and sweet odor — to name a few. Preferring such classification, the critic Philip Wheelright has suggested that, as a manner of speaking, metaphor is often better than simile in that it may differ "in degree of intensity, or in depth of penetration, or in freshness of recombination." [1]

In everyday speech, simile and metaphor are among our most hard-worked resources. We use metaphors ("She's a doll"), implied metaphors ("It's raining pitchforks!"), and similes ("The tickets are selling like hotcakes") without needing to be conscious of them. If, however, we are aware that words possess literal meanings as well as figurative ones, we do not write *died in the wool* for *dyed in the wool*, or *tow the line* for *toe the line*; nor mix our metaphors as did the speaker who urged, "To get ahead, a man should keep his nose to the grindstone, his shoulder to the wheel, his ear to the ground, and his eye on the ball." Perhaps the unintended humor of this statement arises from our realization that the writer who strung together so many stale metaphors was not aware that they had any physical reference. Good poems, which provide us with fresher metaphors, do not suffer if examined in the mind's eye. To help us see what it meant in Victorian England to support a family on a working man's small pay, John Davidson gives us this series of metaphors (in "Thirty Bob a Week"):

> It's a naked child against a hungry wolf;
>> It's playing bowls upon a splitting wreck;
> It's walking on a string across a gulf
>> With millstones fore-and-aft about your neck;
> But the thing is daily done by many and many a one;
>> And we fall, face forward, fighting, on the deck.

The impossibilities coalesce. Though no less literally absurd than the man with his nose to the grindstone, Davidson's man can be visualized, and his balancing act is meaningful.

[1] *The Burning Fountain* (Bloomington: Indiana University Press, 1954), p. 84.

A poem may involve a series of comparisons, like Davidson's; or, as in the following example from Housman, the whole poem may be one extended comparison.

A. E. HOUSMAN (1859–1936)

'From the wash the laundress sends'

> From the wash the laundress sends
> My collars home with raveled ends:
> I must fit, now these are frayed,
> My neck with new ones London-made.   4
>
> Homespun collars, homespun hearts,
> Wear to rags in foreign parts.
> Mine at least's as good as done,
> And I must get a London one.   8

The value to poetry of the use of metaphor may be illustrated by comparing two poems of Tennyson and Blake.

ALFRED, LORD TENNYSON (1809–1892)

Flower in the Crannied Wall

> Flower in the crannied wall,
> I pluck you out of the crannies,
> I hold you here, root and all, in my hand,
> Little flower — but *if* I could understand
> What you are, root and all, and all in all,
> I should know what God and man is.

How many metaphors does Tennyson's poem contain? Not any. Compare this with a still briefer poem on a similar theme: the quatrain that begins Blake's "Auguries of Innocence." (We follow here the opinion of W. B. Yeats who, in editing Blake's poems, thought the lines ought to be printed separately.)

WILLIAM BLAKE (1757–1827)

'To see a world'

> To see a world in a grain of sand
> And a heaven in a wild flower,
> Hold infinity in the palm of your hand
> And eternity in an hour.

Set beside Blake's poem, Tennyson's, short though it is, seems lengthy. And the richness of Blake's comes, doubtless, from his use of a metaphor in every line. Each metaphor is loaded with suggestion; for example, in how many ways our world resembles a grain of sand: in being round, in being one of a myriad (and on and on). Like Blake's grain of sand, a metaphor can contain much within its small circumference.

EMILY DICKINSON (1830–1886)

'It dropped so low – in my Regard'

It dropped so low—in my Regard—
I heard it hit the Ground—
And go to pieces on the Stones
At bottom of my Mind— 4

Yet blamed the Fate that flung it—*less*
Than I denounced Myself,
For entertaining Plated Wares
Upon my Silver Shelf—

QUESTIONS

1. What is *it?* What two things are compared?
2. How much of the poem consists of developing and amplifying this comparison?
3. In another version of this poem, lines 5–6 read: "Yet blamed the Fate that fractured—*less* / Than I reviled Myself . . ." Which version do you prefer? Why?

ANONYMOUS (English; 1784 or earlier)

'There was a man of double deed'

There was a man of double deed
Who sowed his garden full of seed.
When the seed began to grow
'Twas like a garden full of snow,
When the snow began to melt 5
'Twas like a ship without a belt,
When the ship began to sail
'Twas like a bird without a tail,
When the bird began to fly
'Twas like an eagle in the sky, 10
When the sky began to roar
'Twas like a lion at the door,

When the door began to crack
'Twas like a stick across my back,
When my back began to smart   15
'Twas like a penknife in my heart,
And when my heart began to bleed
'Twas death and death and death indeed.

'There was a man of double deed.' This traditional nursery rhyme may
have originated as a chant to the rhythm of a bouncing ball. Its opening
lines echo an old proverb: "A man of words and not of deeds is like a
garden full of weeds." 6. *belt:* a series of armored plates at a ship's water
line.

QUESTION

Does this seem no more than rigmarole or do you find it making any
sense? Consider possible meanings of the phrase *double deed* and ways in
which the objects joined in similes might be truly similar.

ROBERT GRAVES (b. 1895)

A Civil Servant

While in this cavernous place employed
    Not once was I aware
Of my officious other-self
    Poised high above me there,   4

My self reversed, my rage-less part,
    A slimy yellowish cone —
Drip, drip; drip, drip — so down the years
    I stalagmized in stone.   8

Now pilgrims to the cave, who come
    To chip off what they can,
Prod me with child-like merriment:
    "Look, look! It's like a man!"   12

QUESTIONS

1. What is the difference between a stalactite and a stalagmite? What
does Graves liken to each of them?
2. How are they formed? To what is Graves comparing the process of
their formation?
3. What is the theme of the poem?
4. How would you explain the relationship between theme and metaphors in this poem?

EDMUND SPENSER (1552?–1599)

'What guile is this'

What guile is this, that those her golden tresses
    She doth attire under a net of gold
    And with sly skill so cunningly them dresses,
    That which is gold or hair, may scarce be told?   4
Is it that men's frail eyes, which gaze too bold,
    She may entangle in that golden snare
    And being caught may craftily enfold
    Their weaker hearts, which are not well aware?   8
Take heed therefore, mine eyes, how ye do stare
    Henceforth too rashly on that guileful net
    In which if ever ye entrappèd are,
    Out of her bands ye by no means shall get.   12
Fondness° it were for any being free   *folly*
    To covet fetters, though they golden be.

QUESTIONS

1. What is the extended figure of speech in this poem? Would you call it a metaphor or a simile?
2. To what are men's eyes compared (lines 5–8)? In what is the similarity?

ELIZABETH JENNINGS (b. 1926)

Delay

The radiance of that star that leans on me
Was shining years ago. The light that now
Glitters up there my eye may never see
And so the time lag teases me with how   4
Love that loves now may not reach me until
Its first desire is spent. The star's impulse
Must wait for eyes to claim it beautiful
And love arrived may find us somewhere else.   8

QUESTIONS

1. What are the two terms in this metaphor?
2. Why would not the metaphor have been available to a poet in Shakespeare's time?
3. What is the tone of the poem? How does the speaker feel about the "radiance of that star" — simply joyous and glad, as we might expect?
4. What connotations has the word *impulse* (line 6)? What is the implied metaphor here?

OGDEN NASH (b. 1902)

Very Like a Whale

One thing that literature would be greatly the better for
Would be a more restricted employment by authors of simile
and metaphor.
Authors of all races, be they Greeks, Roman, Teutons or
Celts,
Can't seem just to say that anything is the thing it is but
have to go out of their way to say that it is like some-
thing else.
What does it mean when we are told   5
That the Assyrian came down like a wolf on the fold?
In the first place, George Gordon Byron had had enough
experience
To know that it probably wasn't just one Assyrian, it was a
lot of Assyrians.
However, as too many arguments are apt to induce apoplexy
and thus hinder longevity,
We'll let it pass as one Assyrian for the sake of brevity.   10
Now then, this particular Assyrian, the one whose cohorts
were gleaming in purple and gold,
Just what does the poet mean when he says he came down
like a wolf on the fold?
In heaven and earth more than is dreamed of in our philosophy there are a great many things,
But I don't imagine that among them there is a wolf with
purple and gold cohorts or purple and gold anythings.
No, no, Lord Byron, before I'll believe that this Assyrian was   15
actually like a wolf I must have some kind of proof;
Did he run on all fours and did he have a hairy tail and a big
red mouth and big white teeth and did he say Woof
woof woof?
Frankly I think it very unlikely, and all you were entitled to
say, at the very most,
Was that the Assyrian cohorts came down like a lot of
Assyrian cohorts about to destroy the Hebrew host.
But that wasn't fancy enough for Lord Byron, oh dear me
no, he had to invent a lot of figures of speech and then
interpolate them,
With the result that whenever you mention Old Testament   20
soldiers to people they say Oh yes, they're the ones that
a lot of wolves dressed up in gold and purple ate them.
That's the kind of thing that's being done all the time by
poets, from Homer to Tennyson;

94

They're always comparing ladies to lilies and veal to venison.
How about the man who wrote,
Her little feet stole in and out like mice beneath her petti-
    coat?
Wouldn't anybody but a poet think twice   25
Before stating that his girl's feet were mice?
Then they always say things like that after a winter storm
The snow is a white blanket. Oh it is, is it, all right then,
    you sleep under a six-inch blanket of snow and I'll sleep
    under a half-inch blanket of unpoetical blanket material
    and we'll see which one keeps warm,
And after that maybe you'll begin to comprehend dimly
What I mean by too much metaphor and simile.   30

Very Like a Whale. The title is from *Hamlet* (Act III, scene 2): feign-
ing madness, Hamlet likens the shape of a cloud to a whale. "Very like
a whale," says Polonius, who, to humor his prince, will agree to the accuracy of any figure at all. Nash's art has been described by Max
Eastman in *Enjoyment of Laughter* (New York, 1936):

> If you have ever tried to write rhymed verse, you will rec-
> ognize in Nash's writing every naïve crime you were ever tempted
> to commit — artificial inversions, pretended rhymes, sentences
> wrenched and mutilated to bring the rhyme-word to the end of
> the line, words assaulted and battered into rhyming whether they
> wanted to or not, ideas and whole dissertations dragged in for the
> sake of a rhyme, the metrical beat delayed in order to get all the
> necessary words in, the metrical beat speeded up unconscionably
> because there were not enough words to put in.

QUESTIONS

1. Nash alludes to the opening lines of Byron's poem "The Destruction of Sennacherib":

> The Assyrian came down like the wolf on the fold,
> And his cohorts were gleaming in purple and gold;

and to Sir John Suckling's portrait of a bride in "A Ballad Upon a Wedding":

> Her feet beneath her petticoat,
> Like little mice stole in and out,
> As if they feared the light: . . .

Can these metaphors be defended against Nash's quibbles?
2. What valuable functions of simile and metaphor in poetry is Nash
pretending to ignore?

3. OTHER FIGURES

Although rhetoricians have named more than two hundred figures of speech besides metaphor and simile, our concern is with only a few of them. Of particular use to poets are those which (as suggested by the derivation of the word *figure* from the Latin *figura:* form, shape) represent things in definite form and give perceptible shapes to them. Like metaphor and simile, the figures of speech we will consider here may also be of use to writers of prose.

When Shakespeare asks, in a sonnet,

> O! how shall summer's honey breath hold out
> Against the wrackful siege of batt'ring days,

it might seem at first that he mixes metaphors. How can a *breath* confront the battering ram of an invading army? But it is summer's breath, and by giving it one, Shakespeare makes the season a man or woman. It is as if the fragrance of summer were the breath within a person's body — or his very life — and by implication, winter — or the siege of time — the onslaught of old age.

Such is one instance of **personification**: a figure of speech in which an inanimate object, an abstract term (*truth, idleness*), or a force in nature is endowed with humanity. In these lines, a personification is extended throughout a whole short poem:

JAMES STEPHENS (1882–1950)

The Wind

> The wind stood up and gave a shout.
> He whistled on his fingers and
>
> Kicked the withered leaves about
> And thumped the branches with his hand
>
> And said he'd kill and kill and kill,
> And so he will and so he will.

This poet convincingly portrays the wind as a wild man; and evidently it is not just any autumn breeze but a hurricane or at least a stiff gale. In poems that do not work as well as this one, personification may be employed mechanically. Hollow-eyed personifications stalk through the works of lesser English poets of the eighteenth century: Coleridge has quoted the beginning of such a neoclassical ode, "Inoculation! heavenly Maid, descend!" It is hard for the contemporary reader to be excited by William Collins' "The Passions, An Ode for Music" (1747), which personifies, stanza by stanza, Fear, Anger, Despair, Hope, Revenge, Pity, Jealousy, Love, Hate, Melancholy, and Cheerfulness, and has them listen to Music, until even "Brown Exercise rejoiced to hear, / And Sport leapt up, and seized his beechen spear." However, using a figure of speech from custom rather than from inspiration does not necessarily discredit it. The portrayals of the Seven Deadly Sins in the fourteenth-century poem *Piers Plowman* remain memorable: "Thanne come Slothe al bislabered, with two slimy eiyen . . ." John Keats, too, made an abstraction come alive in personifying Fame as "a wayward girl." Sometimes confused with personification is another valuable device, **animism:** attributing life, but not human life, to an inanimate thing or natural object. Tennyson employs it in "The Eagle" in telling us that the wrinkled sea "crawls."

Hand in hand with personification, we often find **apostrophe:** a figure of speech in which the poet addresses by name some inanimate object ("Spade! with which Wilkinson hath tilled his lands") or abstract quality; or addresses a deity ("Great God! I'd rather be a pagan"), or some dead or absent individual ("Milton! thou shouldst be living at this hour") — to take examples from Wordsworth. With an apostrophe, a poet usually announces a lofty and serious tone; he may even put an "O" in front of it ("O moon. . . !"). We tend to be skeptical of such a tone nowadays, perhaps unnecessarily so. As the poet W. D. Snodgrass has remarked, every poet is entitled to say "O" once in his life.

Hyperbole or **overstatement**, another name for exaggeration, is common in Elizabethan sonnets, when lovers claim that their sighs are gales, that in the transports of love they burn, they freeze, they fry. Subtler, but also hyperbolic, is Tennyson's statement that the eagle is "close to the sun." The opposite is **understatement,** implying more than one says. In *Life on the Mississippi* Mark Twain recalls how, as an apprentice steamboat-pilot asleep when supposed to be on watch, he was roused by the pilot and sent clambering to the pilot house: "Mr. Bixby was close behind, commenting." Another example is Robert Frost's line "One could do worse than be a swinger of birches" — the conclusion of a poem which has suggested that to swing on a birch tree is one of the most deeply satisfying activities in the world. Because in both hyperbole and understatement we notice a discrepancy between what the writer says and what he means, both are forms of verbal irony; and either may be extended throughout an entire poem.

In **metonymy**, the name of a thing is substituted for that of another closely associated with it: we say, "The White House decided," and mean the President did. When John Dyer writes in "Grongar Hill,"

> A little rule, a little sway,
> A sun beam on a winter's day,
> Is all the proud and mighty have
> Between the cradle and the grave,

we recognize that *cradle* and *grave* signify birth and death. A special kind of metonymy, **synecdoche** is the use of a part of a thing to stand for the whole of it, or vice-versa. We say, "He lent a hand," and mean that he lent his entire presence. Milton in "Lycidas" refers to greedy clergymen as "blind mouths"; and in Shakespeare's sonnet we also find synecdoche in the figures of summer's "honey breath" and Time's "swift foot." (Nowadays, the term *synecdoche* seems to be yielding to *metonymy*, the slight distinction between the two being generally ignored.) A special kind of metonymy is the **transferred epithet**: a device of emphasis in which the poet takes some characteristic of a thing and attributes it to another thing closely associated with it. When Thomas Gray observed that, in the evening pastures, "drowsy tinklings lull the distant folds," probably he well knew that sheep's bells do not drowse, but sheep do. Similarly, when Hart Crane, describing the earth as seen from an airplane, spoke of "nimble blue plateaus," he attributed the airplane's motion to the earth.

Paradox occurs in a statement that at first strikes us as self-contradictory, but that is true or on reflection makes some sense. "The peasant," said G. K. Chesterton, "lives in a larger world than the globe-trotter." Here, two different meanings of the word *larger* are contrasted: "greater in spiritual values" versus "greater in miles." Such a paradox is a form of verbal irony, in that it requires us to distinguish between one meaning of a word and another one really meant. Some paradoxical statements, however, refer to an absurd or ironic situation — one in which there is some sort of wry contrast — such as that seen by the seventeenth-century poet Fulke Greville, Lord Brooke:

> Oh, wearisome condition of humanity,
> Born under one law, to another bound;
> Vainly begot, and yet forbidden vanity,
> Created sick, commanded to be sound.

What paradoxes do you find in the following poem? For each, explain the sense that underlies the statement. What kind or kinds of irony does the poem contain? Which paradoxical statements are also metaphors?

CHIDIOCK TICHBORNE (1558?–1586)

Elegy, Written with His Own Hand
in the Tower before His Execution

My prime of youth is but a frost of cares,
    My feast of joy is but a dish of pain,
My crop of corn is but a field of tares,
    And all my good is but vain hope of gain:
The day is past, and yet I saw no sun,
And now I live, and now my life is done.   6

My tale was heard, and yet it was not told,
    My fruit is fall'n, and yet my leaves are green,
My youth is spent, and yet I am not old,
    I saw the world, and yet I was not seen:
My thread is cut, and yet it is not spun,
And now I live, and now my life is done.   12

I sought my death, and found it in my womb,
    I looked for life, and saw it was a shade,
I trod the earth, and knew it was my tomb,
    And now I die, and now I was but made:
My glass is full, and now my glass is run,
And now I live, and now my life is done.   18

Ironic poems often will use, together with paradox, a figure known to classical rhetoricians as *paranomasia*, to us as the **pun** or play on words. Asked by a lady to define the difference between men and women, Samuel Johnson replied, "I can't conceive, madam, can you?" As in this example, a pun calls to mind another word (or other words) of the same or similar sound, but of different denotation. Puns may be mere quibbles, but at their best they can point to resemblances. The name of a dentist's country home, Tooth Acres, is accurate: quite literally, the land was paid for by patients with aching teeth. In verse and poetry, the use of two or more denotations may be facetious, as in Thomas Hood's ballad of "Faithless Nelly Gray":

Ben Battle was a soldier bold,
    And used to war's alarms;
But a cannon-ball took off his legs,
    So he laid down his arms!

or serious, as in E. E. Cummings' lines on war:

> the bigness of cannon
> is skilful,

is skilful becoming *is kill-ful* when read aloud. The effect of the following poem depends on serious punning. To read it with understanding, sort out the various meanings of the word *rest*. (The title suggests a metaphor: the pulley is man's weariness, with which God draws him home.)

GEORGE HERBERT (1593–1633)

The Pulley

> When God at first made man,
> Having a glass of blessings standing by —
> Let us (said he) pour on him all we can;
> Let the world's riches, which dispersèd lie,
> Contract into a span.   5
>
> So strength first made a way,
> Then beauty flowed, then wisdom, honor, pleasure:
> When almost all was out, God made a stay,
> Perceiving that, alone of all His treasure,
> Rest in the bottom lay.   10
>
> For if I should (said he)
> Bestow this jewel also on My creature,
> He would adore My gifts instead of Me,
> And rest in Nature, not the God of Nature:
> So both should losers be.   15
>
> Yet let him keep the rest,
> But keep them with repining restlessness;
> Let him be rich and weary, that at least,
> If goodness lead him not, yet weariness
> May toss him to My breast.   20

To sum up: figures of speech are not to be taken literally, but they may direct us to things we can see and touch. By doing so, they can make an abstraction more definite, more clearly apprehensible. In *personifying* an eagle, the poet reminds us that the world of nature and that of men have something in common; by *animizing* the sea, he gives it life. By *metonymy* he can focus our attention on a particular detail in a large, complicated object that otherwise might be a blur to us; by *hyperbole* and *understatement*, *pun* and *paradox*, he can emphasize the physical actuality in back of his words. By *apostrophe*, he animates the inanimate and makes it listen; he speaks directly to an immediate God or to the revivified dead. Put to such uses, a figure of speech has power. It is more than just a manner of playing with words.

ROBERT FROST (1874–1963)

Tree at My Window

Tree at my window, window tree,
My sash is lowered when night comes on;
But let there never be curtain drawn
Between you and me.   4

Vague dream-head lifted out of the ground,
And thing next most diffuse to cloud,
Not all your light tongues talking aloud
Could be profound.   8

But, tree, I have seen you taken and tossed,
And if you have seen me when I slept,
You have seen me when I was taken and swept
And all but lost.   12

That day she put our heads together,
Fate had her imagination about her,
Your head so much concerned with outer,
Mine with inner, weather.   16

QUESTIONS

1. What is the central metaphor of this poem? Is it explicit or implied?

2. What is meant by *light tongues* (line 7)? What resemblances does this comparison point out?

3. What do you understand from the *inner weather* by which the speaker was "taken and swept"?

4. What use does Frost make of personification? What does it contribute to the poem?

ANDREW MARVELL (1621–1678)

The Definition of Love

My love is of a birth as rare
As 'tis for object strange and high:
It was begotten by Despair
Upon Impossibility.   4

101

Magnanimous Despair alone
Could show me so divine a thing,
Where feeble Hope could ne'er have flown
But vainly flapped its tinsel wing.   8

And yet I quickly might arrive
Where my extended soul is fixed,
But Fate does iron wedges drive,
And always crowds itself betwixt.   12

For fate with jealous eyes does see
Two perfect loves, nor lets them close°:   *come together*
Their union would her ruin be,
And her tyrannic power depose.   16

And therefore her decrees of steel
Us as the distant poles have placed,
(Though love's whole world on us doth wheel)
Not by themselves to be embraced,   20

Unless the giddy heaven fall,
And earth some new convulsion tear,
And, us to join, the world should all
Be cramped° into a planisphere.   *forced flat*   24

As lines, so loves oblique may well
Themselves in every angle greet;
But ours, so truly parallel,
Though infinite, can never meet.   28

Therefore the love which us doth bind,
But Fate so enviously debars,
Is the conjunction of the mind,
And opposition of the stars.   32

The Definition of Love. 24. *planisphere*: a map of the globe projected on a plane surface. 31. *conjunction*: a term from astrology and astronomy, the seeming closeness of two heavenly bodies in the same celestial longitude. 32. *opposition*: A planet is said to be in opposition to the sun when its longitude and the sun's are 180° apart.

QUESTIONS

1. What personifications does Marvell employ? Which of them seems most nearly central?
2. To what is *Hope* compared in lines 7–8?
3. What figure of speech is *decrees of steel* (17)? Explain this phrase.
4. What meanings do you find in *oblique* (25) and *parallel* (27)? To what does Marvell refer?
5. What use is made of hyperbole?

EDMUND WALLER (1606–1687)

On a Girdle

That which her slender waist confined,
Shall now my joyful temples bind;
No monarch but would give his crown,
His arms might do what this has done.   4

It was my heaven's extremest sphere,
The pale° which held that lovely deer,   *enclosure*
My joy, my grief, my hope, my love,
Did all within this circle move!   8

A narrow compass! and yet there
Dwelt all that's good, and all that's fair!
Give me but what this riband bound,
Take all the rest the sun goes round!   12

On a Girdle. 1–2. *That which . . . temples bind:* A courtly lover might
bind his brow with a lady's ribbon, to signify he was hers. 5. *extremest
sphere:* in Ptolemaic astronomy, the outermost of the concentric spheres
that surround the earth. In its wall the farthest stars are set.

QUESTIONS

1. To what things is the girdle compared?
2. Explain the pun in line 4. What effect does it have upon the tone
of the poem?
3. Why is the effect of this pun different from that of Thomas Hood's
play on the same word in "Faithless Nelly Gray" (quoted on p. 99)?
4. What does *compass* denote in line 9?
5. What paradox occurs in lines 9–10?
6. How many of the poem's statements are hyperbolic? Is the compliment he pays his lady too grandiose to be believed? Explain.

STEPHEN TROPP (b. 1930)

My Wife Is My Shirt

My wife is my shirt
I put my hands through her armpits
slide my head through her mouth
& finally button her blood around my hands

QUESTIONS

1. How consistently is this metaphor elaborated?
2. Why can this metaphor be said to work in exactly the opposite way
from a personification?
3. A paraphrase might discover this simile: "My wife is as intimate,
familiar, and close to me as the shirt on my back." If this is the idea, and
the poem is supposed to be a love poem, how successfully is its attitude expressed?

WILLIAM MEREDITH (b. 1919)

The Open Sea

We say the sea is lonely; better say
Ourselves are lonesome creatures whom the sea
Gives neither yes nor no for company.

Oh, there are people, all right, settled in the sea;
It is as populous as Maine today,
But no one who will give you the time of day.　　　　6

A man who asks there of his family
Or a friend or teacher gets a cold reply
Or finds him dead against that vast majority.

Nor does it signify that people who stay
Very long, bereaved or not, at the edge of the sea
Hear the drowned folk call: that is mere fancy,　　　　12

They are speechless. And the famous noise of sea
Which a poet has beautifully told us in our day
Is hardly a sound to speak comfort to the lonely.

Although not yet a man given to prayer, I pray
For each creature lost since the start at sea,
And give thanks it was not I, nor yet one close to me.　　　　18

QUESTIONS

    1. Find at least one example in this poem of a statement to be taken as irony. Find at least one statement to be taken at face value.
    2. What puns occur? Describe their effect.
    3. In what respects does the speaker insist on a literal rather than an imaginative view of the sea? What reasons does he give for so insisting?
    4. Taking the poem as a whole, how would you describe its tone? By what particular elements (diction, connotation, imagery, figures of speech, etc.) is this tone communicated?

EXERCISE TWO

    In each of the following poems, what uses are made of these figures of speech: metaphor, simile, personification, apostrophe, metonymy, hyperbole? In any metaphor or simile, what two things are compared? In any use of metonymy, what is represented?

ANONYMOUS (English; time of the Crimean War, 1854–1856)

'The fortunes of war'

The fortunes of war, I tell you plain,
Are a wooden leg — or a golden chain.

ANONYMOUS (English; traditional nursery rime)

'Robinets and Jenny Wrens'

> Robinets and Jenny Wrens
> Are God Almighty's cocks and hens.
> The martins and the swallows
> Are God Almighty's bows and arrows.

DAVID McCORD (b. 1897)

On a Waiter

> By and by
> God caught his eye.

WILLIAM BLAKE (1757–1827)

A Divine Image

> Cruelty has a human heart,
> And Jealousy a human face;
> Terror the human form divine,
> And Secrecy the human dress.   4
>
> The human dress is forgèd iron,
> The human form a fiery forge,
> The human face a furnace sealed,
> The human heart is hungry gorge.   8

WILLIAM SHAKESPEARE (1564–1616)

'Shall I compare thee to a summer's day?'

> Shall I compare thee to a summer's day?
> Thou art more lovely and more temperate.
> Rough winds do shake the darling buds of May,
> And summer's lease hath all too short a date.   4
> Sometime too hot the eye of heaven shines,
> And often is his gold complexion dimmed;
> And every fair from fair sometime declines,
> By chance, or nature's changing course, untrimmed.   8
> But thy eternal summer shall not fade,
> Nor lose possession of that fair thou ow'st°;   *ownest, has*
> Nor shall death brag thou wand'rest in his shade,
> When in eternal lines to time thou grow'st.   12
>   So long as men can breathe or eyes can see,
>   So long lives this, and this gives life to thee.

ROBERT BURNS (1759–1796)

A Red, Red Rose

O, my luve is like a red, red rose,
    That's newly sprung in June;
O, my luve is like the melody
    That's sweetly played in tune.   4

As fair art thou, my bonny lass,
    So deep in luve am I,
And I will luve thee still, my dear,
    Till a'° the seas gang° dry.   *all; go* 8

Till a' the seas gang dry, my dear,
    And the rocks melt wi' the sun;
And I will luve thee still, my dear,
    While the sands o' life shall run.   12

And fare thee weel, my only luve,
    And fare thee weel a while;
And I will come again, my luve,
    Though it were ten thousand mile!   16

THOMAS CAMPION (1567–1620)

'There is a garden in her face'

There is a garden in her face
Where roses and white lilies grow;
    A heav'nly paradise is that place
Wherein all pleasant fruits do flow.
    There cherries grow which none may buy
    Till "Cherry-ripe" themselves do cry.   6

Those cherries fairly do enclose
Of orient pearl a double row,
    Which when her lovely laughter shows,
They look like rose-buds filled with snow;
    Yet them nor° peer nor prince can buy,   *neither*
    Till "Cherry-ripe" themselves do cry.   12

Her eyes like angels watch them still;
Her brows like bended bows do stand,
    Threat'ning with piercing frowns to kill
All that attempt, with eye or hand
    Those sacred cherries to come nigh
    Till "Cherry-ripe" themselves do cry.   18

'There is a garden in her face.' 6. "*Cherry-ripe*": cry of fruit-peddlers in London streets.

SEVEN

SYMBOL AND ALLEGORY

1. SYMBOL

When a black cat crosses his path, the superstitious man shivers, foreseeing bad luck. When a national flag is paraded by, onlookers are supposed to bestir their patriotic feelings. To each of these things, by custom, our society attaches a familiar and expected response. A flag, a black cat's crossing one's path — each is a **symbol**: a visible object or action that suggests some further meaning in addition to itself, besides its being a piece of cloth or the motion of an animal. In literature, too, a symbol does more than meet the eye. It cannot be, of course, a flag we can carry or a cat that can scratch, but instead might be the *word* "flag," or the words "a black cat crossed his path," or every description of flag or cat in an entire novel, story, play, or poem.

A flag and the crossing of a black cat may be called **conventional symbols,** since they can have a conventional or customary effect on us. Conventional symbols are also part of the language of poetry, as we know when we meet the red rose, emblem of love, in many a lyric; or the Christian cross in the devotional poems of George Herbert. More often, however, symbols in literature have no conventional, long-established meaning, but particular meanings of their own. In Melville's novel *Moby Dick,* to take a rich example, whatever we associate with the great white whale is *not* attached unmistakably to white whales by custom. Though Melville tells us that men have long regarded whales with awe, and relates Moby Dick to the celebrated fish that swallowed Jonah, the reader's response is mostly due to one particular whale, the creature of Herman Melville. Only the experience of reading the novel in its entirety can give Moby Dick his particular meaning.

We should say *meanings*, for as Eudora Welty has observed, it is a good thing Melville made Moby Dick a whale, therefore large enough to contain all that critics have found in him. A symbol in literature, if not conventional, has more meanings than just one that leaps instantly to mind. In "The Raven," by Edgar Allan Poe, the appearance of a strange black bird in the narrator's study is evidently sinister; and indeed, if we take the poem seriously, we may even respond with a sympathetic shiver of dread. Does it mean death, fate, melancholy, the loss of a loved one, knowledge in the service of evil? All these, perhaps. Like any well-chosen symbol, Poe's raven sets going within the reader an unending train of feelings and associations.

We miss the value of a symbol, however, if we think it can mean absolutely anything we wish. If a poet has any control over our reactions, his poem will guide our responses in a certain direction.

T. S. ELIOT (1888–1965)

The Boston Evening Transcript

> The readers of the *Boston Evening Transcript*
> Sway in the wind like a field of ripe corn.
>
> When evening quickens faintly in the street,
> Wakening the appetites of life in some
> And to others bringing the *Boston Evening Transcript*,   5
> I mount the steps and ring the bell, turning
> Wearily, as one would turn to nod good-bye to La Roche-
>   foucauld,
> If the street were time and he at the end of the street,
> And I say, "Cousin Harriet, here is the *Boston Evening
>   Transcript*."

The newspaper, whose name Eliot purposely repeats so monotonously, indicates what this poem is about. Now defunct, the *Transcript* covered in detail the slightest activity of Boston's leading families, and was noted for the great length of its obituaries. Eliot, then, uses the newspaper as a symbol for an existence of boredom, fatigue ("Wearily"), petty and unvarying routine (since an evening newspaper, like night, arrives on schedule). The *Transcript* must be a way of life without zest or passion, for, opposed to people who read it, Eliot sets people who do not: those whose desires revive, not expire, when the working day is through. Suggestions abound in the ironic comparison of the *Transcript's* readers to a cornfield in late summer. To mention only a few: the readers sway because they are sleepy; they vegetate, they are drying up; each makes a rattling sound when turning his page. It is not necessary that we know the remote and similarly disillusioned friend to whom the speaker might nod: La Rochefoucauld, whose cynical *Maxims* entertained Parisian society under Louis XIV (sample: "All of us have enough strength to endure the misfortunes of others"). We understand the nod as symbolic of an immense weariness of spirit. We know nothing about Cousin Harriet, whom the speaker addresses, but imagine from the greeting she inspires that she is probably a bore.

If, then, Eliot wishes to say that certain Bostonians lead lives of sterile boredom, why does he couch his meaning in symbols? Why doesn't he *tell* us what he means? Such an objection implies two assumptions not necessarily true: first, that Eliot has a message to impart; second, that he is concealing it. We have reason to think that Eliot did not usually have a message in mind when beginning a poem, for as he once told a critic: "The conscious problems with which one is concerned in the actual writing are more those of a quasi musical nature . . . than of a conscious exposition of ideas." A poet sometimes discovers what he has to say while in the act of saying it. And it may be that in his *Transcript* poem, Eliot is indeed saying exactly what he means. By communicating his meaning through symbols instead of statements, he may be choosing the only kind of language appropriate to an idea of great subtlety and complexity. (The paraphrase "Certain Bostonians are bored" hardly begins to describe the poem in all its possible meaning.) And by his use of symbolism, Eliot affords us the pleasure of finding our own entrances to his poem. Another great strength of a symbol is that, like some figures of speech, it renders the abstract in concrete terms; and, like any other image, refers to what we can perceive — an object like a newspaper, a gesture like a nod. Eliot might, like Robert Frost, have called himself a "synecdochist." Frost explained: "Always a larger significance. A little thing touches a larger thing."

This power of suggestion that a symbol contains is, perhaps, its greatest advantage. Sometimes, as in the following poem by Emily Dickinson, a symbol will lead us from a visible object to something whose dimensions are too vast to be perceived.

EMILY DICKINSON (1830–1886)

'The Lightning is a yellow Fork'

> The Lightning is a yellow Fork
> From Tables in the sky
> By inadvertent fingers dropt
> The awful Cutlery

Of mansions never quite disclosed
And never quite concealed
The Apparatus of the Dark
To ignorance revealed.   8

If the lightning is a fork, then whose are the fingers that drop it, the table from which it slips, the household to which it belongs? The poem implies this question without giving an answer. An obvious answer is "God," but can we be sure? We are left wondering, too, about these partially lighted mansions: if our vision were clearer, what would we behold?

In its suggestion of an infinite realm that mortal eyes cannot quite see, but whose nature can be perceived partially and fleetingly through things visible, Emily Dickinson's poem, by coincidence, resembles the work of that school of later nineteenth-century French poets called **Symbolism**. To a Symbolist the shirt-tail of Truth is continually seen disappearing around a corner. With their Neoplatonic view of ideal realities existing in a great beyond, whose corresponding symbols are the perceptible cats that bite us and tangible stones we stumble over, such French poets as Charles Baudelaire, Jules Laforgue, and Stéphane Mallarmé were profoundly to affect poets writing in English, notably Yeats (who said a poem "entangles . . . a part of the Divine essence") and Eliot. But we deal in this chapter with symbolism as an element in certain poems, not with Symbolism, the literary movement.

To respond to a symbol in literature, we need not even believe, with the French and English Symbolists and Emily Dickinson, in the existence of a world beyond the world of matter. Our understanding of a symbol may emerge from the depths of our unconscious. Even the disbeliever may be impressed by F. Scott Fitzgerald's symbol of an oculist's advertising sign in *The Great Gatsby*: two enormous eyes, like the eyes of God, brooding across a desert made by man.

Understandably appalled by the complexity of their problem, students sometimes ask, "But how am I supposed to know a symbol when I see one?" The best approach is to read poems closely, taking comfort in the likelihood that it is better not to notice metaphors at all than to find significance in every literal stone and symbols in every thing. A few suggestions, however, may help at least some of the time. First, in looking for the symbols in a poem, pick out all the references to concrete objects — newspapers, black cats, twisted pins. Consider these with special care. Note any that the poet emphasizes by describing in detail, by repeating, or by placing at the very beginning or end of the poem. Ask: What is the poem about, what does it

110

add up to? If, when the poem is paraphrased, the paraphrase depends mainly upon the meaning of certain concrete objects, these richly suggestive objects may be the symbols. There are some things a literary symbol usually is *not*. The following list, at best a crude guide, may help a reader resist the understandable temptation to make a symbol of *everything* in a poem.

1. A symbol is not an abstraction. Such terms as *truth, death, love,* and *justice* cannot work as symbols (unless personified, as in the traditional figure of Justice holding a scales). Most often, a symbol is a thing we can see in the mind's eye: a newspaper, a lightning bolt, a gesture of nodding good-bye.

2. In narratives, a well-developed character who speaks much dialogue and is not the least bit mysterious is usually not a symbol. But watch out for an executioner in a black hood; a character named for a Biblical prophet, who does little but utter a prophecy; a trio of old women who resemble the Three Fates. (It has been argued, with good reason, that Milton's fully rounded character of Satan in *Paradise Lost* is a symbol embodying evil, man's pride, etc.; but we suggest here a narrower definition of symbol as more frequently useful.) A symbol *may* be a part of a person's body (the baleful eye of the murder victim in Poe's story "The Tell-Tale Heart"), or a look, a voice, a mannerism.

3. A symbol usually is not the second term of a metaphor. In the line "The lightning is a yellow fork," the symbol is the lightning, not the fork.

Sometimes a symbol, like any other image, may refer to a sense experience other than sight: the sound of a mysterious harp at the end of Chekhov's play *The Cherry Orchard*; or, in William Faulkner's tale "A Rose for Emily," the odor of decay which surrounds the house of the last survivor of a town's leading family — suggestive not only of physical dissolution, but also of the decay of a social order. A symbol is a special kind of image, for it exceeds the usual image in the richness of its connotations. The image of the dead wife's cold comb in the haiku of Buson (discussed on pp. 76–77) works symbolically, suggesting among other things the chill of the grave, the contrast between the living and the dead.

Holding a narrower definition than that used in this book, some readers of poetry prefer to say that a symbol is always a concrete object, never an act. They would deny the label "symbol" to Ahab's breaking his tobacco pipe before setting out to pursue Moby Dick (suggesting, perhaps, his determination to allow no pleasure to distract him from the chase) or to any larger motion (as Ahab's whole quest). This distinction, while confining, does have the merit of spar-ing one from expecting all motion to be possibly symbolic. Some would call Ahab's gesture not a symbol but a **symbolic act**.

To sum up: a symbol is a thing that radiates hints — or casts long shadows (to use Henry James's metaphor). We are unable to say it "stands for" or "represents" a meaning. It evokes, it suggests, it manifests. It demands no single necessary interpretation, such as the interpretation a driver gives to a red traffic light. Rather, like Emily Dickinson's lightning bolt, it points toward an indefinite meaning, which may lie in part beyond the reach of words. In a symbol, as Thomas Carlyle said in *Sartor Resartus*, "the Infinite is made to blend with the Finite, to stand visible, and as it were, attainable there."

EMILY DICKINSON (1830–1886)

'I heard a Fly buzz—when I died'

> I heard a Fly buzz—when I died—
> The Stillness in the Room
> Was like the Stillness in the Air—
> Between the Heaves of Storm—   4
>
> The Eyes around—had wrung them dry—
> And Breaths were gathering firm
> For that last Onset—when the King
> Be witnessed—in the Room—   8
>
> I willed my Keepsakes—Signed away
> What portion of me be
> Assignable—and then it was
> There interposed a Fly—   12
>
> With Blue—uncertain stumbling Buzz—
> Between the light—and me—
> And then the Windows failed—and then
> I could not see to see—   16

QUESTIONS

1. Why is the poem written in the past tense? Where is the speaker at present?
2. What do you understand from the repetition of the word *see* in the last line?
3. What does the poet mean by *Eyes around, that last Onset, the King,* and *What portion of me be/Assignable?*
4. In line 13, how can a sound be called *blue* and *stumbling?*
5. What further meaning might *the Windows* suggest, in addition to denoting the windows of the room?
6. What connotations of the word *fly* seem relevant to an account of a death?
7. Summarize your interpretation of the poem. What does the fly mean?

112

LOUIS SIMPSON (b. 1923)

The Boarder

The time is after dinner. Cigarettes
    Glow on the lawn;
Glasses begin to tinkle; TV sets
    Have been turned on.   4

The moon is brimming like a glass of beer
    Above the town,
And love keeps her appointments — "Harry's here!"
    "I'll be right down."   8

But the pale stranger in the furnished room
    Lies on his back
Looking at paper roses, how they bloom,
    And ceilings crack.   12

QUESTIONS

1. What symbolism do you find in this poem, if any? Is the pale stranger a symbolic figure or not?

2. For what possible effect does Simpson bring together the simile of the moon as beer and the quoted conversation?

3. Compare "The Boarder" with "The *Boston Evening Transcript*." In what respects are the two poems similar?

THOMAS HARDY (1840–1928)

Neutral Tones

We stood by a pond that winter day,
And the sun was white, as though chidden of God,
And a few leaves lay on the starving sod;
    — They had fallen from an ash, and were gray.   4

Your eyes on me were as eyes that rove
Over tedious riddles of years ago;
And some words played between us to and fro
    On which lost the more by our love.   8

The smile on your mouth was the deadest thing
Alive enough to have strength to die;
And a grin of bitterness swept thereby
    Like an ominous bird a-wing. . . .   12

Since then, keen lessons that love deceives,
And wrings with wrong, have shaped to me
Your face, and the God-curst sun, and a tree,
    And a pond edged with grayish leaves.   16

1. Sum up the story told in this poem. In lines 1–12, what is the dramatic situation? What has happened in the interval between the experience related in these lines and the reflection in the last stanza?

2. What meanings do you find in the title?

3. Explain in your own words the metaphor in line 2.

4. What connotations appropriate to this poem does the word *ash* have, that *oak* or *maple* would lack?

5. What visible objects in the poem function symbolically? What actions or gestures?

2. ALLEGORY

Closely akin to symbolism is **allegory**: a description — usually narrative — in which persons, places, and things are employed in a continuous system of equivalents. If we read of a ship, its captain, its sailors, and the rough seas, and we realize we are reading about a commonwealth and how its rulers and workers keep it going even in difficult times, then we are reading an allegory.

Although more strictly limited in its suggestions than symbolism, allegory need not be thought inferior. Few poems continue to interest readers more than Dante's allegorical *Divine Comedy*. Sublime evidence of the appeal of allegory may be found in Christ's use of the **parable**: a brief narrative — usually allegorical but sometimes not — that teaches a moral.

MATTHEW 13:24–30 (Authorized or King James Version, 1611)

The Parable of the Good Seed

The kingdom of heaven is likened unto a man which sowed good seed in his field:

But while men slept, his enemy came and sowed tares among the wheat, and went his way.

But when the blade was sprung up, and brought forth fruit, then appeared the tares also.

So the servants of the householder came and said unto him, "Sir, didst not thou sow good seed in thy field? From whence then hath it tares?"

He said unto them, "An enemy hath done this." The servants said unto him, "Wilt thou then that we go and gather them up?"

But he said, "Nay; lest while ye gather up the tares, ye root up also the wheat with them.

"Let both grow together until the harvest: and in the time of harvest I will say to the reapers, 'Gather ye together first the tares,

114

and bind them in bundles to burn them: but gather the wheat into my barn.' "

An explanation follows: The sower is the Son of man, the field is the world, the good seed are the children of the Kingdom, the tares are the children of the wicked one, the enemy is the devil, the harvest is the end of the world, the reapers are angels. "As therefore the tares are gathered and burned in the fire; so shall it be in the end of this world." (Matthew 13:36–42.)

Usually, as in this parable, the meanings of an allegory are plainly labeled or thinly disguised. In John Bunyan's allegorical narrative *The Pilgrim's Progress*, it is clear that the hero Christian, on his journey through places with such pointed names as Vanity Fair, the Valley of the Shadow of Death, and Doubting Castle, is the soul, traveling the road of life on his way toward Heaven. An allegory, when carefully built, is systematic. It makes one principal comparison, the working out of whose details may lead to further comparisons, then still further comparisons: Christian, thrown by Giant Despair into the dungeon of Doubting Castle, escapes by means of a key called Promise. Such a complicated design may take great length to unfold, as does that of Spenser's *Faerie Queene*; however, an allegory may be as short as this:

SIR WALTER RALEGH (1552?–1618)

'What is our life?'

What is our life? A play of passion,
Our mirth the music of division.
Our mothers' wombs the tiring-houses° be,   *attiring-houses*
Where we are dressed for this short comedy.
Heaven the judicious sharp spectator is,   5
That sits and marks still who doth act amiss.
Our graves that hide us from the searching sun
Are like drawn curtains when the play is done.
Thus march we, playing, to our latest rest,
Only we die in earnest, that's no jest.   10

Like the basic metaphor of *The Pilgrim's Progress* — life is a pilgrimage — that of Ralegh's poem represents an abstract concept in terms of something tangible: all the world's a theater. What we recognize as the method of allegory is Ralegh's use of several other metaphors to develop his central one: life is a play, mirth is the music, wombs are dressing-rooms, etc. This method distinguishes an allegory from a poem containing a single extended metaphor or simile, such as the following:

WILLIAM DRUMMOND OF HAWTHORNDEN (1585–1649)

Madrigal

> This life which seems so fair
> Is like a bubble blown up in the air
> By sporting children's breath,
> Who chase it everywhere
> And strive who can most motion it bequeath;   5
> And though it sometime seem of its own might,
> Like to an eye of gold, to be fixed there,
> And firm to hover in that empty height,
> That only is because it is so light;
> But in that pomp it doth not long appear,   10
>   For even when most admired, it in a thought
>   As swelled from nothing, doth dissolve in nought.

"Madrigal," despite its added image of the children's breath (the whims of fate?) and its second, descriptive simile ("like to an eye of gold"), lacks the ramifications we expect of an allegory. An extended simile, it recalls a shorter simile of Shakespeare: "As flies to wanton boys, are we to the gods; / They kill us for their sport."

An object in allegory is like a bird whose cage is clearly lettered with its identity — "RAVEN, *Corvus corax*; habitat of specimen, Maine." A symbol, by contrast, is a bird with piercing eyes that mysteriously appears one evening in your library. It is there, you can touch it, but what does it mean? You look at it. It continues to look at you.

Whether an object in literature is a symbol, part of an allegory, or no such thing at all, it has at least one sure meaning: Moby Dick is first a whale; the *Boston Evening Transcript*, a newspaper. Besides deriving a multitude of intangible suggestions from the title symbol in Eliot's long poem *The Waste Land*, none of its readers can fail to carry away a sense of the land's physical appearance: a river choked with sandwich papers and cigarette ends; London Bridge "under the brown fog of a winter dawn." A virtue of *The Pilgrim's Progress* is that its walking abstractions are not merely abstractions, but are also persuasively human; Giant Despair, for instance, is a henpecked husband. The most vital element of a literary work may pass us by, unless, before seeking further depths in a thing, we look to the thing itself.

116

SIR PHILIP SIDNEY (1554–1586)

'You that with allegory's curious frame'

You that with allegory's curious frame
  Of others' children changelings use to make,
  With me those pains, for God's sake, do not take;
  I list not° dig so deep for brazen fame.   *I do not*   4
When I say Stella, I do mean the same   *choose to*
  Princess of beauty for whose only sake
  The reins of love I love, though never slake,
  And joy therein, though nations count it shame.   8
I beg no subject to use eloquence,
  Nor in hid ways do guide philosophy;
  Look at my hands for no such quintessence,   12
But know that I in pure simplicity
  Breathe out the flames which burn within my heart,
  Love only reading unto me this art.

GEORGE HERBERT (1593–1633)

Redemption

Having been a tenant long to a rich Lord,
  Not thriving, I resolvèd to be bold,
  And make a suit unto him to afford
A new small-rented lease and cancel th' old.   4
In heaven at his manor I him sought.
  They told me there that he was lately gone
  About some land which he had dearly bought
Long since on earth, to take possessiòn.   8
I straight returned, and knowing his great birth,
  Sought him accordingly in great resorts,
  In cities, theaters, gardens, parks, and courts.
At length I heard a ragged noise and mirth   12
  Of thieves and murderers; there I him espied,
  Who straight "Your suit is granted," said, and died.

QUESTIONS

1. In this allegory, what equivalents does Herbert give each of these terms: *tenant, Lord, not thriving, suit, new lease, old lease, manor, land, dearly bought, take possession, his great birth*?
2. What scene is depicted in the last three lines? How would you account for the difference in effect between the ending of the poem and what has gone before?
3. What figure of speech is "a ragged noise"?

117

ROBERT FROST (1874–1963)

Departmental

An ant on the tablecloth
Ran into a dormant moth
Of many times his size.
He showed not the least surprise.
His business wasn't with such.   5
He gave it scarcely a touch,
And was off on his duty run.
Yet if he encountered one
Of the hive's enquiry squad
Whose work is to find out God   10
And the nature of time and space,
He would put him onto the case.
Ants are a curious race;
One crossing with hurried tread
The body of one of their dead   15
Isn't given a moment's arrest —
Seems not even impressed.
But he no doubt reports to any
With whom he crosses antennae,
And they no doubt report   20
To the higher up at court.
Then word goes forth in Formic:
"Death's come to Jerry McCormic,
Our selfless forager Jerry.
Will the special Janizary°   *soldier*   25
Whose office it is to bury
The dead of the commissary
Go bring him home to his people.
Lay him in state on a sepal.
Wrap him for shroud in a petal.   30
Embalm him with ichor of nettle.
This is the word of your Queen."
And presently on the scene
Appears a solemn mortician;
And taking formal position   35
With feelers calmly atwiddle,
Seizes the dead by the middle,
And heaving him high in air,
Carries him out of there.
No one stands round to stare.   40
It is nobody else's affair.

It couldn't be called ungentle.
But how thoroughly departmental.

118

1. Why do you suppose that in his book *A Further Range*, Frost included "Departmental" in a section of poems called "Taken Doubly"?
2. Is this narrative a parable? Has it a moral? If so, what?

EXERCISE

After reading each of the following poems, decide which one of these descriptions is most nearly accurate:

(1) The poem makes central use of symbolism.
(2) The whole poem develops a consistent allegory.
(3) The whole poem draws one extended metaphor or simile.
(4) The poem does none of these things.

WALLACE STEVENS (1879–1955)

The Curtains in the House of the Metaphysician

It comes about that the drifting of these curtains
Is full of long motions; as the ponderous
Deflations of distance; or as clouds
Inseparable from their afternoons;
Or the changing of light, the dropping   5
Of the silence, wide sleep and solitude
Of night, in which all motion
Is beyond us, as the firmament,
Up-rising and down-falling, bares
The last largeness, bold to see.   10

ROBERT FROST (1874–1963)

The Silken Tent

She is as in a field a silken tent
At midday when a sunny summer breeze
Has dried the dew and all its ropes relent,
So that in guys it gently sways at ease,   4
And its supporting central cedar pole,
That is its pinnacle to heavenward
And signifies the sureness of the soul,
Seems to owe naught to any single cord,   8
But strictly held by none, is loosely bound
By countless silken ties of love and thought
To everything on earth the compass round,
And only by one's going slightly taut   12
In the capriciousness of summer air
Is of the slightest bondage made aware.

STEPHEN CRANE (1871–1900)

The Heart

> In the desert
> I saw a creature, naked, bestial,
> Who, squatting upon the ground,
> Held his heart in his hands,
> And ate of it.   5
>
> I said, "Is it good, friend?"
> "It is bitter — bitter," he answered;
> "But I like it
> Because it is bitter,
> And because it is my heart."   10

JOHN MASEFIELD (b. 1878)

The Lemmings

> Once in a hundred years the Lemmings come
> Westward, in search of food, over the snow,
> Westward, until the salt sea drowns them dumb,
> Westward, till all are drowned, those Lemmings go.   4
> Once, it is thought, there was a westward land
> (Now drowned) where there was food for those starved
>   things,
> And memory of the place has burnt its brand
> In the little brains of all the Lemming Kings.   8
> Perhaps, long since, there was a land beyond
> Westward from death, some city, some calm place,
> Where one could taste God's quiet and be fond
> With the little beauty of a human face;   12
> But now the land is drowned, yet still we press
> Westward, in search, to death, to nothingness.

JOHN DONNE (1572–1631)

A Burnt Ship

> Out of a fired ship which by no way
> But drowning could be rescued from the flame
> Some men leaped forth, and ever as they came
> Near the foe's ships, did by their shot decay;
> So all were lost, which in the ship were found,
>   They in the sea being burnt, they in the burnt ship
>   drowned.

120

WALT WHITMAN (1819–1892)

A *Noiseless Patient Spider*

A noiseless patient spider,
I mark'd where on a little promontory it stood isolated,
Mark'd how to explore the vacant vast surrounding,
It launch'd forth filament, filament, filament, out of itself,
Ever unreeling them, ever tirelessly speeding them.   5

And you O my soul where you stand,
Surrounded, detached, in measureless oceans of space,
Ceaselessly musing, venturing, throwing, seeking the spheres
    to connect them,
Till the bridge you will need be form'd, till the ductile
    anchor hold,
Till the gossamer thread you fling catch somewhere, O my   10
    soul.

EIGHT

SOUND

1. SOUND AS MEANING

Isak Dinesen, in a memoir of her life on a plantation in East Africa, tells how some Kikuyu tribesmen reacted to their first hearing of rimed verse:

> The Natives, who have a strong sense of rhythm, know nothing of verse, or at least did not know anything before the times of the schools, where they were taught hymns. One evening out in the maize-field, where we had been harvesting maize, breaking off the cobs and throwing them on to the ox-carts, to amuse myself, I spoke to the field laborers, who were mostly quite young, in Swahili verse. There was no sense in the verses, they were made for the sake of rime — "Ngumbe na-penda chumbe, Malaya mbaya. Wakamba na-kula mamba." The oxen like salt — whores are bad — The Wakamba eat snakes. It caught the interest of the boys, they formed a ring round me. They were quick to understand that meaning in poetry is of no consequence, and they did not question the thesis of the verse, but waited eagerly for the rime, and laughed at it when it came. I tried to make them themselves find the rime and finish the poem when I had begun it, but they could not, or would not, do that, and turned away their heads. As they had become used to the idea of poetry, they begged: "Speak again. Speak like rain." Why they should feel verse to be like rain I do not know. It must have been, however, an expression of applause, since in Africa rain is always longed for and welcomed.[1]

[1] "Natives and Verse," *Out of Africa* (New York, 1937).

122

What the natives had discovered is that poetry, in common with music, appeals to the ear. However limited in comparison with the sound of an orchestra — or a tribal drummer — the sound of words in itself gives pleasure. We might doubt, however, that "meaning in poetry is of no consequence." In the response of the Kikuyu, there may have been the agreeable surprise of finding that things usually not associated had been brought together. "With a hey nonny-nonny" and other such nonsense can have its place in poetry, and we too might take a certain pleasure in hearing rimes in Swahili; but most good poetry has meaningful sound as well as musical sound. The French poet Isodore Isou, who in 1947 started a literary movement called *lettrisme*, has maintained that poems can be written not in words but in letters alone (sample lines: *xyl, xyl, / prprali dryl / znglo trpylo pwi*). Sound has not sufficed to keep many Letterist poems memorable.

More powerful when in the company of meaning, not apart from it, the sounds of consonants and vowels can contribute greatly to a poem's effect. The sound of *s*, which can suggest the swishing of water, has rarely been used more accurately than in Surrey's line "Calm is the sea, the waves work less and less." When, in a poem, the sound of words pleases mind and ear, by working together with meaning, the effect is **euphony,** as in the following lines from Tennyson's "Come down, O maid":

> The moan of doves in immemorial elms,
> And murmuring of innumerable bees.

A harsh, discordant effect is **cacophony,** which may, however, be relevant to what is said, as in Milton's contemptuous reference in "Lycidas" to corrupt clergymen whose songs "Grate on their scrannel pipes of wretched straw." (Read aloud this line and one of Tennyson's two, and see which requires more work of lips, teeth, and tongue. But note that although Milton's line is cacophonous because it includes an unpleasant combination of sounds, the line in its context is pleasing because it is artful.) Appropriately smooth or harsh as these lines may seem, the sound in each of these examples is not identical with the meaning. In Tennyson's lines, the cooing of doves is not *quite* a moan; and, as John Crowe Ransom has pointed out, the sound would be almost the same but the meaning quite different in "The murdering of innumerable beeves." Relating sound more closely to meaning, **onomatopoeia** is an attempt to represent a thing by a word that

123

sounds like it: *zoom, whiz, crash, bang, ding, dong, pitter-patter, yakety-yak.* It is often effective in poetry, as in Emily Dickinson's line on the fly with its "uncertain stumbling *Buzz*," or in Robert Lowell's transcription of a birdcall: *yuck-a, yuck-a, yuck-a,* in "Falling Asleep over the Aeneid." (In Miss Dickinson's line, the nasal and sibilant sounds — *n, n, m, ng; c, s* — in the first two words also contribute to the buzz.)

Evidently the sounds of words can have a close bond to their denotation, but it is a mistake to expect such a relationship to occur regularly. While it is true that the consonant sound *sl-* will often begin a word that conveys the ideas of wetness and smoothness — *slick, slimy, slippery, slush* — we are so used to hearing it in words that convey nothing of the kind — *slave, sledgehammer, sleeve, slow* — that it is doubtful the sound in itself communicates anything very definitely. Asked by lexicographer Wilfred Funk to nominate the most beautiful word in the English language, a wit once suggested not *sunrise* or *silvery*, but *syphilis.*

Like the Kikuyu tribesmen, others who care for poetry have discovered in the sound of words something of the refreshment of cool rain. Dylan Thomas, telling how he began to write poetry, said that from early childhood words were to him "as the notes of bells, the sounds of musical instruments, the noises of wind, sea, and rain, the rattle of milkcarts, the clopping of hooves on cobbles, the fingering of branches on the window pane, might be to someone, deaf from birth, who has miraculously found his hearing." [2] For readers, too, the sound of words can have a magical spell, the more powerful when it points toward meaning. James Weldon Johnson in *God's Trombones* has told of an old-time preacher who began his sermon, "Brothers and sisters, this morning I intend to explain the unexplainable — find out the indefinable — ponder over the imponderable — and unscrew the inscrutable!" The repetition of a syllable in *unscrew* and *inscrutable* has instant appeal, but the magic of the words is all the greater if they lead us to imagine the universe as something mysteriously held together by an enormous screw which the preacher's mind, like a screw-driver, will loosen. We might conclude that, although either the sound of a word or the meaning of a word may have value all by itself, both become more memorable, taken together.

[2] "Notes on the Art of Poetry," *The Texas Quarterly*, 1961; reprinted in *Modern Poetics*, James Scully, ed. (New York, 1965).

WILLIAM BUTLER YEATS (1865–1939)

Who Goes with Fergus?

> Who will go drive with Fergus now,
> And pierce the deep wood's woven shade,
> And dance upon the level shore?
> Young man, lift up your russet brow,
> And lift your tender eyelids, maid,
> And brood on hopes and fear no more.   6
>
> And no more turn aside and brood
> Upon love's bitter mystery;
> For Fergus rules the brazen cars,
> And rules the shadows of the wood,
> And the white breast of the dim sea
> And all dishevelled wandering stars.   12

Who Goes with Fergus? *Fergus:* Irish king who gave up his throne to be a wandering poet.

QUESTIONS

1. In what lines do you find euphony?
2. In what lines, cacophony?
3. How do the sounds of these lines help enforce what is said in them?

2. ALLITERATION AND ASSONANCE

In music, sound gives pleasure by repetition. Listening to a symphony in which distinct themes are repeated throughout each movement, we enjoy both their recurrence and their variation. We take similar pleasure in the repetition of a phrase or a single chord. Frequently, something like this pleasure is afforded us by poetry.

Analogies between poetry and music, it is true, tend to break down when carried far; since poetry — to mention a single difference — has denotation. But like musical compositions, poems have patterns of sounds. Among such patterns long popular in English poetry is **alliteration**, which has been defined as "a succession of similar sounds." More exactly, alliteration is said to occur in the repetition of the same consonant sound at the beginnings of successive words — "round and round the rugged rocks the ragged rascal ran" — or inside the words, as in Milton's description of the gates of Hell:

> On a sudden open fly
> With impetuous recoil and jarring sound

125

The infernal doors, and on their hinges grate
Harsh thunder, that the lowest bottom shook
Of Erebus.

The former kind is called **initial alliteration**; the latter, **internal alliteration** or **hidden alliteration**. We recognize alliteration by sound, not
by spelling: *know* and *nail* alliterate, *know* and *key* do not.

Incidentally, the letter *r* does not *always* lend itself to cacophony:
elsewhere in *Paradise Lost* Milton said that

> Heaven opened wide
> Her ever-during gates, harmonious sound
> On golden hinges moving . . .

By itself, a letter-sound has no particular meaning. This is a truth
forgotten by people who would attribute the effectiveness of Milton's
lines on the Heavenly Gates to, say, "the mellow O's and liquid *L* of
harmonious and *golden*." Mellow O's and liquid L's occur also in the
phrase "moldy cold oatmeal," which may have quite a different effect.
Meaning depends on larger units of language than letters of the
alphabet.

Today good prose writers usually avoid alliteration; in the past, some
have cultivated it. "There is nothing more swifter than time, nothing
more sweeter," wrote John Lyly in *Euphues* (1579); and went on —
playing especially with the sounds of *v, n, t, s, l,* and *b* — "we have
not, as Seneca saith, little time to live, but we lose much; neither have
we a short life by nature, but we make it shorter by naughtiness."
Poetry, too, formerly contained more alliteration: in Old English
verse, each line was held together by alliteration, a basic pattern still
evident in the fourteenth century, as in the following description of
the world as a "fair field" in *Piers Plowman:*

> A feir feld ful of folk fond I ther bi-twene,
> Of alle maner of men, the mene and the riche . . .

Some impact of an older system of versification may be heard, too,
in this song by John Skelton. Pronunciation in Skelton's day differed
from our own, but it is still possible to utter this poem aloud without
technical training. (*Ywis* is pronounced ĭ · wis. *Pole hatchet*, line 36,
probably means one who loitered at an alehouse, which had as its
sign a pole.)

JOHN SKELTON (1460?–1529)

Lullay

> With lullay, lullay, like a child,
> Thou sleep'st too long, thou art beguiled.

> My darling dear, my daisy flower,
>   Let me, quod° he, lie in your lap.   *quoth*
> Lie still, quod she, my paramour,   5
>   Lie still hardily°, and take a nap.   *trustingly*
> His head was heavy, such was his hap,
> All drowsy dreaming, drowned in sleep,
>   That of his love he took no keep°,   *notice*
>   With hey, lullay, lullay, like a child,   10
>   Thou sleep'st too long, thou art beguiled.

> With ba, ba, ba! and bas°, bas, bas!   *kiss*
>   She cherished him both cheek and chin,
> That he wist° never where he was: *knew*
>   He had forgotten all deadly sin.   15
>   He wanted wit her love to win.
> He trusted her payment and lost all his pay;
> She left him sleeping and stale away,
>   With hey, lullay, lullay, like a child,
>   Thou sleep'st too long, thou art beguiled.   20

> The rivers rough, the waters wan,
>   She sparèd not to wet her feet.
> She waded over, she found a man
>   That halsèd° her heartily and kissed her sweet: *embraced*
>   Thus after her cold she caught a heat.   25
> My love, she said, routeth° in his bed;   *snores*
> Ywis° he hath an heavy head,   *surely*
>   With hey, lullay, lullay, like a child,
>   Thou sleep'st too long, thou art beguiled.

> What dream'st thou, drunkard, drowsy pate?   30
>   Thy lust and liking is from thee gone.
> Thou blinkard° blowboll°, thou wakest too late,   *blinking, sleepy; drunkard*
>   Behold thou liest, luggard, alone!
>   Well may thou sigh, well may thou groan,
> To deal with her so cowardly: 35
> Ywis, pole hatchet, she bleared thine eye,
>   With hey, lullay, lullay, like a child,
>   Thou sleep'st too long, thou art beguiled.

127

Relating this sad story, Skelton does more with alliteration than just bind his poem into a pattern. Evidently it is a great deal more insulting to call a man a blinkard blowboll than to call him a sleepy drunk.

Most later poets have saved alliteration for very special occasions. They may use it to give emphasis, as in Edward Lear's lines "*Far* and *few*, *far* and *few*, / Are the *lands* where the Jumblies *live*." With its aid they can point out the relationship between two things placed side by side, as in Pope's line on things of little worth: "The courtier's *p*romises, and sick man's *p*rayers." Alliteration, too, can be a powerful aid to memory. It is hard to forget such tongue twisters as "Peter Piper picked a peck of pickled peppers," or such common expressions as "all black and blue," "from stem to stern," and "cool as a cucumber." In fact, because alliteration directs our attention to something memorable and worthy of emphasis, it had better not be used thoughtlessly or merely for decoration, lest it appear empty and ludicrous. A case in point may be the line by Philip James Bailey, in which he reacts to a weeping lady: "I saw, but *sp*ared to *sp*eak." If the poet chooses the word *spared* for any meaningful reason other than that it alliterates, he fails to make such a reason clear.

As we have seen, to repeat the sound of a consonant is to produce alliteration; but to repeat the sound of a *vowel* is to produce **assonance**. Like alliteration, assonance may occur either initially — "*a*ll the *a*wful *au*guries" [3] — or internally — Spenser's "Her goodly *eyes* *like* sapph*i*res sh*i*ning br*i*ght, / Her forehead *i*vory wh*i*te . . ." Like alliteration, it can help slow the reader down and focus his attention.

EXERCISE ONE

Noticing especially the various sounds of *a*, *i*, and *o*, try reading aloud as rapidly as possible the following poem by Tennyson. From the difficulties you encounter, you may be able to sense the slowing effect of assonance. Then read the poem aloud a second time, with due consideration.

ALFRED, LORD TENNYSON (1809–1892)

'*The splendor falls*'

> The splendor falls on castle walls
>   And snowy summits old in story;
> The long light shakes across the lakes,
>   And the wild cataract leaps in glory.
> Blow, bugle, blow, set the wild echoes flying,
> Blow, bugle; answer, echoes, dying, dying, dying.   6

[3] Some prefer to call the repetition of an initial vowel-sound alliteration: "apt alliteration's artful aid."

O hark, O hear! how thin and clear,
  And thinner, clearer, farther going!
O sweet and far from cliff and scar
  The horns of Elfland faintly blowing!
Blow, let us hear the purple glens replying:
Blow, bugle; answer, echoes, dying, dying, dying.   12

O love, they die in yon rich sky,
  They faint on hill or field or river;
Our echoes roll from soul to soul,
  And grow for ever and for ever.
Blow, bugle, blow, set the wild echoes flying,
And answer, echoes, answer, dying, dying, dying.   18

Tennyson's poem, like many others that depend upon sound for much of their effect, mingles alliteration and assonance in a complicated network of relationships. Words set up echoes with other words, like various bells ringing together. So, too, the ornate line from Poe's "Raven" reverberates: "And the silken, soft, uncertain rustle of each purple curtain." Alliteration and assonance are not the only elements that make poetry memorable, but in some poems they can help.

EXERCISE TWO

In the following two-line poem, pick out the patterns of alliteration and assonance. Describe their usefulness to the poem.

ALEXANDER POPE (1688–1744)

Epitaph Intended for Sir Isaac Newton

Nature and Nature's laws lay hid in night.
God said, *Let Newton be!* and all was light.

EXERCISE THREE

Which of these translations of the same passage from Petrarch do you think the better poetry? Why? What does sound have to do with your preference?

A. Love that liveth and reigneth in my thought,
   That built his seat within my captive breast,
   Clad in the arms wherein with me he fought,
   Oft in my face he doth his banner rest.
          — Henry Howard, Earl of Surrey (1517?–1547)

B. The long love that in my thought doth harbor,
   And in mine heart doth keep his residence,
   Into my face presseth with bold pretense
   And therein campeth, spreading his banner.
          — Sir Thomas Wyatt (1503?–1542)

129

3. RIME

Isak Dinesen's natives, to whom rime was a new phenomenon, recognized at once that rimed language is a special language. So do we; for, although much English poetry is unrimed, rime is one means to set poetry apart from ordinary conversation. A **rime** (or **rhyme**), defined most narrowly, occurs when two or more words or phrases contain an identical or similar vowel-sound, usually accented, and the consonant-sounds (if any) that follow the vowel-sound are identical: *hay* and *sleigh, prairie schooner* and *piano tuner*.[4] From these examples it will be seen that rime depends not on spelling but on sound.

To be excellent, rime should surprise. It is all very well that a reader may anticipate which vowel-sound is coming next, for patterns of rime give him pleasure by satisfying his expectations; but riming becomes dull clunking if, at the end of every line, the reader can predict the very word that will end the next. Hearing many a jukebox tune for the first time, a listener can do so: *charms* lead to *arms, skies above* to *love, madness* to *sadness* or *gladness*. But who, given the opening line of this child-composed jingle, could expect it to arrive where it did?

ANONYMOUS (English; twentieth century)

'*Julius Caesar*'

> Julius Caesar,
> The Roman geezer,
> Squashed his wife with a lemon squeezer.

As Robert Herrick also knew, and demonstrated in the following lines, a pair of rimes may join terms that ordinarily we might not expect to find together:

> Then while time serves, and we are but decaying,
> Come, my Corinna, come, let's go a-Maying.

Though good rimes will seem fresh, not all will startle, and probably very few will call to mind things of such striking contrast as *May* and *decay, Caesar* and *lemon squeezer*. Some masters of rime will link un-

---

[4] Some definitions of *rime* would apply the term to the repetition of any identical or similar sound, not only a vowel-sound. In this sense, assonance is a kind of rime; so is alliteration (called **initial rime**).

obtrusive words, which, taken out of context, may seem common and unevocative. Here, for instance, is Alexander Pope's comment on a trifling and effeminate courtier:

> Yet let me flap this bug with gilded wings,
> This painted child of dirt, that stinks and stings;
> Whose buzz the witty and the fair annoys,
> Yet wit ne'er tastes, and beauty ne'er enjoys:
> So well-bred spaniels civilly delight
> In mumbling of the game they dare not bite.
> Eternal smiles his emptiness betray,
> As shallow streams run dimpling all the way.

The rime-words in themselves are not especially memorable — and yet the lines are, because (among other reasons) they rime. Wit may be driven home without rime, but it is rime that rings the doorbell when she arrives. Admittedly, some rimes — like old coins — wear thin from too much use. More difficult to use freshly than before the establishment of Tin Pan Alley, such rimes as *moon / June / croon* seem leaden, and to ring true would need an extremely powerful context. *Death* and *breath* are a rime that poets have used with wearisome frequency; another is *birth, earth,* and *mirth.* And yet we cannot exclude these from the diction of poetry, for they might be the very words a poet would need in order to say something new and original. This poem by Blake remains fresher than its rimes (taken out of context) would suggest:

WILLIAM BLAKE (1757–1827)

'The Angel that presided o'er my birth'

> The Angel that presided o'er my birth
> Said, "Little creature, formed of Joy and Mirth,
> Go love without the help of any thing on earth."

What matters to rime is freshness — not of a word, but of the poet's way of seeing.

Good poets, according to John Dryden, have learned to make their rime "so properly a part of the verse, that it should never mislead the sense, but itself be led and governed by it." The comment may remind us that skillful rime — unlike poor rime — is much more than a distracting ornament. It gives emphasis and, like other patterns

131

of sound, can help to weave a poem together. It sets up reverberations between words and invites us to look for relationships of meaning. Such a relationship between two rimed words may be a contrast, as in a hymn by Isaac Watts:

> Like flowery fields the nations stand
> Pleased with the morning *light;*
> The flowers beneath the mower's hand
> Lie withering ere 'tis *night.*

And rime can help organize ideas. (For a detailed treatment of this subject see chap. 10.)

Rime comes in several varieties:

To have an **exact rime,** any sounds following the vowel sound have to be the same in both rimed words or phrases: *red* and *bread, wealthily* and *stealthily, walk to her* and *talk to her.* If final consonant sounds are the same, but the vowel sounds are different, the result is a **slant-rime,** also called **near-rime, off-rime,** or **partial rime.** An instance would be *stone* riming with *sun, moon, rain, green, gone, thin,* etc. By not satisfying the reader's expectation that there is going to be an exact chime, but instead giving him a clunk, a slant-rime calls attention to itself in a way that may occasionally help a poet say something more meaningfully. It works especially well for negations and denials, as in Blake's couplet:

> He who the ox to wrath has moved
> Shall never be by woman loved.

Consonance is a particular sort of slant-rime. It occurs when the rimed words or phrases have identical consonant sounds but a different vowel, as in *chitter* and *chatter.* It is used in a traditional nonsense poem, "The Cutty Wren": " 'O where are you going?' says *Milder* to *Malder."* W. H. Auden wrote a variation on it that begins, " 'O where are you going?' said *reader* to *rider,"* thus keeping the consonance.

End-rime, not surprisingly, comes at the ends of lines; **internal rime,** within them. Most rime tends to be end-rime. Few recent poets have used internal rime so heavily as Wallace Stevens in the beginning of "Bantams in Pine-Woods": "Chieftain Iffucan of Azcan in caftan / Of tan with henna hackles, halt!" (lines also heavy on alliteration). A poet may employ both end-rime and internal rime in the same poem, as in Stevens' lines and in Robert Burns's satiric ballad "The Kirk's Alarm": "Orthodox, orthodox, wha believe in John Knox." The effect is a powerful emphasis.

Masculine rime is a rime of monosyllabic words or of stressed final syllables in words of more than one syllable: *nail* and *quail, compare* and

132

affair. Though a **feminine rime** — a stressed riming syllable followed by one or more unstressed syllables identical in sound (as in *turtle* and *fertile*) — often lends itself to light verse, it can also be valuable in serious poems like "Desert Places" by Robert Frost:

> They cannot scare me with their empty spaces
> Between stars — on stars where no human race is.

(Not quite an exact rime, but feminine.) In English, serious poems containing three-syllable feminine rimes have been attempted, notably by Thomas Hood in "The Bridge of Sighs":

> Take her up tenderly,
> Lift her with care;
> Fashioned so slenderly,
> Young, and so fair!

But the pattern is hard to sustain without lapsing into unintentional comedy, as in the same poem:

> Still, for all slips of hers,
> One of Eve's family —
> Wipe those poor lips of hers,
> Oozing so clammily.

It works better when comedy is meant:

HILAIRE BELLOC (1870–1953)

The Hippopotamus

> I shoot the Hippopotamus
>   with bullets made of platinum,
> Because if I use leaden ones
>   his hide is sure to flatten 'em.

In **eye-rime**, spellings look alike but pronunciations differ — *rough* and *dough*. Strictly speaking, eye-rime is not rime at all.

In the 1960's, American poetry has seen a great turning away from rime, with Louis Simpson, James Wright, Robert Lowell, W. S. Merwin, and others who in the past have favored rime, often quitting it for free or unrimed verse. Indeed, it has been suggested that rime in the English language is exhausted. Such a view may be a reaction against the wearing-thin of rimes by overuse, or the mechanical and meaningless application of a rime scheme. Yet anyone who listens to children skipping rope in the street, making up rimes to delight themselves as they go along, may doubt that the pleasures of rime are ended; and certainly the practice of Yeats and Emily Dickinson, to name only two, suggests that the possibilities of slant-rime may be nearly infinite. If successfully employed, as it has been employed at times by a majority of English-speaking poets whose work we care to save, rime runs through its poem like a spine: the creature moves by means of it.

JOHN MALCOLM BRINNIN (b. 1916)

Song for Strangers in Wales

Between Red Roses and St. Clears
I met an old man all eyes and ears;
Hands trembling twigs, head snowing snow,
He had no mortal place to go
To lay his cheek or say his prayers
Between Red Roses and St. Clears.   6

Between Red Roses and St. Clears,
"Father," I said, "persuade your tears
Toward one who has sore need of them."
"Son," he replied, "do not condemn
The spittle and phlegm of all these years
Between Red Roses and St. Clears."   12

Between Red Roses and St. Clears,
Hail-fellow-met, we palmed our fears,
His for the world, mine for me,
Two blossoms on the apple tree,
Then linked our arms and clinked our beers
Between Red Roses and St. Clears.   18

Between Red Roses and St. Clears,
I said so long to his white hairs
And watched him go, humped in his age,
Under the stars and over the bridge.
Nobody knows, nobody cares
Between Red Roses and St. Clears.   24

Between Red Roses and St. Clears,
I skulked for owls and polar bears.
The sun rose sober, as did I.
Something was smoking in the sky:
"Beware yourselves! my dears, my dears,
Between Red Roses and St. Clears."   30

1. Red Roses and St. Clears are names of Welsh villages; the latter exactly rimes with *bears*. What portion of this poem is made of lines ending in this rime or in slant-rime variations?
2. Read the poem aloud. Do you find this frequency of the same rime successful or monotonous?
3. Point out the slant-rimes. How would you describe their effect?
4. What patterns of assonance and alliteration are established? What help are they to the effectiveness of the poem?
5. If Red Roses were named Red Pansies what would be lost? Would this loss be a loss in sound only?
6. Would you agree or disagree with the contention that in this poem sound is the only element that matters?

GERARD MANLEY HOPKINS (1844–1889)

God's Grandeur

The world is charged with the grandeur of God.
 It will flame out, like shining from shook foil;
 It gathers to a greatness, like the ooze of oil
Crushed. Why do men then now not reck his rod?   4
Generations have trod, have trod, have trod;
 And all is seared with trade; bleared, smeared with toil;
 And wears man's smudge and shares man's smell: the soil
Is bare now, nor can foot feel, being shod.   8

And for all this, nature is never spent;
 There lives the dearest freshness deep down things;
 And though the last lights off the black West went
Oh, morning, at the brown brink eastward, springs —   12
Because the Holy Ghost over the bent
 World broods with warm breast and with ah! bright wings.

1. In a letter Hopkins explained *shook foil* (line 2): "I mean foil in its sense of leaf or tinsel . . . Shaken goldfoil gives off broad glares like sheet lightning and also, and this is true of nothing else, owing to its zigzag dints and creasings and network of small many cornered facets, a sort of fork lightning too." What do you think he meant by line 3, *ooze of oil?* Is this phrase an example of alliteration?
2. What instances of internal rime does the poem contain? How would you describe their effects?
3. Point out some of the poet's uses of alliteration and assonance. Does he go too far in his heavy use of devices of sound, or would you defend his practice?

EMANUEL MORGAN [WITTER BYNNER] (b. 1881)

Opus 6

If I were only dafter
    I might be making hymns
To the liquor of your laughter
    And the lacquer of your limbs.   4

But you turn across the table
    A telescope of eyes,
And it lights a Russian sable
    Running circles in the skies . . . ⁻   8

Till I go running after,
    Obeying all your whims —
For the liquor of your laughter
    And the lacquer of your limbs.   12

QUESTIONS

1. This deliberately baffling poem was attributed to the Pittsburgh
bohemian Morgan by Witter Bynner, who invented him. (For an entertaining history of this 1916 literary prank, see William Jay Smith, *The
Spectra Hoax*, Wesleyan University Press, 1961.) In what demonstrations
of sound effects do these lines revel?

2. How do you account for this poem's being comic in effect, while
Hopkins' "God's Grandeur," though more heavily laden with devices of
sound, is not?

4. READING POEMS ALOUD

Thomas Moore's "The light that lies in women's eyes" — a line rich
in internal rime, alliteration, and assonance — is harder to forget than
"The light burning in the gaze of a woman." Because of sound, it
is possible to remember the obscure line Christopher Smart wrote
while in an insane asylum: "Let Ross, house of Ross rejoice with the
Great Flabber Dabber Flat Clapping Fish with hands." Such lines,
striking as they are even when read silently, become still more effective when addressed to the ear. As was suggested at the beginning of
this book, reading poems aloud is a way to understand them. For
these reasons, the reader will do well to practice the art of lending
poetry his voice. A few points may be helpful to keep in mind:

1. Before trying to read a poem aloud to other people, understand its
meaning as thoroughly as possible. If you know what the poet is saying
and his attitude toward it, you will be better able to find an appropriate
tone of voice, and to give certain parts a proper emphasis.

136

2. Except in the most informal situations, and some exercises in class, read a poem to yourself before trying it on an audience. No actor goes before the footlights without first having studied his script, and the language of poems usually demands even more consideration than the language of most contemporary plays. Prepare your reading in advance. Check pronunciations you are not sure of. Underline things to be emphasized.

3. Read deliberately, more slowly than you would read aloud from a newspaper. Keep in mind that you are saying something to somebody. Don't race through the poem as if anxious to get it over with.

4. Don't fall into singsong. A poem may have a definite swing (the next chapter will go into this), but swing should never be exaggerated at the cost of sense. Again, if you understand what the poem is saying and utter the poem as if you do, the temptation to fall into such a mechanical intonation should not occur. Observe the punctuation, making slight pauses for commas, longer pauses for full stops (periods, question marks, exclamation points).

5. If the poem is rimed, don't raise your voice and make the rimes stand out unnaturally. They should receive no more volume than other words in the poem, though a faint pause at the end of each line will call the listener's attention to them. This advice goes contrary to the school that holds that, reading aloud a line that does not end in any punctuation, one should not pause, but run it right together with the line following. From such a reading, a listener may not be able to tell the rimes; besides, that valuable unit of rhythm, the line, is destroyed. (More about rhythm will be said in chap. 9).

6. Be aware that, in some older poems, rimes that look like slant-rimes may have been exact rimes in their day:

> Still so perverse and opposite,
> As if they worshiped God for spite.
>
> — Samuel Butler, *Hudibras* (1663)

> Soft yielding minds to water glide away,
> And sip, with nymphs, their elemental tea.
>
> — Alexander Pope, "The Rape of the Lock" (1714)

You may wish to establish a consistent policy toward such shifty objects: is it worthwhile to distort current pronunciation for the sake of the rime?

7. Listening to a poem, especially an unfamiliar poem, places considerable demands on your hearers' attention. Seldom — unless you are outstandingly good at it — read poetry aloud to anyone uninterruptedly for more than a few minutes at a time. Reading to audiences, Robert Frost would intersperse his poems with many silences and seemingly casual comments, shrewdly giving the poems a chance to sink in.

8. You may find it helpful to listen to recordings of some poets read-

137

ing their poems. Not all read their own work well, but there is much to be relished in both the highly dramatic reading style of Dylan Thomas and Ezra Pound and in the quiet underplay of Frost, to mention some superior performers. You need feel no obligation to follow the poet's reading of a poem as if it were the letter of a law. It may be necessary to feel about the poem in your own way, in order to read it with conviction and spontaneity.

EXERCISE FOUR

Read the following poems aloud. What devices of sound — alliteration, assonance, onomatopoeia, rime, slant-rime, internal rime — do you find in each? Point out euphony or cacophony. Try to explain what the sound contributes to the total effect of the poem and how it reinforces what the poet is saying.

WILLIAM SHAKESPEARE (1564–1616)

'It was a lover and his lass'

> It was a lover and his lass,
> With a hey, and a ho, and a hey nonny no,
> That o'er the green corn fields did pass
> In spring time, the only pretty ring time,
> When birds do sing, hey ding a ding a ding:
> Sweet lovers love the spring.   6
>
> Between the acres of the rye,
> With a hey, and a ho, and a hey nonny no,
> These pretty country fools would lie,
> In spring time, the only pretty ring time,
> When birds do sing, hey ding a ding a ding:
> Sweet lovers love the spring.   12
>
> This carol they began that hour,
> With a hey, and a ho, and a hey nonny no,
> How that a life was but a flower
> In spring time, the only pretty ring time,
> When birds do sing, hey ding a ding a ding:
> Sweet lovers love the spring.   18
>
> Then pretty lovers take the time
> With a hey, and a ho, and a hey nonny no,
> For love is crownèd with the prime
> In spring time, the only pretty ring time,
> When birds do sing, hey ding a ding a ding:
> Sweet lovers love the spring.   24

138

ROBERT HERRICK (1591–1674)

Soft Music

> The mellow touch of music most doth wound
> The soul, when it doth rather sigh than sound.

LEIGH HUNT (1784–1859)

Rondeau

> Jenny kissed me when we met,
>   Jumping from the chair she sat in;
> Time, you thief, who love to get
>   Sweets into your list, put that in:
> Say I'm weary, say I'm sad,   5
>   Say that health and wealth have missed me,
> Say I'm growing old, but add,
>   Jenny kissed me.

A. E. HOUSMAN (1859–1936)

'With rue my heart is laden'

> With rue my heart is laden
>   For golden friends I had,
> For many a rose-lipt maiden
>   And many a lightfoot lad.   4
>
> By brooks too broad for leaping
>   The lightfoot boys are laid;
> The rose-lipt girls are sleeping
>   In fields where roses fade.   8

JOHN UPDIKE (b. 1932)

Winter Ocean

> Many-maned scud-thumper, tub
> of male whales, maker of worn wood, shrub-
> ruster, sky-mocker, rave!
> portly pusher of waves, wind-slave.

NINE

RHYTHM

1. STRESS

Rhythms affect us powerfully. The sound of a band with a definite beat can set our feet tapping, and the rising and falling of waves and tides continue in memory long after we return from the beach. We are lulled to sleep by the sway of a hammock, or perhaps driven almost crazy by the vibration of a power drill in the street. How essential rhythm can be to poetry, too, is illustrated in the folk songs of railroad work-gangs (in which words were sung and chanted in time to the lifting and dropping of a sledge-hammer) and in verse that soldiers shout while marching:

> Your left! Two! Three! Four!
> Your left! Two! Three! Four!
> You left your wife and twenty-one kids
> And you left! Two! Three! Four!
> You'll never go home tonight!

It is also seen in some Mother Goose rimes, to which children have been responding with glee for hundreds of years. This one is chanted while jogging a child up and down:

> Here goes my lord
> A trot, a trot, a trot, a trot!
> Here goes my lady
> A canter, a canter, a canter, a canter!
> Here goes my young master
> Jockey-hitch, jockey-hitch, jockey-hitch, jockey-hitch!

Here goes my young miss
An amble, an amble, an amble, an amble!
The footman lags behind to tipple ale and wine
And goes gallop, a gallop, a gallop, to make up his time.

Although on hearing a poem read aloud we perceive its sound and its rhythm simultaneously, rhythm and sound are not identical. Even if totally deaf, a man at a parade can sense, from the beat of drums and the tramp of marching feet, rhythm in the vibrations of the pavement. Rhythms occur in the pulsing of the blood, the succession of the seasons, the motions of the moon and stars, and the alternations of night and day, even when these things occur without a sound.

While **rhythm,** then, may be the recurrence of a sound, it also may be the recurrence of a motion, an emphasis, or a pulsation. In poetry, several kinds of recurrent sound are possible including (as we saw in the last chapter) rime, assonance, and alliteration. But ordinarily, when we speak of the rhythm in poetry, we mean not the recurrence of sound but the recurrence of stresses at equal intervals. A **stress**, also commonly called an **accent**, is a greater amount of force given to one syllable in speaking than is given to another. We favor the stressed syllable with a little more breath and emphasis, with the result that it may come out slightly louder, higher in pitch, or longer in duration than other syllables. In this manner we place a stress on the first syllable of such words as *open, impact, statue, apron*; and on the second syllable of *precise, amount, mistake, until*. The unstressed or unaccented syllable in each of these words actually receives *some* stress, of course, in order to be heard; but less. It is often called a **slack syllable**.

Every word in English carries at least one stress, except the articles *the, a, an* and usually such prepositions as *of, from, by, at, to,* and *with* (but not *a · gaínst, u · pón*). Even these may bear stress occasionally, as when a suitor declares, "You are THE girl for me," or in the expression "Get WITH it"; and, depending on where they occur in syntax, these words will often be given at least a half-stress: "Ī'm dówn at thē óf · fīce." (This book will use the mark **/** for a whole stress, **/** for a half-stress, and **–** for a slack syllable.) To indicate where stresses occur in a line is to **scan** it; the art of doing so is **scansion**.

The existence of such half-stresses (and, indeed, much more subtle gradations can be distinguished in a laboratory) suggests that scansion is an inexact but useful rule of thumb. If we wanted to describe rhythms with slightly more accuracy, we might recognize that (as a dictionary will indicate) such a word as díc · tion · ár · y takes a **primary** (greater) **stress** on its first syllable, a **secondary stress** on its third. But to keep the rule of thumb from becoming impracticably complicated, half-stresses are usually ignored in scansion and counted as wholes.

Whenever two readers find differences in their understandings of a poem, they are likely to differ in the way each will scan it. To scan a poem is more than a matter of syllable-counting: it is to place an interpretation upon it and to offer a way to read the poem aloud.

In general, it is of little use to speak of the rhythm of a *word*, most words being too short for us to perceive much recurrence of stress. Usually we refer to the rhythm of a phrase, a line, a passage, or an entire poem. Add a few other words to the word *dictionary* — say, for instance, "Ī sét thē díc · tīon · ár · y clóse āt hánd" — and the result is that stresses recur regularly — in this example, on every second syllable in the line. Such a recurrence of stresses at regular intervals makes a pattern, a **meter.** (Our concern at this point is with rhythm in general; a discussion of particular meters common to English verse will be saved for the second part of this chapter.)

Reading a poem aloud or silently scanning it, we pay special attention to places where stressed syllables occur together or predominate. The poet is placing greater emphasis on them — and their meaning — as surely as if he had underlined them. Consider the following lines from Donne's sonnet (see p. 9):

> Bát · tēr mý héart, thrée-pér · sōned Gód, fōr yóu
>
> Ās yét būt knóck, bréathe, shíne, ānd séek tō ménd;
>
> Thāt Ī māy ríse ānd stánd, o'er · thrów mé, ānd bénd
>
> Yōur fórce tō bréak, blów, búrn, ānd máke mē néw.

Slack syllables also may direct our attention to certain words. But the poet may be after an effect, not of power, but of hesitation; not of force, but of delicacy. Yeats in "Among School Children" asks: What youthful mother, if she could see her son grown old, would think him

> A compensation for the pang of his birth
>
> Ōr thē ūn · cér · taīn · ty ōf hīs sét · tīng fórth?

Whenever slack syllables recur in pairs, they introduce rhythmic trippings and bounces:

For the moon nev · er beams, with · out bring · ing me dreams

Of the beau · ti · ful An · na · bel Lee;

A bunch of the boys were whoop · ing it up in the Mal · a · mute

sa · loon.

An effect heavier, but also rocking, is produced by recurrent pairs of stresses:

"sweet spring is your

time is my time is our

time for spring · time is love · time

and vi · va sweet love"

In this passage of E. E. Cummings, paired stresses link lines together (*your / time, our / time*) into a continuous pattern of rhythm.

Apart from the words that convey it, the rhythm of a poem has no meaning. There are no essentially sad rhythms, nor any essentially happy ones. But some rhythms belong with some meanings better than others do. The bouncing rhythm of Cummings' lines seems appropriate to a song about spring, but it might be a disaster if chosen for a solemn elegy.

EXERCISE ONE

In each of the following passages, decide whether (1) rhythm enforces meaning and tone; or (2) rhythm works against these elements and, consequently, against the poem's effectiveness. What is the overall effect of the rhythm in each passage?

A. Roll on, thou deep and dark blue Ocean — roll!
    Ten thousand fleets sweep over thee in vain;
    Man marks the earth with ruin — his control
    Stops with the shore; — upon the watery plain
    The wrecks are all thy deed, nor doth remain
    A shadow of man's ravage, save his own,
    When, for a moment, like a drop of rain,
    He sinks into thy depths with bubbling groan —
    Without a grave — unknelled, uncoffined, and unknown.

                        — George Gordon, Lord Byron,
                          "Childe Harold's Pilgrimage"

B.   Then my heart it grew ashen and sober
            As the leaves that were crispèd and sere —
            As the leaves that were withering and sere,
     And I cried: "It was surely October
         On *this* very night of last year
         That I journeyed — I journeyed down here —
         That I brought a dread burden down here —
         On this night of all nights in the year,
         Ah, what demon has tempted me here?"
                     — Edgar Allan Poe, "Ulalume"

C.   Weep eyes, break heart!
     My love and I must part.
                     — Thomas Middleton, song from
                     the play *Chaste Maid in Cheapside*

D.   Many a lip is gaping for drink,
         And madly calling for rain;
     And some hot brains are beginning to think
         Of a messmate's opened vein.
                     — Eliza Cook, "Song of the Sea-Weed"

E.   The master, the swabber, the boatswain, and I,
     The gunner and his mate
     Loved Moll, Meg, and Marian, and Margery,
     But none of us cared for Kate;
     For she had a tongue with a tang
     Would cry to a sailor "Go hang!" —
     She loved not the savor of tar nor of pitch
     Yet a tailor might scratch her where'er she did itch;
     Then to sea, boys, and let her go hang!
                     — William Shakespeare, song from *The Tempest*

Rhythm in English poetry is due not only to stresses but also to stops. When a line ends in a pause, usually indicated by some mark of punctuation, it is **end-stopped.** Every line is end-stopped in this passage by Alexander Pope:

    Hither the heroes and the nymphs resort,
    To taste awhile the pleasures of a court;
    In various talk th' instructive hours they passed,
    Who gave the ball, or paid the visit last;
    One speaks the glory of the British Queen,
    And one describes a charming Indian screen;
    A third interprets motions, looks, and eyes;
    At every word a reputation dies.

Any line that has no punctuation at its end, and which therefore is read with only the slightest pause after it, is **run-on;** and the running-on of its thought into the next line, **enjambment.** We cannot stop reading at the end of a run-on line without doing violence to the sense; we are given only part of a phrase, whose conclusion is still to come. Robert Browning wrote:

> That's my last Duchess painted on the wall
> Looking as if she were alive. I call
> That piece a wonder, now: Frà Pandolf's hands
> Worked busily a day, and there she stands.

Lines 2 and 3 are clearly run-on lines; line 1 may be run-on also, but makes such a complete and self-contained statement that we may want to pause at the end of it, despite its lack of final punctuation.

A poem with many end-stopped lines has a different rhythm from that of a poem with much enjambment, even if, in both poems, individual lines contain the same pattern of stressed syllables. Compare, for instance, these two passages. (In the first, *heavens* and *powers* are pronounced as words of one syllable: "heav'ns," "pow'rs.")

> And ye high heavens, the temple of the gods,
> In which a thousand torches flaming bright
> Do burn, that to us wretched earthly clods,
> In dreadful darkness lend desirèd light;
> And all ye powers which in the same remain   5
> More than we men can feign°,   *imagine*
> Pour out your blessing on us plentiously . . .
> — Edmund Spenser, "Epithalamion"

> Let seed be grass, and grass turn into hay:
> I'm martyr to a motion not my own;
> What's freedom for? To know eternity.
> I swear she cast a shadow white as stone.
> But who would count eternity in days?   5
> These old bones live to learn her wanton ways:
> (I measure time by how a body sways).
> — Theodore Roethke, "I Knew a Woman"

Both passages (with some variation) are in iambic pentameter — lines of ten syllables with every second syllable given a heavier stress than that given to the previous syllable — but the rhythm of Roethke's seven end-stopped lines is more halting or disconnected than the rhythm of Spenser's long sentence with its run-on lines 2 and 5. There are other devices, besides, that make for particular effects of rhythm here: Roethke's full stop at the question mark inside line 3; and Spenser's use of short line 6, in which, by leading us to expect

145

another ten-syllable line, then drawing us up short, the poet gives his words special emphasis. In this line, too, the fact that every word is a monosyllable helps shift the rhythm and compels us to read more slowly and carefully. This is no more than we might do if we were to meet such a line in prose, where it might slow the eye, strike the ear of the mind, and make us pick our way through each word one by one — with all the care it takes to cross a brook that has stones to step on. Effects of rhythm also may be created by the poet's choosing words that take less time to pronounce, or more. Milton ends *Paradise Lost:*

> They hand in hand with wand'ring steps and slow,
> Through Eden took their solitary way.

We can preserve the meter and yet alter the duration thus:

> They hip to hip with wand'ring steps and slow,
> Through Eden took their solitary walk.[1]

In summary: rhythm is not sound but a pattern of recurrence and, in poetry, is made up of stressed and relatively unstressed syllables. It can be affected by the poet's doing any of several things: making the intervals between his stresses regular or varied; making his lines short or long; end-stopping his lines or running them over; choosing words more easy (or less easy) to say; choosing polysyllabic words or monosyllables. Most important of all: rhythm conveys meaning.

ROBERT FROST (1874–1963)

Never Again Would Birds' Song Be the Same

> He would declare and could himself believe
> That the birds there in all the garden round
> From having heard the daylong voice of Eve
> Had added to their own an oversound,   4
> Her tone of meaning but without the words.
> Admittedly an eloquence so soft
> Could only have had an influence on birds
> When call or laughter carried it aloft.   8

[1] John Oliver Perry, who kindly provided this illustration, added a word of caution: The meanings of the words are in part responsible for the length that we give them.

Be that as may be, she was in their song.
Moreover her voice upon their voices crossed
Had now persisted in the woods so long
That probably it never would be lost.   12
Never again would birds' song be the same.
And to do that to birds was why she came.

QUESTIONS

1. Who is *he?*
2. In reading aloud line 9, do you stress *may?* (Do you say *as MAY be* or *as may BE?*) What guide do we have to the poet's wishes here?
3. Which lines does Frost cast mostly or entirely into monosyllables? How would you describe the impact of these lines?
4. In his "Essay on Criticism," Alexander Pope made fun of the poets who wrote mechanically, without wit: "And ten low words oft creep in one dull line." Is this criticism applicable to Frost's lines of monosyllables? Explain.

BEN JONSON (1573?–1637)

'*Slow, slow, fresh fount*'

Slow, slow, fresh fount, keep time with my salt tears;
    Yet slower yet, oh faintly, gentle springs;
List to the heavy part the music bears,
    Woe weeps out her division° when she sings.   *a part in a song*
        Droop herbs and flowers,   5
        Fall grief in showers;
        Our beauties are not ours;
            Oh, I could still,
Like melting snow upon some craggy hill,
        Drop, drop, drop, drop,   10
Since nature's pride is now a withered daffodil.

QUESTIONS

1. The nymph Echo sings this lament over the youth Narcissus in Jonson's play *Cynthia's Revels.* In mythology, Nemesis, goddess of vengeance, to punish Narcissus for loving his own beauty, caused him to pine away, then transformed him into a narcissus (another name for a *daffodil,* line 11). What qualities do the particular objects in the poem (*fountain, tears, springs, music, herbs, flowers,* etc.) all have in common?
2. Try reading the first line aloud as rapidly as you can. Why is it difficult to do so?
3. Which lines rely most heavily on stressed syllables?
4. In general, how would you describe the rhythm of this poem? How is it appropriate to what is said?

147

ROBERT LOWELL (b. 1917)

At the Altar

>I sit at a gold table with my girl
>Whose eyelids burn with brandy. What a whirl
>Of Easter eggs is colored by the lights,
>As the Norwegian dancer's crystalled tights
>Flash with her naked leg's high-booted skate,   5
>Like Northern Lights upon my watching plate.
>The twinkling steel above me is a star;
>I am a fallen Christmas tree. Our car
>Races through seven red-lights — then the road
>Is unpatrolled and empty, and a load   10
>Of ply-wood with a tail-light makes us slow.
>I turn and whisper in her ear. You know
>I want to leave my mother and my wife,
>You wouldn't have me tied to them for life . . .
>Time runs, the windshield runs with stars. The past   15
>Is cities from a train, until at last
>Its escalating and black-windowed blocks
>Recoil against a Gothic church. The clocks
>Are tolling. I am dying. The shocked stones
>Are falling like a ton of bricks and bones   20
>That snap and splinter and descend in glass
>Before a priest who mumbles through his Mass
>And sprinkles holy water; and the Day
>Breaks with its lightning on the man of clay,
>*Dies amara valde.* Here the Lord   25
>Is Lucifer in harness: hand on sword,
>He watches me for Mother, and will turn
>The bier and baby-carriage where I burn.

At the Altar. In a public reading of this poem, Robert Lowell once made some remarks cited by George P. Elliott in *Fifteen Modern American Poets* (New York, 1956). Lit up like a Christmas tree, the speaker finds himself in a Boston nightclub, watching a skating floorshow. Then he and his girl drive (or does he only dream they drive?) to a church where a priest, saying a funeral Mass, sprinkles a corpse with holy water. The Day (line 23) is the Day of Judgment. 25. *Dies amara valde:* "day bitter above all others," a phrase from a funeral hymn, the *Dies Irae*, in which sinners are warned to fear God's wrath. 28. *baby-carriage:* the undertaker's silver dolly, supporting a coffin.

QUESTIONS

1. Which of the lines in this poem are end-stopped?
2. What effects does Lowell obtain by so much enjambment?
3. What besides enjambment contributes to the rhythm of the poem?
4. How is this rhythm appropriate to what the poet is saying? Explain.

148

Both of the following compositions in verse have lines of similar length, yet they differ greatly in rhythm. Explain how they differ, and why.

SIR THOMAS WYATT (1503?–1542)

'With serving still'

> With serving still°   *continually*
>   This have I won,
> For my goodwill
>   To be undone;   4
>
> And for redress
>   Of all my pain,
> Disdainfulness
>   I have again;   8
>
> And for reward
>   Of all my smart
> Lo, thus unheard,
>   I must depart!   12
>
> Wherefore all ye
>   That after shall
> By fortune be,
>   As I am, thrall,   16
>
> Example take
>   What I have won,
> Thus for her sake
>   To be undone!   20

DOROTHY PARKER (b. 1893)

Résumé

> Razors pain you;
> Rivers are damp;
> Acids stain you;
> And drugs cause cramp.
> Guns aren't lawful;   5
> Nooses give;
> Gas smells awful;
> You might as well live.

2. METER

To become more aware of the rhythms of poetry, to be able to speak of them with greater accuracy, and to acquire an instrument for reading poems aloud more effectively, we need to know more about meter. To tell the meter of a given line is to name which pattern of stressed and unstressed syllables predominates, and also to tell the length of the line. Here, for instance, are four lines of Thomas Gray's "Elegy in a Country Church-Yard," in one of the most familiar of English meters:

> The cúr / few tólls / the knéll / of párt / ing dáy,
>
> The lów / ing hérd / wind slów / ly o'ér / the léa,
>
> The plów / man hóme / ward plóds / his wéar / y wáy,
>
> And léaves / the wórld / to dárk / ness ánd / to mé.

This is a crude notation of how the lines might be read aloud. Of course, if the reader speaks a poem with a view toward sense, he will not deliver it in a mechanical singsong; some stresses might receive more weight than others. The basic unit here — the combination most frequent — is one stress with one slack syllable before it. Such a unit is a **foot**: a kind of rhythmic molecule out of which meters are made. Feet, as in this example, are not necessarily made up of complete words. Notice, for instance, that the first foot consists of one word and one half of the next word. A foot consists usually of one stressed *syllable* with one or two unstressed syllables, or two stressed syllables with one unstressed syllable; this particular foot is an **iamb**, and, because the line is made up of five iambs, it is **iambic pentameter**. Note that in these lines the pattern is not fulfilled quite perfectly. In line 2, the middle foot has two stresses; in line 4, the next to last foot has two slack syllables. How can these lines be iambic pentameter? They are, just as a waltz that includes an extra step or two, or leaves a few steps out, remains a waltz. In these lines, the basic iambic rhythm has been set by the preceding lines and feet. Though the pattern is varied, it does not altogether disappear. Meter is determined not by unanimous consent but by majority rule. Like a basic dance-step, a meter exists to be followed for much of the time; and when the poet wishes to kick up his heels and display a bit of joy and ingenuity, the meter is there, to be departed from. It continues to exist and, indeed, to run on in the reader's mind for a while, simultaneous with the variation. If the poet does not stay away from it too long, it will be there when he chooses to come back again.

In fact, by comparison with some lines of iambic pentameter, Thomas Gray's four lines seem almost monotonously regular. Note the variation in line 3 of this passage by Christopher Marlowe:

Wās thís thē fáce thāt laúnched ā thóu · sānd shíps

Ānd búrnt thē tóp · lēss tów'rs ōf Íl · ī · um?

Swéet Hél · ēn, máke mē ím · mór · tāl wīth ā kíss.

And yet the rhythm of the passage is iambic pentameter. A common misunderstanding is that there is something at fault in a poem whose metrical pattern is not followed with undeviating regularity. The contrary is more frequently true: if a line of iambic pentameter goes exactly "da-DUM, da-DUM, da-DUM, da-DUM, da-DUM," and is followed by several more lines of the same, it is possible that the entire poem is marching right over the brink of doom and that the poet does not much care about it. Nothing more clearly indicates the poet's control of his poem than its rhythm. Robert Frost once disclosed that in writing a poem he could tell it was going wrong and that he himself did not believe what he was saying whenever he found the rhythm becoming monotonously regular. It would seem that together with a shifting, various, now-and-then emphatic rhythm go a certain energy of mind and an agility of feeling.

An exception is the passage of metrical monotony that has a deliberate effect. In Gray's lines, the rhythm is quite right. An almost unvarying iambic pentameter seems appropriate to convey the ideas of a tolling bell and a plowman wearily setting down one foot after the other.

Here, with examples, are the four kinds of feet from which meters in English most commonly are made:

1. The **iamb** (- /):

   Thē fál / līng oút / ōf faíth / fūl friénds, / rēnéw / ing is / ōf
   lóve.   7 iambs (*iambic heptameter*)

2. The **anapest** (-- /):

   Ī am món / ārch ōf áll / Ī súrvey   3 anapests (*anapestic
                                                        trimeter*)

151

3. The **trochee** (**/** -):

    Double, / double, / toil and / trouble   4 trochees (*trochaic tetrameter*)

4. The **dactyl** (**/** --):

    Take her up / tenderly   2 dactyls (*dactylic dimeter*)

Iambic and anapestic meters are sometimes called **rising** because their movement supposedly rises from slack syllable (or syllables) to stress; trochaic and dactylic meters are called **falling**. Often called feet, though they contain no unaccented syllables, are the **monosyllabic foot** (**/**) and the **spondee** (**//**). Meters are not ordinarily made up of them; if one were, it would be like the steady impact of nails being hammered into a board — no pleasure to hear, nor dance to. But inserted now and then, they can lend emphasis and variety to a meter, as Yeats well knew when he broke up a poem, predominantly iambic tetrameter, with the line "And the white breast of the dim sea," which has two spondees. (See "Who Goes with Fergus?" p. 125.) A pair of unaccented syllables, like *and the* and *of the* in this line, is called a **pyrrhic foot**.

To tell a dactyl from an anapest, recall that *dactyl* comes from the Greek word for *finger* and, like its namesake with one long joint and two short ones, has one stressed syllable and two unstressed syllables. It may be helpful to keep in mind at least the opening lines of Coleridge's jingle, which also defines two less familiar feet. (The scansion marks are by Coleridge, who apparently meant to illustrate only the metrical feet he lists, not to scan the entire poem.)

SAMUEL TAYLOR COLERIDGE (1772–1834)

Metrical Feet

    Trochee trips from long to short;

    From long to long in solemn sort

    Slow Spondee stalks: strong foot! yet ill able

    Ever to come up with Dactyl trisyllable;

    Iambics march from short to long;

    With a leap and a bound the swift Anapests throng;   5

    One syllable long, with one short at each side,

Āmphibrachȳs hástes with a státely stride;

First and last being long, middle short, Amphimacer

Strikes his thundering hoofs like a proud high-bred racer.   10

EXERCISE THREE

Go back to the Mother Goose rime 'Here goes my Lord' (pp. 140–141) and identify the various metrical feet you find in it.

Meters are named as follows:

1. **Monometer:** a line of one foot, as in these anonymous trochees on microbes:

> Adam
> Had 'em.

2. **Dimeter:** a line of two feet.
3. **Trimeter:** a line of three feet.
4. **Tetrameter:** a line of four feet.
5. **Pentameter:** a line of five feet.
6. **Hexameter:** a line of six feet.
7. **Heptameter:** a line of seven feet.
8. **Octameter:** a line of eight feet.

Lines longer than eight feet are possible, but to a listener they tend to break up into shorter lengths.

A **caesura** is a definite pause within a line, usually indicated in scansion by a double line (||). It may occur either at a mark of punctuation, or if no punctuation is present, where a meaningful unit of syntax is completed, as at the beginning or end of a phrase or clause:

> Must helpless man, || in ignorance sedate,
> Roll darkling || down the torrent of his fate?

Lines of tetrameter, pentameter, and hexameter tend to have just one caesura; though sometimes, as in the following line, there are more:

> Cover her face: || mine eyes dazzle: || she died young.

Occasionally there are difficulties in scanning a poem. Sometimes a line may be scanned as either iambic or trochaic, depending on where the divisions are made. But reading aloud the line in doubt, two or three times, slowly and carefully, may reveal one dominant rhythm. If there is none, better to call the line doubtful or irregular than to buckle it into a pattern like a Procrustean bed.

Another temptation in scanning is to make the lines of a poem conform to the basic metrical pattern emerging, rather than read them the way one would *ordinarily* say the words aloud. This is an inaccurate scansion:

$$\text{Th}\bar{a}\text{t's m}\acute{y}\text{ l}\bar{a}\text{st D}\acute{u}\text{ch}\bar{e}\text{ss p}\acute{a}\text{int}\bar{e}\text{d }\acute{o}\text{n th}\bar{e}\text{ w}\acute{a}\text{ll,}$$

because no speaker of English would say it that way. (He would be likely to stress *That's* and *last*.) Most of the time, in scanning poetry, place the stresses exactly where they would be placed in a line of prose read aloud.

Sometimes, however, it seems as if a tug-of-war were going on between the meter and our habits of pronounciation. Consider, for instance, this passage by John Wilmot, Earl of Rochester:

> Were I, who to my cost already am
> One of those strange, prodigious creatures, man,
> A spirit free to choose for my own share
> What sort of flesh and blood I pleased to wear,
> I'd be a dog, a monkey, or a bear,
> Or anything but that vain animal
> Who is so proud of being rational.

The one-syllable words *am, man, share, wear,* and *bear* so clearly demand to be stressed that we fall into the habit of stressing every line-ending, and so give a stress to the final syllables of *animal* and *rational* as well.

The reader might well refuse to distort his language to the extent of saying "aniMAL," but it seems here that he will have to give in to the meter to the extent, at least, of allowing the final syllable a half-stress in order for the lines to rime at all. But this is not a constant problem, and it is certainly better to follow our ordinary pronunciation than to let the meter have its own way whenever it likes. Still, such a tension between habit and meter can have the valuable effect — as in Rochester's lines — of giving words an unusual emphasis.

EXERCISE FOUR

> Scan these lines, the beginning of Walt Whitman's "Song of the Broad-Axe." What do you find yourself doing in the last line? Why?
>
> Weapon shapely, naked, wan,
> Head from the mother's bowels drawn,
> Wooded flesh and metal bone, limb only one and lip only one,
> Gray-blue leaf by red-heat grown, helve produced from a little
> seed sown,
> Resting the grass amid and upon,
> To be lean'd and to lean on.

154

Let us consider a poem in which rhythm and meaning are closely bound.

THOMAS HARDY (1840–1928)

The Five Students

> The sparrow dips in his wheel-rut bath,
>> The sun grows passionate-eyed,
> And boils the dew to smoke by the paddock-path;
>> As strenuously we stride, —
> Five of us; dark He, fair He, dark She, fair She, I,
>> All beating by.   6

> The air is shaken, the high-road hot,
>> Shadowless swoons the day,
> The greens are sobered and cattle at rest; but not
>> We on our urgent way, —
> Four of us; fair She, dark She, fair He, I, are there,
>> But one — elsewhere.   12

> Autumn moulds the hard fruit mellow,
>> And forward still we press
> Through moors, briar-meshed plantations, clay-pits yellow
>> As in the spring hours — yes,
> Three of us; fair He, fair She, I, as heretofore,
>> But — fallen one more.   18

> The leaf drops: earthworms draw it in
>> At night-time noiselessly,
> The fingers of birch and beech are skeleton-thin
>> And yet on the beat are we, —
> Two of us; fair She, I. But no more left to go
>> The track we know.   24

> Icicles tag the church-aisle leads,
>> The flag-rope gibbers hoarse,
> The home-bound foot-folk wrap their snow-flaked heads,
>> Yet I still stalk the course —
> One of us. . . . Dark and fair He, dark and fair She, gone:
>> The rest — anon.   30

Probably, the countdown becomes apparent after reading the first two stanzas. Indeed, so mathematical is the outline of Hardy's poem that it may recall the nursery rime, "Ten little Indians went out to dine, / One fell in the gravy pot / And then there were nine . . ." But much more is happening. Besides the progress (toward the grave) of the narrator and his fellow students, a change is taking place among the

155

images: a hot, steamy landscape of spring or summer is yielding to
ripening fruit, then falling leaf, and finally frozen winter. And as the
poem moves along, a comparable progress and alteration of rhythm
is going on in it. The opening four lines, in which there are more
slack than stressed syllables, might be scanned like this:

> The sparrow dips in his wheel-rut bath,
> The sun grows passionate-eyed,
> And boils the dew to smoke by the paddock-path;
> As strenuously we stride.

Here, in each line, two or more unstressed syllables occur together.
Whenever they do, the effect is a kind of bounding or tripping. It
is somewhat like the effect encountered in such light verse as W. S.
Gilbert's "Nightmare Song," with its predominantly anapestic beat:

> When you're lying awake with a dismal headache, and repose is
>   tabooed by anxiety,
> I conceive you may use any language you choose to indulge in,
>   without impropriety;
> For your brain is on fire — the bedclothes conspire of usual slum-
>   ber to plunder you:
> First your counterpane goes, and uncovers your toes, and your
>   sheet slips demurely from under you . . .

But in Hardy's poem the rhythms are more various. In line five,
every syllable except *of* takes a stress. It is as if the poet were speaking
with more emphasis. Stressed syllables predominate in the fifth line of
each stanza, the line in which the speaker tells us of another death.

In the beginning of the second stanza, bounding anapests are still
possible. (It is no coincidence that here Hardy is talking about
walkers striding along urgently.) In stanzas three and four the light
feet become fewer. Then in the final stanza:

> Icicles tag the church-aisle leads,
> The flag-rope gibbers hoarse,
> The home-bound foot-folk wrap their snow-flaked heads,
> Yet I still stalk the course.

156

As the speaker's memory of the original five students draws to a close, as he faces his own extinction, and as the natural world itself lies buried in a freezing snow that assails the living, home-bound walkers, tripping rhythms no longer are possible.

There is, of course, a tripping dactyl in the first word, *icicles*. And an overzealous reader might say: "Ah! with the word *icicles* the rhythm lightens, for the poet is introducing a merry note." But a single foot doesn't make a meter; it stands out as a variation. Had he wanted to, Hardy could have made the rhythm in the last two lines even heavier. He might have stressed nearly every syllable for, say, ten lines running. Had he done so, all emphasis would have vanished, for everything would be emphasized; and the poem would sound like a piece of music with every note played *fortissimo* — one prolonged thunder, loud but monotonous.

As the names of the feet indicate, the idea of meter was taken over from the Greek by scholar-critics of the English Renaissance, who wanted to find laws for English prosody like those available to poets in the classical languages. Difficulty arose in this attempt: Latin and Greek prosodists were dealing with a language *not* measured by stressed and unstressed syllables but by long and short vowels. (An iamb in Greek verse is one short vowel followed by a longer one.) It has been charged that the imposition of classical meters upon English prosody was a wholesale conspiracy: an attempt to make a Parthenon out of English wattles. And, indeed, plenty of outstanding poetry can be found that owes no evident obligation to conventional ideas of meter; for instance, the authors of folk ballads and of nursery rimes probably were unaware of the names of the meters they used. And yet this importation has the advantage of a long tradition behind it: all major poets since Shakespeare have been influenced by it, and if we are to read their works closely and sensitively we need to know of it. Whatever the deficiencies of the classical terminology, it — like meter — endures. As a recent critic, Paul Fussell, Jr., has observed, "No element of a poem is more basic — and I mean physical — in its effect upon the reader than the metrical element, and perhaps no technical triumphs reveal more readily than the metrical the poet's sympathy with that universal human nature . . . which exists outside his own."[2] Another view of the value of meter is summarized in an old jazz lyric: "It don't mean a thing if you ain't got that swing." The "swing" of poetry is not the swing of a metronome. Ordinarily, it should not be. But for a poet, like a musician, there are

[2] *Poetic Meter and Poetic Form* (New York, 1965), p. 110.

few more powerful instruments than a driving, forceful, and fundamental rhythm, which engages both our conscious and our unconscious attention.

WALTER SAVAGE LANDOR (1775–1864)

On Seeing a Hair of Lucretia Borgia

Borgia, thou once wert almost too august
And high for adoration; now thou'rt dust.
All that remains of thee these plaits unfold,
Calm hair, meandering in pellucid gold.

QUESTIONS

1. Who was Lucretia Borgia and when did she live? What connotations that add meaning to Landor's poem has her name?
2. What does *meander* mean? How can a hair meander?
3. Scan the poem, indicating stressed syllables. What is the basic meter of most of the poem? What happens to this meter in the last line? Note especially *meandering in pel-*. How many light, unstressed syllables are there in a row? Does rhythm in any way reinforce what Landor is saying in this poem?

EXERCISE FIVE

In each of the following quotations, what is the basic meter? At what point or points does the poet deviate from it, and to what meaningful effect?

A. Where'er you find "the cooling western breeze,"
In the next line it "whispers through the trees";
If crystal streams "with pleasing murmurs creep,"
The reader's threatened (not in vain) with "sleep";
Then, at the last and only couplet fraught   5
With some unmeaning thing they call a thought,
A needless Alexandrine ends the song
That, like a wounded snake, drags its slow length along.
Leave such to tune their own dull rimes, and know
What's roundly smooth or languishingly slow;   10
And praise the easy vigor of a line
Where Denham's strength and Waller's sweetness join.
True ease in writing comes from art, not chance,
As those move easiest who have learned to dance.
'Tis not enough no harshness gives offence.   15
The sound must seem an echo to the sense:
Soft is the strain when Zephyr gently blows,
And the smooth stream in smoother numbers° flows;   *metrical*
But when loud surges lash the sounding shore,   *rhythm*
The harsh, rough verse should like the torrent roar: 20
When Ajax strives some rock's vast weight to throw,
The line too labors, and the words move slow;
Not so, when swift Camilla scours the plain,
Flies o'er the unbending corn, and skims along the main.

— Alexander Pope, "An Essay on Criticism"

158

B.   Shadwell alone of all my sons is he
     Who stands confirmed in full stupidity.
     The rest to some faint meaning make pretense,
     But Shadwell never deviates into sense.

— John Dryden, "Mac Flecknoe" (speech
of Flecknoe, prince of Nonsense, referring
to Thomas Shadwell, poet and playwright)

C.   'Tis true, with shame and grief I yield,
     Thou like the van° first tookst the field,   *vanguard*
     And gotten hath the victory
     In thus adventuring to die
     Before me, whose more years might crave   5
     A just precedence in the grave.
     But hark! my pulse like a soft drum
     Beats my approach, tells thee I come;
     And slow howe'er my marches be,
     I shall at last sit down by thee.   10

— Henry King, "The Exequy"
(an apostrophe to his wife)

D.   . . . Half-way up the hill, I see the Past
     Lying beneath me with its sounds and sights, —
     A city in the twilight dim and vast,
    With smoking roofs, soft bells, and gleaming lights, —
     And hear above me on the autumnal blast
     The cataract of Death far thundering from the heights.

— Henry Wadsworth Longfellow, "Mezzo Cammin"

EXERCISE SIX

Some latter-day critics have charged Sir Thomas Wyatt with being a careless poet because some of his lines seem faltering and metrically inconsistent. It is uncertain whether the final *e*'s in English spelling were still pronounced in Sir Thomas Wyatt's day, as they were in Chaucer's, but if so, perhaps Wyatt's work has been misread. In the text below, spellings have been modernized except in words where the final *e* would make a difference in rhythm. To sense how it matters, try reading the poem aloud each way: leaving out the final *e*'s, and then putting them in wherever indicated. Sound them like the *a* in *sofa*. Which way of reading the poem do you prefer? Why?

SIR THOMAS WYATT (1503?–1542)

'They flee from me that sometime did me seke'

They flee from me that sometime did me sekë
    With naked fotë° stalking in my chamber.   *foot*
I have seen them gentle, tame and mekë
    That now are wild, and do not remember
    That sometime they put themself in danger   5
To take bread at my hand; and now they range
Busily seeking with a continual change.

Thanked be fortune, it hath been otherwise
    Twenty times better; but once in speciàll,
In thin array, after a pleasant guise,   10
    When her loose gown from her shoulders did fall,
    And she me caught in her armës long and small,
Therewith all sweetly did me kiss,
And softly said, *Dear heart, how like you this?*

It was no dremë: I lay broadë waking.   15
    But all is turned thorough° my gentleness   *through*
Into a strangë fashion of forsaking;
    And I have leave to go of her goodness,
    And she also to use newfangleness°.   *to seek novelty*
But since that I so kindëly° am served   *naturally (according* 20
I would fain knowë what she hath deserved.   *to woman's nature)*

EXERCISE SEVEN

    Which of the following poems contain regular meters? In which are
the rhythms varying or alternating? How would you describe the effect
of rhythm in each poem, whether regular or irregular? What elements
besides rhythm give each poem its total effect?

GERARD MANLEY HOPKINS (1844–1889)

Inversnaid

This darksome burn°, horseback brown,   *brook*
His rollrock highroad roaring down,
In coop° and in comb° the fleece of his foam   *hollow; ravine*
Flutes and low to the lake falls home.   4

A windpuff-bonnet of fáwn-fróth
Turns and twindles over the broth
Of a pool so pitchblack, féll-frówning,
It rounds and rounds Despair to drowning.   8

Degged° with dew, dappled with dew   *sprinkled*
Are the groins of the braes that the brook treads through,
Wiry heathpacks, flitches° of fern,   *ragged clumps*
And the beadbonny ash that sits over the burn.   12

What would the world be, once bereft
Of wet and of wildness? Let them be left,
O let them be left, wildness and wet;
Long live the weeds and the wilderness yet.   16

Inversnaid is a hilly place in Scotland, lying along Loch Lomond. 6.
twindles: W. H. Gardner, who has edited Hopkins' poems, thinks this
word may be a coinage made up of *dwindles* and *twists*.

ALFRED, LORD TENNYSON (1809–1892)

'Dark house'

Dark house, by which once more I stand
   Here in the long unlovely street,
   Doors, where my heart was used to beat
So quickly, waiting for a hand,   4

A hand that can be clasped no more —
   Behold me, for I cannot sleep,
   And like a guilty thing I creep
At earliest morning to the door.   8

He is not here; but far away
   The noise of life begins again,
   And ghastly through the drizzling rain
On the bald street breaks the blank day.   12

'Dark house.' This poem is one part of the series *In Memoriam*.

WILLIAM CARLOS WILLIAMS (1883–1963)

'To freight cars in the air'

To freight cars in the air

all the slow
   clank, clank
   clank, clank
moving above the treetops   5

the
   wha, wha
of the hoarse whistle

   pah,   pah,   pah
   pah, pah, pah, pah, pah   10
   piece and piece
   piece and piece
moving still trippingly
through the morningmist

long after the engine   15
has fought by
        and disappeared
in silence
          to the left

GEORGE PEELE (1558?–1597?)

'Hot sun, cool fire'

Hot sun, cool fire, tempered with sweet air,
Black shade, fair nurse, shadow my white hair.
Shine, sun; burn, fire; breathe, air, and ease me;
Black shade, fair nurse, shroud me and please me;
Shadow, my sweet nurse, keep me from burning,   5
Make not my glad cause cause of mourning.
       Let not my beauty's fire
       Inflame unstaid desire,
       Nor pierce any bright eye
       That wand'reth lightly.   10

'Hot sun, cool fire.' In Peele's play *Love of King David and Fair Bethsabe*,
the heroine sings this song while bathing.

WALT WHITMAN (1819–1892)

Beat! Beat! Drums!

Beat! beat! drums! — blow! bugles! blow!
Through the windows — through doors — burst like a ruth-
    less force,
Into the solemn church, and scatter the congregation,
Into the school where the scholar is studying;
Leave not the bridegroom quiet — no happiness must he   5
    have now with his bride,
Nor the peaceful farmer any peace, ploughing his field or
    gathering his grain,
So fierce you whirr and pound you drums — so shrill you
    bugles blow.

Beat! beat! drums! — blow! bugles! blow!
Over the traffic of cities — over the rumble of wheels in the
    streets;
Are beds prepared for sleepers at night in the houses? no   10
    sleepers must sleep in those beds,
No bargainers' bargains by day — no brokers or speculators —
    would they continue?
Would the talkers be talking? would the singer attempt to
    sing?
Would the lawyer rise in the court to state his case before the
    judge?
Then rattle quicker, heavier drums — you bugles wilder blow.

Beat! beat! drums! — blow! bugles! blow!   15
Make no parley — stop for no expostulation,
Mind not the timid — mind not the weeper or prayer,
Mind not the old man beseeching the young man,
Let not the child's voice be heard, nor the mother's en-
    treaties,
Make even the trestles to shake the dead where they lie   20
    awaiting the hearses,
So strong you thump O terrible drums — so loud you bugles
    blow.

JOHN KEATS (1795–1821)

'The Gothic looks solemn'

The Gothic looks solemn —
The plain Doric column
Supports an old bishop and crosier;
    The moldering arch,
    Shaded o'er by a larch,
Lives next door to Wilson the Hosier.   6

Vicè — that is, by turns —
O'er pale faces mourns
The black tassel trencher or common hat:
    The chauntry° boy sings,   *chauntry, chapel*
    The steeple-bell rings,
And as for the Chancellor — *dominat*°.   *he rules*   12

    There are plenty of trees,
    And plenty of ease,
And plenty of fat deer for parsons;
    And when it is venison
    Short is the benison, —
Then each on a leg or thigh fastens.   18

'The Gothic looks solemn.' 9. *trencher:* nickname for the academic hat
also known as the mortarboard. (A trencher is a board, platter, or slab of
bread for serving food on.) 12. *Chancellor:* the head of the University.
Keats enclosed these lines in an 1817 letter to his friend John Hamilton
Reynolds, remarking, "Wordsworth sometimes, though in a fine way,
gives us sentences in the style of school exercises — for instance

> The lake doth glitter
> Small birds twitter &c.

Now I think this is an excellent method of giving a very clear description
of an interesting place such as Oxford is."

TEN

FORM

Form, as a general idea, denotes the shape or design of a thing as a whole, the configuration of its parts. Among its connotations is that of order made from chaos: "In the beginning God created the heaven and the earth. And the earth was without form, and void . . ."

Like *irony*, the word *form* has been favored in literary criticism with several meanings. This chapter will deal with five of these: (1) form as a pattern of sound and rhythm, (2) form as a shape that meets the eye, (3) flexible form or free verse, (4) form in the sense of a genre, or particular kind of poem, and (5) form as the structure of a poem — the ways in which its materials are organized.

1. PATTERNS OF SOUND AND RHYTHM

"Rime the rudder is of verses, / With which, like ships, they steer their courses," wrote the seventeenth-century poet Samuel Butler. Not merely a matter of sound, rime (discussed in detail in chap. 8) helps the poet bind together his poem and bring an order to it. The poet may use a **rime scheme**, a pattern according to which the rimes recur, or he may choose to construct more or less elaborate interconnections of assonance and alliteration. He has rhythm, too, with which to give his poem a pattern — and, indeed, no poem can avoid having some kind of pattern, whether its lines be in lengths as various as broomstraws or all in hexameter. These devices of sound and rhythm result in form. To put it another way: If we listened to a poem being read aloud in a foreign language, whatever we could perceive would be the form of the poem.

The great value of a fixed pattern to poetry has long been recognized. Among its advantages, the pattern helps make a poem memorable. The **epic** poems of nations — long narratives tracing the episodic adventures of popular heroes: the Greek *Iliad* and *Odyssey*, the French *Song of Roland*, the Spanish *Cid* — tend to occur in patterns of fairly consistent line-length or number of stresses because these works (or portions or earlier versions of them) were sometimes transmitted orally. Sung to the music of a lyre or possibly chanted to a drumbeat, they may have been easier to memorize because of their patterns. Besides, if a singer forgot something, his pattern would fall short; so that rime or fixed meter probably helped prevent an epic from diminishing when passed along from one singer to another. It is no coincidence that so many English playwrights of Shakespeare's day favored iambic pentameter, since companies of actors, often called upon to perform a different play daily, could count on the aid of a fixed line-length to prod their burdened memories.

Taking *form* to mean a pattern of sound and rhythm, we find it useful to the study of poetry to speak of **verse form** and **stanza form**. The former is a rhythmic pattern of a **verse** (another name for a line; sometimes popularly but inaccurately used to denote stanza: "All join in and sing the second verse!"). An example would be any meter: the verse form of blank verse is iambic pentameter. A **stanza** (in Italian, "a stopping place") is a group of a certain number of lines, having a rime scheme or a particular rhythm or both. This pattern is normally repeated at least once in a poem, but a fairly short poem without such repetition may be said to consist entirely of a single stanza. In printed poetry, stanzas are usually set off separately by the use of white space; in sung or spoken poetry, by a pause or by the introduction of a chorus or refrain. If printed, the indentations of lines usually (but not always) indicate which rimes go together:

> Round, round, the roof does run;
> And being ravished thus,
> Come, I will drink a tun
> To my Propertius.

Stanzas may be either rimed or unrimed. If rimed, the riming words usually recur with relative frequency. To most readers, end-rimes probably pass unnoticed if too few and too far apart (separated by more than, say, five or six lines). Stanzas in such hard-to-hear rime schemes have been contrived, however, notably by Marianne Moore. Perhaps the poet needs some kind of form to struggle with, whether or not the reader cares to look for it.

By its repetition, a stanzaic pattern can be a powerful implement to rhythm. Any fixed line length, repeated through all or part of a poem, has a rhythmic effect (as we have seen in chap. 9); and, in a stanza, greater emphasis tends to fall upon the last line and upon its last word. The poet can, if he likes, make this emphasis still stronger by choosing a stanza whose last line is shorter than the rest (see Keats's "La Belle Dame sans Merci," pp. 212–213); or he may choose the rhythmic variety of a stanza in which line-lengths differ radically. The rhythmic effects of this ingenious stanza by John Donne, for instance, may best be heard aloud.

JOHN DONNE (1572–1631)
Song

> Go and catch a falling star,
>   Get with child a mandrake root,
> Tell me where all past years are,
>   Or who cleft the Devil's foot,
> Teach me to hear mermaids singing,   5
>   Or to keep off envy's stinging,
>   And find
>   What wind
> Serves to advance an honest mind.
>
> If thou be'st borne to strange sights,   10
>   Things invisible to see,
> Ride ten thousand days and nights,
>   Till age snow white hairs on thee,
> Thou, when thou return'st, wilt tell me
>   All strange wonders that befell thee,   15
>   And swear
>   Nowhere
> Lives a woman true, and fair.
>
> If thou findst one, let me know,
>   Such a pilgrimage were sweet —   20
> Yet do not, I would not go,
>   Though at next door we might meet;
> Though she were true, when you met her,
>   And last, till you write your letter,
>   Yet she   25
>   Will be
> False, ere I come, to two, or three.

The most familiar English stanzas are the couplet, the tercet, and the quatrain, called by the critic Paul Fussell, Jr., the basic building blocks of English poetry, since longer forms can be made up of them.

166

Here are some common patterns of English poetry, listed by order of their number of lines.

1. The best-known, repeated one-line pattern for an English poem is **blank verse**, or unrimed iambic pentameter. (This pattern, of course, is not a stanza, since stanzas have more than one line.) Much distinguished poetry has taken it: most portions of Shakespeare's plays, Milton's *Paradise Lost*, Tennyson's "Ulysses" (pp. 353–354), some of the dramatic monologues of Robert Browning and Robert Frost.

2. The **couplet** is a two-line stanza, usually rimed. Its lines often tend to be equal in length, whether short or long. Here are two examples:

Why
I?

As I in hoary winter's night stood shivering in the snow,
Surprised I was with sudden heat which made my heart to glow.

(Actually, any pair of rimed lines is called a couplet, even if not a stanza: the *couplet* that ends a sonnet of Shakespeare.) Unlike other stanzas, couplets are often printed solid, not separated by white space. This practice is usual in printing the **heroic couplet** — or **closed couplet** — two rimed lines of iambic pentameter, the first ending in a light pause, the second more heavily end-stopped. George Crabbe, in *The Parish Register*, described a shotgun wedding:

Next at our altar stood a luckless pair,
Brought by strong passions and a warrant there:
By long rent cloak, hung loosely, strove the bride,
From every eye, what all perceived, to hide;
While the boy bridegroom, shuffling in his place,
Now hid awhile and then exposed his face.
As shame altèrnately with anger strove
The brain confused with muddy ale to move,
In haste and stammering he performed his part,
And looked the rage that rankled in his heart.

Though employed by Chaucer, the heroic couplet was named from its later use by Dryden and others in poems, translations of classical epics, and verse plays of epical heroes. It continued in favor through most of the eighteenth century. Much of our pleasure in reading good heroic couplets comes from the seemingly easy precision with which a skilled poet unites statements and strict pattern. In doing so, he may place a pair of words, phrases, clauses, or sentences side by side in agreement or similarity, forming a **parallel;** or in contrast and opposition, forming an **anthithesis**. The effect is neat. For such skill in manipulating parallels and antitheses, John Denham's lines on the river Thames were much admired:

O could I flow like thee, and make thy stream
My great example, as it is my theme!

> Though deep, yet clear; though gentle, yet not dull;
> Strong without rage, without o'erflowing full.

These lines were echoed by Pope, ridiculing a poetaster, in two heroic couplets in *The Dunciad*:

> Flow, Welsted, flow! like thine inspirer, Beer:
> Though stale, not ripe; though thin, yet never clear;
> So sweetly mawkish, and so smoothly dull;
> Heady, not strong; o'erflowing, though not full.

The rhythms of so precise a form can become monotonous unless the poet does something to vary them; one means is to shift the position of the caesura (see p. 153) from line to line.

3. The **tercet** is a three-line stanza which, if rimed, usually keeps to one rime sound:

> The witch that comes (the withered hag)
> To wash the steps with pail and rag,
> Was once the beauty Abishag . . .

Tercets linked together by a rime scheme are called **terza rima**, the form chosen by Dante for *The Divine Comedy*. In it, the middle line of a tercet rimes with the first and third lines of the next: *aba, bcb, cdc*, and so on. (By this convenient algebra, the letters *a* denote lines that rime with each other; similarly, the *b* lines rime.) More difficult to fulfill in English than in Italian, which offers a poet a wider choice of riming words, the form nevertheless has been well managed by Shelley in "Ode to the West Wind" (pp. 343–345) and recently by John Heath-Stubbs in *The Triumph of the Muse*.

4. Probably the favorite of all English stanzas is the **quatrain**, whose four lines come sometimes short, sometimes long. A certain quatrain, the **ballad stanza**, rimed *abcb*, has four iambic feet in lines 1 and 3, three in lines 2 and 4:

> Clerk Saunders and Maid Margaret
> Walked owre yon garden green,
> And deep and heavy was the love
> That fell thir twa between.

Though not the only possible stanza for a **ballad** (a story told in stanzas of any kind), this easily singable quatrain has continued to attract poets since the Middle Ages. For an example from a modern folk song, see "Frankie and Johnny" (p. 278). Sung or read aloud, such a poem in couplets of long lines will tend to fall into quatrains, since its recurrent caesuras sound like pauses at the ends of lines. **Common meter** is another name sometimes given to the ballad stanza, especially when it occurs in hymns. Other poets besides ballad singers and hymnists have been fond of it, among them A. E. Housman and Emily Dickinson.

Speaking of ballads, it may be well to notice a special pattern of rhythm and sound often accompanying the ballad stanza, sometimes even forming part of it: the **refrain** (lines or a line repeated as a chorus). Frequent not only in ballads but also in other kinds of song, it may occur following a stanza of any kind; if it does, it is called **terminal refrain**. Sometimes an internal refrain appears *within* a stanza, usually in a position that stays fixed throughout the poem (as in the ballad "Johnny, I Hardly Knew Ye," pp. 18–19, and in Yeats's "Long Legged Fly," p. 376). Both internal and terminal refrain occur in the following nursery rime:

ANONYMOUS (English; before 1658)

'There was a lady loved a swine'

> There was a lady loved a swine.
>   Honey, quoth she,
> Pig-hog, wilt thou be mine?
>   *Hoogh*, quoth he.   4
>
> I'll build thee a silver sty,
>   Honey, quoth she,
> And in it thou shalt lie.
>   *Hoogh*, quoth he.   8
>
> Pinned with a silver pin,
>   Honey, quoth she,
> That thou may go out and in.
>   *Hoogh*, quoth he.   12
>
> Wilt thou have me now,
>   Honey? quoth she.
> Speak or my heart will break.
>   *Hoogh*, quoth he.   16

This terminal refrain makes a point: as we might expect, the lady's passion is hopeless. Another refrain that works an ironic contrast is that of the ballad "The Cruel Mother" (p. 280), which recounts the murder of a child while, in the refrain, Nature is seen going indifferently about her chores. A refrain whose words change slightly with each reappearance, as in "Frankie and Johnny" (pp. 278–280), is called an **incremental refrain**. Often refrains seem tedious in a poem read silently, then suddenly leap into life when spoken or sung. Similar in effect to a refrain is the repetition of a word or words at the beginning of successive lines, as in Walt Whitman's "When Lilacs Last . . ." (pp. 357–364) and some Biblical Psalms.

  5. Less familiar than any of the preceding stanzas, five-line stanzas appear now and again in English poetry, no particular one having achieved wide acceptance. We except the frivolous and very popular *limerick* (see p. 188) as not being a stanza but a whole poem — although, as it has been said, a short poem of a single unit may be called one stanza. An

example of a serious poem in five-line stanzas is Yvor Winters' "At the San Francisco Airport" (p. 367).

6. Six-line stanzas are more common, but like five-line stanzas, most are nameless. Examples: Wordsworth's "I Wandered Lonely as a Cloud" (p. 12) and Yeats's "Crazy Jane Talks with the Bishop" (p. 377). The **sestina**, an unrimed poem in six six-line stanzas and a tercet, repeats in each stanza the same six end-words in a different order. (If interested, look up Ezra Pound's "Sestina: Altaforte" in his *Personae* or Rudyard Kipling's "Sestina of the Tramp-Royal.")

7. **Rime royal** (called royal because it appears in the poems of James I of Scotland, even though Chaucer had used it earlier) is the best known seven-line stanza, having been used by Shakespeare for "The Rape of Lucrece." Its iambic pentameter lines rime *ababbcc*.

8. **Ottava rima**, a borrowing from Italy, is an eight-line stanza of iambic pentameter riming *abababcc*. Byron chose it for *Don Juan*.

9. The **Spenserian stanza** of nine lines, riming *ababbcbcc*, has eight lines of iambic pentameter and concludes with an **Alexandrine** (a line of iambic hexameter). Invented by Spenser for *The Faerie Queene*, it was later employed by Keats in "The Eve of St. Agnes," Byron in "Childe Harold," and Shelley in "Adonais."

Many stanzas of more than nine lines will be found in English poetry; but there does seem to be a limit to how long a stanza can go on and still, when read aloud, have a perceptible pattern.

New stanzas continue to be invented in twentieth-century poetry, though few if any seem to take root and spread. Recently in vogue has been **syllabic verse**, usually stanzaic, in which the poet establishes a pattern of a certain number of syllables to a line. Either rimed or rimeless, syllabic verse has been hailed as a way for the poet to escape "the tyranny of the iamb" and discover less conventional rhythms, since, if he takes as his line length an *odd* number of syllables, iambs and trochees, being feet of *two* syllables, cannot fit perfectly into it. Offbeat victories have been scored in syllabics by such poets as W. H. Auden, W. D. Snodgrass, Donald Hall, Thom Gunn, and Marianne Moore. Here is a well-known poem in syllabics:

DYLAN THOMAS (1914–1953)

Fern Hill

Now as I was young and easy under the apple boughs
About the lilting house and happy as the grass was green,
 The night above the dingle° starry,   *wooded valley*
 Time let me hail and climb
 Golden in the heydays of his eyes,   5

And honored among wagons I was prince of the apple towns
And once below a time I lordly had the trees and leaves
   Trail with daisies and barley
  Down the rivers of the windfall light.

And as I was green and carefree, famous among the barns   10
About the happy yard and singing as the farm was home,
   In the sun that is young once only,
   Time let me play and be
  Golden in the mercy of his means,
And green and golden I was huntsman and herdsman, the   15
  calves
Sang to my horn, the foxes on the hills barked clear and cold,
   And the sabbath rang slowly
  In the pebbles of the holy streams.

All the sun long it was running, it was lovely, the hay
Fields high as the house, the tunes from the chimneys, it   20
  was air
   And playing, lovely and watery
   And fire green as grass.
   And nightly under the simple stars
As I rode to sleep the owls were bearing the farm away,
All the moon long I heard, blessed among stables, the night-   25
  jars
   Flying with the ricks, and the horses
   Flashing into the dark.

And then to awake, and the farm, like a wanderer white
With the dew, come back, the cock on his shoulder: it was all
   Shining, it was Adam and maiden,   30
   The sky gathered again
  And the sun grew round that very day.
So it must have been after the birth of the simple light
In the first, spinning place, the spellbound horses walking
  warm
   Out of the whinnying green stable   35
   On to the fields of praise.

And honored among foxes and pheasants by the gay house
Under the new made clouds and happy as the heart was long,
   In the sun born over and over,
   I ran my heedless ways,   40
   My wishes raced through the house high hay
And nothing I cared, at my sky blue trades, that time allows
In all his tuneful turning so few and such morning songs
   Before the children green and golden
   Follow him out of grace,   45

Nothing I cared, in the lamb white days, that time would
 take me
Up to the swallow thronged loft by the shadow of my hand,
 In the moon that is always rising,
 Nor that riding to sleep
 I should hear him fly with the high fields   50
And wake to the farm forever fled from the childless land.
Oh as I was young and easy in the mercy of his means,
 Time held me green and dying
 Though I sang in my chains like the sea.

Some poets, novice poets in particular, complain that stanza patterns and fixed forms are nuisances. They want to declare, as did the
author of one very lazy book of verbal forget-me-nots, that "the poet
must dispense with the obligations of rime and stanza, as encum-
brances to fullest poetic expression." But other poets feel that, like
fires held fast in a narrow space, thoughts stated in a tightly binding
form may take on a heightened intensity. "Limitation makes for
power," according to one contemporary practitioner of strict forms,
Richard Wilbur; "the strength of the genie comes of his being confined in a bottle." Sometimes it is a benefit to a poet not to be allowed
to say whatever first comes into his mind. Compelled by a strict
form, whether traditional or invented, to arrange and rearrange his
words, delete and exchange them, the poet must focus on them his
keenest attention. Wrestling a poem into a difficult pattern, he stands
a better chance of discovering stronger and more meaningful words
than the ones he started out with. And at times, in obedience to a
rime scheme, the poet may surprise himself by saying something he
had not expected to say at all. He is like a blindfolded man walking
down a dark road, his hand in the hand of an inexorable guide. With
the logical, conscious portion of his mind, he may wish to express
what he thinks would be a good idea to express. But having written
a line ending in *year*, he must follow it with another ending in *atmosphere, beer, bier, bombardier, cashier, deer, friction-gear, frontier,* or
some other rime which otherwise might not have entered his head.
That is why he may find, in rime schemes and stanza patterns, mighty
allies and valuable disturbers of the unconscious. As Rolfe Hum-
phries has said about a strict form: "It makes you think of better
things than you would all by yourself."
Patterns of sound and rhythm can be mechanically striven after,
and sometimes not much else gets into the poem. Swinburne, who
loved alliterations and tripping meters, had enough detachment to
poke fun at his own formal excesses:

172

> From the depth of the dreamy decline of the dawn through a
>   notable nimbus of nebulous noonshine,
>   Pallid and pink as the palm of the flag-flower that flickers with
>   fear of the flies as they float,
> Are the looks of our lovers that lustrously lean from a marvel of
>   mystic miraculous moonshine,
>   These that we feel in the blood of our blushes that thicken and
>   threaten with throbs through the throat?

This is bad, but bad deliberately. If any good at all, a poem in a fixed pattern, such as a sonnet, is created not only by the craftsman's chipping away at it, but by the explosion of a sonnet-shaped idea in his mind. Viewed mechanically, as so many empty boxes somehow to be filled up, stanzas can impose the most hollow sort of discipline; and a poem written in these stanzas becomes no more than finger-exercise. This comment (although on fiction) may be applicable:

ROY CAMPBELL (1901–1957)

On Some South African Novelists

> You praise the firm restraint with which they write —
>   I'm with you there, of course.
> They use the snaffle and the curb all right;
>   But where's the bloody horse?

But some of the finest poems in our language are distinguished simultaneously by the firm restraint of form and by towering passion. For a Shakespeare or a Blake, a strict form may be a means to put in order and thereby contain the thoughts and emotions that throng within him. He is a powerful horseman upon a sturdy horse.

For the reader, verse forms and stanzas bring with them tremendous resources of appeal. They establish rhythms, engage the unconscious mind, and give us the pleasures of fulfilled expectations. Part of the joy of reading a fine poem in a strict form, like the heroic couplet, comes from observing the seemingly effortless way in which the poet persuades words to tumble into a graceful accommodation. It is a pleasure like that of seeing any difficult thing done smoothly: a perfect pitch in a ball game, a dancer's pirouette. More important still, the discipline of a pattern calls forth more of the poet's emotional and intellectual energy. Such a form may help him sing excellently for us even though, with Dylan Thomas, he may sing in his chains like the sea.

173

Proud Maisie

Proud Maisie is in the wood,
   Walking so early;
Sweet Robin sits on the bush,
   Singing so rarely.   4

"Tell me, thou bonny bird,
   When shall I marry me?" —
"When six braw° gentlemen   *brave*
   Kirkward° shall carry ye."   *to the church*

"Who makes the bridal bed,   9
   Birdie, say truly?" —
"The gray-headed sexton
   That delves the grave duly.   12

"The glow-worm o'er grave and stone
   Shall light thee steady;
The owl from the steeple sing,
   'Welcome, proud lady.' "   16

QUESTIONS

1. What comparisons are drawn between a wedding and a funeral?
2. How is the particular stanza form of this poem useful to the poet in setting things side by side?
3. How is the pattern of the poem ballad-like? What other elements (besides pattern) in "Proud Maisie" remind you of a folk ballad?

APHRA BEHN (1640–1689)

'When maidens are young'

When maidens are young, and in their spring,
Of pleasure, of pleasure let 'em take their full swing,
   Full swing, full swing,
And love, and dance, and play, and sing,
For Silvia, believe it, when youth is done,
There's nought but hum-drum, hum-drum, hum-drum,
There's nought but hum-drum, hum-drum, hum-drum.

QUESTIONS

1. What patterns of rhythm and sound are evident in this brief song (from Mrs. Behn's play *The Emperor of the Moon*)?
2. How do these patterns contribute to what is said?

ALEXANDER POPE (1688–1744)

[*Atticus*]

How did they fume, and stamp, and roar, and chafe!
And swear, not Addison himself was safe.
 Peace to all such! but were there one whose fires
True genius kindles, and fair fame inspires;
Blest with each talent, and each art to please,   5
And born to write, converse, and live with ease,
Should such a man, too fond to rule alone,
Bear, like the Turk, no brother near the throne,
View him with scornful, yet with jealous eyes,
And hate for arts that caused himself to rise;   10
Damn with faint praise, assent with civil leer,
And, without sneering, teach the rest to sneer;
Willing to wound, and yet afraid to strike,
Just hint a fault, and hesitate dislike;
Alike reserved to blame, or to commend,   15
A timorous foe, and a suspicious friend;
Dreading e'en fools, by flatterers besieged,
And so obliging, that he ne'er obliged;
Like Cato, give his little Senate laws,
And sit attentive to his own applause: 20
While wits and Templars every sentence raise,
And wonder with a foolish face of praise —
Who but must laugh, if such a man there be?
Who would not weep, if Atticus were he?

Atticus. In this selection from "An Epistle to Dr. Arbuthnot," Pope has
been referring to dull versifiers and their angry reception of his satiric
thrusts at them. With "Peace to all such!" he turns to his celebrated
portrait of a rival man of letters, Joseph Addison. 19. *Cato:* Roman
senator about whom Addison had written a tragedy. 21. *Templars:* London lawyers who dabbled in literature.

QUESTIONS

 1. What positive virtues, as Pope implies, does Addison lack?
 2. What effects does the form of the heroic couplet have upon Pope's
organization of his argument?
 3. What antitheses are contained in these couplets, either within a
line or between two lines? What parallels?
 4. Point out the caesuras, line by line. What, in this passage taken as a
whole, is their effect?

2. VISUAL PATTERNS

How can we tell the difference between poetry and prose? Legend has it that a schoolboy, asked this puzzler on a test, made an inspired reply. "Poetry," he wrote, "is when the lines don't come out even to the right-hand side of the page." He may not have known that the word *verse* is from *versus*, "a turning"; and he may not have realized that by the poet's turning back to the left margin a pattern of rhythm is formed. But he knew at least one true thing: a printed poem has a form addressed to the eye.

Ever since the invention of the alphabet, poems have existed not only as rhythmic sounds upon the air, but also as visual patterns: arrangements of lines upon two-dimensional surfaces. Beginning to write a poem, the poet finds his blank page lying in wait, much like a painter's canvas. At times he may try to be a graphic artist and to entertain the eye as well as the ear. To at least some extent, our pleasure in silently reading a poem comes from looking at the way a poet adorns his empty page with pieces of type. We notice how he indents lines, how he uses white space to set off certain words and place them in positions of emphasis. And after all, as designers of advertising well know,

aren't
you more greatly
tempted

to read
words

strewn about

like this
than if they were set

as a
solid
block
?

Let us look at a famous example of a poem with a very distinctive visible shape. In the seventeenth century, ingenious poets went as far as to trim their lines into the silhouettes of altars and crosses, pillars and pyramids. Here is one: is it anything more than a demonstration of ingenuity?

176

GEORGE HERBERT (1593–1633)

Easter Wings

Lord, who createdst man in wealth and store,
Though foolishly he lost the same,
Decaying more and more
Till he became
Most poor;   5
With thee
Oh, let me rise
As larks, harmoniously,
And sing this day thy victories;
Then shall the fall further the flight in me.   10

My tender age in sorrow did begin;
And still with sicknesses and shame
Thou didst so punish sin,
That I became
Most thin.   15
With thee
Let me combine,
And feel this day thy victory;
For if I imp my wing on thine,
Affliction shall advance the flight in me.   20

In the next-to-last line, *imp* is a term from falconry, meaning to repair the wing of an injured bird by grafting feathers into it. As if to make its wing-shapes all the more apparent, the poem originally was printed sideways, its lines running vertically.[1]

Considered merely as a picture, we will have to admit, Herbert's word-design does not go far. It renders, with difficulty, shapes that a sketcher's pencil could set down in a flash. The pencil sketch might have more detail, might be more accurate. Was Herbert's effort wasted? It might have been — were there not more to his poem than meets the eye. The mind, too, is engaged by the visual pattern; by the realization in line 15, for instance, that the words *most thin* are given emphasis by their narrow form. Here, visual pattern points out

1 For a few more recent, facetious specimens of shaped verse, see Lewis Carroll's mouse's tail in chap. 3 of *Alice in Wonderland*; and some of Guillaume Apollinaire's *Caligrammes* (Paris, 1918). John Hollander has filled with serious words the shapes of a bottle and an hourglass in *Movie-Going* (New York, 1962). E. E. Cummings has tried to convey by word-arrangements not fixed shapes but the paths of things in motion: birds, snow, a falling leaf. See his collections *No Thanks* and *50 Poems*, both reprinted in *Poems 1923–1954* (New York, 1954).

meaning. Heard aloud, too, "Easter Wings" takes on additional depths. Its rimes, its pattern of varied line-lengths are audible. It gives pleasure as any poem in a symmetrical stanza may do: by setting up a pattern that leads the hearer to anticipate when another rime or a pause will arrive, then fulfilling his expectation.

A whole poem, however, does not need to be such a verbal silhouette to have meaningful appearances. In part of a longer poem, William Carlos Williams has conveyed the way a bellhop runs downstairs:

> ta tuck a
> > ta tuck a
> > > ta tuck a
> > > > ta tuck a
> > > > > ta tuck a

This is not only good onomatopoeia and an accurate description of a rhythm; the step-like appearance of the lines goes together with their meaning. While too much importance can be given to the visual element of poetry, and while many poets seem hardly to care about it, it can be another dimension that sets apart poetry from prose. It is at least arguable that some of Walt Whitman's long-line, page-filling descriptions of the wide ocean, open landscapes, and broad streets of his America, which meet the eye as wide expanses of words, would lose something — besides what would be lost in rhythm — if couched in lines of three or four syllables, in stanzas three lines long.

The way a poem looks, though significant, is hardly enough in itself to make a poem succeed. The poem has to appeal to us in other ways as well: in sound, rhythm, literal meaning, and connotation. These together with a distinctive visual pattern may help the poem speak to us, striking both eye and mind.

HENRY VAUGHAN (1622–1695)

Ascension Hymn

> Dust and clay,
> Man's ancient wear!
> Here you must stay,
> But I elsewhere;
> Souls sojourn here, but may not rest;
> Who will ascend, must be undressed.   6

> And yet some
> That know to die

Before death come,
Walk to the sky
Even in this life; but all such can
Leave behind them the old Man.   12

If a star
Should leave the sphere,
She first must mar
Her flaming wear,
And after fall, for in her dress
Of glory, she cannot transgress.   18

Man of old
Within the line
Of Eden could
Like the sun shine
All naked, innocent and bright,
And intimate with Heav'n as light;   24

But since he
That brightness soiled,
His garments be
All dark and spoiled,
And here are left as nothing worth,
Till the Refiner's fire breaks forth.   30

Then comes He!
Whose mighty light
Made his clothes be
Like Heav'n, all bright:
The Fuller, whose pure blood did flow
To make stained man more white than snow.   36

He alone
And none else can
Bring bone to bone
And rebuild man,
And by His all-subduing might
Make clay ascend more quick than light.   42

QUESTION

What reasons can be found for the poet's casting his poem into this
visual form? Would the poem be equally meaningful if printed with each
stanza arranged, say, like this?

Dust and clay, man's ancient wear!
Here you must stay, but I elsewhere;
Souls sojourn here, but may not rest;
Who will ascend, must be undressed.

179

ROBERT HERRICK (1591–1674)

Upon Prew His Maid

> In this little urn is laid
> Prudence Baldwin (once my maid)
> From whose happy spark here let
> Spring the purple violet.

QUESTIONS

1. What possible meanings has the phrase *this little urn?*
2. What does the visual appearance of this poem have to do with the meaning of it?
3. What sense do you make of *happy spark?* What metaphor binds together lines 3 and 4? What characteristics do *spark* and *violet* have in common?
4. This well-wrought poem is bound together also by certain vowel-sounds and consonant-sounds running through it. Try to trace them.

3. FREE VERSE

Free verse, or poetry written in a **flexible form,** is bound by no conventional patterns of rime, stanza, or meter. In fact, the lines of some experimental free verse may look as if scattered about by accident. On inspection, sometimes, we will find this apparent disarray to be deliberate. The poet is conveying thoughts that conventions would not have aided. Here is an unchaotic example:

DENISE LEVERTOV (b. 1923)

Six Variations (iii)

> Shlup, shlup, the dog
> as it laps up
> water
> makes intelligent
> music, resting
> now and then to take breath in irregular
> measure.

Wittily, the poet has cast her description into a pattern neatly appropriate. All one sentence, the poem interrupts itself now and then by line-breaks, at which anyone reading aloud can catch his breath. Thoughts, sound, and rhythm are one; the result is an "intelligent music."

To some eyes, the variety of a free verse pattern may be more attractive than that of stanzas laid down like so many bricks in a row. As the poet Cid Corman once argued, "Doesn't it *look* more interesting?" Even granting this, we need to remember that in free verse, as in other poetry, visual pattern is not nearly so important an element of appeal as sound and rhythm; therefore, lacking the powerful appeal of rime, lacking any fixed line-length with its rhythmic effects, the free verse poet has to work harder to capture the reader's attention and hold on to it. He must discover, by his own unaided wits, the most meaningful words available. He has to fix them on the page in positions that look impregnable. He must pay far more conscious attention to rhythm and sound than he would if he were writing prose or stanzaic verse. As W. H. Auden put it: "The poet who writes 'free verse' is like Robinson Crusoe on his desert island: he must do all his cooking, laundry and darning for himself. In a few exceptional cases, this manly independence produces something original and impressive, but more often the result is squalor — dirty sheets on the unmade bed and empty bottles on the unswept floor." [2]

The pattern of free verse, however, does afford the poet certain advantages. He has white space with which to set words off and stress them. (One word all alone on a line may stand out more than it would in a line of hexameter. This means that if so much attention is to be paid to it, it had best be an extremely accurate word.) He may introduce pauses or break off his line unexpectedly. If his ear is keen, he may discover rhythms of great subtlety and variety.

Some poets, especially beginners, wish to write free verse because it looks as though it requires no skill and imposes no obligations. Fine examples of free verse for the novice to emulate are the *Psalms* and the *Song of Solomon* in the King James Bible; Walt Whitman's *Leaves of Grass*; and much of the work of such twentieth-century poets as William Carlos Williams, E. E. Cummings, Ezra Pound, Charles Olson, and Robert Lowell. In this poetry, lines are cast now and again into a regular pattern of similar lengths, of repeated words and phrases. (For a masterful instance of such repetition, see Whitman's "When Lilacs Last . . . ," pp. 357–364, especially sec. 6.) But the aspiring poet should study conventional forms as well. Then if he wishes to write in free verse, he can do so because he does not *choose* to write a sonnet, not because he cannot. "Writing free verse," said Robert Frost, who distrusted it, "is like playing tennis without a net." And yet, high scores can be made in such an unconventional game — provided it can be kept from straggling all over the court.

[2] *The Dyer's Hand* (New York, 1962), p. 22.

EMILY DICKINSON (1830–1886)

'Victory comes late'

> Victory comes late–
> And is held low to freezing lips–
> Too rapt with frost
> To take it–
> How sweet it would have tasted– 5
> Just a Drop–
> Was God so economical?
> His Table's spread too high for Us–
> Unless We dine on tiptoe–
> Crumbs–fit such little mouths– 10
> Cherries–suit Robins–
> The Eagle's Golden Breakfast strangles–Them–
> God keep His Oath to Sparrows–
> Who of little Love–know how to starve–

QUESTIONS

1. In this specimen of free verse, can you see any other places at which Emily Dickinson might have broken off any of her lines? To place a word last in a line gives it a greater emphasis; she might, for instance, have ended line 12 with *Breakfast* and for the word *strangles*, begun a new line. Discuss: Do you think she knows what she is doing here or does the pattern of this poem seem decided by whim?

2. Read the poem aloud. Try pausing for a fraction of a second at every dash. Is there any possible justification for her unorthodox punctuation?

WILLIAM CARLOS WILLIAMS (1883–1963)

The Dance

> In Breughel's great picture, The Kermess,
> the dancers go round, they go round and
> around, the squeal and the blare and the
> tweedle of bagpipes, a bugle and fiddles
> tipping their bellies (round as the thick- 5
> sided glasses whose wash they impound)
> their hips and their bellies off balance
> to turn them. Kicking and rolling about
> the Fair Grounds, swinging their butts, those
> shanks must be sound to bear up under such 10
> rollicking measures, prance as they dance
> in Breughel's great picture, The Kermess.

182

1. Pieter Breughel (1520?–1569), Flemish painter known for his scenes of peasant activities, painted "The Kermess" to represent the feast day of a local patron saint. Scan the poem metrically and describe the effect of its rhythms.

2. Williams, widely admired for his free verse, insisted for many years that what he sought was a form not in the least bit free. What effect does he achieve by ending lines on such weak words as the articles *and* and *the*? By splitting *thick-/sided*? By splitting the prepositional phrase by the break at the end of line 8? By using line-breaks to split *those* and *such* from what they modify? What do you think he is trying to convey?

3. Is there any point in his making line 12 a repetition of the opening line?

4. FIXED FORMS

When we speak of "the sonnet form" and "French courtly forms such as the ballad and villanelle," we use *form* as a synonym for a **genre** or a kind of literature. So intended, *a form* can mean a kind of poem with a familiar and expected pattern running through the whole of it; for instance, the **sonnet,** a fourteen-line poem in iambic pentameter. But the term can also imply — especially in the case of the sonnet — not only such a pattern, but also a certain arrangement of thought, and perhaps the use of certain **conventions:** habitual devices, subjects, attitudes, and figures of speech. For example, in that ingenious courtly form, the **ballade** (see "The Complaint of Chaucer to His Purse," p. 292), the arrangement calls for a short last stanza containing a plea or a compliment, which conventionally is addressed to a prince. A form, in this sense, is sometimes called a **fixed form** rather than a genre. For a sonnet, with its notable tradition, the term *genre* might not seem too grand; but it would be hard to speak of "the genre of the limerick" without pomposity.[3]

Originally an Italian form (*sonnetto:* "little song"), the sonnet owes much of its prestige to Petrarch (1304–1374), who cast into it his expressions of longing for his unattainable Laura. So great was the vogue for sonnets in England at the end of the sixteenth century that a gentleman courtier might have been thought a boor if he proved unable to write a decent sonnet when a lady demanded one. Not content to adopt only the pattern of the sonnet, poets assumed

[3] *Genre* may refer also to such large inclusive "kinds" of literature as drama, narrative, and lyric; or, for example, one can speak of the genres of tragedy, comedy, melodrama, and farce; or of the genres of novel, epic, and short story; or of the genres of elegy, epitaph, and ode. For a discussion of the term and its uses, see René Wellek and Austin Warren, *Theory of Literature* (New York, 1956), chap. 17.

the conventional mask of the suffering lover, imitated the Italian master's similes, and invented others. The result was a great surplus of Petrarchan **conceits**, or comparisons (from the Italian *concetto*: concept, idea, bright thought). A lady's eyes were suns; her hair, gold wires; her lips, coral; her cheeks, roses or cherries. A lover's heart was a storm-tossed ship; love, the star he steered by. The lover was a fleeing deer hunted by love; and, in a favorite use of hyperbole, his tears were rain, his sighs gales. Contrary to what you might expect, fine poems were written with the aid of these conventions (see some of the poems in this book by Wyatt, Marlowe, Shakespeare, Sidney, Spenser, Herrick, and Campion). In the following sonnet, Shakespeare, who helped himself generously from the Petrarchan stockpile, pokes fun at poets who use such conventions thoughtlessly:

WILLIAM SHAKESPEARE (1564–1616)

'My mistress' eyes are nothing like the sun'

My mistress' eyes are nothing like the sun;
Coral is far more red than her lips' red;
If snow be white, why then her breasts are dun;
If hairs be wires, black wires grow on her head.   4
I have seen roses damasked red and white,
But no such roses see I in her cheeks;
And in some perfumes is there more delight
Than in the breath that from my mistress reeks.   8
I love to hear her speak, yet well I know
That music hath a far more pleasing sound;
I grant I never saw a goddess go:
My mistress, when she walks, treads on the ground.   12
   And yet, by heaven, I think my love as rare
   As any she, belied with false compare.

Not long after English poets imported the sonnet form in the middle of the sixteenth century, they worked out their own rime scheme. In the preceding sample of an **English sonnet**, sometimes called a **Shakespearean sonnet**, the rimes cohere in four clusters: *abab cdcd efef gg*. Because a rime scheme tends to shape the poet's statements to it, encouraging sentences to end upon the last word of a group of rimes, the English sonnet has three places where a shift in thought is likely to occur. Within its form, a poet may pursue one idea throughout the three quatrains, then in the couplet whip out a surprise ending.

184

MICHAEL DRAYTON (1563–1631)

'Since there's no help'

Since there's no help, come let us kiss and part;
Nay, I have done, you get no more of me,
And I am glad, yea, glad with all my heart
That thus so cleanly I myself can free;   4
Shake hands for ever, cancel all our vows,
And when we meet at any time again,
Be it not seen in either of our brows
That we one jot of former love retain.   8
Now at the last gasp of Love's latest breath,
When, his pulse failing, Passion speechless lies,
When Faith is kneeling by his bed of death,
And Innocence is closing up his eyes,   12
  Now if thou wouldst, when all have given him over,
  From death to life thou mightst him yet recover.

Less frequently met in English poetry, the **Italian sonnet,** or **Petrarchan sonnet,** follows the rime scheme *abbaabba* in its first eight lines, the **octave,** then adds new rime sounds in the last six lines, the **sestet.** The sestet may rime *cdcdcd, cdecde, cdccdc,* or in almost any other variation that does not end in a couplet. This organization into two parts is often reflected in the poem's arrangement of thought. One conventional method is to introduce a statement of some problem in the octave, then in the sestet offer some resolution. A lover, for example, may lament that his loved one neglects him; then in line 9 begin to foresee some kind of outcome: he'll die, or accept the inevitability of unhappiness, or trust that the lady will yield in time. For certain effects, however, the poet may wish to vary the location of the break between the thought of the octave and that of the sestet.

ELIZABETH BARRETT BROWNING (1806–1861)

Grief

I tell you, hopeless grief is passionless;
  That only men incredulous of despair,
  Half-taught in anguish, through the midnight air
Beat upward to God's throne in loud access   4
Of shrieking and reproach. Full desertness
  In souls, as countries, lieth silent-bare
  Under the blanching, vertical eye-glare

185

Of the absolute Heavens. Deep-hearted man, express
Grief for the Dead in silence like to death:
  Most like a monumental statue set
In everlasting watch and moveless woe
Till itself crumble to the dust beneath.   12
  Touch it: the marble eyelids are not wet —
If it could weep, it could arise and go.

In this Italian sonnet, the division in thought comes a bit early: in the middle of line 8. Few English-speaking poets who have used the form seem to feel strictly bound by it.

"The sonnet," in the view of Robert Bly, a recent critic, "is where old professors go to die." And yet the use of the form by such twentieth-century poets as Yeats, Frost, Auden, Thomas, Pound, Cummings, Snodgrass and Robert Lowell suggests that its vitality is far from exhausted. Like the hero of the popular ballad "Finnegan's Wake," literary forms declared dead (though not professors) have a habit of springing up again.

EXERCISE ONE

Find other sonnets in this book. Which are English in form? Which are Italian? Which are variations on either form, or combinations of the two? In which sonnet form, the English or the Italian, is it more difficult and demanding for an English-speaking poet to write? Explain. (You may wish to try your hand at both forms and find out for yourself.)

Oscar Wilde once said that a cynic is "a man who knows the price of everything and the value of nothing." Such a terse, pointed statement is called an epigram. In poetry, however, an **epigram** is a form: "A short poem ending in a witty or ingenious turn of thought, to which the rest of the composition is intended to lead up" (according to the *Oxford English Dictionary*). Often it is a malicious gibe with an unexpected stinger in the final line.

GEORGE GRANVILLE, LORD LANSDOWNE (1667–1725)
Cloë

Bright as the day, and like the morning fair,
Such Cloë is — and common as the air.

Like any other heroic couplet, this particular epigram has a stanza form into which a parallel and an antithesis fit beautifully.

Cultivated by the Roman poet Martial, for whom the epigram was a short poem, sometimes satiric but not always, this form has been especially favored by English poets who know Latin. Few characteristics of the English epigram seem fixed. Its pattern tends usually to be brief and rimed; its tone, playfully merciless.

MARTIAL (A.D. 40?–102?)

A Hinted Wish

> You told me, Maro, whilst you live
> You'd not a single penny give,
> But that, whene'er you chanced to die,
> You'd leave a handsome legacy:
> You must be mad beyond redress
> If my next wish you cannot guess!
>
> *(Translated by Samuel Johnson)*

SIR JOHN HARINGTON (1561?–1612)

Of Treason

> Treason doth never prosper; what's the reason?
> For if it prosper, none dare call it treason.

JOHN DONNE (1572–1631)

Antiquary

> If in his study he hath so much care
> To hang all old strange things, let his wife beware.

THOMAS BANCROFT (fl. 1633–1658)

A Drunken Brabbler°   brawler

> Who only in his cups will fight is like
> A clock, that must be oiled well ere it strike.

J. V. CUNNINGHAM (b. 1911)

'The Elders'

> The Elders at their services begin
> With paper offerings. They release from sin
> The catechumens on the couches lying
> In visions, testimonies, prophesying:
> Not, "Are you saved?" they ask, but in informal
> Insistent query, "Brother, are you normal?"

187

Rewrite any of the preceding epigrams, taking them out of rime and adding a few more words to them. See if your revisions have nearly the same effect as the originals.

Exercise Three

Read all the sonnets by Shakespeare in this book. How do the final couplets of some of them resemble epigrams? Does this diminish their effect of "seriousness"?

In English the only other fixed form to rival the sonnet and the epigram in favor is the **limerick**: a pattern of five anapestic lines usually riming *aabba*, the third and fourth lines having two stresses, the other lines three.

> There was an old man of Pantoum
> Who kept a live sheep in his room.
> "It reminds me," he said,
> "Of a loved one long dead,
> But I never can quite recall whom."

The limerick was made popular by Edward Lear (1812–1888), English humorist and painter, whose own practice was to make the last line echo the first: "That oppressive old man of Pantoum."

Exercise Four

The **clerihew**, a fixed form named for its inventor, Edmund Clerihew Bentley (1875–1956), has straggled behind the limerick in popularity. Here are four examples: how would you define the form and what are its rules? Who or what is its conventional subject matter? Try writing your own examples.

James Watt
Was the hard-boiled kind
      of Scot:
He thought any dream
Sheer waste of steam.
            —W. H. Auden

Sir Christopher Wren
Said, "I am going to dine with
      some men.
If anybody calls
Say I am designing St. Paul's."
            —Edmund Clerihew Bentley

Old Andy Jackson
Was half Anglo-Saxon.
He was so full of beans
That he took New Orleans.
            —Anonymous

Clara Barton
Gnawed on a bandage carton
Whenever at a loss
Over the Red Cross.
            —Hope Camp Wiebe

188

When Dylan Thomas wrote a poem addressed to his father, whom he felt had grown tame in old age, he cast it into a **villanelle**: a fixed form of French courtly origin. From this example, sum up its rules. In obeying them, does Thomas commit himself to write nothing more than what a villanelle so easily can be: an elaborate and trivial exercise?

DYLAN THOMAS (1914–1953)

Do Not Go Gentle into That Good Night

Do not go gentle into that good night,
Old age should burn and rave at close of day;
Rage, rage against the dying of the light.

Though wise men at their end know dark is right,
Because their words had forked no lightning they
Do not go gentle into that good night.   6

Good men, the last wave by, crying how bright
Their frail deeds might have danced in a green bay,
Rage, rage against the dying of the light.

Wild men who caught and sang the sun in flight,
And learn, too late, they grieved it on its way,
Do not go gentle into that good night.   12

Grave men, near death, who see with blinding sight
Blind eyes could blaze like meteors and be gay,
Rage, rage against the dying of the light.

And you, my father, there on the sad height,
Curse, bless, me now with your fierce tears, I pray.
Do not go gentle into that good night.   18
Rage, rage against the dying of the light.

EDGAR LEE MASTERS (1869–1950)

Petit, the Poet

> Seeds in a dry pod, tick, tick, tick,
> Tick, tick, tick, like mites in a quarrel —
> Faint iambics that the full breeze wakens —
> But the pine tree makes a symphony thereof.
> Triolets, villanelles, rondels, rondeaus.   5
> Ballades by the score with the same old thought:
> The snows and the roses of yesterday are vanished;
> And what is love but a rose that fades?
> Life all around me here in the village:
> Tragedy, comedy, valor and truth,   10
> Courage, constancy, heroism, failure —
> All in the loom, and, oh, what patterns!
> Woodlands, meadows, streams and rivers —
> Blind to all of it all my life long.
> Triolets, villanelles, rondels, rondeaus,   15
> Seeds in a dry pod, tick, tick, tick,
> Tick, tick, tick, what little iambics,
> While Homer and Whitman roared in the pines!

QUESTIONS

1. The speaker is a local poet of the village that Masters celebrates in *Spoon River Anthology*. What does his name suggest?

2. Summarize Petit's criticism of his own work. Does he mean that major poetry cannot be written in iambs?

3. Like the *villanelle*, just seen in the example by Dylan Thomas, the other fixed forms mentioned are those of French courtly verse. For a *ballade*, see Chaucer's "Complaint" (p. 292). For a *rondeau* (so called, though it is not one strictly according to the French pattern), see Leigh Hunt's "Rondeau" (p. 139). What is a *rondel*? A *triolet*?

5. STRUCTURE

"We'll build in sonnets pretty rooms," said John Donne, speaking for himself and other poets; and thus suggesting that, in some ways, the making of poems resembles architecture. So far, in considering some different kinds of form in poetry—patterns of sound and rhythm, visual patterns, flexible forms, fixed forms — we have seen that it is characteristic of a formal pattern to help arrange and give order to the thoughts expressed in it. In Drayton's sonnet (p. 185), in which the lover protests for twelve lines that the affair is through, then abruptly decides that it might be rescued after all, the rime scheme functions in this way. The shift from a series of quatrains to the final

190

couplet seems to encourage the procession of thought to turn off in another direction. This organization of thought within a poem, while bound up intimately with the patterns we have studied, is a kind of form we have yet to deal with. Much else makes up this configuration called a poem besides visual shapes and line lengths, patterns of stresses and sounds. Arrangements of thought are part of it; also syntax, any allusions, symbols, figures of speech, and much more.

Within a poem, this organization of materials *other than stresses, sounds, and visual shapes* is the kind of form called **structure**. Since structure is an arrangement found in whole poems and passages, we usually speak of the structure of a poem, a stanza, a section, rather than that of an individual word or line.[4] Seeing the structure of a poem entails seeing relationships between its parts, between these parts and the poem as a whole. We may have to decide, for instance, which thought in a poem is most important and what details are subordinate to it.

As a leaf, to the casual eye indistinguishable from any other of a thousand leaves on a tree, on being examined will reveal an arrangement of veins and markings distinctively its own, so any poem carefully studied will be seen to contain a structure in some ways unique. For this reason, brief descriptions of the structures of poems can be no more than rough sketches; but certain general types of structure are encountered frequently. A poem, like many a piece of expository prose, may open with a general statement, which it then illustrates and amplifies by particulars, as does Mrs. Browning's sonnet beginning "I tell you, hopeless grief is passionless" (p. 185). Or it might move from details to more general statement, as does Keats's "Ode on a Grecian Urn" (p. 321), presenting details of the urn's pattern and arriving at the conclusion, "Beauty is truth, truth beauty." A poem may set two elements in parallel structure:

ALEXANDER POPE (1688–1744)

Epigram Engraved on the Collar of a Dog
Which I Gave to His Royal Highness

> I am his Highness' dog at Kew;
> Pray tell me, sir, whose dog are you?

---

4 To refer to words, feet, individual concrete details and images considered apart from a poem's structure, John Crowe Ransom has suggested the word **texture**. See *The New Criticism* (New York, 1941).

191

A poem may also set two elements in an antithesis, as the two halves of Robert Frost's short poem quoted at the beginning of this book: "We dance round in a ring and suppose, / But the Secret sits in the middle and knows." (Not all poems containing parallels or antitheses need be so brief; and some contain other things in addition to statements set side by side.) There may be an overall coherence in a poem's imagery and figures of speech, as in Dylan Thomas' "Fern Hill," with its "simple stars," "lamb white days," "new made clouds," and allusions to "Adam and maiden" — all relating to one another by their mutual connotations of freshness and innocence, and contributing to the central theme of childhood as being joyous but certain to pass. If a poem tells a story, it may build to a **crisis** or turning point in the action, as might a novel or play. These are just a few kinds of structure possible. Here is a poem containing — like most poems — more than one kind:

ROBERT HERRICK (1591–1674)

Divination by a Daffodil

> When a daffodil I see
> Hanging down his head t'wards me,
> Guess I may, what I must be:
> First, I shall decline my head;
> Secondly, I shall be dead;
> Lastly, safely burièd.   5

This poem is arranged in two halves, bound together by a metaphor. In the first three lines, the speaker sees a drooping daffodil; in the last three, he foresees his own eventual drooping in like manner. There is another relationship, too: the second half of the poem explains the first half, it specifies "what I must be." Furthermore, the last three lines make a one-two-three listing of the stages of dying and being buried. There is also in these lines a progression of narrative: the events take place one after another.

How do we look for structure? Here are some suggested methods of approach to a poem and some questions that may be asked:

1. Paraphrase the poem.
2. Try to divide it into sections. Where do ideas stop and start? How do sections relate to one another? (By parallel, antithesis, metaphor, simile, cause and effect, enumeration, or what?)
3. Is the poem as a whole an extended metaphor? Is it an allegory?
4. If the poem contains symbols, which if any is most centrally important? How do other symbols in the poem relate to it?

192

5. If the poem tells a story, what are its events? Can the action be divided into beginning, middle, and conclusion?

6. Do the statements in a poem display any ascending or descending order of abstraction? That is, do they move from generalizations to particular details, or vice versa?

7. Is anything concealed from the reader at the beginning of the poem — any knowledge or understanding — and revealed to him by the time he reaches the end? At what point is it revealed? All at once? Bit by bit along the way?

8. What relationships may be drawn between the poem's images? Which ones have similar connotations? Which ones help communicate the poem's theme?

9. What is the tone? Is it consistent throughout the poem or does it, at any point, seem to change? If so, at what point?

10. Does the poem shift at any point from direct or literal statement, to be taken at face value, to irony? Why does such a shift come where it does — no sooner, no later?

11. Are we given the speeches of two or more voices or characters? If they are not clearly identified, tell them apart.

12. At what points does the poet address the reader or some other party? At what points is he talking to himself?

13. Separate passages of objective description from subjective meditation. What do the two have to do with each other?

14. Has the poem an overall frame or setting (such as the situation in "My Last Duchess" of Browning, pp. 289–290, in which the duke is telling his story to a visitor)? If so, which parts of the poem are devoted to this frame, which to whatever goes into it?

A poem that could answer to all these questions, or even to most, would be a rare animal; do not expect these questions to be universally applicable. All this might look like dull work without reward — and it would be if, having summed up the structure of a poem, we were to stop there. Looking for structure, however, is only a way to read poems more closely and intently, and to read them whole. Unless, having made our summary of a poem's structure, we return to the poem for another reading — for the pleasure that comes with seeing parts and whole together — then our summary is no more than fossil evidence. Often such a summary can be a means of entrance into the most difficult of poems, whether conventional in form or flexible, whether an epic or an epigram.

EXERCISE SIX

Try some of the preceding questions and methods of approach on some poem or poems in the Anthology.

The following puzzle is meant not as a parlor game but as a way to see the structure of a poem. (It mistreats a masterpiece little in size, but sinewy enough to survive.) Here is the garbled text of a poem of Wordsworth. Without looking up the original, try to determine the order in which the stanzas ought to be read. You will need to remove two unnecessary stanzas by Poe. What has determined the order you have given the stanzas? What have you left out and why is it extraneous?

EDGAR ALLAN WORDSWORTH

Lucy Lee

> She lived unknown, and few could know
>   When Lucy ceased to be;
> But she is in her grave, and, oh,
>   The difference to me!   4
>
> She dwelt among the untrodden ways
>   Beside the springs of Dove,
> A maid whom there were none to praise
>   And very few to love: 8
>
> Ah, broken is the golden bowl!
>   The spirit flown forever!
> Let the bell toll! — a saintly soul
>   Floats on the Stygian river;   12
>
> A violet by a mossy stone
>   Half hidden from the eye!
> — Fair as a star, when only one
>   Is shining in the sky.   16
>
> And so, all the night-tide, I lie down by the side
> Of my darling — my darling — my life and my bride,
>   In the sepulchre there by the sea,
>   In her tomb by the sounding sea.   20

T. S. ELIOT (1888–1965)

Rhapsody on a Windy Night

> Twelve o'clock.
> Along the reaches of the street
> Held in a lunar synthesis,
> Whispering lunar incantations
> Dissolve the floors of memory   5
> And all its clear relations
> Its divisions and precisions,
> Every street-lamp that I pass
> Beats like a fatalistic drum,
> And through the spaces of the dark   10
> Midnight shakes the memory
> As a madman shakes a dead geranium.

194

Half-past one,
The street-lamp sputtered,
The street-lamp muttered,   15
The street-lamp said, "Regard that woman
Who hesitates toward you in the light of the door
Which opens on her like a grin.
You see the border of her dress
Is torn and stained with sand,   20
And you see the corner of her eye
Twists like a crooked pin."

The memory throws up high and dry
A crowd of twisted things;
A twisted branch upon the beach   25
Eaten smooth, and polished
As if the world gave up
The secret of its skeleton,
Stiff and white.
A broken spring in a factory yard,   30
Rust that clings to the form that the strength has left
Hard and curled and ready to snap.

Half-past two,
The street-lamp said,
"Remark the cat which flattens itself in the gutter,   35
Slips out its tongue
And devours a morsel of rancid butter."
So the hand of the child, automatic,
Slipped out and pocketed a toy that was running along the
        quay.
I could see nothing behind that child's eye.   40
I have seen eyes in the street
Trying to peer through lighted shutters,
And a crab one afternoon in a pool,
An old crab with barnacles on his back,
Gripped the end of a stick which I held him.   45

Half-past three,
The lamp sputtered,
The lamp muttered in the dark.
The lamp hummed:
"Regard the moon,   50
La lune ne garde aucune rancune,
She winks a feeble eye,
She smiles into corners.
She smooths the hair of the grass.
The moon has lost her memory.   55

A washed-out smallpox cracks her face,
Her hand twists a paper rose,
That smells of dust and eau de Cologne,
She is alone
With all the old nocturnal smells   60
That cross and cross across her brain."
The reminiscence comes
Of sunless dry geraniums
And dust in crevices,
Smells of chestnuts in the streets,   65
And female smells in shuttered rooms,
And cigarettes in corridors
And cocktail smells in bars.

The lamp said,
"Four o'clock,
Here is the number on the door.   70
Memory!
You have the key,
The little lamp spreads a ring on the stair.
Mount.   75
The bed is open; the tooth-brush hangs on the wall,
Put your shoes at the door, sleep, prepare for life."

The last twist of the knife.

QUESTIONS

1. Comment on the title. What sort of utterance is a rhapsody? What does the term mean in musical composition? Is it any more appropriate that the speaker's experience occurs on a windy night instead of on, say, a clear day at noon?

2. What happens to *memory* in the opening dozen lines? What uses of memory are made throughout the remainder of the poem?

3. Into what sections or episodes can the poem clearly be divided? What marks the beginning of each episode?

4. In each episode, what happens? What parallel organization do the second and succeeding episodes have?

5. In general, how would you describe the process by which, in the second and each succeeding episode, one image leads to others?

6. In lines 33–45, what do cat, child, peering eyes, and crab have in common?

7. The description of a street lamp in lines 8–9 is not a hallucination. Gas-burning street lamps *did* pulsate and make a drumming sound. What other symbols in the poem also seem products of exact observation?

8. How do you visualize the comparison in lines 21–22?

9. Line 51 is a quotation from the French Symbolist poet Laforgue: "The moon holds no grudge." What does the moon, as personified in this episode, have in common with the woman in the doorway (lines 16–22)? What does it have in common with the street-lamp?

10. What patterns of sound and rhythm help bind the poem together?

11. What do you make of the tooth-brush on the wall (line 76)? What does it have to do with the "last twist of the knife"?

12. Compare this poem with "The *Boston Evening Transcript*" (p. 108) and with "The Love Song of J. Alfred Prufrock" (pp. 302–306). Do the symbols in these poems point to any mutual themes?

WALLACE STEVENS (1879–1955)

Thirteen Ways of Looking at a Blackbird

I

Among twenty snowy mountains,
The only moving thing
Was the eye of the blackbird.

II

I was of three minds,
Like a tree   5
In which there are three blackbirds.

III

The blackbird whirled in the autumn winds.
It was a small part of the pantomime.

IV

A man and a woman
Are one.   10
A man and a woman and a blackbird
Are one.

V

I do not know which to prefer,
The beauty of inflections
Or the beauty of innuendoes,   15
The blackbird whistling
Or just after.

VI

Icicles filled the long window
With barbaric glass.
The shadow of the blackbird   20
Crossed it, to and fro.
The mood
Traced in the shadow
An indecipherable cause.

VII

O thin men of Haddam,   25
Why do you imagine golden birds?

Do you not see how the blackbird
Walks around the feet
Of the women about you?

VIII

I know noble accents   30
And lucid, inescapable rhythms;
But I know, too,
That the blackbird is involved
In what I know.

IX

When the blackbird flew out of sight,   35
It marked the edge
Of one of many circles.

X

At the sight of blackbirds
Flying in a green light,
Even the bawds of euphony   40
Would cry out sharply.

XI

He rode over Connecticut
In a glass coach.
Once, a fear pierced him,
In that he mistook   45
The shadow of his equipage
For blackbirds.

XII

The river is moving.
The blackbird must be flying.

XIII

It was evening all afternoon.   50
It was snowing
And it was going to snow.
The blackbird sat
In the cedar-limbs.

QUESTIONS

1. The Biblical-sounding name in line 25 is that of a town in Connecticut. What is the speaker's attitude toward the men of Haddam? What attitude — or failure of comprehension — toward their world does he condemn? What attitude toward this world does he suggest they lack? What is implied by calling them "thin"?

2. What do the landscapes of winter contribute to the poem's effectiveness? If instead Stevens had chosen images of summer lawns, what would have been lost?

3. In which stanzas does Stevens suggest that a unity exists between human being and blackbird, between blackbird and the entire natural world? Can we say that Stevens "philosophizes"? What role does the imagery of this poem play in the poet's statement of his ideas?

4. What sense can you make of Part X of the poem? Make an enlightened guess.

5. Consider any one of the thirteen parts. What patterns of sound and rhythm do you find in it? What kind of structure does it have?

6. If the thirteen parts were arranged in some different order, would the poem be just as good? Or can we find a justification for its beginning with Part I and ending with Part XIII?

7. Does the poem seem an arbitrary combination of thirteen separate poems? Or is there any reason to call it a whole?

ANONYMOUS (English; traditional popular ballad)

The Cherry-Tree Carol

Joseph was an old man,
    And an old man was he,
When he wedded Mary,
    In the land of Galilee.   4

Joseph and Mary walked
    Through an orchard good,
Where was cherries and berries,
    So red as any blood.   8

Joseph and Mary walked
    Through an orchard green,
Where was berries and cherries,
    As thick as might be seen.   12

O then bespoke Mary,
    So meek and so mild:
"Pluck me one cherry, Joseph,
    For I am with child."   16

O then bespoke Joseph,
    With words most unkind:
"Let him pluck thee a cherry
    That brought thee with child."   20

O then bespoke the babe,
    Within his mother's womb:
"Bow down then the tallest tree,
    For my mother to have some."   24

Then bowed down the highest tree
    Unto his mother's hand;
Then she cried, "See, Joseph,
    I have cherries at command."   28

O then bespoke Joseph:
  "I have done Mary wrong;
But cheer up, my dearest,
  And be not cast down." 32

Then Mary plucked a cherry,
  As red as the blood,
Then Mary went home
  With her heavy load. 36

Then Mary took her babe,
  And sat him on her knee,
Saying, "My dear son, tell me
  What this world will be." 40

"O I shall be as dead, mother,
  As the stones in the wall;
O the stones in the streets, mother,
  Shall mourn for me all. 44

"Upon Easter day, mother,
  My uprising shall be;
O the sun and the moon, mother,
  Shall both rise with me." 48

QUESTIONS

1. Narratives in folk ballads sometimes leap from one event to another without a transition (possibly because subsequent singers recall the more vivid stanzas, forget others; possibly because further stanzas have been added). Such a lapse in time occurs between the ninth and tenth stanzas. What has happened? Do you find that this gap seriously impairs the continuity of the poem?

2. According to some apocryphal versions of the nativity story, Joseph at first did not know that Mary's pregnancy was due to divine intervention. How would you describe the characterization of Joseph in this ballad?

3. What is the tone of this poem? Do you find the characterization of Joseph inconsistent with it?

4. What is the basic stanza pattern? Point out lines in which the poem does not strictly adhere to it. Are any particular effects ever gained by the lines' falling short?

5. What repetitions of sound (besides the rime scheme) help bind the poem together?

6. What relationships are possible between the imagery in the last two stanzas? (Between the stones and Christ's rising from the tomb; between Him and the sun and moon?)

7. What connections are possible between the imagery of the last two stanzas and the imagery of cherries and cherry tree?

8. Is it necessary to think that the composer of this carol consciously intended these connections, for such connections to be there? Explain.

ELEVEN

MYTH

1. TRADITIONAL MYTH

Poets have long been fond of retelling **myths,** narrowly defined as traditional stories of immortal beings. Such stories taken collectively may also be called **myth** or **mythology.** In one of the most celebrated collections of myth ever assembled, the *Metamorphoses,* the poet Ovid has told — to take one example from many — how Phaeton, child of the sun god, rashly tried to drive his father's fiery chariot on its daily round, lost control of the horses, and caused disaster both to himself and to the world. Our use of the term *myth* in discussing poetry, then, differs from its use in such common expressions as "the myth of communism" or "the myth of democracy." In these examples, myth, in its broadest sense, is any idea people believe in, whether true or false. Nor do we mean — to take another familiar use of the word — a cock-and-bull story: "Professor Jones doesn't roast students alive; that's just a *myth.*" In the following discussion, myth will mean — as the critic Northrop Frye has put it — "the imitation of actions near or at the conceivable limits of desire." Myths tell us of the exploits of the gods — their battles, the ways in which they live, love, and perhaps suffer — all on a scale of magnificence larger than our life. We envy their freedom and power; they enact our wishes and dreams. Whether we believe in them or not, their adventures are myths: Ovid, it seems, placed no credence in the stories he related, for he declared, "I prate of ancient poets' monstrous lies."

And yet it is characteristic of a myth that it *can* be believed. Throughout history, myths have accompanied religious doctrines and

201

rituals. They have helped sanction or recall to men the reasons for religious observances. A sublime instance is the New Testament account of the Last Supper. Because of it, and its record of the words of Jesus, "This do in remembrance of Me," Christians have continued to re-enact the offering and partaking of the body and blood of their Lord, under the appearances of bread and wine. It is essential to recall that, just because a *myth* narrates the acts of a god, we do not necessarily mean by the term a false or fictitious narrative. When we speak of the "myth of Islam" or "the Christian myth," we do so without implying either belief or disbelief. Myths can also help sanction customs and institutions other than religious ones. At the same time the baking of bread was introduced to ancient Greece — one theory goes — there was introduced the myth of Demeter, goddess of grain, who had kindly sent her emissary Triptolemus to teach man this valuable art — thus helping to persuade the distrustful that bread was a good thing.

Some myths, however, seem made to divert and regale, not to sanction anything. Such may be the story of the sculptor Pygmalion, whose statue of the beautiful Galatea was brought to life by Venus (which myth we know in modern dress as *My Fair Lady*). Tales of the marvelous feats of a warrior — Siegfried, Beowulf, Jason, the Ulysses of the *Odyssey* — may affirm the pride of such a hero's nation or people, but they also abound in entertainment.

How does a myth begin? Several theories have been proposed, none universally credited. One is that myth is a way in which primitive man explains to himself some natural phenomenon. In this view, myth is rudimentary science. Winter comes and the vegetation perishes because Persephone, child of Demeter, must return to the underworld for four months every year. This theory, as classical scholar Edith Hamilton has pointed out, may lead us to think incorrectly that Greek mythology was the creation of a primitive people. Tales of the gods of Mount Olympus may reflect an earlier inheritance, but Greek myths known to us were transcribed in an era of high civilization. Anthropologists have questioned whether primitive people generally find beauty in the mysteries of nature. "From my own study of living myths among savages," wrote Bronislaw Malinowski, "I should say that primitive man has to a very limited extent the purely artistic or scientific interest in nature; there is but little room for symbolism in his ideas and tales; and myth, in fact, is not an idle rhapsody . . . but a hard-working, extremely important cultural force." [1] Such a practical

[1] *Myth in Primitive Psychology* (New York, 1926); reprinted in *Magic, Science and Religion* (New York, 1954), p. 97.

function was seen by Sir James Frazer in *The Golden Bough*: myths were originally expressions of man's hope that nature would be fertile. Still another theory is that, once upon a time, heroes of myth were human prototypes. The Greek philosopher Euhemerus declared myths to be tales of real persons, which poets had exaggerated. Most present-day historians of myth would seek no general explanation but would say that different myths probably had different origins.

Poets have many coherent mythologies on which to draw; perhaps those most frequently consulted by British and American poets are the classical, the Christian, the Norse, and folk myth of the frontier (embodying the deeds of such superhuman characters as Paul Bunyan). Some poets have taken inspiration from primitive mythology as well; T. S. Eliot's *The Waste Land*, for example, is enriched by allusions to pagan vegetation-cults.

Myth has made possible much of the graphic art of Western civilization, as a tour through any good museum of painting will demonstrate. In literature, one evidence of its continuing value to recent poets and storytellers is the frequency with which myths — both primitive and civilized — are retold. William Faulkner's *The Bear* recalls tales of Indian totem animals; John Updike's novel *The Centaur* presents the horse-man Chiron as a modern high school teacher; Hart Crane's poem "For the Marriage of Faustus and Helen" unites two figures of different myths, who dance to jazz; T. S. Eliot's plays bring into the drawing-room the myths of Alcestis (*The Cocktail Party*) and the Eumenides (*The Family Reunion*); Jean Cocteau's film *Orphée* shows us a Eurydice who goes to the underworld with an escort of motorcycles. Popular interest in such works may testify to the profound appeal such myths continue to hold for us. Like any other large body of knowledge that can be alluded to, myth offers the poet an instant means of communication — if his reader also knows the particular myth cited. Writing "Lycidas," John Milton could depend upon his readers — mostly gentlemen of similar classical learning — to understand him without footnotes. Today, a poet referring to a traditional myth must be sure to choose a reasonably well-known one, or else write as well as T. S. Eliot, whose work has compelled critics and readers to single out his allusions and look them up. Like other varieties of poetry, myth is a kind of knowledge, not at odds with scientific knowledge, but existing in addition to it.

203

WILLIAM WORDSWORTH (1770–1850)

The World Is Too Much with Us

The world is too much with us; late and soon,
Getting and spending, we lay waste our powers:
Little we see in Nature that is ours;
We have given our hearts away, a sordid boon!   4
This Sea that bares her bosom to the moon;
The winds that will be howling at all hours,
And are up-gathered now like sleeping flowers;
For this, for everything, we are out of tune;   8
It moves us not. — Great God! I'd rather be
A Pagan suckled in a creed outworn;
So might I, standing on this pleasant lea,
Have glimpses that would make me less forlorn;   12
Have sight of Proteus rising from the sea;
Or hear old Triton blow his wreathèd horn.

EDGAR ALLAN POE (1809–1849)

Sonnet — To Science

Science! true daughter of Old Time thou art!
   Who alterest all things with thy peering eyes.
Why preyest thou thus upon the poet's heart,
   Vulture, whose wings are dull realities?   4
How should he love thee? or how deem thee wise,
   Who wouldst not leave him in his wandering
To seek for treasure in the jewelled skies,
   Albeit he soared with an undaunted wing?   8
Hast thou not dragged Diana from her car?
   And driven the Hamadryad from the wood
To seek a shelter in some happier star?
   Hast thou not torn the Naiad from her flood,   12
The Elfin from the green grass, and from me
   The summer dream beneath the tamarind tree?

Sonnet — To Science. 9. *Diana:* Roman goddess of hunting and of chastity. The moon was her chariot. 10, 12: *Hamadryad, Naiad:* in Greek myth, feminine spirits who live in — and give life to — objects in nature. A Hamadryad inhabits a tree; a Naiad, a lake or stream.

QUESTIONS

1. In these sonnets by Wordsworth and Poe, what does each poet complain about? To what does he attribute his complaint?
2. How does it affect him as an individual?

204

WILLIAM BUTLER YEATS (1865–1939)

Leda and the Swan

> A sudden blow: the great wings beating still
> Above the staggering girl, her thighs caressed
> By the dark webs, her nape caught in his bill,
> He holds her helpless breast upon his breast.
>
> How can those terrified vague fingers push   5
> The feathered glory from her loosening thighs?
> And how can body, laid in that white rush,
> But feel the strange heart beating where it lies?
>
> A shudder in the loins engenders there
> The broken wall, the burning roof and tower   10
> And Agamemnon dead.
>   Being so caught up,
> So mastered by the brute blood of the air,
> Did she put on his knowledge with his power
> Before the indifferent beak could let her drop?

QUESTIONS

1. According to Greek mythology, the god Zeus in the form of a swan descended upon Leda, a Spartan queen. Among the offspring of this union were Clytemnestra, Agamemnon's unfaithful wife who conspired in his murder; and Helen, on whose account the Trojan war was fought. What does a knowledge of these allusions contribute to our understanding of the poem's last two lines?

2. The slant-rime *up/drop* may seem accidental or inept. Is it? Would this poem have ended nearly so well if Yeats had made an exact rime like *up/cup* or *stop/drop*?

2. PERSONAL MYTH

When Plato in *The Republic* relates the Myth of Er, he presents a philosophic discussion in terms of supernatural characters he himself originated. It is worth noting that poets, too, have been inspired to make up myths of their own, for their own purposes. "I must create a system or be enslaved by another man's," said William Blake, who in his *Prophetic Books* peopled the cosmos with supernatural beings with names like Urthona, Luvah, and Tharmas (side by side with recognizable figures from the Old and New Testaments). This kind of system-making probably has both advantages and drawbacks. T. S. Eliot, in his essay on Blake, expressed his wish that the author of the *Prophetic Books* had been more willing to inherit myths from other

205

men; compared Blake's thinking to a piece of homemade furniture and complained that Blake's obligation to construct a myth of his own diverted energy that might instead have been given to poetry. Others — notably William Butler Yeats — have found Blake's untraditional mythology a high accomplishment. At the very least, Blake's long poems remain a startling demonstration of the poet as inventor of myth, as well as reteller of myth.

It may be difficult to say whether a poet creating his own myth does so to have something to live by or to have something to write about. Robert Graves, who has professed his belief in the myth of the White Goddess ("the Mother of All Living, the ancient power of love and terror"), has made it known that he has written poetry in a state of trance, inspired by the Goddess-Muse.[2] Luckily, we do not have to know what a poet believes in order to read his poems. Probably most personal myths, as they appear in poetry, are not personal confessions but conscious works of art: attempts to relate stories that will resemble traditional myths. C. M. Doughty, the late Victorian English poet whose long epic *The Dawn in Britain* today sits neglected in a few libraries, was an inventor of supernatural beings whose myths seem handed down from remote antiquity. Here is Belisama, kindly goddess of the wilderness who protects such wayfarers as Caradoc (a sleeping hero):

> It night of the moon-measurer of the year
> Is, wherein Belisama, eyebright goddess,
> Girded in kirtle blue, with woodwives sheen,
> Wont to fare forth; and her shield-maidens' train,
> And loud hounds in the forest-skies above.
> She, Caradoc seeing, stays her aery wain:
> And marveling! in cloud-cliff, her divine team
> She bound: so lights this faery queen, benign,
> (Like her sire Belin), to the kin of men.
> She goddess, leaning on her spear-staff, wakes
> In this his loneliness, in cold midnight grove,
> Over the hero's sleep . . .

Despite the pseudo-archaic style — or perhaps with the aid of it — an attractive new divinity has been born. Though her hounds and nocturnal habits recall Artemis, Greek goddess of the moon, Belisama

[2] If interested, see Graves's *The White Goddess* (New York, 1948; paperbound reprint, New York, 1958); or for a shorter and more readily understandable statement of Graves's position, his lecture "The Personal Muse," in *Oxford Addresses on Poetry* (New York, 1962).

clearly has a personality and a function all her own. More recently the English scholar and storyteller J. R. R. Tolkien has transcribed the mythology of an ancient world of elves, wizards, and hobbits in his trilogy *The Lord of the Rings*. This fictive world contains, besides heroes, creatures as disgusting as the Mewlips, about whom Tolkien has written in rime:

> The shadows where the Mewlips dwell
> Are dark and wet as ink,
> And slow and softly rings their bell,
> As in the slime you sink.

Myths, as the Mewlips remind us, can be invented playfully.

In constructing a whole private myth — as Tolkien has done — a poet may help himself to tradition. Designing his symbol of the Great Wheel, whose moonlike phases help account for the vicissitudes of history and human nature, William Butler Yeats in *A Vision* drew upon his acquaintance with Eastern religion, occultism, and Rosicrucianism (also upon what voices from the spirit world dictated). The completed symbol apparently helped Yeats write poems embodying coherent myths. Graves has found evidence of the worship of the White Goddess dating back, in his opinion, to the Old Stone Age. Blake accepted at least part of the Biblical account of the fallen angels, but his version gives a characteristic twist to it. Defying God, Satan had the good fortune to win his rebellion; but being crafty, he gave out the false news of his own defeat and proceeded to govern under the name of the Almighty he had displaced. Whether as playful as Tolkien or as earnest as Blake, whether creating a single goddess or a whole pantheon, poets have sometimes based remarkable poems on individual mythologies.

JOHN HEATH-STUBBS (b. 1918)

A Charm against the Toothache

> Venerable Mother Toothache
> Climb down from the white battlements,
> Stop twisting in your yellow fingers
> The fourfold rope of nerves;
> And tomorrow I will give you a tot of whisky   5
> To hold in your cupped hands,
> A garland of anise-flowers,
> And three cloves like nails.

207

And tell the attendant gnomes
It is time to knock off now,
To shoulder their little pick-axes,
Their cold-chisels and drills.
And you may mount by a silver ladder
Into the sky, to grind
In the cracked polished mortar
Of the hollow moon.

By the lapse of warm waters,
And the poppies nodding like red coals,
The paths on the granite mountains,
And the plantation of my dreams.

10

15

20

QUESTIONS

1. This poem shows us a poet inventing his own mythology. What powers and characteristics does he attribute to Mother Toothache? What facts of common experience does she help account for?

2. In what ways does the poem recall any myths and rituals that already exist?

3. What is the tone of the poem?

3. A NOTE ON THE THEORY OF ARCHETYPES

Earlier, in looking at symbols, we saw that certain concrete objects in poetry can convey suggestions to which we respond without quite being able to tell why. Such, perhaps, are Emily Dickinson's forked lightning bolt, dropped from celestial tables, and her buzzing fly that arrives together with death. Indefinite power may be present also in an **archetype** (Greek: "first-molded"), which can mean "an original model or pattern from which later things are made." The word acquired a special denotation through the work of the Swiss psychologist Carl Gustav Jung (1875–1961). Recently, it has occurred so frequently in literary criticism that students of poetry may wish to be aware of its significance.

An archetype, in Jung's view, is generally some particular story, character, symbol, or situation that recurs again and again in worldwide myth, literature, and dream. Some of these — as defined by Jung or others — might be such figures as the cruel mother (Cinderella's stepmother, the White Goddess), the creature half human and half animal (centaurs, satyrs, mermaids), the beautiful garden (Eden, Arcadia, the myth of the Golden Age, most concepts of paradise), the story of the hero who by slaying a monster delivers a country from its curse (as in the romance of Parsifal, the Old

English heroic narrative *Beowulf*, the myth of Perseus, the legend of Saint George and the dragon, most Hollywood monster movies), the story of the beast who yearns for the love of a woman (the fairy tale of "Beauty and the Beast," the movie *King Kong*), the story of the fall from innocence and initiation into life (the account in Genesis of the departure from Eden, J. D. Salinger's novel *The Catcher in the Rye*).

Like Sigmund Freud, Jung saw myth as an aid to the psychiatrist seeking to understand his patients' dreams. But Jung went further and postulated the existence of a "collective unconscious" or racial memory, in which archetypes lie. "These fantasy-images," said Jung, referring to archetypal dreams not traceable to anything a patient himself has ever experienced, "correspond to certain *collective* (not personal) structural elements in the human psyche in general, and, like the morphological elements of the human body, are *inherited*. . . . The archetype — let us never forget this — is a psychic organ present in all of us." [3]

What this means to the study of poetry is that, if we accept Jung's view, poems containing recognizable archetypes are likely to stir us more profoundly than those that do not. Archetypes being our inheritance from what Shakespeare called "the dark backward and abysm of time," most men can perceive them and respond to them. Some critics have found Jung's theory helpful in fathoming poems. In *Archetypal Patterns in Poetry* (1934), Maud Bodkin found similar archetypes in such dissimilar poems as "Kubla Khan" and *Paradise Lost*. Recently the French critic Paul Ginestier discovered common archetypes in certain classical myths and in modern poetry dealing with the machine.[4]

Not all psychologists and students of literature agree with the theories of Jung. Some would maintain that archetypes, because they tend to disappear with the disintegration of a culture in which they had prospered, are transmitted by word of mouth, not by racial memory.[5] Even Jung, in *Psychology and Religion*, has told of one tribal medicine man who confessed he had stopped having dreams ever since the tribe had been given a District Commissioner.

In literature, it is doubtful that an archetype alone can make a bad or mediocre poem valuable. One of the perils of expecting such a

[3] "The Psychology of the Child Archetype," in *Psyche and Symbol*, Violet S. de Laszlo, ed. (New York, 1958), pp. 117, 123.

[4] *The Poet and the Machine*, trans. Martin B. Friedman (University of North Carolina Press, 1961).

[5] See J. S. Lincoln, *The Dream in Primitive Cultures* (London, 1935), p. 24.

recognizable element is that we may be tempted to oversimplify a poem, forcing it into a shape we wish to see and valuing it because we see a shape. And yet, if we approach poetry with due respect for its complications, recognizing familiar elements may lead to worthwhile comparisons between poems. Even readers who take no stock in Jung's theory of the collective unconscious may find the word *archetype* a useful and convenient name for something which, since antiquity, has exerted a continuing appeal to makers of myth — including poets and storytellers.

ANONYMOUS (Scottish; traditional folk ballad)

Thomas the Rimer

True Thomas lay on Huntlie bank,
  A ferlie° he spied wi' his ee,   *wondrous thing*
And there he saw a lady bright,
  Come riding down by the Eildon Tree.   4

Her shirt was o' the grass-green silk,
  Her mantle o' the velvet fine,
At ilka tett° of her horse's mane   *every lock*
  Hang fifty siller bells and nine.   8

True Thomas, he pulled aff his cap,
  And louted° low down to his knee: *bowed*
"All hail, thou mighty Queen of Heaven!
  For thy peer on earth I never did see."   12

"O no, O no, Thomas," she said,
  "That name does not belang to me;
I am but the queen of fair Elfland,
  That am hither come to visit thee.   16

"Harp and carp°, Thomas," she said,   *sing ballads*
  "Harp and carp along wi' me,
And if ye dare to kiss my lips,
  Sure of your body I will be."   20

"Betide me weal, betide me woe,
  That weird° shall never daunton me";   *fate*
Syne° he has kissed her rosy lips,   *then*
  All underneath the Eildon Tree.   24

"Now, ye maun° go wi' me," she said,   *must*
  "True Thomas, ye maun go wi' me,
And ye maun serve me seven years,
  Thro weal or woe, as may chance to be."   28

She mounted on her milk-white steed,
    She's taen True Thomas up behind,
And aye° whene'er her bridle rung,   *always*
    The steed flew swifter than the wind.   32

O they rade on, and farther on —
    The steed gaed swifter than the wind —
Until they reached a desart wide,
    And living land was left behind.   36

"Light down, light down, now, True Thomas,
    And lean your head upon my knee;
Abide and rest a little space,
    And I will shew you ferlies three.   40

"O see ye not yon narrow road,
    So thick beset with thorns and briars?
That is the path of righteousness,
    Though after it but few enquires.   44

"And see not ye that braid° braid road,   *broad*
    That lies across that lily leven°?   *lovely lawn*
That is the path of wickedness,
    Though some call it the road to heaven.   48

"And see not ye that bonny road,
    That winds about the ferny brae°?   *hillside*
That is the road to fair Elfland,
    Where thou and I this night maun gae.   52

"But, Thomas, ye maun hold your tongue,
    Whatever ye may hear or see,
For, if you speak word in Elflyn land,
    Ye'll ne'er get back to your ain countrie."   56

O they rade on, and farther on,
    And they waded thro rivers aboon the knee,
And they saw neither sun nor moon,
    But they heard the roaring of the sea.   60

It was mirk° mirk night, and there was nae   *murky*
        stern° light,   *star*
    And they waded thro red blude to the knee;
For a' the blude that's shed on earth
    Rins thro the springs o' that countrie.   64

Syne they came on to a garden green,
    And she pu'd an apple frae a tree:
"Take this for thy wages, True Thomas,
    It will give the tongue that can never lie."   68

"My tongue is mine ain," True Thomas said;
  "A gudely gift ye wad gie to me!
I neither dought° to buy nor sell,   *would be able*
  At fair or tryst° where I may be.   *market*   72

"I dought neither speak to prince or peer,
  Nor ask of grace from fair ladye":
"Now hold thy peace," the lady said,
  "For as I say, so must it be."   76

He has gotten a coat of the even cloth,
  And a pair of shoes of velvet green,
And till seven years were gane and past
  True Thomas on earth was never seen.   80

Thomas the Rimer. Thomas of Erceldoune, popularly called True
Thomas or Thomas the Rimer, was an actual Scottish minstrel of the
thirteenth century. He was said to have received the power of prophecy as
a gift from the queen of the elves.

QUESTIONS

1. From what kinds of traditional myth does the poem derive? Point
out Christian and pagan elements.
2. What impression do we receive of the queen? Is she benevolent or
sinister? What popular attitudes toward the supernatural might this
characterization reveal?
3. What do you make of the magic apple in lines 66–68? What other
celebrated apples does it recall?
4. What statements seem ironies?

JOHN KEATS (1795–1821)

La Belle Dame sans Merci

O what can ail thee, knight-at-arms,
  Alone and palely loitering?
The sedge has withered from the lake,
  And no birds sing.   4

O what can ail thee, knight-at-arms,
  So haggard and so woe-begone?
The squirrel's granary is full,
  And the harvest's done.   8

I see a lily on thy brow
  With anguish moist and fever dew,
And on thy cheek a fading rose
  Fast withereth too.   12

212

"I met a lady in the meads,
    Full beautiful — a faery's child;
Her hair was long, her foot was light,
    And her eyes were wild.   16

"I made a garland for her head,
    And bracelets too, and fragrant zone°;   *belt, sash*
She looked at me as she did love,
    And made sweet moan.   20

"I set her on my pacing steed,
    And nothing else saw all day long,
For sidelong would she bend, and sing
    A faery's song.   24

"She found me roots of relish sweet,
    And honey wild, and manna dew,
And sure in language strange she said —
    'I love thee true!'   28

"She took me to her elfin grot,
    And there she wept and sighed full sore,
And there I shut her wild eyes
    With kisses four.   32

"And there she lullèd me asleep,
    And there I dreamed — ah! woe betide!
The latest dream I ever dreamed
    On the cold hill's side.   36

"I saw pale kings and princes too,
    Pale warriors, death-pale were they all;
They cried — 'La Belle Dame sans Merci
    Hath thee in thrall!'   40

"I saw their starved lips in the gloam,
    With horrid warning gapèd wide,
And I awoke and found me here,
    On the cold hill's side.   44

"And this is why I sojourn here,
    Alone and palely loitering,
Though the sedge is withered from the lake
    And no birds sing."   48

La Belle Dame sans Merci. Keats borrowed this title, "The Merciless
Beauty," from a medieval French poem. The text given above is his earlier
version.

1. What happens in this ballad? What is indicated by the contrast between the imagery from nature in lines 17, 18, 25, and 26 and that in lines 3–4 7–8, 44, and 47–48? How do you interpret the knight's "latest dream"?

2. What do we know about this beautiful lady without pity? What supernatural powers does she possess?

3. In what respects does she resemble the Queen of Elfland in the ballad of "Thomas the Rimer"? In what respects does she differ?

4. What other *dames sans merci* do you find in other poems in this book? In what respects are they similar? In what respects, if any, is Keats's lady an individual?

5. What other relentless beauties with supernatural powers do you know from myth, folklore, literature, movies, or television? In what respects, if any, do they resemble the *Belle Dame* or Thomas the Rimer's queen?

JOHN MILTON (1608–1674)

Lycidas

In this monody the author bewails a learned friend, unfortunately drowned in his passage from Chester on the Irish Seas, 1637. And by occasion foretells the ruin of our corrupted clergy then in their height.

> Yet once more, O ye laurels, and once more,
> Ye myrtles brown°, with ivy never sere,   *dark*
> I come to pluck your berries harsh and crude°,   *immature*
> And with forced fingers rude
> Shatter your leaves before the mellowing year.   5
> Bitter constraint and sad occasion dear
> Compels me to disturb your season due;
> For Lycidas is dead, dead ere his prime,
> Young Lycidas, and hath not left his peer.
> Who would not sing for Lycidas? he knew   10
> Himself to sing, and build the lofty rhyme.
> He must not float upon his wat'ry bier
> Unwept, and welter° to the parching wind,   *toss about*
> Without the meed° of some melodious tear.   *tribute*
>   Begin, then, Sisters of the Sacred Well   15
> That from beneath the seat of Jove doth spring,
> Begin, and somewhat loudly sweep the string.
> Hence with denial vain and coy excuse:
> So may some gentle Muse°   *poet*
> With lucky words favor my destined urn,   20

Lycidas. This was a conventional name for a young shepherd in pastoral poetry. Milton refers to Edward King, scholar and poet, a fellow student at Cambridge, who had planned a career in the ministry. A *monody*, in the epigraph, is a song for a single voice. 1–2. *laurels, myrtles:* evergreens in the crowns traditionally awarded to poets.

And, as he passes, turn,
And bid fair peace be to my sable shroud!
For we were nursed upon the self-same hill,
Fed the same flocks, by fountain, shade, and rill;
   Together both, ere the high lawns appeared   25
Under the opening eyelids of the Morn,
We drove a-field, and both together heard
What time the gray-fly winds° her sultry horn,   *sounds*
Batt'ning° our flocks with the fresh dews of night,   *feeding*
Oft till the star that rose at evening bright   30
Toward Heav'n's descent had sloped his westering wheel.
Meanwhile the rural ditties were not mute,
Tempered to the oaten° flute,   *made of an*
Rough satyrs danced, and fauns with cloven heel   *oat stalk*
From the glad sound would not be absent long;   35
And old Damaetas loved to hear our song.
   But, O the heavy change, now thou art gone,
Now thou art gone, and never must return!
Thee, Shepherd, thee the woods and desert caves,
With wild thyme and the gadding° vine o'ergrown,   *wandering*
And all their echoes mourn.   41
The willows, and the hazel copses green,
Shall now no more be seen
Fanning their joyous leaves to thy soft lays.
As killing as the canker to the rose,   45
Or taint-worm to the weanling herds that graze,
Or frost to flowers, that their gay wardrobe wear
When first the white thorn blows°;   *blossoms*
Such, Lycidas, thy loss to shepherd's ear.
   Where were ye, Nymphs, when the remorseless deep   50
Closed o'er the head of your loved Lycidas?
For neither were ye playing on the steep
Where your old bards, the famous Druids, lie,
Nor yet on the shaggy top of Mona high,
Nor yet where Deva spreads her wizard stream.   55
Ay me! I fondly° dream!   *foolishly*
"Had ye been there" — for what could that have done?
What could the Muse herself that Orpheus bore,
The Muse herself, for her enchanting son,
Whom universal Nature did lament,   60
When, by the rout° that made the hideous roar,   *mob*
His gory visage down the stream was sent,

36. *Damaetas:* perhaps some Cambridge tutor. 53. *Druids:* priests and poets of the Celts in pre-Christian Britain. 54. *Mona:* Roman name for the Isle of Man, near which King was drowned. 55. *Deva:* the river Dee, flowing between England and Wales. Its shifts in course were said to augur good luck for one country or the other.

Down the swift Hebrus to the Lesbian shore?
    Alas! what boots it° with uncessant care   *what good does*
To tend the homely, slighted, shepherd's trade,   *it do* 65
And strictly meditate the thankless Muse?
Were it not better done, as others use°,   *do*
To sport with Amaryllis in the shade,
Or with the tangles of Neaera's hair?
Fame is the spur that the clear spirit doth raise   70
(That last infirmity of noble mind)
To scorn delights and live laborious days;
But the fair guerdon when we hope to find,
And think to burst out into sudden blaze,
Comes the blind Fury with th' abhorrèd shears,   75
And slits the thin-spun life. "But not the praise,"
Phoebus replied, and touched my trembling ears:
"Fame is no plant that grows on mortal soil,
Nor in the glistering° foil   *glittering*
Set off to the world, nor in broad rumor° lies,   *reputation* 80
But lives and spreads aloft by those pure eyes
And perfect witness of all-judging Jove;
As he pronounces lastly on each deed,
Of so much fame in Heav'n expect thy meed."

    O fountain Arethuse, and thou honored flood,   85
Smooth-sliding Mincius, crowned with vocal reeds,
That strain I heard was of a higher mood:
But now my oat proceeds,
And listens to the Herald of the Sea,
That came in Neptune's plea.   90
He asked the waves, and asked the felon winds,
What hard mishap hath doomed this gentle swain?
And questioned every gust of rugged wings
That blows from off each beakèd promontory:
They knew not of his story;   95
And sage Hippotades their answer brings,
That not a blast was from his dungeon strayed:
The air was calm, and on the level brine
Sleek Panope with all her sisters played.
It was that fatal and perfidious bark,   100

68–69. *Amaryllis, Neaera:* conventional names for shepherdesses. 70. *the clear spirit doth raise:* doth raise the clear spirit. 77. *touched . . . ears:* gesture signifying "Remember!" 79. *foil:* a setting of gold or silver leaf, used to make a gem appear more brilliant. 85–86. *Arethuse, Mincius:* a fountain and river near the birthplaces of Theocritus and Virgil, respectively, hence recalling the most celebrated writer of pastorals in Greek and the most celebrated in Latin. 90. *in Neptune's plea:* bringing the sea-god's plea, "not guilty." 99. *Panope:* a sea nymph. Her name means "one who sees all."

Built in th' eclipse, and rigged with curses dark,
That sunk so low that sacred head of thine.
    Next, Camus, reverend sire, went footing slow,
His mantle hairy, and his bonnet sedge,
Inwrought with figures dim, and on the edge   105
Like to that sanguine flower inscribed with woe.
"Ah! who hath reft," quoth he, "my dearest pledge?"
Last came, and last did go,
The pilot of the Galilean lake;
Two massy keys he bore of metals twain   110
(The golden opes, the iron shuts amain°).   *with force*
He shook his mitered locks, and stern bespake: —
"How well could I have spared for thee, young swain,
Enow° of such, as for their bellies' sake,   *enough*
Creep, and intrude, and climb into the fold!   115
Of other care they little reck'ning make
Than how to scramble at the shearers' feast,
And shove away the worthy bidden guest.
Blind mouths! that scarce themselves know how to hold
A sheep-hook, or have learned aught else the least   120
That to the faithful herdsman's art belongs!
What recks it them? What need they? they are sped°; *prosperous*
And, when they list°, their lean and flashy songs   *so incline*
Grate on their scrannel° pipes of wretched straw;   *feeble, harsh*
The hungry sheep look up, and are not fed,   125
But, swoll'n with wind and the rank mist they draw,
Rot inwardly, and foul contagion spread;
Besides what the grim wolf with privy° paw   *stealthy*
Daily devours apace, and nothing said;
But that two-handed engine at the door   130
Stands ready to smite once, and smite no more."
    Return, Alpheus; the dread voice is past
That shrunk thy streams; return, Sicilian Muse,
And call the vales, and bid them hither cast

101. *eclipse:* thought to be an omen of evil fortune. 103. *Camus:* spirit of
the river Cam and personification of Cambridge University. 109–112.
pilot: Saint Peter, once a fisherman in Galilee, to whom Christ gave the
keys of Heaven (Matthew 16:19). As first Bishop of Rome, he wears the
miter, a bishop's emblematic head-covering. 115. *fold:* the Church of
England. 120. *sheep-hook:* a bishop's staff or crozier, which resembles a
shepherd's crook. 128. *wolf:* probably the Church of Rome. Jesuits in
England at the time were winning converts. 130. *two-handed engine:*
This disputed phrase may refer (among other possibilities) to the punish-
ing sword of The Word of God (Revelation 19:15). Perhaps Milton vis-
ualizes it as a lightningbolt, as does Spenser, to whom Jove's wrath is a
"threeforked engine" (*Faerie Queene,* VIII, 9). 131. *smite once . . . no
more:* because, in the proverb, lightning never strikes twice in the same
place? 133. *Sicilian Muse:* who inspired Theocritus, a native of Sicily.

217

Their bells and flow'rets of a thousand hues.   135
Ye valleys low, where the mild whispers use°   *resort*
Of shades, and wanton winds, and gushing brooks,
On whose fresh lap the swart star sparely looks,
Throw hither all your quaint enameled eyes,
That on the green turf suck the honied showers,   140
And purple all the ground with vernal flowers.
Bring the rathe° primrose that forsaken dies,   *early*
The tufted crow-toe, and pale jessamine,
The white pink, and the pansy freaked° with jet,   *streaked*
The glowing violet,   145
The musk-rose, and the well-attired woodbine,
With cowslips wan that hang the pensive head,
And every flower that sad embroidery wears;
Bid amaranthus all his beauty shed,
And daffadillies fill their cups with tears,   150
To strew the laureate hearse where Lycid lies.
For so, to interpose a little ease,
Let our frail thoughts dally with false surmise,
Ay me! whilst thee the shores and sounding seas
Wash far away, where'er thy bones are hurled;   155
Whether beyond the stormy Hebrides,
Where thou, perhaps, under the whelming tide
Visit'st the bottom of the monstrous° world;   *full of sea-*
Or whether thou, to our moist vows° denied,   *monsters; prayers*
Sleep'st by the fable of Bellerus old,   160
Where the great Vision of the guarded mount
Looks toward Namancos and Bayona's hold°:   *stronghold*
Look homeward, angel, now, and melt with ruth°;   *pity*
And, O ye dolphins, waft the hapless youth.
        Weep no more, woeful shepherds, weep no more,   165
For Lycidas, your sorrow, is not dead,
Sunk though he be beneath the wat'ry floor:
So sinks the day-star in the ocean bed
And yet anon repairs his drooping head,
And tricks° his beams, and with new-spangled ore°   *arrays; gold*
Flames in the forehead of the morning sky: 171
So Lycidas sunk low, but mounted high,
Through the dear might of Him that walked the waves,
Where, other groves and other streams along,

---

138. *swart star:* Sirius, at its zenith in summer, was thought to turn vegetation black. 153. *false surmise:* futile hope that the body of Lycidas could be recovered. 160. *Bellerus:* legendary giant of Land's End, the far tip of Cornwall. 161. *guarded mount:* Saint Michael's Mount, off Land's End, said to be under the protection of the archangel. 162. *Namancos, Bayona:* on the coast of Spain. 164. *dolphins:* in several Greek legends, these kindly fish delivered to shore the drowned or the drowning.

With nectar pure his oozy locks he laves,   175
And hears the unexpressive nuptial song,
In the blest kingdoms meek of Joy and Love.
There entertain him all the Saints above,
In solemn troops, and sweet societies,
That sing, and singing in their glory move,   180
And wipe the tears forever from his eyes.
Now, Lycidas, the shepherds weep no more;
Henceforth thou art the Genius° of the shore,   *guardian spirit*
In thy large recompense, and shalt be good
To all that wander in that perilous flood.   185

    Thus sang the uncouth° swain to th' oaks and rills,   *rustic (or*
While the still Morn went out with sandals gray;   *little-known)*
He touched the tender stops of various quills°,   *reeds of a*
With eager thought warbling his Doric lay: *shepherd's pipe*
And now the sun had stretched out all the hills,   190
And now was dropped into the western bay.
At last he rose, and twitched° his mantle blue: *donned*
Tomorrow to fresh woods and pastures new.

176. *unexpressive nuptial song*: inexpressibly beautiful song for the marriage feast of the Lamb (Revelation 19:9). 189. *Doric lay*: pastoral
poem. Doric is the dialect of Greek employed by Theocritus.

QUESTIONS AND EXERCISES

    1. With the aid of an encyclopedia or a handbook of classical myth-
ology (such as Bulfinch's *Mythology*, Edith Hamilton's *Mythology*, or
H. J. Rose's *Handbook of Greek Mythology*) learn more about the following myths or mythical figures and places to which Milton alludes:

Line 15   Sisters of the Sacred Well (Muses)
    16   seat of Jove (Mount Olympus)
    58   the Muse . . . that Orpheus bore (Calliope)
  61–63   (the death of Orpheus)
    75   Fury with the . . . shears (Atropos, one of the three
          Fates)
    77   Phoebus
    89   Herald of the Sea (Triton)
    90   Neptune
    96   Hippotades
   106   (Hyacinthus)
   132   Alpheus

Then reread Milton's poem. As a result of your familiarity with these
myths, what details become clear?
    2. Read the parable of the Good Shepherd (John 10:1–18). What re-
lationships does Milton draw between the Christian idea of the shepherd
and pastoral poetry?
    3. "With these trifling fictions [allusions to classical mythology],"
wrote Samuel Johnson about "Lycidas," "are mingled the most awful and
sacred truths, such as ought never to be polluted with such irreverend
combinations." Does this mingling of paganism and Christianity detract
from Milton's poem? Discuss.

TWELVE

EVALUATING POETRY: POEMS THAT FLY AND POEMS THAT FLOUNDER

1. IMPRECISION

"The bulk of English poetry is bad," a critic [1] has said, referring to all verse printed over the past six hundred years, not only that which survives in anthologies. As his comment reminds us, excellent poetry is at least as scarce as gold. Though the reader who seeks it for himself can expect to pan through much shale, such labor need not discourage him from prospecting. Only the naïve reader assumes, "This poem must be good, or else why would it appear in a leading magazine?" Only the reader whose mind is coasting in neutral says, "Who knows if this poem is good? Who cares? It all depends upon your point of view." Open-minded, skeptical, and alert, the critical reader will make his own evaluations.

To **evaluate** a poem means to judge it, to place a value on it in relation to other poems of similar length and kind. We say similar, for it would hardly be fair to an epigram to demand that it match an epic in grandeur and complexity. Much as a jeweler may estimate the worth of two diamonds by scratching them together, a means to evaluate two poems is to place them side by side and test them against each other. A poor poem is not in itself worth reading (unless, perhaps, it causes laughter unintentionally). Since, however, fine diamonds need weaker ones to scratch, this chapter will offer a few

[1] Christopher Adams in prefacing his anthology, *The Worst English Poets* (London, 1958).

220

clear-cut gems and a few clinkers, on the theory that in learning to judge for oneself it is well to begin with unmistakable specimens.

Why do we call some poems "bad"? We are not, certainly, talking about their moral implications. Rather, we mean that, for one or more of many possible reasons, the poem has failed to move us or engage our sympathies. Instead, it has made us doubt that the poet is in control of his language and his vision; perhaps it has aroused our antipathies or unwittingly appealed to our sense of the comic, though the poet is serious. Most often, such a poem ails from some kind of imprecision in its conception and execution. It may be inaccurate in its observation of people and nature; inexact in its diction; inept in its figures of speech; discordant in sound; inappropriate in its choice of rhythm; ill-fitted to its pattern; inadequate or excessive in its statement of feeling. And nearly always it reveals only a dim and distorted awareness of its possible effect upon a reader.

A poet whose work over the years wins him a devoted readership may have even his slightest and feeblest efforts collected; consequently, some lines in the canon of the most celebrated English poets may make us wonder, "How could he possibly have written this?" Wordsworth, Keats, Shelley, Whitman, and Browning are among the great whose weakest efforts can be painful; and lapses of awareness may occur even in poems that, taken entire, are excellent. To be unwilling to read them, though, would be as ill-advised as to decline a trip to Venice just because the Grand Canal is said to contain impurities. The seasoned reader of poetry thinks no less of Tennyson for having written, "Form, Form, Riflemen Form! . . . Look to your butts, and take good aims!" The collected works of a duller poet may contain no such lines of unconscious double-meaning, but neither do they contain, perhaps, any poem as good as "Ulysses." If the duller poet never had a spectacular failure, it may be because he never dared take risks.

We flatter ourselves if we think all imprecise poetry the work of centuries gone by. Poetry editors of current magazines find that about nine hundred out of a thousand unsolicited poems are, at a glance, unworthy of a second reading. Although the editor may have nightmares in which he ignorantly rejects the poems of some new Gerard Manley Hopkins or Emily Dickinson, he sends them back at once with a printed "thank you" slip, then turns to the hundred that look interesting. How does he winnow them so quickly? Often, inept poems fall into familiar categories. At one extreme is the poem written entirely in conventional diction, dimly echoing lines from Shakespeare, Wordsworth, and the Bible, but garbling them and flattening them out. Couched in a rhythm that ticks along like a metronome, this kind of poem shows no sign that its author has ever taken a hard look at any particular concrete objects that can be tasted, handled, and felt. It employs loosely and thoughtlessly the most abstract of words: *love, beauty, life, death, time, eternity.* Littered with old-fashioned contractions (*'tis, o'er, where'er*), it may end in a simple platitude or preachment, as if the poet expected us to profit from his wisdom and moral superiority. George Orwell's complaint against much contemporary writing (not only poetry) is applicable: "As soon as certain topics are raised" — and one thinks of such standard topics for poetry as spring, a first kiss, and stars — "the concrete melts into the abstract and no one seems able to think of turns of speech that are not hackneyed." Writers, Orwell charged, too often make their sentences out of tacked-together phrases "like the sections of a pre-fabricated hen-house." ² Versifiers often do likewise.

At the opposite extreme is the poem that displays no acquaintance with poetry of the past but manages, instead, to fabricate its own clichés. Slightly paraphrased, a manuscript once submitted to *The Paris Review* began:

> Vile
>
>   rottenflush
>
>   o   *— screaming —*
>   f CORPSEBLOOD!!   ooze
>
> STRANGLE my
>   *eyes . . .*   H E L L 's
>   O, ghastly   stench * * !!!

At most, such a work has only a private value. The writer has vented his personal frustrations upon words, instead of kicking stray dogs or smashing furniture. Poems offer, of course, many varieties of failure between these two extremes. Perhaps the least interesting failure of all is the poem good enough to be printed in many a literary quarterly: the poem that contains no glaring faults — nor anything great to inspire, to excite, or to please. "In poetry," said Ronsard, "the greatest vice is mediocrity."

Let us turn to some kinds of imprecision and consider how to recognize them. At the outset we must admit that some poems can be

² "Politics and the English Language," from *Shooting an Elephant and Other Essays* (New York, 1945).

said to succeed despite burdensome faults. But in general these faults are often symptoms of deep malady, of some weakness in the poem's basic conception. Perhaps the sound of words may clash with what a poem is saying, as in the jarring last word of this opening line of a tender lyric (author unknown, quoted by Richard Wilbur): "Come into the tent, my love, and close the flap." Perhaps a metaphor may fail by calling to mind more differences than similarities, such as Emily Dickinson's lines "Our lives are Swiss — / So still — so cool." A bad poem usually overshoots or falls short of its mark by the poet's thinking too little or too much. Thinking much, he contrives such an excess of ingenuity as that quoted by Alexander Pope in *Peri Bathous*, or *Of the Art of Sinking in Poetry*: a hounded stag who "Hears his own feet, and thinks they sound like more; / And fears the hind feet will o'ertake the fore." Or perhaps, his energy flagging, a simple idea will dawdle along for line after line after line. Even Wordsworth must have nodded when he wrote in "The Thorn": "And they had fixed the wedding-day, / The morning that must wed them both."

In a poem that has a rime scheme or a set line length, when all is well, pattern and structure move inseparably with the rest of their poem, the way a tiger's skin and bones move with the tiger. But sometimes, in such a poem that fails, the poet evidently has had difficulty in persuading his statements to fit a formal pattern. English poets have long felt free to invert word order for a special effect, but the poet having trouble keeping to a rime scheme may invert his syntax for no apparent reason but convenience. Needing a rime for *barge*, he ends his next line with *a policedog large* instead of *a large policedog*. Another sign of trouble is a profusion of adjectives. If a line of iambic pentameter reads, "Her lovely skin, like dear sweet white old silk," we suspect the poet of stuffing the line to make it long enough. Whenever two adjectives stand together in poetry or in prose, both need to be charged with meaning. Though the line may be heavy with adjectives, there is no padding in the conclusion of Matthew Arnold's "To Marguerite": "The unplumbed, salt, estranging sea."

In judging a poem, remember that excellence is never due simply to regularity and architectural symmetry. Variety is essential to the life of a poem; and a competent poet often will depart from a pattern, not because he finds it too difficult to follow, but because a departure helps him to say something new. There is satisfaction, said Robert Frost, in things not mechanically straight: "We enjoy the straight crookedness of a good walking stick."

Here is a small anthology of bad moments in poetry. For what reasons does each selection fail? In which instances do you attribute the failure to inappropriate sound or diction? To monotony of meter? To padding? To forced rime? To simple-mindedness or excessive ingenuity?

1. From Sir Richard Blackmore's *Paraphrase of the Book of Job*:

> I cannot stifle this gigantic woe,
> Nor on my raging grief a muzzle throw.

2. One alumnus writes an elegy for another (from Irving Bacheller, "To a Dead Classmate"):

> I love to tell of the last farewell, and this is the way it ran:
> "I don't know when I'll see you again — take care of
>   yourself, ol' man."
>
> Put the Beta pin upon his breast, with rosemary and rue,
> The cap and gown, the scarlet and brown and the symbol
>   of '82 . . .

3. A lover's lament (from Harry Edward Mills, *Select Sunflowers*):

> I see her in my fondest moods,
>   She haunts the parlor hallway;
> And yet her form my clasp eludes,
>   Her lips my kisses alway.

4. A suffering swain makes a vow (from "the poem of a young trades-man" quoted by Coleridge in *Biographia Literaria*):

> No more will I endure love's pleasing pain,
> Or round my heart's leg tie his galling chain.

5. From an elegy for Queen Victoria by one of her Indian subjects:

> Dust to dust, and ashes to ashes,
> Into the tomb the Great Queen dashes.

6. This poem, "Purple Grapes," given in its entirety, is attributed to an unknown student of creative writing at the University of Michigan:

> Purple grapes in the marketplace,
> Purple grapes at home
> Remind me of the pyramids
> And of the hills of Rome.

7. The opening lines of Alice Meynell's "The Shepherdess":

> She walks — the lady of my delight —
> A shepherdess of sheep.

8. From a juvenile poem of John Dryden, "Upon the Death of the Lord Hastings" (a victim of smallpox):

> Blisters with pride swelled; which through's flesh did sprout
> Like rose-buds, stuck i' th'lily-skin about.
> Each little pimple had a tear in it,
> To wail the fault its rising did commit . . .

9. A poet discusses the pity he feels for the newborn (from J. W. Scholl, *The Light-Bearer of Liberty*):

> Gooing babies, helpless pygmies,
> Who shall solve your Fate's enigmas?
> Who shall save you from Earth's stigmas?

10. A metaphor from Edgar A. Guest's "The Crucible of Life":

> Sacred and sweet is the joy that must come
> From the furnace of life when you've poured off the scum.

11. A stanza composed by Samuel Johnson as a deliberately bad example:

> I put my hat upon my head
> And walked into the Strand;
> And there I met another man
> Whose hat was in his hand.

12. A lover describes his lady (from Thomas Holley Chivers, "Rosalie Lee"):

> Many mellow Cydonian suckets,
>   Sweet apples, anthosmial, divine,
> From the ruby-rimmed beryline buckets,
>   Star-gemmed, lily-shaped, hyaline:
> Like the sweet golden goblet found growing
>   On the wild emerald cucumber-tree,
> Rich, brilliant, like chrysoprase glowing,
>   Was my beautiful Rosalie Lee.

13. Lines on a sick gipsy, author unknown (quoted in *The Stuffed Owl, an Anthology of Bad Verse*, D. B. Wyndham Lewis and Charles Lee, eds.):

> There we leave her,
> There we leave her,
> Far from where her swarthy kindred roam,
> In the Scarlet Fever,
> Scarlet Fever,
> Scarlet Fever Convalescent Home.

2. SENTIMENTALITY

Sentimentality is the failure of a writer who implies that he feels great emotion but who gives us insufficient grounds for sharing it. His emotion may be an anger greater than its object seems to call for, as in these lines to a girl who caused scandal (the exact nature of her act never being specified): "The gossip in each hall / Will curse your name . . . / Go! better cast yourself right down the falls!" [3] Or it may be an enthusiasm quite unwarranted by its subject: in *The Fleece* John Dyer temptingly describes the pleasures of life in a workhouse for the poor. The sentimental poet is especially prone to tenderness. Great tears fill his eyes at a glimpse of an aged grandmother sitting by a hearth. For all he knows, she may be the well-to-do manager of a casino in Las Vegas, who would be startled to find herself an object of pity; but the sentimentalist seems not to care to know much about the lady herself. He employs her as a general excuse for feeling

[3] Ali S. Hilmi, "The Preacher's Sermon," in *Verse at Random* (Larnaca, Cyprus, 1953).

maudlin. Any other conventional object will serve him as well: a faded valentine, the strains of an old song, a baby's cast-off pacifier. A celebrated instance of such emotional self-indulgence is "The Old Oaken Bucket," by Samuel Woodworth, a stanza of which goes:

> How sweet from the green, mossy brim to receive it,
> As, poised on the curb, it inclined to my lips!
> Not a full-blushing goblet could tempt me to leave it,
> Tho' filled with the nectar that Jupiter sips.
> And now, far removed from the loved habitation,
> The tear of regret will intrusively swell,
> As fancy reverts to my father's plantation,
> And sighs for the bucket that hung in the well.

After all, this is only a bucket. As a symbol, it might conceivably be made to hold the significance of the past and the speaker's regret at being caught in the destroying grip of time. But the staleness of the phrasing and imagery (Jove's nectar, "tear of regret") suggests that the speaker is not even seeing the actual physical bucket; and the tripping meter of the lines is inappropriate to an expression of tearful regret. Perhaps the poet's nostalgia is genuine. We need not doubt it; indeed, as the critic Bernard Waldrop has put it, "a bad poem is always utterly and profoundly sincere." But such sincerity is not that of a poet deeply committed to his craft. Sincere in his feelings, the sentimental poet is insincere in his art — otherwise, he might take the trouble to write a better poem or at least to burn the one he wrote. By the vagueness of his language and the monotony of his rhythms, Woodworth fails to persuade us that we ought to care. Wet-eyed and sighing for a bucket, he achieves not pathos but **bathos**: a description that can move us to laughter instead of tears.[4]

Tears, of course, can be shed for good reason. A piece of sentimentality is not to be confused with a well-wrought poem whose tone is tenderness. At first glance, the following poem by Burns might strike you as sentimental. If so, your suspicions are understandable, for it is a rare poet who can speak honestly or effectively on the theme

---

[4] *Bathos* in poetry can also mean an abrupt fall from the sublime to the trivial or incongruous. A sample, from Nicholas Rowe's play *The Fair Penitent:* "Is it the voice of thunder, or my father?" When, however, such a let-down from grandeur is used for a *desirable* effect of humor or contrast, it is usually called an **anti-climax**: as in Alexander Pope's lines on the queen's palace, "Here thou, great Anna! whom three realms obey, / Dost sometimes counsel take — and sometimes tea."

that love grows deeper as lovers grow old. Many a popular song-writer has seen the process of aging as valuable: "Darling, I am growing old, / Silver threads among the gold." According to such songs, to grow decrepit is a privilege. What is fresh in Burns's poem, however, is that no attempt is made to gloss over the ravages of age and the inevitability of death. The speaker expresses no self-pity, no comment *about* her feelings, only a simple account of what has befallen her and her John, and what is still to follow.

ROBERT BURNS (1759–1796)

'John Anderson my jo'

John Anderson my jo°, John,	*dear*
When we were first acquent°,	*acquainted*
Your locks were like the raven,	
Your bonny brow was brent°;	*unwrinkled* 4
But now your brow is beld°, John,	*bald*
Your locks are like the snaw;	
But blessings on your frosty pow°,	*head*
John Anderson my jo.	8
John Anderson my jo, John,	
We clamb the hill thegither;	
And mony a canty° day, John,	*happy*
We've had wi' ane anither:	12
Now we maun° totter down, John,	*must*
And hand in hand we'll go,	
And sleep thegither at the foot,	
John Anderson my jo.	16

EXERCISE TWO

Which of the following poems, if any, do you find sentimental? Which would you defend? Why? (Suggestion: At least one kind of evidence to look for is minute, detailed observation of physical objects. In a successful poem, the poet is likely at least occasionally to notice the world beyond his own skin; in a sentimental poem, this world is likely to be ignored while the poet contemplates his feelings.)

JOHN FREDERICK NIMS (b. 1914)

Love Poem

My clumsiest dear, whose hands shipwreck vases,
At whose quick touch all glasses chip and ring,
Whose palms are bulls in china, burs in linen,
And have no cunning with any soft thing   4

227

Except all ill-at-ease fidgeting people:
The refugee uncertain at the door
You make at home; deftly you steady
The drunk clambering on his undulant floor.   8

Unpredictable dear, the taxi drivers' terror,
Shrinking from far headlights pale as a dime
Yet leaping before red apoplectic streetcars —
Misfit in any space. And never on time.   12

A wrench in clocks and the solar system. Only
With words and people and love you move at ease.
In traffic of wit expertly manoeuvre
And keep us, all devotion, at your knees.   16

Forgetting your coffee spreading on our flannel,
Your lipstick grinning on our coat,
So gayly in love's unbreakable heaven
Our souls on glory of spilt bourbon float.   20

Be with me, darling, early and late. Smash glasses —
I will study wry music for your sake.
For should your hands drop white and empty
All the toys of the world would break.   24

J. W. SCHOLL (1869–1947?)

Betrothal

My pure one, my White Lily, whose chaste lips
    Drank morning dew, where life's cool shadows brood!
    My perfect flower of noble womanhood!
From out thy wanton sisterhood, where dips   4
With touch promiscuous the lustful bee
    Just prizing loveliness for what it yields
    When rifled of the treasure that it shields,
I chose thee, spotless one, to cherish thee   8
Less for ephemeral uses than to fill
    Life with perennial sweetness. Love, place thou
    With thy pure lips a seal upon my brow
To keep my thoughts from straying into ill!   12
    Chasten my soul till life's realities
    Accord with thy soul's idealities!

IRVING LAYTON (b. 1912)

The Bull Calf

The thing could barely stand. Yet taken
from his mother and the barn smells
he still impressed with his pride,
with the promise of sovereignty in the way
his head moved to take us in.   5
The fierce sunlight tugging the maize from the ground
licked at his shapely flanks.
He was too young for all that pride.
I thought of the deposed Richard II.

"No money in bull calves," Freeman had said.   10
The visiting clergyman rubbed the nostrils
now snuffing pathetically at the windless day.
"A pity," he sighed.
My gaze slipped off his hat toward the empty sky
that circled over the black knot of men,   15
over us and the calf waiting for the first blow.

Struck,
the bull calf drew in his thin forelegs
as if gathering strength for a mad rush . . .
tottered . . . raised his darkening eyes to us,   20
and I saw we were at the far end
of his frightened look, growing smaller and smaller
till we were only the ponderous mallet
that flicked his bleeding ear
and pushed him over on his side, stiffly,   25
like a block of wood.

Below the hill's crest
the river snuffled on the improvised beach.
We dug a deep pit and threw the dead calf into it.
It made a wet sound, a sepulchral gurgle,   30
as the warm sides bulged and flattened.
Settled, the bull calf lay as if asleep,
one foreleg over the other,
bereft of pride and so beautiful now,
without movement, perfectly still in the cool pit,   35
I turned away and wept.

D. H. LAWRENCE (1885–1930)

Piano

Softly, in the dusk, a woman is singing to me;
Taking me back down the vista of years, till I see
A child sitting under the piano, in the boom of the tingling
    strings
And pressing the small, poised feet of a mother who smiles   4
    as she sings.

In spite of myself, the insidious mastery of song
Betrays me back, till the heart of me weeps to belong
To the old Sunday evenings at home, with winter outside
And hymns in the cozy parlor, the tinkling piano our guide.   8

So now it is vain for the singer to burst into clamor
With the great black piano appassionato. The glamor
Of childish days is upon me, my manhood is cast
Down in the flood of rememberance, I weep like a child   12
    for the past.

ALFRED, LORD TENNYSON (1809–1892)

'Tears, idle tears'

    Tears, idle tears, I know not what they mean,
Tears from the depth of some divine despair
Rise in the heart, and gather to the eyes,
In looking on the happy autumn-fields,
And thinking of the days that are no more.   5

    Fresh as the first beam glittering on a sail,
That brings our friends up from the under-world,
Sad as the last which reddens over one
That sinks with all we love below the verge;
So sad, so fresh, the days that are no more.   10

    Ah, sad and strange as in dark summer dawns
The earliest pipe of half-awakened birds
To dying ears, when unto dying eyes
The casement slowly grows a glimmering square;
So sad, so strange, the days that are no more.   15

    Dear as remembered kisses after death,
And sweet as those by hopeless fancy feigned
On lips that are for others; deep as love,
Deep as first love, and wild with all regret;
O Death in Life, the days that are no more.   20

230

3. PARODY

A sentimental poem is particularly vulnerable to **parody**: a kind of literary composition in which one writer pokes fun at another by imitating him. A parody implies some definite attitude toward its original. In skilled hands, it can be a terse, forceful, and detailed evaluation. Generally the parodist imitates the characteristic tone, form, diction and other features of the original; but applies them to ludicrously inappropriate matter, as in E. B. White's take-off on Walt Whitman, "A Classic Waits for Me," which employs the rhetoric of the chest-thumping bard in a pledge of allegiance to a mail-order book club.[5] Rather than fling abuse at his original, the skilled parodist imitates it with understanding, perhaps with affection. The many inadequate parodies of T. S. Eliot's professedly obscure poem *The Waste Land* show the parodists mocking what they do not understand: their effect is not to illuminate the original but to belittle it. Parody can be aimed at poems good and bad; but there are poems of such splendor and dignity that no parodist seems able to touch them without looking like a small dog defiling a cathedral, and poems so illiterate that parody would be squandered on them. In the following original by T. E. Brown, what failings does the parodist jump upon? (*God wot* is an archaism for "God knows.")

T. E. BROWN (1830–1897)
My Garden

A garden is a lovesome thing,
  God wot!
Rose plot,
Fringed pool,
Ferned grot —
The veriest school
Of peace; and yet the fool
Contends that God is not —
Not God! in gardens! when
  the eve is cool?
Nay, but I have a sign;
'Tis very sure God walks in
  mine.

J. A. LINDON (fl. 1959)
My *Garden*

A garden is a *lovesome* thing?
  What rot!
Weed plot,
Scum pool,
Old pot,
Snail-shiny stool
In pieces; yet the fool
Contends that snails are not —
Not snails! in gardens! when
  the eve is cool?
Nay, but I see their trails!
'Tis very sure *my* garden's full
  of snails!

[5] For this and other specimens, see the anthology *Parodies*, Dwight Macdonald, ed. (New York, 1960). Macdonald's dedicatory note to this volume, by the way, is a parody on dedications:

> To my dear sons
> **Michael and Nicholas**
> without whose school bills
> this anthology would not have been made

HUGH KINGSMILL [HUGH KINGSMILL LUNN] (1889–1949)

'What, still alive at twenty-two?'

What, still alive at twenty-two,
A clean, upstanding chap like you?
Sure, if your throat 'tis hard to slit,
Slit your girl's, and swing for it. 4

Like enough, you won't be glad
When they come to hang you, lad:
But bacon's not the only thing
That's cured by hanging from a string. 8

So, when the spilt ink of the night
Spreads o'er the blotting-pad of light,
Lads whose job is still to do
Shall whet their knives, and think of you. 12

QUESTIONS

1. A. E. Housman considered this the best of many parodies of his
poetry. Read his poems in this book, particularly "To an Athlete Dying
Young" and 'Terence, this is stupid stuff' (pp. 316–319). What characteristics of theme, form, and language does Kingsmill's parody convey?

2. What does Kingsmill exaggerate?

WILLIAM WORDSWORTH (1770–1850)

'The sun has long been set'

The sun has long been set,
    The stars are out by twos and threes,
The little birds are piping yet
    Among the bushes and trees;
There's a cuckoo, and one or two thrushes, 5
And a far-off wind that rushes,
And a sound of water that gushes,
And the cuckoo's sovereign cry
Fills all the hollow of the sky.
    Who would go "parading" 10
In London, "and masquerading,"
On such a night of June
With that beautiful soft half-moon,
And all these innocent blisses?
On such a night as this is! 15

232

J. K. STEPHEN (1859–1892)

A *Sonnet*

Two voices are there: one is of the deep;
It learns the storm-cloud's thunderous melody,
Now roars, now murmurs with the changing sea,
Now bird-like pipes, now closes soft in sleep: 4
And one is of an old half-witted sheep
Which bleats articulate monotony,
And indicates that two and one are three,
That grass is green, lakes damp, and mountains steep: 8
And, Wordsworth, both are thine: at certain times
Forth from the heart of thy melodious rhymes,
The form and pressure of high thoughts will burst:
At other times — good Lord! I'd rather be   12
Quite unacquainted with the ABC
Than write such hopeless rubbish as thy worst.

QUESTIONS

1. Evaluate Wordsworth's poem. Specifically, what in the poem leads you to your opinion?
2. Stephen's parody echoes Wordsworth's "Thought of a Briton on the Subjugation of Switzerland," which begins: "Two voices are there; one is of the sea, / One of the mountains; each a mighty voice. . ." Of what other poems by Wordsworth are you reminded?
3. Considering not only 'The sun has long been set' but other poems by Wordsworth in this book, comment on the justice or injustice of Stephen's criticism.
4. Wordsworth, according to Dwight Macdonald, was the most frequently parodied serious poet of the nineteenth century. What qualities of his work — not necessarily defects — might a parodist find attractive?

EXERCISE THREE

Write a parody of Walt Whitman, Emily Dickinson, Robert Frost, or any other modern poet whose work interests you and whose forms you feel yourself skillful enough to imitate. In preparation, read all the poet's work included in this book; see also his collected poems; then carefully evaluate the poet's strengths and weaknesses. You may find it simplest to choose one particular poem as the model for your parody, or you may wish to echo many poems. In either case, it might be helpful to select a characteristic subject or theme.

233

JULIA A. MOORE (1847–1920)

Little Libbie

One more little spirit to Heaven has flown,
  To dwell in that mansion above,
Where dear little angels, together roam,
  In God's everlasting love.   4

One little flower has withered and died,
  A bud near ready to bloom,
Its life on earth is marked with pride;
  Oh, sad it should die so soon.   8

Sweet little Libbie, that precious flower
  Was a pride in her parents' home,
They miss their little girl *every* hour,
  Those friends that are left to mourn.   12

Her sweet silvery voice no more is heard
  In the home where she once roamed;
Her place is *vacant* around the hearth,
  Where her friends are mourning lone.   16

They are mourning the loss of a little girl,
  With black eyes and auburn hair,
She was a treasure to them in this world,
  This beautiful child so fair.   20

One morning in April, a short time ago,
  Libbie was active and gay;
Her Saviour called her, she had to go,
  Ere the close of that pleasant day.   24

While eating dinner, this dear little child
  Was choked on a piece of beef.
Doctors came, tried their skill awhile,
  But none could give relief.   28

She was ten years of age, I am told,
  And in school stood very high.
Her little form now the earth enfolds,
  In her embrace it must ever lie.   32

Her friends and schoolmates will not forget
  Little Libbie that is no more;
She is waiting on the shining step,
  To welcome home friends once more.   36

234

HILAIRE BELLOC (1870–1953)

Henry King

The Chief Defect of Henry King
Was chewing little bits of String.
At last he swallowed some which tied
Itself in ugly Knots inside.
Physicians of the Utmost Fame   5
Were called at once; but when they came
They answered, as they took their Fees,
"There is no Cure for this Disease.
Henry will very soon be dead."
His Parents stood about his Bed   10
Lamenting his Untimely Death,
When Henry, with his Latest Breath,
Cried — "Oh, my Friends, be warned by me,
That Breakfast, Dinner, Lunch and Tea
Are all the Human Frame requires . . ."   15
With that the Wretched Child expires.

QUESTIONS

1. Mrs. Moore, who called herself "The Sweet Singer of Michigan,"
anticipated some of the techniques of Ogden Nash (pp. 94–95), but apparently she was in earnest. How does the tone of "Little Libbie" compare
with that of "Henry King"?
2. In Mrs. Moore's piece, how many varieties of failure can you list?
3. How would you argue with a critic who condemned "Henry King"
on the grounds that its subject cannot possibly be comic?

ANONYMOUS (English; about 1900)

'O Moon'

O Moon, when I gaze on thy beautiful face,
Careering along through the boundaries of space,
The thought has often come into my mind
If I ever shall see thy glorious behind.

QUESTIONS

1. Which words seem chosen with too little awareness of their denotations or connotations?
2. Sir Edmund Gosse, the English critic (1849–1928), offered this
quatrain as the work of his maidservant, but there is reason to suspect him
of having written it himself. If, having first thought it the work of a
naïve person, you later discovered the piece to have been deliberately contrived, would your evaluation of it be affected? If so, how?

GRACE TREASONE (fl. 1963)

Life

Life is like a jagged tooth
that cuts into your heart;
fix the tooth and save the root,
and laughs, not tears, will start.

WILLIAM ERNEST HENLEY (1849–1903)

'Madam Life's a piece in bloom'

Madam Life's a piece in bloom
    Death goes dogging everywhere:
She's the tenant of the room,
    He's the ruffian on the stair.   4

You shall see her as a friend,
    You shall bilk him once or twice;
But he'll trap you in the end,
    And he'll stick you for her price.   8

With his kneebones at your chest,
    And his knuckles in your throat,
You would reason — plead — protest!
    Clutching at her petticoat;   12

But she's heard it all before,
    Well she knows you've had your fun,
Gingerly she gains the door,
    And your little job is done.   16

QUESTIONS

1. Try to paraphrase the two preceding poems. What is the theme of
each?
2. Which statement of theme do you find the more convincing? Why?
3. Which poem is the more consistent in working out its metaphor?

EXERCISE FOUR

Here are three poems roughly similar in theme and dramatic situation.
Compare them and try to describe their relative effectiveness. In any of
them, is there a skillful flight, or a definite floundering? If so, how do you
account for it?

ALEXANDER KERR, LITT. D. (c. 1855–1914)

Mary and Her Dead Canary

SAD WORDS TO A JOVIAL AIR

I weep when the gay are around me,
I'm sad when my slumbers have bound me;
And perchance, ye'll smile to know
That in dreams I often go
    To the weeping willow drooping, where my Jimmie lies so   5
    low.

O, the robin's songs in the wildwood!
They were love in the heart of my childhood.
Yet far sweeter than they
Was the music of the lay
    That my Jimmie used to sing, till his life fled away.   10

It was sad, oh, so fondly to love him,
And to look while the earth fell above him.
Thus, my Jimmie, will it be,
As it ever is with me,
    That the things I love the dearest, best, will wither first,   15
    like thee.

Is there one, who hath tears, one only,
Who could weep for my sorrow so lonely?
Such a friend I'd fondly crave,
Who could feel the griefs I have,
    And would with me shed a tear-drop on my dead Canary's   20
    grave.

JOHN CROWE RANSOM (b. 1888)

Janet Waking

Beautifully Janet slept
Till it was deeply morning. She woke then
And thought about her dainty-feathered hen,
To see how it had kept.   4

One kiss she gave her mother,
Only a small one gave she to her daddy
Who would have kissed each curl of his shining baby;
No kiss at all for her brother.   8

"Old Chucky, Old Chucky!" she cried,
Running on little pink feet upon the grass
To Chucky's house, and listening. But alas,
Her Chucky had died.   12

It was a transmogrifying° bee   *change-working*
Came droning down on Chucky's old bald head
And sat and put the poison. It scarcely bled,
But how exceedingly   16

And purply did the knot
Swell with the venom and communicate
Its rigor! Now the poor comb stood up straight
But Chucky did not.   20

So there was Janet
Kneeling on the wet grass, crying her brown hen
(Translated far beyond the daughters of men)
To rise and walk upon it.   24

And weeping fast as she had breath
Janet implored us, "Wake her from her sleep!"
And would not be instructed in how deep
Was the forgetful kingdom of death.   28

GERARD MANLEY HOPKINS (1844–1889)

Spring and Fall

TO A YOUNG CHILD

Márgarét, are you gríeving
Over Goldengrove unleaving°?   *shedding its leaves*
Leáves, líke the things of man, you
With your fresh thoughts care for, can you?
Ah! ás the heart grows older   5
It will come to such sights colder
By and by, nor spare a sigh
Though worlds of wanwood leafmeal lie;
And yet you wíll weep and know why.
Now no matter, child, the name: 10
Sórrow's spríngs áre the same.
Nor mouth had, no nor mind, expressed
What heart heard of, ghost° guessed: *spirit*
It ís the blight man was born for,
It is Margaret you mourn for.   15

238

THIRTEEN

EVALUATING POETRY: ON KNOWING EXCELLENCE

How can we distinguish an excellent poem from any other? Aware that no critic has yet proposed a wholly satisfactory answer, let us try to find at least a partial one. To give reasons for excellence in poetry is harder than to give reasons for failure in poetry (so often due to familiar, old-hat sorts of imprecision and sentimentality). A bad poem tends to be stereotyped; an excellent poem, unique. In judging either, we can have no absolute pre-existing specifications. A poem is not a simple mechanism like an electric toaster that an inspector in a factory can test by a check-off list. It has to be judged on the basis of what it evidently is trying to be and how well it succeeds in its effort.

To judge a poem we first have to understand it. At least, we need to understand it *almost* all the way; there is, to be sure, such a poem as Hopkins' "Windhover" (p. 316), which most readers probably would call excellent even though its meaning is still being debated. While it is a good idea to give a poem at least a couple of considerate readings before judging it, sometimes our very first encounter with a poem starts turning into an act of evaluation. Moving along into the poem, becoming more deeply involved in it as we go along, we may begin forming an opinion of it. In general, the more a poem contains for us to understand, the more rewarding we are likely to find it. This does not mean that an obscure and highly demanding poem is always to be preferred to a relatively simple and accessible one. Difficult poems may be pretentious and incoherent, but there is something to be said for the poem complicated enough to leave us something to discover on our fifteenth reading (unlike most clerihews, which yield their all at a single look). Here is such a poem: one not readily fathomed and exhausted. (Byzantium was the capital of the Byzantine Empire, the city now called Istanbul. Yeats means, though, not merely the physical city: Byzantium is also a name for his conception of paradise.)

WILLIAM BUTLER YEATS (1865–1939)

Sailing to Byzantium

That is no country for old men. The young
In one another's arms, birds in the trees
— Those dying generations — at their song,
The salmon-falls, the mackerel-crowded seas,   4
Fish, flesh, or fowl, commend all summer long
Whatever is begotten, born, and dies.
Caught in that sensual music all neglect
Monuments of unaging intellect.   8

An aged man is but a paltry thing,
A tattered coat upon a stick, unless
Soul clap its hands and sing, and louder sing
For every tatter in its mortal dress,   12
Nor is there singing school but studying
Monuments of its own magnificence;
And therefore I have sailed the seas and come
To the holy city of Byzantium.   16

O sages standing in God's holy fire
As in the gold mosaic of a wall,
Come from the holy fire, perne in a gyre°,   *spin down in a spiral*
And be the singing-masters of my soul.   20
Consume my heart away; sick with desire
And fastened to a dying animal
It knows not what it is; and gather me
Into the artifice of eternity.   24

Once out of nature I shall never take
My bodily form from any natural thing,
But such a form as Grecian goldsmiths make
Of hammered gold and gold enameling   28
To keep a drowsy Emperor awake;
Or set upon a golden bough to sing
To lords and ladies of Byzantium
Of what is past, or passing, or to come.   32

Though the "salmon falls" suggest Yeats's native Ireland, the poem (as we find out for sure in line 25) is about escaping from the entire natural world. If the poet desires this escape, then probably the *country* mentioned in the opening line is no political nation but the cycle of birth and death in which human beings are trapped; and, indeed, the poet says his heart is "fastened to a dying animal." Imaginary landscapes, it would seem, are merging with the historical Byzantium. Lines 17–18 refer to mosaic images, adornments of the Byzantine cathedral of St. Sophia, in which the figures of saints are inlaid against backgrounds of gold. The clockwork bird of the last stanza is also a reference to something actual. Yeats noted: "I have read somewhere that in the Emperor's palace at Byzantium was a tree made of gold and silver, and artificial birds that sang." This description of the role the poet would seek — that of a changeless, immortal singer — directs us back to the earlier references to music and singing. Taken all together, they point toward the central metaphor of the poem: the craft of writing poetry is a kind of singing. One kind of monument to the soul's magnificence (and perhaps it is worth noting that Yeats entertained the idea that there exists one soul for the entire race) is a great poem. To study masterpieces of poetry is the only "singing school" — the only way to learn to write a poem.

We have no more than skimmed through a few of this poem's suggestions: enough to show that, out of allusion and imagery, Yeats has woven at least one elaborate metaphor. Surely one thing the poem achieves is that, far from merely puzzling us, it makes us aware of relationships between what a man can imagine and his physical world. There is the statement that a man's heart is bound to the body that perishes; and yet it is possible for him to see his consciousness for a moment independent of flesh, to sing with joy at the very fact that his body is crumbling from under him. Expressing a similar view of mortality, the Japanese artist Hokusai has shown a withered tree letting go of its few remaining leaves, while under it, two gray-beards shake with laughter. Like Hokusai's view, that of Yeats is by no means simple. Much of the power of his poem comes from the physical terms with which he states the ancient quarrel between body and spirit, body being a "tattered coat upon a stick." That so vigorous a mind and so piercing an eye are in this poem, alive and moving, is a reason for its excellence.

There is all the difference in the world between the work of the poet whose eye is on the living thing and whose mind is awake and passionate, and that of the slovenly poet whose dull eye and sleepy mind focus on nothing more than some book he long ago read hastily. The former writes a poem as if he would die if he did not; the latter, as if he thinks it might be a nice idea to write something.

241

Yeats has achieved, too, the excellence of a thing that has — as Thomas Aquinas said in a famous definition of beauty — "wholeness, harmony, and radiance." His poem is one; it is consistent and its parts get along with one another; it "radiates" a certain emotional intensity. Its unity comes from its *structure* (discussed on pp. 190–193), composed of images that relate to each other (to recall just one such relationship: "dying generations" of birds, "dying animal" of the poet's body, and changeless and supernatural golden bird in Byzantium — all having evident similarities, and all pointing to the central metaphor, "the artifice of eternity"). There is coherent form, too, in the stanza pattern that repeats itself and in the basic rhythm of iambic pentameter. These things cannot in themselves make a poem excellent, but they help. "Sailing to Byzantium" is interesting all the way through; it is not like a poem that has — in Pope's words — "One simile, that solitary shines / In the dry desert of a thousand lines." Yeats's whole poem is a metaphor, with further metaphors as its tributaries. "Only emotion endures," his friend Ezra Pound said of poetry. Yeats's poem should endure because, reading it, we experience some of its emotional intensity. Being human and aware that we too are perishing, we can be stirred by the prayer: "Consume my heart away, sick with desire / And fastened to a dying animal . . ." (Either you feel this emotion or you do not. If you do not, try another poem. No *reasons* to be moved by this one can possibly pick you up and shake you.)

Yeats's poem is an excellent lyric — the match, some think, of any in English. It could be argued that it is inferior to an epic (to *Paradise Lost*, say, or *The Iliad*), but this is to lead us into a different argument: whether certain genres are inherently better than others. Such an argument is likely to lead nowhere. Evidently Milton's masterpiece has more size, range, variety, matter — in fact more of nearly everything — than a limerick of Edward Lear. But this does not mean that limericks cannot be admirable; any poem — a lyric, or an epic, or a limerick — ought to be judged by how well it fulfills the design of whatever it undertakes to be. God, who created both fleas and whales, pronounced all good: fleas (like man-made epigrams) have no reason to feel inferior.

So far, we have considered a few qualities that make for excellence in a poem: richness of meaning and suggestion, a manifest vigor of mind and eye, unity, emotional intensity. It ought to be clear that, while an excellent poem may be expected to have these qualities, they can be sought only by thoughtful, careful, sympathetic readers. Our standards are subjective ones. We can never take them as yardsticks that poems can be pushed up against. Evidently there is no use in trying to judge poems by how much emotion they communicate. How could we measure such emotion? At a large university, so the story goes, a psychologist once invented an apparatus to register the emotional reactions of a person reading a poem. Somewhat like a lie detector, it recorded pulsebeat, nervous twitches, respiration. The psychologist's intent was to evaluate poems by claiming that "Sailing to Byzantium" scored 200 on the emotion-meter, while "Ozymandias" rated only 170. His grand design was shattered when a subject (whose father, incidentally, was a vice-president of General Cement) caused the needle to break 400. While reading a poem on a newspaper page, the subject's eye had fallen upon an adjoining column. There lay what the apparatus declared the greatest poem ever written: "General Cement Corporation today declared bankruptcy."

"Sailing to Byzantium" has a theme that is significant for all of us, the wish of mortal man for immortality. Most excellent poems, it might be argued, have significant themes; but such a theme cannot be demanded of a poem any more than emotion can be, and its presence is not enough to render a poem excellent. Very bad poems can have significant themes; for instance, Julia A. Moore's "Little Libby" expresses grief at the death of a child and the comfort of believing in her immortality. Robert Herrick has written poems on the same theme, which are excellent. It is not theme alone that makes a good poem but how well the theme is stated and developed.

EXERCISE ONE

Here are two pieces of verse expressing a similar theme. Try to state the theme as you find it in each one. Which piece contains more of the qualities of excellent poetry? Decide whether the other is bad or whether it may be praised for achieving something different.

ARTHUR GUITERMAN (1871–1943)

On the Vanity of Earthly Greatness

The tusks that clashed in mighty brawls
Of mastodons, are billiard balls.

The sword of Charlemagne the Just
Is ferric oxide, known as rust.

4

The grizzly bear whose potent hug
Was feared by all, is now a rug.

Great Caesar's bust is on the shelf,
And I don't feel so well myself.

8

PERCY BYSSHE SHELLEY (1792–1822)

Ozymandias

> I met a traveler from an antique land
> Who said: Two vast and trunkless legs of stone
> Stand in the desert. Near them, on the sand,
> Half sunk, a shattered visage lies, whose frown,
> And wrinkled lip, and sneer of cold command,   5
> Tell that its sculptor well those passions read
> Which yet survive, stamped on these lifeless things,
> The hand that mocked° them and the heart that fed;   *imitated*
> And on the pedestal these words appear:
> "My name is Ozymandias, king of kings: 10
> Look on my works, ye Mighty, and despair!"
> Nothing beside remains. Round the decay
> Of that colossal wreck, boundless and bare
> The lone and level sands stretch far away.

Some people believe that they can tell the excellence of a poem by the moral uplift of its message. By this standard, Longfellow's "A Psalm of Life" is certainly notable for its cheerful exhortations, "Life is real! Life is earnest!" and for its conclusion,

> Let us, then, be up and doing,
>   With a heart for any fate;
> Still achieving, still pursuing,
>   Learn to labor and to wait.

Such a view was more common a century ago than today. Recent critics have felt that Longfellow elsewhere wrote much better poetry. Their complaint is not that a poem must not preach but that a poem must do much more besides. "We must love one another or die," said W. H. Auden in "September 1, 1939." "The woods are lovely, dark and deep, / But I have promises to keep," said Robert Frost. No less than Longfellow's "Life is real! Life is earnest!" these statements are didactic. In their contexts, however, Auden and Frost's lines — unlike Longfellow's — work with all the emotional power and richness of connotation that we expect of poetry.

Akin to the fallacy that poems have to preach is the fallacy that poems must fulfill a political purpose. Literature, according to some Marxist theorists, is valuable insofar as it contributes to social revolution. As crudely applied by some Red Chinese commissars, this may mean that a good poem is one that inspires factory workers to turn out more tractors. A critic who applies the standard of political usefulness — as does Vernon L. Parrington in his socially oriented history of American literature, *Main Currents in American Thought* — may have a cogent argument. But to judge a poem by its political value is to assume that the function of a poem lies somewhere outside itself and outside the immediate experience of the reader. In this view, the worth of poetry is finally measurable by some later effect it has on us. What this book assumes is that the poem's worth is on the page, at present. Often, it is true, we may improve our understanding of a poem and the quality of our response to it by reading it again later, by continuing to think about it. But if we do so, it is we, not the poems, that change and become better.

The best poems, like "Sailing to Byzantium," may offer a kind of religious experience. (This does not mean that reading poetry has to be a substitute for church- or temple-going). In this sixth decade of the twentieth century, some of us may rarely set foot on grass. Whizzing down four-lane superhighways, we observe grass in the distance and are far removed from any sense of immediate contact with the natural world. In a way, our cities are to us as anthills are to ants, as Frost reminds us in "Departmental." No less than anthills, they are "natural" structures. But the "unnatural" world of school or business is, as Wordsworth says, too much with us. Locked in the shells of our ambitions, our self-esteem, we forget our very real kinship to the far stars and the sea. We fabricate intellectual self-justifications. But a great poem shocks us into another order of perception. It helps us know ourselves, but it does more. Perhaps it may even offer a momentary sense of some everlasting unity.

While no one takes language more seriously than a good poet, perhaps it is true that a good poem is one that points beyond words to something still more essential. The best poem ushers us into an experience so profoundly moving that we feel (to quote King Lear) "cut to the brain." A bad or indifferent poem fails to do so. In such a poem, words are all there is.

We make judgments, of course, while admitting that readers of the future may reverse them; many of us no longer hold, for instance, an opinion of Whitman like the following, written by one of his contemporaries:

> WALT WHITMAN (1819–1892), by some regarded as a great poet; by others, as no poet at all. Most of his so-called poems are mere catalogues of things, without meter or rime, but in a few more regular poems and in lines here and there he is grandly poetical, as in "O Captain! My Captain!" [1]

[1] J. Willis Westlake, A.M., in *Common-school Literature, English and American, with Several Hundred Extracts to be Memorized* (Philadelphia, 1898).

There is nothing to do but commit ourselves and judge, and, if need be, let time erase our error. In a sense, all readers of poetry are constantly re-examining the judgments of the past just by choosing the poems they care to go on reading. By choosing well, we too take part in the continuing life of excellent poetry.

EDWARD TAYLOR (1642?–1729)

The Preface

Infinity, when all things it beheld
In nothing, and of nothing all did build,
Upon what base was fixed the lathe wherein
He turned this globe, and riggled it so trim?
Who blew the bellows of His furnace vast?   5
Or held the mold wherein the world was cast?
Who laid its corner stone? Or whose command?
Where stand the pillars upon which it stands?
Who laced and filletted the earth so fine,
With rivers like green ribbons smaragdine°?   *emerald-* 10
Who made the seas its selvage, and it locks   *colored*
Like a quilt ball within a silver box?
Who spread its canopy? Or curtains spun?
Who in this bowling alley bowled the sun?
Who made it always when it rises set   15
To go at once both down, and up to get?
Who th' curtain rods made for this tapestry?
Who hung the twinkling lanthorns in the sky?
Who? who did this? or who is He? Why, know
Its only Might Almighty this did do.   20
His hand hath made this noble work which stands
His glorious handiwork not made by hands;
Who spake all things from nothing; and with ease
Can speak all things to nothing, if He please;
Whose little finger at His pleasure can   25
Out mete ten thousand worlds with half a span;
Whose Might Almighty can by half a looks
Root up the rocks and rock the hills by th' roots;
Can take this mighty world up in His hand,
And shake it like a squitchen° or a wand;   *twig*   30
Whose single frown will make the heavens shake
Like as an aspen leaf the wind makes quake;
Oh! what a Might is this Whose single frown
Doth shake the world as it would shake it down?
Which all from nothing fet°, from nothing, all; *fetched* 35
Hath all on nothing set, lets nothing fall;

246

Gave all to nothing Man indeed, whereby
Through nothing Man all might Him glorify;
In nothing then embossed the brightest gem
More precious than all preciousness in them.   40
But nothing Man did throw down all by sin
And darkenèd that lightsome gem in him;
    That now his brightest diamond is grown
    Darker by far than any coalpit stone.

The Preface. This poem stands as preface to a group of Taylor's poems
entitled *God's Determinations*. Lines 3–4 borrow metaphors from the
craft of pottery (and perhaps carpentry); lines 9–11, from dressmaking.
3. *lathe:* a potter's wheel (or possibly a wood-worker's lathe). 4. *riggled:*
marked with a ring-like mark or groove, a finishing touch (as the maker's
imprint might have been placed on a pot). 11. *selvage:* the border on a
piece of fabric, put on to prevent unraveling.

QUESTIONS

    1. Is *locks* (line 11) a noun or a verb? Is *nothing* a noun or an ad-
jective in line 37? In line 38?
    2. Explain the analogy in the last four lines. What is the *gem?*
    3. This poem has been called the American "Tyger." Why? Evaluate
it in relation to Blake's poem (p. 288). Which poem, Taylor's or Blake's,
seems more closely organized around one basic metaphor? (Do you think
a poem has to be so organized in order to be excellent?)
    4. An anthologist once printed this poem with lines 15 through 44
omitted. Can the first fourteen lines stand as a self-contained poem? In
what respects does the poem improve by being read in its entirety?

CARL SANDBURG (b. 1878)

Fog

    The fog comes
on little cat feet.
It sits looking
over harbor and city
on silent haunches
and then moves on.

QUESTION

    In lines 15–22 of "The Love Song of J. Alfred Prufrock" (pp. 302–
306), T. S. Eliot also likens fog to a cat. Compare Sandburg's lines and
Eliot's. Which passage tells us more about fogs and cats?

EXERCISE TWO

    Here are two poems no longer in the mainstream of living poetry (that
is, rarely reprinted in anthologies), with some questions to help in examining them. Decide whether their merits commend them to be restored
or whether the curtain of time has been rung down on them mercifully.

CHARLES SPRAGUE (1791–1874)

To My Cigar

Yes, social friend, I love thee well,
   In learned doctors' spite;
Thy clouds all other clouds dispel,
   And lap me in delight.   4

What though they tell, with phizzes° long,   *faces*
   My years are sooner passed?
I would reply, with reason strong,
   They're sweeter while they last.   8

And oft, mild friend, to me thou art
   A monitor, though still;
Thou speak'st a lesson to my heart,
   Beyond the preacher's skill.   12

Thou'rt like the man of worth, who gives
   To goodness every day,
The odor of whose virtues lives
   When he has passed away.   16

When, in the lonely evening hour,
   Attended but by thee,
O'er history's varied page I pore,
   Man's fate in thine I see.   20

Oft as thy snowy column grows,
   Then breaks and falls away,
I trace how mighty realms thus rose,
   Thus tumbled to decay.   24

A while, like thee, earth's masters burn
   And smoke and fume around,
And then, like thee, to ashes turn,
   And mingle with the ground.   28

Life's but a leaf adroitly rolled,
   And time's the wasting breath,
That late or early, we behold,
   Gives all to dusty death.   32

From beggar's frieze to monarch's robe,
   One common doom is passed:
Sweet nature's works, the swelling globe,
   Must all burn out at last.   36

And what is he who smokes thee now? —
   A little moving heap,

That soon like thee to fate must bow,
  With thee in dust must sleep.   40

But though thine ashes downward go,
. Thine essence rolls on high;
Thus, when my body must lie low,
  My soul shall cleave the sky.   44

To My Cigar. Text from Rufus W. Griswold, ed., *The Poets and Poetry of America* (Philadelphia, 1845). In this large anthology Sprague's portrait appears on the frontispiece along with those of Longfellow, William Cullen Bryant, Fitz-Greene Halleck, and Richard Henry Dana. Sprague was a Boston banker.

QUESTIONS

 1. What figure of speech occurs in the opening line?
 2. To what things, in succession, is the cigar compared?
 3. What is the tone of this poem? How is it indicated?
 4. In some respects, "To My Cigar" may remind you of a kind of poetry prevalent in the seventeenth century (for instance, that of Donne, Marvell, and Edward Taylor). Is Sprague in the same league? What are the resemblances?

JOSEPH SKIPSEY (1832–1903)

Get Up!

"Get up!" the caller calls, "Get up!"
  And in the dead of night,
To win the bairns their bite and sup,
  I rise a weary wight.   4

My flannel dudden° donned, thrice o'er   *clothing*
  My birds are kissed, and then
I with a whistle shut the door
  I may not ope again.   8

Get Up! Text from John Heath-Stubbs and David Wright, eds., *The Forsaken Garden* (London, 1950), an anthology of Victorian poetry not included in *The Oxford Book of Victorian Verse*. From childhood, Skipsey spent much of his life in the coal mines of North Shielding, England.

QUESTIONS

 1. Is this statement sentimental and full of self-pity, or is it not? Discuss, with specific reference to the poem.
 2. In its diction, this poem mingles dialect words (*bairns, dudden*) with "poetic" contractions (*o'er, ope*) and an archaism (*wight*). Does this inconsistency negate the poem's success? Why or why not?
 3. Evaluate the poem.

249

WILLIAM BLAKE (1757–1827)

The Little Black Boy

My mother bore me in the southern wild,
And I am black, but O! my soul is white;
White as an angel is the English child,
But I am black, as if bereaved of light.   4

My mother taught me underneath a tree,
And sitting down before the heat of day,
She took me on her lap and kissèd me,
And pointing to the east, began to say: 8

"Look on the rising sun: there God does live,
And gives his light, and gives his heat away;
And flowers and trees and beasts and men receive
Comfort in morning, joy in the noonday.   12

"And we are put on earth a little space,
That we may learn to bear the beams of love;
And these black bodies and this sunburnt face
Is but a cloud, and like a shady grove.   16

"For when our souls have learned the heat to bear,
The cloud will vanish; we shall hear his voice,
Saying: 'Come out from the grove, my love and care,
And round my golden tent like lambs rejoice.' "   20

Thus did my mother say, and kissèd me;
And thus I say to little English boy:
When I from black and he from white cloud free,
And round the tent of God like lambs we joy,   24

I'll shade him from the heat, till he can bear
To lean in joy upon our Father's knee;
And then I'll stand and stroke his silver hair,
And be like him, and he will then love me.   28

QUESTIONS

1. Summarize the metaphor that extends throughout this poem. What stands for what?

2. Do you or do you not find the various parts of this extended metaphor consistent with one another? Is this a well unified or a badly unified poem?

3. What is the speaker's attitude toward the fact that he is black? Is he sorry, glad, or both? Justify your answer by pointing to particulars in the poem.

4. In *A Child's Garden of Verses*, Robert Louis Stevenson makes a little white English child say:

Little Indian, Sioux or Crow,
Littly frosty Eskimo,
Little Turk or Japanee,
Oh! don't you wish that you were me? . . .

You have curious things to eat,
I am fed on proper meat;
You must dwell beyond the foam,
But I am safe and live at home.

How would you compare this attitude with that of Blake's little boy toward the English child? Which attitude do you find the more attractive?
5. The mutual love of a black child and a white child is a notion that can lend itself to a treatment of the utmost sentimentality (for example, in *Uncle Tom's Cabin* by Harriet Beecher Stowe, the treatment given Topsy the slave girl and Little Eva). Is Blake's poem sentimental or is it not?
6. Is this poem as good as "The Tyger" (p. 288)? Explain. (The word *good* here should be taken to mean "good in relation to Blake's other work." It is possible that what is good for Blake, for Charles Sprague or Joseph Skipsey would be excellent.)

JOHN KEATS (1795–1821)

'Bright star!'

Bright star! would I were steadfast as thou art —
    Not in lone splendor hung aloft the night,
And watching, with eternal lids apart,
    Like nature's patient, sleepless Eremite°   *hermit* 4
The moving waters at their priest-like task
    Of pure ablution round earth's human shores,
Or gazing on the new soft-fallen mask
    Of snow upon the mountains and the moors —   8
No — yet still steadfast, still unchangeable,
    Pillowed upon my fair love's ripening breast,
To feel for ever its soft fall and swell,
    Awake for ever in a sweet unrest,   12
Still, still to hear her tender-taken breath,
And so live ever — or else swoon to death.

QUESTIONS

1. Stars are conventional symbols for love, a loved one. (Love, Shakespeare tells us in a sonnet, "is the star to every wandering bark.") In this sonnet, why is it not possible for the star to have this meaning? How does Keats use it?
2. What seems concrete and particular in the speaker's observations?
3. Suppose Keats had said *slow and easy* instead of *tender-taken* in line 13? What would have been lost?
4. Many readers have been bothered by the latter half of the last line. Does it lose your sympathy? If so, why? If not, how do you defend it?

ANONYMOUS (English; Middle Ages)

The Unquiet Grave

"The wind doth blow today, my love,
    And a few small drops of rain;
I never had but one true-love,
    In cold grave she was lain.   4

"I'll do as much for my true-love
    As any young man may;
I'll sit and mourn all at her grave
    For a twelvemonth and a day."   8

The twelvemonth and a day being up,
    The dead began to speak:
"Oh who sits weeping on my grave,
    And will not let me sleep?"   12

" 'Tis I, my love, sits on your grave,
    And will not let you sleep;
For I crave one kiss of your clay-cold lips,
    And that is all I seek."   16

"You crave one kiss of my clay-cold lips,
    But my breath smells earthy strong;
If you have one kiss of my clay-cold lips,
    Your time will not be long.   20

" 'Tis down in yonder garden green,
    Love, where we used to walk,
The finest flower that ere° was seen   *ever*
    Is withered to a stalk.   24

"The stalk is withered dry, my love,
    So will our hearts decay;
So make yourself content, my love,
    Till God calls you away."   28

QUESTIONS

1. Why do you suppose the first two lines of this folk song have been so greatly admired?

2. What connection might be drawn between these lines and the withered flower in stanza six?

3. A different version, in which the second speaker is a murdered man, ends:

"Your lips are cold as clay, dear love,
    Your breath doth smell so strong;
I am afraid, my pretty, pretty maid,
    Your time will not be long."

Do you prefer this version? Why or why not?

MARK ALEXANDER BOYD (1563–1601)

'Fra bank to bank'

Fra bank to bank, fra wood to wood I rin°   *run*
Ourhailit° with my feeble fantasie   *overcome*
Like til° a leaf that fallis from a tree   *to*
Or til a reed ourblawin with the wind,

Two gods guides me, the ane of them is blin,   5
Yea, and a bairn° brocht up in vanitie,   *child*
The next a wife ingenrit° of the sea   *engendered*
And lichter nor° a dauphin° with her fin.   *than; dolphin*

Unhappy is the man for evermair
That tills the sand and sawis° in the air,   *sows* 10

But twice unhappier is he, I lairn,
That feidis° in his heart a mad desire   *feeds*
And follows on a woman throw the fire
Led by a blind and teachit by a bairn.

QUESTIONS

1. Explain the allusions in lines 5–8.
2. What has Boyd's poem in common with other love poetry in the Petrarchan tradition (discussed on pp. 183–184)?
3. Ezra Pound has called this the most beautiful sonnet in the English language. What is there in it to admire?

J. V. CUNNINGHAM (b. 1911)

Epitaph

When I shall be without regret
And shall mortality forget,
When I shall die who lived for this,
I shall not miss the things I miss.
And you who notice where I lie   5
Ask not my name. It is not I.

QUESTION

To an anthology (*Poet's Choice*, Paul Engle and Joseph Langland, eds. New York, 1962), J. V. Cunningham contributed this note:

> I like this poem because it is all denotation and no connotation; because it has only one level of meaning; because it is not ironic, paradoxical, complex, or subtle; and because the meter is monotonously regular.

He might have added that neither does it contain any image, symbol, allegory, or allusion. What does it have to recommend it?

253

FRED EMERSON BROOKS (fl. 1894)

Pat's Opinion of Flags

Every man in the world thinks his banner the best,
      And his national song
      Is often too long,
Yet in praising his flag he makes sport of the rest,
Though there's many a truth that is spoken in jest,   5
      Save wid malice prepense
      There should be no offense.

There's the Hawaiian kingdom stuck out in the ocean;
      'Twas made as a site
      For the seabirds to light;   10
There they worship their colors wid colored devotion,
And they never have war, but internal commotion,
      For those islands contain, O,
      Queen Lilli's volcano.

For the honor of flags how much blood has been spilt!   15
      Yet humanity clings
      To those queer-looking things.
Take the flag of Japan that's all covered wid gilt,
And the Austrian flag, like a new "crazy quilt,"
      And that bit of caprice   20
      That is all over Greece.

         .   .   .

There's the flag of the Chinese, as everywan knows,
      Cut three-cornered wid care,
      Like they'd no cloth to spare;
Yet they seem to have plenty when makin' their clothes;   25
Havin' no fashion plate, they've cut big, I suppose;
      Hangin' loose roundabout
      So the fleas will drop out.

You can judge of those men by the wardrobe they wear:
      They don't look to get fits   30
      For a "dollar six bits."
Their flag was made yellow, as people declare,
Because they've the smallpox so much over there;
      Be warned, if ye're wise,
      By the dragon it flies.   35

But one of the prettiest flags that I know
      Is the great oroflam
      Of our old Uncle Sam;

Wid the red and white bars all laid out in a row,
And a nice pasture blue for the bright stars to grow;   40
      Wid the eagle above
      And around it the dove.

Of the Star-spangled Banner alone, it is said
      She has earned this renown —
      She was niver pulled down.   45
With the green on my grave and that flag overhead
I think I'll rest aisy! But wait till I'm dead!
      Wid that flag in the sky
      I'm in no haste to die.

ANTHONY HECHT (b. 1923)

Japan

It was a miniature country once
To my imagination; Home of the Short,
And also the academy of stunts
      Where acrobats are taught
    The famous secrets of the trade: 5
      To cycle in the big parade
While spinning plates upon their parasols,
Or somersaults that do not touch the ground,
      Or tossing seven balls
In Most Celestial Order round and round.   10

A child's quick sense of the ingenious stamped
All their invention: toys I used to get
At Christmastime, or the peculiar, cramped
      Look of their alphabet.
    Fragile and easily destroyed,   15
      Those little boats of celluloid
Driven by camphor round the bathroom sink,
And delicate the folded paper prize
      Which, dropped into a drink
Of water, grew up right before your eyes.   20

Now when we reached them it was with a sense
Sharpened for treachery compounding in their brains
Like mating weasels; our Intelligence
      Said: The Black Dragon reigns
    Secretly under yellow skin,   25
      Deeper than dyes of atabrine
And deadlier. The War Department said:
Remember you are Americans; forsake
      The wounded and the dead
At your own cost; remember Pearl and Wake.   30

And yet they bowed us in with ceremony,
Told us what brands of Sake were the best,
Explained their agriculture in a phony
    Dialect of the West,
    Meant vaguely to be understood 35
    As a shy sign of brotherhood
In the old human bondage to the facts
Of day-to-day existence. And like ants,
    Signaling tiny pacts
With their antennae, they would wave their hands. 40

At last we came to see them not as glib
Walkers of tightropes, worshipers of carp,
Nor yet a species out of Adam's rib
    Meant to preserve its warp
    In Cain's own image. They had learned 45
    That their tough eye-born goddess burned
Adoring fingers. They were very poor.
The holy mountain was not moved to speak.
    Wind at the paper door
Offered them snow out of its hollow peak. 50

Human endeavor clumsily betrays
Humanity. Their excrement served in this;
For, planting rice in water, they would raise
    Schistosomiasis
    Japonica, that enters through 55
    The pores into the avenue
And orbit of the blood, where it may foil
The heart and kill, or settle in the brain.
    This fruit of their nightsoil
Thrives in the skull, where it is called insane. 60

Now the quaint early image of Japan
That was so charming to me as a child
Seems like a bright design upon a fan,
    Of water rushing wild
    On rocks that can be folded up, 65
    A river which the wrist can stop
With a neat flip, revealing merely sticks
And silk of what had been a fan before,
    And like such winning tricks,
It shall be buried in excelsior. 70

1. The preceding poems by Brooks and Hecht may be evaluated in comparison with each other. Pat opens with an advance apology for what he is about to say. Do you find this apology satisfactory?

2. Consider the attitude toward flags described in Brooks's lines 15–17 and the attitude toward Old Glory in the last two stanzas. What contradiction occurs between the two passages? To what do you attribute it?

3. Do you find any evidence that Brooks writes from an ironic point of view and that Pat's views are clearly not to be taken as his own? Or do you feel as if you are expected to share Pat's sentiments? Discuss, with specific reference to the poem.

4. A word worth knowing is *jingoism*. It comes from the refrain of a patriotic song from British music halls: "We don't want to fight, but by jingo, if we do / We've got the ships, we've got the men, and got the money too!" For what reasons may Brooks's piece be regarded as jingoistic?

5. In Hecht's poem, the *Black Dragon* (line 24) was a militarist organization that had urged the expansion of the Japanese empire. Pearl Harbor and Wake Island (30) were attacked by the Japanese on Dec. 7, 1941. Wake fell after a prolonged defense by a small garrison of Marines. Does the poem gain anything from our sense of its time and the speaker's situation? If the same feelings were expressed by a present-day tourist visiting Japan, would they have the same effect on us? Why or why not?

6. What is the speaker's attitude toward the Japanese at the beginning of the poem? At the end? What changes it?

7. *Atabrine* (line 26) is a drug used against malaria. A side effect is that it gives a yellow tinge to the user's skin. *Schistosomiasis Japonica* (54–55) is a disease caused by parasitic worms in the bloodstream. What do these medical references contribute? How does the speaker feel toward victims of the disease? Compare this with the reference to smallpox in "Pat's Opinion of Flags," line 33.

8. Both Hecht and Brooks try to write in ingenious stanza forms. Which more successfully makes us forget his ingenuity? Which displays greater mastery of rime?

9. What is the theme of each poem? To what extent does each poet implement his theme by detailed observation?

10. A subject to discuss, with reference to these poems: How is the excellence of a poem related to the poet's moral awareness?

FOURTEEN

ALTERNATIVES

1. THE POET'S REVISIONS

"He / Who casts to write a living line must sweat, / . . . and strike the second heat / Upon the Muse's anvil," wrote Ben Jonson. Indeed, few if any immortal poems can have been perfected with the first blow. The labor of revising seems the usual practice of most bards (other than the Bard of Avon, if we believe the famous rumor that in "whatsoever he penned, he never blotted out line"). As a result, a poet sometimes leaves us two or more versions of a poem. A study of these versions is valuable to anyone who cares to observe how a finished poem comes to be. More important to anyone who simply wishes to read poetry well, we stand to learn something about the rightness of a poem by comparing its successive drafts. If the poet is a master who kept revising his work over many years, as Yeats did, we may learn a great deal. Revising his work, the poet has had to make some merciless evaluations. By setting earlier and later versions side by side, we may see the difference between the weak line, merely decent line, or even very good line he discarded, and the line he finally chose. A novice poet who regards his first draft as inviolable sometimes loses interest in a poem if anyone suggests he do more work on it. But other poets have found excitement in the task. ("What bliss!" Yeats exclaimed, looking forward to weeks of laborious rewriting.) Indeed, "the work of correction is often quite as inspired as 'the first onrush of words and ideas,' " as A. F. Scott remarks on revisions by English poets (in *The Poet's Craft*).

A master of inspired revising, Yeats discarded lines that a lesser poet would have been grateful for. In some cases — an example follows — his final version was practically a new poem.

WILLIAM BUTLER YEATS (1865–1939)

The Sorrow of Love (1892 text)

> The quarrel of the sparrows in the eaves,
> The full round moon and the star-laden sky,
> And the loud song of the ever-singing leaves
> Has hid away earth's old and weary cry.   4
>
> And then you came with those red mournful lips,
> And with you came the whole of the world's tears,
> And all the sorrows of her laboring ships,
> And all burden of her myriad years.   8
>
> And now the sparrows warring in the eaves,
> The crumbling moon, the white stars in the sky,
> And the loud chanting of the unquiet leaves,
> Are shaken with earth's old and weary cry.   12

The Sorrow of Love (1939 text)

> The brawling of a sparrow in the eaves,
> The brilliant moon and all the milky sky,
> And all that famous harmony of leaves,
> Had blotted out man's image and his cry.   4
>
> A girl arose that had red mournful lips
> And seemed the greatness of the world in tears,
> Doomed like Odysseus and the laboring ships
> And proud as Priam murdered with his peers;   8
>
> Arose, and on the instant clamorous eaves,
> A climbing moon upon an empty sky,
> And all that lamentation of the leaves,
> Could but compose man's image and his cry.   12

Notice that a few of the revised lines seem less colorful than they were: "brilliant moon" (line 2) may be more flat, less suggestive than "full round moon" (or "curd-pale moon," in another version). Referring to this poem, Yeats made a revealing comment on his method in revision:

> In dream poetry, in "Kubla Khan," . . . every line, every word can carry its unanalyzable, rich associations; but if we dramatize some possible singer or speaker we remember that he is moved by one thing at a time, certain words must be dull and numb. Here and there in correcting my early poems I have introduced such numbness and dullness, turned, for instance, the "curd-pale moon"

into the "brilliant moon," that all might seem, as it were, remembered with indifference, except some one vivid image. When I began to rehearse a play I had the defects of my early poetry; I insisted upon obvious all-pervading rhythm. Later on I found myself saying that only in those lines or words where the beauty of the passage came to its climax, must rhythm be obvious.[1]

Not all revisions are successful. An instance might be the later alterations Keats made in "La Belle Dame sans Merci" (pp. 212–213), which some critics have lamented. But when he revises effectively — when we agree with his second thoughts — the poet is changing his meaning for the better. He enriches it, he finds words that speak with a greater precision and economy. A "spindrift gaze" really is not the same kind of look as a "sky-wide sea-foam gaze."

When Mark Antony begins his funeral oration, "Friends, Romans, countrymen: lend me your ears," Shakespeare makes him ask something quite different from the modernized version in one high-school English textbook: "Friends, Romans, countrymen: listen to me." Strictly speaking, any revised version of a poem is a different poem, even if its only change is a single word.

We need not rummage through the poet's wastebasket, and we need not feel thwarted if no early versions survive. We can follow a suggestion once made by the critic Austin Warren: Take any fine poem and make some changes in it. Then compare the changes to the original to see why the poet wrote what he did instead of anything else.

EXERCISE ONE

In each of the following pairs, italics indicate portions of one text not found in the other. In what respects does each revised version show an improvement over the earlier? Or has something been lost?

1. Robert Herrick, "To Anthea, Who May Command Him Anything," first two stanzas:

> A. Bid me *but* live, and I will live
> Thy *Votary* to be:
> Or bid me love, and I will give
> A loving heart to thee.   4
>
> A heart as soft, a heart as kind,
> A heart as *soundly* free,
> As in the world thou canst *not* find,
> That heart I'll give to thee.   (*earlier version*)   8

[1] "Dramatis Personae, 1896–1902," in *The Autobiography of William Butler Yeats* (New York, 1953).

260

B. Bid me *to* live, and I will live
     Thy *Protestant* to be:
    Or bid me love, and I will give
     A loving heart to thee.   4

    A heart as soft, a heart as kind,
     A heart as *sound* and free,
    As in the *whole* world thou canst find,
     That heart I'll give to thee.   *(1648 version)* 8

2. Samuel Taylor Coleridge, "The Rime of the Ancient Mariner," from Part III:

A. With *never a* whisper *in* the Sea
    Off *darts* the Specter-*ship*;
    While clombe above the Eastern bar
    The hornèd Moon, with one bright star
    Almost atween the tips.   5

    One after one by the hornèd Moon
     (*Listen, O Stranger! to me*)
    Each turn'd his face with a ghastly pang
    And curs'd me with his *ee.*   *(1799 version)*

B. *The Sun's rim dips; the stars rush out:*
    At one stride comes the dark;
    With *far-heard* whisper, *o'er* the sea,
    Off *shot* the specter *bark.*

    We listened and looked sideways up!   5
    Fear at my heart, as at a cup,
    My life-blood seemed to sip!
    The stars were dim, and thick the night,
    The steersman's face by his lamp gleamed white;
    From the sails the dew did drip —   10
    Till clomb above the eastern bar
    The hornèd Moon, with one bright star
    Within the nether tip.

    One after one, by the *star-dogged* Moon,
    Too quick for groan or sigh,   15
    Each turned his face with a ghastly pang
    And cursed me with his *eye.*   *(1817 version)*

3. Matthew Arnold, the poem first called "Sonnet"; later, "Quiet Work":

A. *Two lessons*, Nature, let me learn of thee —
    Two lessons that in every wind *are* blown;
    Two *blending* duties, *harmonized* in one,
    Though the loud world proclaim their enmity;
      Of toil unsevered from tranquillity: 5
    Of labor, that in *one short hour* outgrows
    Man's noisy schemes, accomplished in repose,
    Too great for haste, too high for rivalry.
    Yes, while on earth a thousand discords ring,
    Man's *weak complainings* mingling with his toil,   10
    Still do thy sleepless ministers move on,
    Their glorious *course* in silence perfecting;
    Still working, *chiding* still our vain turmoil,
    Laborers that shall not fail, when man is gone.
                                    (1849 version)

B. *One lesson*, Nature, let me learn of thee,
    One lesson which in every wind *is* blown,
    One lesson of two duties *kept at* one
    Though the loud world proclaim their enmity —

    Of toil unsevered from tranquillity!   5
    Of labor, that in *lasting fruit* outgrows
    Far noisier schemes, accomplished in repose,
    Too great for haste, too high for rivalry!

    Yes, while on earth a thousand discords ring,
    Mans' *fitful uproar* mingling with his toil,   10
    Still do thy sleepless ministers move on,

    Their glorious *tasks* in silence perfecting;
    Still working, *blaming* still our vain turmoil,
    Laborers that shall not fail, when man is gone.

                                        (*1885 version*)

WILLIAM BUTLER YEATS (1865–1939)

The Old Pensioner (1890 text)

    I had a chair at every hearth,
    When no one turned to see
    With 'Look at that old fellow there;
    And who may he be?'
    And therefore do I wander on,
    And the fret is on me.   6

    The road-side trees keep murmuring —
    Ah, wherefore murmur ye
    As in the old days long gone by,
    Green oak and poplar tree!
    The well-known faces are all gone,
    And the fret is on me.   12

The Lamentation of the Old Pensioner (1939 text)

    Although I shelter from the rain
    Under a broken tree
    My chair was nearest to the fire
    In every company
    That talked of love or politics,   5
    Ere Time transfigured me.

    Though lads are making pikes again
    For some conspiracy,
    And crazy rascals rage their fill
    At human tyranny,   10
    My contemplations are of Time
    That has transfigured me.

262

There's not a woman turns her face
Upon a broken tree,
And yet the beauties that I loved   15
Are in my memory;
I spit into the face of Time
That has transfigured me.

QUESTIONS

1. "The Old Pensioner" is this poem's first printed version; "Lamentation," its last. From the original, what elements has Yeats in the end retained?
2. What does the final version add to our knowledge of the old man (his character, attitudes, circumstances)?
3. Compare in sound and rhythm the refrain in the "Lamentation" with the original refrain.
4. Why do the statements in the final version seem to follow one another more naturally, and the poem as a whole seem more tightly woven together?

DONALD HALL (b. 1928)

My Son, My Executioner

My son, my executioner,
   I take you in my arms,
Quiet and small and just astir,
   And whom my body warms.   4

Sweet death, small son, our instrument
   Of immortality,
Your cries and hungers document
   Our bodily decay.   8

We twenty-five and twenty-two,
   Who seemed to live forever,
Observe enduring life in you
   And start to die together.   12

QUESTIONS

1. The first line introduces a paradoxical truth, the basic theme of the poem. How would you sum up this truth in your own words?
2. Exactly what do these words denote: *instrument* (line 5), *document* (7)?
3. When first published, this poem had a fourth stanza:

    I take into my arms the death
      Maturity exacts,
    And name with my imperfect breath
      The mortal paradox.

Do you think the poet right or wrong to omit this stanza? Explain.

2. TRANSLATIONS

Like revised versions, translations of the same poem by different hands invite the reader to compare and judge. Unlike the writer of an original poem, the translator begins with a meaning already in existence. To convey it, he may hold sacred the denotations of the original words, or else may depart from them, more or less freely, looking for something he values more. (This latter aim was apparently that of Robert Lowell in his *Imitations*: he said he had been "reckless with literal meaning" and instead had "labored hard to get the tone.") Here it is our purpose to judge a translation, not by its fidelity to its original (which requires a thorough knowledge of the original language), but by the same standards we apply to any other poem written in English.

EXERCISE TWO

Here are three versions of a famous poem from the Greek or Palatine Anthology, that great collection of surviving lyrics and epigrams written between 700 B.C. and A.D. 1000. Which of the three do you prefer? The versions by Cory and Lang reflect a style not much prevalent since the coming of Ezra Pound and T. S. Eliot. This is not to say that one style is intrinsically superior to the other, for it is open to question that there exist, beyond literary fashions, changeless standards of poetic right and wrong. Still, one can prefer one fashion or the other for good reasons. What are yours?

CALLIMACHUS (310?–240? B.C.)

A. *Heraclitus*

> They told me, Heraclitus, they told me you were dead,
> They brought me bitter news to hear and bitter tears to shed.
> I wept as I remembered how often you and I
> Had tired the sun with talking and sent him down the sky.
>
> And now that thou art lying, my dear Old Carian guest,   5
> A handful of grey ashes, long, long ago at rest,
> Still are thy pleasant voices, thy nightingales, awake;
> For Death, he taketh all away, but them he cannot take.
>
> — William Cory (1823–1892)

B. *'One told me, Heraclitus'*

> One told me, Heraclitus, of thy fate;
>   He brought me tears, he brought me memories.
> Alas, my Carian friend, how oft, how late,
>   We twain have talked the sun adown the skies,
> And somewhere thou art dust without a date!   5
>   But of thy songs Death maketh not his prize,
> In Death's despite, that stealeth all, they wait,
>   The new year's nightingale that never dies!
>
> — Andrew Lang (1844–1912)

C. *Elegy on Herakleitos*

One brought me the news of your death, O Herakleitos my
    friend,
And I wept for you, remembering
How often we had watched the sun set as we talked.

And you are ashes now, old friend from Halikarnassos,
Ashes now: 5
            but your nightingale songs live on,
And Death, the destroyer of every lovely thing,
Shall not touch them with his blind all-canceling fingers.

                                        — Dudley Fitts (b. 1903)

EXERCISE THREE

Which English translation of each of the following poems is the best
poetry? The originals may be of interest to some. For those who do not
know the foreign language, the editor's line-by-line prose paraphrases may
help indicate what the translator had to work with, and how much of his
translation is his own idea. In which do you find the diction most
felicitous? In which do pattern and structure best move as one? What
differences in tone are apparent? It is doubtful that any one translation
will surpass the others in every detail.

RAINER MARIA RILKE (1875–1926)

Abend

Der Abend wechselt langsam die Gewänder,
die ihm ein Rand von alten Bäumen hält;
du schaust: und von dir scheiden sich die Länder,
ein himmelfahrendes und eins, das fällt;   4

und lassen dich, zu keinem ganz gehörend,
nicht ganz so dunkel wie das Haus, das schweigt,
nicht ganz so sicher Ewiges beschwörend
wie das, was Stern wird jede Nacht und steigt;   8

und lassen dir (unsäglich zu entwirrn)
dein Leben, bang und riesenhaft und reifend,
so dass es, bald begrenzt und bald begreifend,
abwechselnd Stein in dir wird und Gestirn.   12

Prose translation: 'Evening'

(Line 1) The evening changes slowly the garments (2) that a border
of old trees holds out to it; (3) you watch: and the lands move away
from you, (4) one rising heavenward, and one that falls; (5) and leave
you, to neither one quite belonging, (6) not quite so dark as the house
that is silent, (7) not quite so certainly avowing something eternal (8)
as that which becomes a star each night and rises; (9) and leave you (to
unravel mutely) (10) your life, anxious and gigantic and ripening, (11)
so that it, now confined and now comprehending ['*begreifend*' *can mean
both* understanding *and* containing], (12) becomes within you alternately
stone and stars.

265

A. *Evening*

Slowly now the evening changes his garments
held for him by a rim of ancient trees;
you gaze: and the landscape divides and leaves you,
one sinking and one rising toward the sky.   4

And you are left, to none belonging wholly,
not so dark as a silent house, nor quite
so surely pledged unto eternity
as that which grows to star and climbs the night.   8

To you is left (unspeakably confused)
your life, gigantic, ripening, full of fears,
so that it, now hemmed in, now grasping all,
is changed in you by turns to stone and stars.   12

— C. F. MacIntyre (b. 1890)

B. *Evening*

The evening folds about itself the dark
Garments the old trees hold out to it.
You watch, and the lands are borne from you,
One soaring heavenward, one falling;   4

And leave you here, not wholly either's,
Not quite so darkened as the silent houses,
Not quite so surely summoning the eternal
As that which each night becomes star, and rises;   8

And leave you (inscrutably to disentangle)
Your life: the fearful and ripening and enormous
Being that — bounded by everything, or boundless —
For a moment becomes stone, for a moment stars.   12

— Randall Jarrell (1914–1965)

HORACE (65–8 B.C.)

Odes I, 38

Persicos odi, puer, apparatus,
Displicent nexæ philyra coronæ;
Mitte sectari, rosa quo locorum
        Sera moretur.
Simplici myrto nihil allabores   5
Sedulus curo: neque te ministrum
Dedecet myrtus neque me sub arta
        Vite bibentem.

Prose translation:

(Line 1) Persian pomp, boy, I detest, (2) garlands woven of linden
bark displease me; (3–4) give up searching for the place where the late-
blooming rose is. (5–6) Take care that you put no laborious trimmings
on simple myrtle: (6–7) for myrtle is unbecoming neither to you, a
servant, nor to me, under the shade of this (8) vine, drinking.

266

A. *Simplicity*

> Boy, I hate their empty shows,
>   Persian garlands I detest,
> Bring me not the late-blown rose
>   Lingering after all the rest:
>
> Plainer myrtle pleases me   5
>   Thus outstretched beneath my vine,
> Myrtle more becoming thee,
>   Waiting with thy master's wine.
>
>   — William Cowper (1731–1800)

B. *Fie on Eastern Luxury!*

> Nay, nay, my boy — 'tis not for me,
>   This studious pomp of Eastern luxury;
> Give me no various garlands — fine
>   With linden twine,
> Nor seek, where latest lingering blows,   5
>   The solitary rose.
>
> Earnest I beg — add not with toilsome pain,
> One far-sought blossom to the myrtle plain,
> For sure, the fragrant myrtle bough
>   Looks seemliest on thy brow;   10
> Nor me mis-seems, while, underneath the vine,
> Close interweaved, I quaff the rosy wine.
>
>   — Hartley Coleridge (1796–1849)

C. *From Horace*

> Ah child, no Persian-perfect art!
> Crowns composite and braided bast°   *linden bark*
> They tease me. Never know the part
>   Where roses linger last.
>
> Bring natural myrtle, and have done: 5
> Myrtle will suit your place and mine:
> And set the glasses from the sun
>   Beneath the tackled vine.
>
>   — Gerard Manley Hopkins (1844–1889)

D. *The Preference Declared*

> Boy, I detest the Persian pomp;
>   I hate those linden-bark devices;
> And as for roses, holy Moses!
>   They can't be got at living prices!
> Myrtle is good enough for us, —   5
>   For *you*, as bearer of my flagon;
> For *me*, supine beneath this vine,
>   Doing my best to get a jag on!
>
>   — Eugene Field (1850–1895)

267

CHARLES BAUDELAIRE (1821–1867)

Recueillement

Sois sage, ô ma Douleur, et tiens-toi plus tranquille.
Tu réclamais le Soir; il descend; le voici:
Une atmosphère obscure enveloppe la ville,
Aux uns portant la paix, aux autres le souci.

Pendant que des mortels la multitude vile,   5
Sous le fouet du Plaisir, ce bourreau sans merci,
Va cueillir des remords dans la fête servile,
Ma Douleur, donne-moi la main; viens par ici,

Loin d'eux. Vois se pencher les défuntes Années,
Sur les balcons du ciel, en robes surannées;   10
Surgir du fond des eaux le Regret souriant;

Le Soleil moribond s'endormir sous une arche,
Et, comme un long linceul traînant à l'Orient,
Entends, ma chère, entends la douce Nuit qui marche.

Prose translation: 'Meditation'

(Line 1) Behave yourself [*as a mother would say to her child*], O my
Melancholy, and keep calmer. (2) You called for Evening; he descends;
here he is: (3) a dim atmosphere envelops the city, (4) bringing peace
to some; to others, anxiety. (5) While mortals, the vile multitude, (6)
under the whip of Pleasure, that merciless slave-driver, (7) go to gather
remorse in the servile festival, (8) my Melancholy, give me your hand;
come this way, (9) far from them. See the dead years lean (10) on the
balconies of the sky, in outdated dresses; (11) [see] Regret, smiling,
emerge from the depths of the waters; (12) [see] the dying Sun go to
sleep under an arch; (13) and like a long shroud trailing into the East,
(14) hear, my darling, hear the soft Night walk.

A. 'Peace, be at peace, O thou my heaviness'

Peace, be at peace, O thou my heaviness,
Thou callèdst for the evening, lo! 'tis here,
The City wears a somber atmosphere
That brings repose to some, to some distress.
Now while the heedless throng make haste to press   5
Where pleasure drives them, ruthless charioteer,
To pluck the fruits of sick remorse and fear,
Come thou with me, and leave their fretfulness.
See how they hang from heaven's high balconies,
The old lost years in faded garments dressed,   10
And see Regret with faintly smiling mouth;
And while the dying sun sinks in the west,
Hear how, far off, Night walks with velvet tread,
And her long robe trails all about the south.

       — Lord Alfred Douglas (1870–1945)

B. *Inward Conversation*

Be reasonable, my pain, and think with more detachment.
You asked to see the dusk; it descends; it is here:
A sheath of dark light robes the city,
To some bringing peace, to some the end of peace.

Now while the rotten herds of mankind,   5
Flogged by pleasure, that lyncher without touch,
Go picking remorse in their filthy holidays,
Let us join hands, my pain; come this way,

Far from them. Look at the dead years that lean on
The balconies of the sky, in their clothes long out of date;   10
The sense of loss that climbs from the deep waters with a
    smile;

The sun, nearly dead, that drops asleep beneath an arch;
And listen to the night, like a long shroud being dragged
Toward the east, my love, listen, the soft night is moving.

— Robert Bly (b. 1926)

C. *Meditation*

Calm down, my Sorrow, we must move with care.
You called for evening; it descends; it's here.
The town is coffined in its atmosphere,
bringing relief to some, to others care.

Now while the common multitude strips bare,   5
feels pleasure's cat o' nine tails on its back,
and fights off anguish at the great bazaar,
give me your hand, my Sorrow. Let's stand back;

back from these people! Look, the dead years dressed
in old clothes crowd the balconies of the sky.   10
Regret emerges smiling from the sea,

the sick sun slumbers underneath an arch,
and like a shroud strung out from east to west,
listen, my Dearest, hear the sweet night march!

— Robert Lowell (b. 1917)

FIFTEEN

WHAT IS POETRY?

ARCHIBALD MACLEISH (b. 1892)
Ars Poetica

A poem should be palpable and mute
As a globed fruit,

Dumb
As old medallions to the thumb, 4

Silent as the sleeve-worn stone
Of casement ledges where the moss has grown —

A poem should be wordless
As the flight of birds. 8

A poem should be motionless in time
As the moon climbs,

Leaving, as the moon releases
Twig by twig the night-entangled trees, 12

Leaving, as the moon behind the winter leaves,
Memory by memory the mind —

A poem should be motionless in time
As the moon climbs. 16

A poem should be equal to:
Not true.

For all the history of grief
An empty doorway and a maple leaf. 20

For love
The leaning grasses and two lights above the sea —

A poem should not mean
But be. 24

What is a poem? Having elected at the beginning of this book to place the question in suspended animation, we are obliged to take it out again. Although a definition to fit every poem may be as baggy as a suit to fit every man, some tentative generalization ought now to be possible. Suppose we put it like this: A poem is an arrangement of words in lines which, heard aloud or read silently, can occasion a particular response and occasion it again by being memorable.

What is a "particular response"? A response the poem makes possible. As we read poetry, simultaneously understanding and evaluating, we move along under the poem's direction; and, when we come to its end, we know we have lived through a complete experience. The poem does not allow us to feel just any old way about it. Of course, if we *want* to feel sorrow and gloom while reading Wordsworth's "I Wandered Lonely as a Cloud," we are free to do so; but we will be reading some other poem of our own imagining, our eyes closed to what is on the page.

One might object: Isn't that what a piece of prose also can do? Doesn't it rouse our emotions? When we are involved in a good detective story, aren't our feelings also guided and controlled? And when we finally discover that it was the Eskimo house-boy who murdered old Mr. Bradthwaite with a harpoon of ice that melted and left no trace, don't we feel that some experience we have lived through has come to a satisfying end? Granted. Then we need to make more distinctions. A poem differs from prose in several ways. For one, both writer and reader tend to regard it differently. The poet's attitude is as if, sticking his neck out, he were to say: I offer this piece of writing to be read not as prose but as a poem — that is, more perceptively, thoughtfully, and considerately, with more attention given to sounds and connotations. This is a great deal to expect, but in return, the reader has a right to his own expectations. He approaches the poem in the anticipation of some out-of-the-ordinary knowledge and pleasure. Willing to spend more time finding these than he would spend upon reading prose, he expects to be rewarded accordingly. He assumes that the poet may use certain pleasurable devices of sound and rhythm not available to prose: rime, alliteration, meter, and rhythms — definite, various, or emphatic. (The poet may not *always* choose to employ these things.) He expects the poet to make greater use, perhaps, of such resources of meaning as figurative language, allusion, symbol, and imagery. And the reader expects to derive from poetry a different kind of knowledge and a different order of awareness. If he were reading prose, he might seek no more than meaning: no more than what could be paraphrased without serious loss. If he encounters any figurative language or graceful turns of syntax, he considers them pleasant extras. But in poetry all the "extras" may be as important as the paraphraseable content, if not more important. This is because, in its more extensive use of certain components (sound, symbol, figures of speech, ambiguity), poetry appeals to the unconscious to a greater degree than does prose. For, when we finish reading a good poem, we cannot explain to ourselves *all* we have understood. Nor can we describe *precisely* what we have experienced, without repeating, word for word, the language of the poem itself.

Perhaps, if a poem is very good indeed, it may point beyond words to something still more essential, as Blake's "Tyger" or Yeats's "Sailing to Byzantium" might lead one to some kind of awareness of the natural world and his relation to it. Language has its limits; and Edgar Allan Poe was probably the only poet ever to claim he could always find words for whatever he wished to express. For, of all a man can experience and all he can imagine, words can express only part. "Human speech," said Flaubert, who strove so conscientiously after the best of it, "is like a cracked kettle on which we hammer out tunes to make bears dance, when what we long for is the compassion of the stars." And yet poetry manages to touch more closely man's inmost longings than any other kind of human speech.

Like Yeats's chestnut-tree in "Among School Children" (which — when asked whether it is leaf, blossom, or bole — has no answer), a poem is not to be seen as a confederation of form, rime, image, metaphor, tone, and theme, but as a whole. We study a poem one element at a time because the intellect best comprehends what it can separate. But only our total attention, involving the participation of our blood and marrow, can see all elements in a poem fused, all dancing together. Yeats knew how to make poems and how to read them:

> God guard me from those thoughts men think
> In the mind alone;
> He that sings a lasting song
> Thinks in a marrow-bone.

Throughout this book, we have been working on the assumption that the patient and conscious explication of poems will lead to the sharpening of unconscious perceptions. We can only hope that it will; the final test lies in whether you care to go on by yourself, read other poems, and find in them pleasure and enlightenment. Pedagogy must have a stop; so must the viewing of poems as if their elements fell into chapters. For the total experience of reading a poem surpasses the mind's categories. The wind in the grass, says a proverb, cannot be taken into the house.

272

ANTHOLOGY

ANONYMOUS (English; sixteenth century)

Western Wind

Western wind, when wilt thou blow,
The° small rain down can rain?   (*so that*) *the*
Christ, if my love were in my arms,
And I in my bed again!

ANONYMOUS (Scottish popular ballad)

Edward

"Why dois your brand° sae° drap wi' bluid,   *sword; so*
    Edward, Edward?
Why dois your brand sae drap wi' bluid?
    And why sae sad gang° yee, O?"   *go*
"O, I hae killed my hauke sae guid,   5
    Mither, mither,
O, I hae killed my hauke sae guid,
    And I had nae mair bot° hee, O."   *but*

"Your haukis bluid was nevir sae reid,
    Edward, Edward,   10
Your haukis bluid was nevir sae reid,
    My deir son I tell thee, O."
"O, I hae killed my reid-roan steid,
    Mither, mither,
O, I hae killed my reid-roan steid,   15
    That erst° was sa fair and frie°, O."   *once; free*

"Your steid was auld, and ye hae gat mair,
    Edward, Edward,
Your steid was auld, and ye hae gat mair,
    Sum other dule° ye drie°, O."   *sorrow; suffer* 20
"O, I hae killed my fadir deir,
    Mither, mither,
O, I hae killed my fadir deir,
    Alas, and wae° is mee, O!"   *woe*

"And whatten penance wul ye drie for that,   25
    Edward, Edward?
And whatten penance will ye drie for that?
    My deir son, now tell me, O."
"Ile set my feit in yonder boat,
    Mither, mither,   30
Ile set my feit in yonder boat,
    And Ile fare ovir the sea, O."

"And what wul ye doe wi' your towirs and your ha',
    Edward, Edward,
And what wul ye doe wi' your towirs and your ha',   35
    That were sae fair to see, O?"
"Ile let thame stand tul they doun fa',
    Mither, mither,
Ile let thame stand tul they doun fa',
    For here nevir mair maun° I bee, O."   *must* 40

"And what wul ye leive to your bairns° and your wife,   *children*
    Edward, Edward?
And what wul ye leive to your bairns and your wife,
    When ye gang ovir the sea, O?"
"The warldis° room, late° them beg thrae° life,   *world's;* 45
    Mither, mither,   *let; through*
The warldis room, late them beg thrae life,
    For thame nevir mair wul I see, O."

"And what wul ye leive to your ain° mither deir,   *own*
    Edward, Edward?   50
And what wul ye leive to your ain mither deir?
    My deir son, now tell me, O."
"The curse of hell frae me sall ye beir,
    Mither, mither,
The curse of hell frae me sall ye beir,   55
    Sic° counseils° ye gave to me, O."   *such; counsel*

ANONYMOUS (Irish-American popular ballad)

Finnegan's Wake

Tim Finnegan lived in Walker Street,
    An Irish gentleman mighty odd:
He'd a beautiful tongue both rich and sweet
    And to rise in the world he carried a hod.
But Tim, he'd a sort of a tippling way,   5
    With the love of the liquor the lad was born
And to help him along to his work each day
    He'd a drop of the craythur° every morn.   *creature,*
                                     substance

With a philalloo, hullaboo, whack hurroo, boys.
Didn't we laugh till our jaws did ache!   10
And the talk and the tippling went on till Saturday,
Plenty of fun at Finnegan's Wake!

One morning Tim was a good bit full,
  His head felt heavy, which made him shake.
He fell from the ladder and broke his skull,   15
  So they carried him home, his corpse to wake.
They rolled him up in a nice white sheet
  And laid him out upon the bed
With a gallon of whisky at his feet
  And a barrel of praties° at his head.   *potatoes*   20

His friends assembled at the wake
  And Missus Finnegan sent for a lunch.
First they brought in tay and cake,
  Then pipes, tobacco, and whisky punch.
Miss Biddy O'Brien began to cry,   25
  "Such a neat clean corpse did you ever see?
Arrah, Tim mavourneen°, why did you die?"   *my darling*
  "Ah, hold your gab," said Paddy McGee.

Then Maggie O'Connor took up the job:
  "Biddy," says she, "you're wrong, I'm sure,"   30
But Biddy gave her a belt in the gob°   *mouth*
  And doubled her sprawling on the floor.
Oh, then what a war did soon enrage!
  'Twas woman to woman and man to man,
Shillelagh° law did all engage   *a heavy cudgel*   35
  And a row and a ruction soon began.

Then Mickey Maloney raised his head
  When the gallon of whisky flew at him,
But it missed, and falling on the bed,
  The liquor scattered over Tim.   40
Bedad, he revives, see how he rises,
  And Timothy rising from the bed
Says, "Whirl your liquor round like blazes!
  Arrah, on me life, do you think I'm dead?"

Finnegan's Wake. The chorus is repeated after every stanza. This song
was a favorite of vaudeville comedians in the 1870's. A *wake* is a gathering of mourners who sit up all night with the corpse.

Frankie and Johnny

Frankie she was a good woman, Johnny he was her man,
And every silver dollar Frankie made went straight to her
Johnny's hand.
He was her man, but he done her wrong.

Frankie and Johnny went walking, Johnny in a brand new
suit.
"Cost me a hundred," says Frankie, "but don't my Johnny   5
look cute?"
He was her man, but he done her wrong.

Frankie went down to the corner, she called for a thimble of
gin,
She says to the fat bartender, "Has my lovin' Johnny been
in?
I can't believe he's been doing me wrong."

"Ain't going to tell you no story, ain't going to tell you no   10
lie,
Mister Johnny was in here 'bout an hour ago with a floozy
named Ella Fly.
He is your man, but I believe he's doing you wrong."

Frankie ran down to the pawn shop, she didn't go there for
fun.
She turned in her doorknob diamonds, she took out a forty-
four gun.
He was her man, but he done her wrong.   15

Frankie ran down to the parlor-house, she leaned on the
parlor-house bell.
"Stand out of my way, you floozies, or I'll splash you all over
Hell!
I want my man, he's been doing me wrong."

Frankie looked over the transom, the tears ran out of her eyes.
There was her lovin' Johnny a-lovin' up Ella Fly.   20
He was her man, but he was doing her wrong.

She threw back her red silk kimono, she whipped out that
old forty-four.
Rooty-toot-toot, three times she did shoot, right through
that hardwood door.
He was her man, but he done her wrong.

Johnny grabbed off his Stetson, "O Lord no, Frankie, don't   25
    shoot!"
But Frankie squeezed the trigger three times more and he
    fell down like a stick of wood.
He was her man, but he done her wrong.

The first shot, Johnny staggered; the second shot, he fell;
The third shot took him through the heart and his face
    started coming out in Hell.
He was her man, but he done her wrong.   30

"O roll me over easy, roll me over slow,
Roll me over on my right side, honey, so my heart don't
    overflow.
I was your man, but I done you wrong."

Bring on your rubber-tired hearses, bring on your rubber-
    tired hacks.
There's eight men going to the burying yard and only seven   35
    of 'em coming back.
He was her man, but he done her wrong.

The judge looked hard at the jury, says, "It's plain as plain
    can be,
This woman put some daylight through her man, it's murder
    in the second degree.
He was her man, and she done him wrong."

Now it wasn't murder in the second degree, it wasn't murder   40
    in the third,
All Frankie did was drop her man like a hunter drops a bird.
He was her man, but he done her wrong.

The jury went out on Frankie, sat under an electric fan,
Came back and said, "You're a free woman, go kill yourself
    another man
If he does you wrong, if he does you wrong."   45

"O put me away in a dungeon, put me in a cold, cold cell,
Put me where the north wind blows from the southeast
    corner of Hell.
I shot my man, 'cause he done me wrong."

Frankie she heard a rumbling, away down under the ground.
Maybe it was little Johnny where she had shot him down.   50
He was her man, but he done her wrong.

Frankie went out to the burying yard, just to look her Johnny
    in the face.
"Ain't it hard to see you, Johnny, in this lonesome place?"
He was her man, but he done her wrong.

Well, I looked down the lonesome street, Lord, as far off as   55
    I could see,
All I could hear was a two-string fiddle playing "Nearer,
    My God, to Thee."
He was her man, but he done her wrong.

Frankie and Johnny. Hundreds of versions of this ballad exist; this one
is a composite of many. In the 1890's a murder that took place either in
St. Louis or in Kansas City, Missouri, became famous in folk song as the
story of Frankie and Albert. About 1911, vaudeville singers changed
Albert's name to Johnny, and introduced mock-serious elements. 16. *par-lor-house:* a brothel fancy enough to have a waiting-room.

ANONYMOUS (Scottish popular ballad)

The Cruel Mother

She sat down below a thorn,
    Fine flowers in the valley,
And there she has her sweet babe born
    And the green leaves they grow rarely.

"Smile na sae° sweet, my bonie babe,"   *so* 5
    Fine flowers in the valley,
"And° ye smile sae sweet, ye'll smile me dead."   *if*
    And the green leaves they grow rarely.

She's taen out her little pen-knife,
    Fine flowers in the valley,   10
And twinned° the sweet babe o' its life,   *severed*
    And the green leaves they grow rarely.

She's howket° a grave by the light o' the moon,   *dug*
    Fine flowers in the valley,
And there she's buried her sweet babe in   15
    And the green leaves they grow rarely.

As she was going to the church,
    Fine flowers in the valley,
She saw a sweet babe in the porch
    And the green leaves they grow rarely.   20

"O sweet babe, and thou were mine,"
    Fine flowers in the valley,
"I wad cleed° thee in the silk so fine."   *dress*
    And the green leaves they grow rarely.

"O mother dear, when I was thine,"   25
    Fine flowers in the valley,
"You did na prove to me sae kind."
    And the green leaves they grow rarely.

ANONYMOUS (English popular ballad)

The Three Ravens

There were three ravens sat on a tree,
    Down a down, hay down, hay down,
There were three ravens sat on a tree,
    With a down,
There were three ravens sat on a tree,   5
They were as black as they might be.
    With a down derry, derry, derry, down, down.

The one of them said to his mate,
"Where shall we our breakfast take?"

"Down in yonder greene field,   10
There lies a knight slain under his shield.

"His hounds they lie down at his feet,
So well they can their master keep.

"His hawks they fly so eagerly,
There's no fowl dare him come nigh."   15

Down there comes a fallow doe,
As great with young as she might go.

She lift up his bloody head,
And kist his wounds that were so red.

She got him up upon her back,   20
And carried him to earthen lake°.   *the grave*

She buried him before the prime,
She was dead herself ere evensong time.

God send every gentleman
Such hawks, such hounds, and such a leman°.   *lover*   25

The Three Ravens. The lines of refrain are repeated in each stanza.
"Perhaps in the folk mind the doe is the form the soul of a human
mistress, now dead, has taken," Albert B. Friedman has suggested (in
The Viking Book of Folk Ballads, New York, 1963). "Most probably the
knight's beloved was understood to be an enchanted woman who was
metamorphosed at certain times into an animal." 22–23. *prime, evensong:*
two of the canonical hours set aside for prayer and worship. Prime is at
dawn, evensong at dusk.

ANONYMOUS (Scottish popular ballad)

The Twa Corbies

As I was walking all alane,
I heard twa corbies° making a mane°;   *ravens; moan*
The tane° unto the t'other say,   *one*
"Where sall we gang° and dine today?"   *go*

"In behint yon auld fail dyke°,   *turf wall* 5
I wot° there lies a new slain knight;   *know*
And naebody kens° that he lies there,   *knows*
But his hawk, his hound, and lady fair.

"His hound is to the hunting gane,
His hawk to fetch the wild-fowl hame,   10
His lady's ta'en another mate,
So we may mak our dinner sweet.

"Ye'll sit on his white hause-bane°,   *neck bone*
And I'll pike out his bonny blue een;
Wi' ae° lock o' his gowden hair   *one* 15
We'll theek° our nest when it grows bare.   *thatch*

"Mony a one for him makes mane,
But nane sall ken where he is gane;
O'er his white banes, when they are bare,
The wind sall blaw for evermair."   20

The Twa Corbies. Sir Walter Scott, the first to print this traditional folk
song in his *Minstrelsy of the Scottish Border*, calls it "rather a counter-
part than a copy" of "The Three Ravens." That it might be "a cynical
variation of the tender little English ballad" is the guess of ballad-scholar
F. J. Child.

ANONYMOUS (Scottish popular ballad)

Sir Patrick Spence

The king sits in Dumferling toune,
    Drinking the blude-reid wine:
"O whar will I get guid sailor
    To sail this schip of mine?"

Up and spak an eldern knicht,
    Sat at the kings richt kne: 5
"Sir Patrick Spence is the best sailor
    That sails upon the se."

The king has written a braid letter,
    And signed it wi' his hand,
And sent it to Sir Patrick Spence,   10
    Was walking on the sand.

The first line that Sir Patrick red,
    A loud lauch lauchèd he;
The next line that Sir Patrick red,   15
    The teir blinded his ee.

"O wha° is this has don this deid,   *who*
    This ill deid don to me,
To send me out this time o' the yeir,
    To sail upon the se!   20

"Mak haste, mak haste, my mirry men all,
    Our guid schip sails the morne."
"O say na sae°, my master deir,   *so*
    For I feir a deadlie storme.

"Late late yestreen I saw the new moone,   25
    Wi' the auld moone in hir arme,
And I feir, I feir, my deir master,
    That we will cum to harme."

O our Scots nobles wer richt laith°   *loath*
    To weet° their cork-heild schoone°;   *wet; shoes* 30
Bot lang owre° a' the play wer playd,   *ere*
    Their hats they swam aboone°.   *above (their heads)*

O lang, lang may their ladies sit,
    Wi' their fans into their hand,
Or ere° they se Sir Patrick Spence   *long before* 35
    Cum sailing to the land.

O lang, lang may the ladies stand,
    Wi' their gold kems° in their hair,   *combs*
Waiting for their ain° deir lords,   *own*
    For they'll se thame na mair.   40

Haf owre°, haf owre to Aberdour,   *halfway over*
    It's fiftie fadom deip,
And thair lies guid Sir Patrick Spence,
    Wi' the Scots lords at his feit.

Sir Patrick Spence. 9. *braid:* broad, but broad in what sense? Among guesses are *plain-spoken, official,* and *on wide paper.*

MATTHEW ARNOLD (1822–1888)

Dover Beach

The sea is calm tonight.
The tide is full, the moon lies fair
Upon the straits; — on the French coast the light
Gleams and is gone; the cliffs of England stand,
Glimmering and vast, out in the tranquil bay.   5
Come to the window, sweet is the night-air!
Only, from the long line of spray
Where the sea meets the moon-blanched land,
Listen! you hear the grating roar
Of pebbles which the waves draw back, and fling,   10
At their return, up the high strand,
Begin, and cease, and then again begin,
With tremulous cadence slow, and bring
The eternal note of sadness in.

Sophocles long ago   15
Heard it on the Aegean, and it brought
Into his mind the turbid ebb and flow
Of human misery; we
Find also in the sound a thought,
Hearing it by this distant northern sea.   20

The Sea of Faith
Was once, too, at the full, and round earth's shore
Lay like the folds of a bright girdle furled.
But now I only hear
Its melancholy, long, withdrawing roar,   25
Retreating, to the breath
Of the night-wind, down the vast edges drear
And naked shingles° of the world.   *gravel beaches*

Ah, love, let us be true
To one another! for the world, which seems   30
To lie before us like a land of dreams,
So various, so beautiful, so new,
Hath really neither joy, nor love, nor light,
Nor certitude, nor peace, nor help for pain;
And we are here as on a darkling° plain   *darkened or*   35
Swept with confused alarms of struggle and flight,   *darkening*
Where ignorant armies clash by night.

W. H. AUDEN (b. 1907)

The Quarry

O what is that sound which so thrills the ear
  Down in the valley drumming, drumming?
Only the scarlet soldiers, dear,
  The soldiers coming.

O what is that light I see flashing so clear   5
  Over the distance brightly, brightly?
Only the sun on their weapons, dear,
  As they step lightly.

O what are they doing with all that gear,
  What are they doing this morning, this morning?   10
Only their usual maneuvers, dear,
  Or perhaps a warning.

O why have they left the road down there,
  Why are they suddenly wheeling, wheeling?
Perhaps a change in their orders, dear.   15
  Why are you kneeling?

O haven't they stopped for the doctor's care,
  Haven't they reined their horses, their horses?
Why, they are none of them wounded, dear,
  None of these forces.   20

O is it the parson they want, with white hair,
  Is it the parson, is it, is it?
No, they are passing his gateway, dear,
  Without a visit.

O it must be the farmer who lives so near.   25
  It must be the farmer so cunning, so cunning?
They have passed the farmyard already, dear,
  And now they are running.

O where are you going? Stay with me here!
  Were the vows you swore, deceiving, deceiving?   30
No, I promised to love you, dear,
  But I must be leaving.

O it's broken the lock and splintered the door,
  O it's the gate where they're turning, turning;
Their boots are heavy on the floor   35
  And their eyes are burning.

W. H. AUDEN (b. 1907)

Musée des Beaux Arts

About suffering they were never wrong,
The Old Masters: how well they understood
Its human position; how it takes place
While someone else is eating or opening a window or just
    walking dully along;
How, when the aged are reverently, passionately waiting   5
For the miraculous birth, there always must be
Children who did not specially want it to happen, skating
On a pond at the edge of the wood:
They never forgot
That even the dreadful martyrdom must run its course   10
Anyhow in a corner, some untidy spot
Where the dogs go on with their doggy life and the torturer's
    horse
Scratches its innocent behind on a tree.

In Brueghel's *Icarus*, for instance: how everything turns away
Quite leisurely from the disaster; the ploughman may   15
Have heard the splash, the forsaken cry,
But for him it was not an important failure; the sun shone
As it had to on the white legs disappearing into the green
Water; and the expensive delicate ship that must have seen
Something amazing, a boy falling out of the sky,   20
Had somewhere to get to and sailed calmly on.

JOHN BETJEMAN (b. 1906)

In Westminster Abbey

Let me take this other glove off
    As the *vox humana* swells,
And the beauteous fields of Eden
    Bask beneath the Abbey bells.
Here, where England's statesmen lie,   5
Listen to a lady's cry.

Gracious Lord, oh bomb the Germans.
    Spare their women for Thy Sake,
And if that is not too easy
    We will pardon Thy Mistake.
But, gracious Lord, whate'er shall be,   10
Don't let anyone bomb me.

Keep our Empire undismembered,
  Guide our Forces by Thy Hand,
Gallant blacks from far Jamaica,   15
  Honduras and Togoland;
Protect them Lord in all their fights,
And, even more, protect the whites.

Think of what our Nation stands for:
  Books from Boots' and country lanes,   20
Free speech, free passes, class distinction,
  Democracy and proper drains.
Lord, put beneath Thy special care
One-eighty-nine Cadogan Square.

Although dear Lord I am a sinner,   25
  I have done no major crime;
Now I'll come to Evening Service
  Whensoever I have the time.
So, Lord, reserve for me a crown,
And do not let my shares go down.   30

I will labor for Thy Kingdom,
  Help our lads to win the war,
Send white feathers to the cowards,
  Join the Women's Army Corps,
Then wash the Steps around Thy Throne   35
In the Eternal Safety Zone.

Now I feel a little better,
  What a treat to hear Thy Word,
Where the bones of leading statesmen,
  Have so often been interred.   40
And now, dear Lord, I cannot wait
Because I have a luncheon date.

In Westminster Abbey. Published during World War II. 2. *vox humana:*
an organ stop that makes tones similar to those of the human voice. 20.
Boots': a cut-rate pharmacy.

WILLIAM BLAKE (1757–1827)

Eternity

He who binds to himself a joy
Does the wingèd life destroy;
But he who kisses the joy as it flies
Lives in eternity's sun rise.

WILLIAM BLAKE (1757–1827)

The Sick Rose

O Rose, thou art sick!
The invisible worm
That flies in the night,
In the howling storm,

Has found out thy bed   5
Of crimson joy,
And his dark secret love
Does thy life destroy.

The Tyger

Tyger! Tyger! burning bright
In the forests of the night,
What immortal hand or eye
Could frame thy fearful symmetry?

In what distant deeps or skies   5
Burnt the fire of thine eyes?
On what wings dare he aspire?
What the hand dare seize the fire?

And what shoulder, and what art,
Could twist the sinews of thy heart?   10
And when thy heart began to beat,
What dread hand? and what dread feet?

What the hammer? what the chain?
In what furnace was thy brain?
What the anvil? what dread grasp   15
Dare its deadly terrors clasp?

When the stars threw down their spears,
And watered heaven with their tears,
Did he smile his work to see?
Did he who made the Lamb make thee?   20

Tyger! Tyger! burning bright
In the forests of the night,
What immortal hand or eye
Dare frame thy fearful symmetry?

WILLIAM BLAKE (1757–1827)

Long John Brown and Little Mary Bell

Little Mary Bell had a fairy in a nut,
Long John Brown had the Devil in his gut;
Long John Brown loved Little Mary Bell,
And the fairy drew the Devil into the nut-shell.

Her fairy skipped out and her fairy skipped in;   5
He laughed at the Devil saying "Love is a sin."
The Devil he raged and Devil he was wroth,
And the Devil entered into the young man's broth.

He was soon in the gut of the loving young swain,
For John eat and drank to drive away love's pain;   10
But all he could do he grew thinner and thinner,
Though he eat and drank as much as ten men for his dinner.

Some said he had a wolf in his stomach day and night,
Some said he had the Devil and they guessed right;
The fairy skipped about in his glory, joy and pride,   15
And he laughed at the Devil till poor John Brown died.

Then the fairy skipped out of the old nut-shell,
And woe and alack for pretty Mary Bell!
For the Devil crept in when the fairy skipped out,
And there goes Miss Bell with her fusty old nut.   20

ROBERT BROWNING (1812–1889)

My Last Duchess

FERRARA

That's my last Duchess painted on the wall,
Looking as if she were alive. I call
That piece a wonder, now; Frà Pandolf's hands
Worked busily a day, and there she stands.
Will 't please you sit and look at her? I said   5
"Frà Pandolf" by design, for never read
Strangers like you that pictured countenance,
The depth and passion of its earnest glance,
But to myself they turned (since none puts by
The curtain I have drawn for you, but I)   10
And seemed as they would ask me, if they durst,
How such a glance came there; so, not the first
Are you to turn and ask thus. Sir, 'twas not
Her husband's presence only, called that spot

Of joy into the Duchess' cheek; perhaps   15
Frà Pandolf chanced to say, "Her mantle laps
Over my lady's wrist too much," or "Paint
Must never hope to reproduce the faint
Half-flush that dies along her throat." Such stuff
Was courtesy, she thought, and cause enough   20
For calling up that spot of joy. She had
A heart — how shall I say? — too soon made glad,
Too easily impressed; she liked whate'er
She looked on, and her looks went everywhere.
Sir, 'twas all one! My favor at her breast,   25
The dropping of the daylight in the West,
The bough of cherries some officious fool
Broke in the orchard for her, the white mule
She rode with round the terrace — all and each
Would draw from her alike the approving speech,   30
Or blush, at least. She thanked men, — good! but thanked
Somehow — I know not how — as if she ranked
My gift of a nine-hundred-years' old name
With anybody's gift. Who'd stoop to blame
This sort of trifling? Even had you skill   35
In speech — which I have not — to make your will
Quite clear to such an one, and say, "Just this
Or that in you disgusts me; here you miss,
Or there exceed the mark" — and if she let
Herself be lessoned so, nor plainly set   40
Her wits to yours, forsooth, and made excuse —
E'en then would be some stooping; and I choose
Never to stoop. Oh, sir, she smiled, no doubt,
Whene'er I passed her; but who passed without
Much the same smile? This grew; I gave commands; 45
Then all smiles stopped together. There she stands
As if alive. Will 't please you rise? We'll meet
The company below, then. I repeat,
The Count your master's known munificence
Is ample warrant that no just pretense   50
Of mine for dowry will be disallowed;
Though his fair daughter's self, as I avowed
At starting, is my object. Nay, we'll go
Together down, sir. Notice Neptune, though,
Taming a sea-horse, thought a rarity,   55
Which Claus of Innsbruck cast in bronze for me!

My Last Duchess. Ferrara, a city in northern Italy, is the scene. Browning
may have modeled his speaker after Alonzo, Duke of Ferrara (1533–
1598). 3. *Frà Pandolf* and 56. *Claus of Innsbruck*: fictitious names of
artists.

CHARLES CAUSLEY (b. 1917)

Recruiting Drive

Under the willow the willow
    I heard the butcher-bird sing,
Come out you fine young fellow
    From under your mother's wing.
I'll show you the magic garden   5
    That hangs in the beamy air,
The way of the lynx and the angry Sphinx
    And the fun of the freezing fair.

Lie down lie down with my daughter
    Beneath the Arabian tree,   10
Gaze on your face in the water,
    Forget the scribbling sea.
Your pillow the nine bright shiners,
    Your bed the spilling sand,
But the terrible toy of my lily-white boy   15
    Is the gun in his innocent hand.

You must take off your clothes for the doctor
    And stand as straight as a pin,
His hand of stone on your white breast-bone
    Where the bullets all go in.   20
They'll dress you in lawn and linen
    And fill you with Plymouth gin,
O the devil may wear a rose in his hair,
    I'll wear my fine doe-skin.

My mother weeps as I leave her   25
    But I tell her it won't be long,
The murderers wail in Wandsworth Jail
    But I shoot a more popular song.
Down in the enemy country
    Under the enemy tree   30
There lies a lad whose heart has gone bad
    Waiting for me, for me.

He says I have no culture
    And that when I've stormed the pass
I shall fall on the farm with a smoking arm   35
    And ravish his bonny lass.
Under the willow the willow
    Death spreads her dripping wings
And caught in the snare of the bleeding air
    The butcher-bird sings, sings, sings.   40

GEOFFREY CHAUCER (1340?–1400)

The Complaint of Chaucer to His Purse

To yow, my purse, and to noon other wight°   *person*
Complayne I, for ye be my lady dere!
I am so sory, now that ye been lyght;
For certes, but° ye make me hevy chere,   *unless*
Me were as leef be layd upon my bere;   5
For which unto your mercy thus I crye:
Beth hevy ageyn, or elles moote I dye!

Now voucheth sauf° this day, or° yt be nyght,   *vouchsafe;*
That I of yow the blisful soun may here,   *before*
Or see your colour lyk the sonne bryght,   10
That of yelownesse hadde never pere.
Ye be my lyf, ye be myn hertes stere°,   *rudder*
Quene of comfort and of good companye:
Beth hevy ageyn, or elles moote I dye!

Now purse, that ben to me my lyves lyght   15
And saveour, as° doun in this world here,   *while*
Out of this toune helpe me thurgh your myght,
Syn that ye wole nat ben my tresorere;
For I am shave as nye as any frere.
But yet I pray unto your curtesye: 20
Beth hevy ageyn, or elles moote I dye!

Lenvoy de Chaucer

O conquerour of Brutes Albyon,
Which that by lyne and free eleccion
Been verray° kyng, this song to yow I sende;   *true*
And ye, that mowen° alle oure harmes amende,   *can*   25
Have mynde upon my supplicacion!

The Complaint of Chaucer to His Purse. Chaucer appears to have sent this poem in 1399 to the newly crowned Henry IV, who promptly added forty marks to the poet's annual salary. 19. *I am shave as nye as any frere:* I am as close-shaven (of money) as a friar's head. *Lenvoy de Chaucer:* In a *ballade,* the French form Chaucer imitates here, the *envoy* is usually the poet's parting address to his ruler or patron. 22. *Brutes Albyon:* Albion ("the white land") is another name for white-cliffed England. Old chroniclers thought Britain to have been founded by Brutus (a legendary hero, great-grandson of Aeneas) and named after him.

SAMUEL TAYLOR COLERIDGE (1772–1834)

Kubla Khan

OR, A VISION IN A DREAM. A FRAGMENT.

In Xanadu did Kubla Khan
A stately pleasure-dome decree:
Where Alph, the sacred river, ran
Through caverns measureless to man
    Down to a sunless sea.   5
So twice five miles of fertile ground
With walls and towers were girdled round;
And there were gardens bright with sinuous rills,
Where blossomed many an incense-bearing tree;
And here were forests ancient as the hills,   10
Enfolding sunny spots of greenery.

But oh! that deep romantic chasm which slanted
Down the green hill athwart a cedarn cover!
A savage place! as holy and enchanted
As e'er beneath a waning moon was haunted   15
By woman wailing for her demon-lover!
And from this chasm, with ceaseless turmoil seething,
As if this earth in fast thick pants were breathing,
A mighty fountain momently was forced:
Amid whose swift half-intermitted burst   20
Huge fragments vaulted like rebounding hail,
Or chaffy grain beneath the thresher's flail:
And 'mid these dancing rocks at once and ever
It flung up momently the sacred river.
Five miles meandering with a mazy motion   25
Through wood and dale the sacred river ran,
Then reached the caverns measureless to man,
And sank in tumult to a lifeless ocean:
And 'mid this tumult Kubla heard from far
Ancestral voices prophesying war!   30
    The shadow of the dome of pleasure
    Floated midway on the waves;
    Where was heard the mingled measure
    From the fountain and the caves.
It was a miracle of rare device,   35
A sunny pleasure-dome with caves of ice!

A damsel with a dulcimer
In a vision once I saw:
It was an Abyssinian maid,
And on her dulcimer she played,   40
Singing of Mount Abora.
Could I revive within me
Her symphony and song,
To such a deep delight 'twould win me,
That with music loud and long,   45
I would build that dome in air,
That sunny dome! those caves of ice!
And all who heard should see them there,
And all should cry, Beware! Beware!
His flashing eyes, his floating hair!   50
Weave a circle round him thrice,
And close your eyes with holy dread,
For he on honey-dew hath fed,
And drunk the milk of Paradise.

Kubla Khan. There was an actual Kublai Khan, a thirteenth-century
Mongol emperor, and a Chinese city of Xamdu; but Coleridge's dream
vision also borrows from travelers' descriptions of such other exotic places
as Abyssinia and America. 51. *circle:* a magic circle drawn to keep away
evil spirits.

ELIZA COOK (1818–1889)

The Old Arm-Chair

I love it, I love it! and who shall dare
To chide me for loving that old arm-chair?
I've treasured it long as a sainted prize,
I've bedewed it with tears, I've embalmed it with sighs,
'Tis bound by a thousand bands to my heart;   5
Not a tie will break, not a link will start.
Would you know the spell? — a mother sat there!
And a sacred thing is that old arm-chair.

In childhood's hour I lingered near
The hallowed seat with listening ear;   10
And gentle words that mother would give
To fit me to die and teach me to live.
She told me that shame would never betide
With truth for my creed, and God for my guide;
She taught me to lisp my earliest prayer,   15
As I knelt beside that old arm-chair.

I sat and watched her many a day,
When her eyes grew dim, and her locks were gray;
And I almost worshiped her when she smiled,
And turned from her Bible to bless her child.   20
Years rolled on, but the last one sped, —
My idol was shattered, my earth-star fled!
I learned how much the heart can bear,
When I saw her die in her old arm-chair.

'Tis past, 'tis past! but I gaze on it now,   25
With quivering breath and throbbing brow;
'Twas there she nursed me, 'twas there she died,
And memory flows with a lava tide.
Say it is folly, and deem me weak,
Whilst scalding drops start down my cheek;   30
But I love it, I love it! and cannot tear
My soul from a mother's old arm-chair.

E. E. CUMMINGS (1894–1962)

'when serpents bargain for the right to squirm'

when serpents bargain for the right to squirm
and the sun strikes to gain a living wage —
when thorns regard their roses with alarm
and rainbows are insured against old age

when every thrush may sing no new moon in   5
if all screech-owls have not okayed his voice
— and any wave signs on the dotted line
or else an ocean is compelled to close

when the oak begs permission of the birch
to make an acorn — valleys accuse their   10
mountains of having altitude — and march
denounces april as a saboteur

then we'll believe in that incredible
unanimal mankind(and not until)

EMILY DICKINSON (1830–1886)

'I started Early–Took my Dog'

I started Early–Took my Dog–
And visited the Sea–
The Mermaids in the Basement
Came out to look at me–

And Frigates–in the Upper Floor   5
Extended Hempen Hands–
Presuming Me to be a Mouse–
Aground–upon the Sands–

But no Man moved Me–till the Tide
Went past my simple Shoe–   10
And past my Apron–and my Belt
And past my Bodice–too–

And made as He would eat me up–
As wholly as a Dew
Upon a Dandelion's Sleeve–   15
And then–I started–too–

And He–He followed–close behind–
I felt His Silver Heel
Upon my Ankle–Then my Shoes
Would overflow with Pearl–   20

Until We met the Solid Town–
No One He seemed to know–
And bowing–with a Mighty look–
At me–The Sea withdrew–

'The Soul selects her own Society'

The Soul selects her own Society–
Then–shuts the Door–
To her divine Majority–
Present no more–

Unmoved–she notes the Chariots–pausing–   5
At her low Gate–
Unmoved–an Emperor be kneeling
Upon her Mat–

I've known her—from an ample nation—
Choose One—
Then—close the Valves of her attention—
Like Stone—

EMILY DICKINSON (1830–1886)

'Because I could not stop for Death'

Because I could not stop for Death—
He kindly stopped for me—
The Carriage held but just Ourselves—
And Immortality.

We slowly drove—He knew no haste   5
And I had put away
My labor and my leisure too,
For His Civility—

We passed the School, where Children strove
At Recess—in the Ring—   10
We passed the Fields of Gazing Grain—
We passed the Setting Sun—

Or rather—He passed Us—
The Dews drew quivering and chill—
For only Gossamer, my Gown—   15
My Tippet—only Tulle—

We paused before a House that seemed
A Swelling of the Ground—
The Roof was scarcely visible—
The Cornice—in the Ground—   20

Since then—'tis Centuries—and yet
Feels shorter than the Day
I first surmised the Horses' Heads
Were toward Eternity—

'**Because I could not stop for Death.**' In the version of this poem printed by Emily Dickinson's first editors in 1890, stanza four was left out. In line 9 *strove* was replaced by *played*; line 10 was made to read "Their lessons scarcely done"; line 20, "The cornice but a mound"; line 21, "Since then 'tis centuries, but each"; and capitalization and punctuation were made conventional.

JOHN DONNE (1572–1631)

A Valediction: Forbidding Mourning

As virtuous men pass mildly away,
 And whisper to their souls to go,
Whilst some of their sad friends do say
 The breath goes now, and some say no:

So let us melt, and make no noise,   5
 No tear-floods, nor sigh-tempests move;
'Twere profanation of our joys
 To tell the laity our love.

Moving of th' earth° brings harms and fears;   *earthquake*
 Men reckon what it did and meant;   10
But trepidation of the spheres,
 Though greater far, is innocent°.   *harmless*

Dull súblunary lovers' love
 (Whose soul is sense) cannot admit
Absence, because it doth remove   15
 Those things which elemented° it.   *constituted*

But we, by a love so much refined
 That ourselves know not what it is,
Inter-assurèd of the mind,
 Care less, eyes, lips, and hands to miss.   20

Our two souls, therefore, which are one,
 Though I must go, endure not yet
A breach, but an expansiòn,
 Like gold to airy thinness beat.

If they be two, they are two so   25
 As stiff twin compasses are two:
Thy soul, the fixed foot, makes no show
 To move, but doth, if th' other do.

And though it in the center sit,
 Yet when the other far doth roam,   30
It leans and harkens after it,
 And grows erect as that comes home.

Such wilt thou be to me, who must,
 Like th' other foot, obliquely run;
Thy firmness makes my circle just°,   *perfect* 35
 And makes me end where I begun.

A Valediction: Forbidding Mourning. 11. *spheres:* in Ptolemaic astronomy, the concentric spheres surrounding the earth. The trepidation or
motion of the ninth sphere was thought to change the date of the
equinox.

JOHN DONNE (1572–1631)

A Lecture upon the Shadow

Stand still, and I will read to thee
A lecture, love, in love's philosophy.
   These three hours that we have spent
   Walking here, two shadows went
Along with us, which we ourselves produced;   5
   But, now the sun is just above our head,
   We do those shadows tread,
And to brave clearness all things are reduced.
   So whilst our infant loves did grow,
   Disguises did, and shadows, flow   10
   From us and our cares, but now 'tis not so.

That love hath not attained the high'st degree,
Which is still diligent lest others see.

Except our loves at this noon stay,
We shall new shadows make the other way.   15
   As the first were made to blind
   Others, these which come behind
Will work upon ourselves, and blind our eyes.
   If our loves faint, and westwardly decline,
   To me thou falsely thine,   20
And I to thee, mine actions shall disguise.
   The morning shadows wear away,
   But these grow longer all the day;
   But oh, love's day is short, if love decay.

Love is a growing, or full constant light,   25
And his short minute after noon, is night.

JOHN DONNE (1572–1631)

The Bait

Come live with me and be my love,
And we will some new pleasures prove
Of golden sands and crystal brooks,
With silken lines and silver hooks.

There will the river whispering run   5
Warmed by thy eyes more than the sun;
And there the enamored fish will stay,
Begging° themselves they may betray.   *begging that*

When thou wilt swim in that live bath,
Each fish, which every channel hath,   10
Will amorously to thee swim,
Gladder to catch thee, than thou him.

If thou to be so seen be'st loath,
By sun or moon, thou dark'nest both;
And if myself have leave to see,   15
I need not their light, having thee.

Let others freeze with angling reeds°,   *rods*
And cut their legs with shells and weeds,
Or treacherously poor fish beset
With strangling snare or windowy net.   20

Let coarse bold hands from slimy nest
The bedded fish in banks out-wrest,
Or curious traitors, sleave-silk° flies,   *silk thread*
Bewitch poor fishes' wand'ring eyes.

For thee, thou need'st no such deceit,   25
For thou thyself art thine own bait;
That fish that is not catched thereby,
Alas, is wiser far than I.

The Bait. A reply to Marlowe's "Passionate Shepherd" (see p. 325).

CHARLES SACKVILLE, EARL OF DORSET (1638–1706)

A Paraphrase from the French

In grey-haired Celia's withered arms
  As mighty Louis lay,
She cried, "If I have any charms,
  My dearest, let's away!
For you, my love, is all my fear,   5
  Hark how the drums do rattle;
Alas, sir! what should you do here
  In dreadful day of battle?
Let little Orange stay and fight,
  For danger's his diversion;   10
The wise will think you in the right
  Not to expose your person,
Nor vex your thoughts how to repair
  The ruins of your glory:
You ought to leave so mean a care   15
  To those who pen your story.
Are not Boileau and Corneille paid
  For panegyric writing?
They know how heroes may be made,
  Without the help of fighting.   20
When foes too saucily approach,
  'Tis best to leave them fairly;
Put six good horses in your coach,
  And carry me to Marly.
Let Boufflers, to secure your fame,   25
  Go take some town, or buy it;
Whilst you, great sir, at Notre Dame
  Te Deum sing in quiet!"

A Paraphrase from the French. This free translation, attributed without
certainty to Dorset, pokes fun at Louis XIV. 1. *Celia:* Madame de Main-
tenon, who became the wife (not queen) of Louis in 1685, said to have
influenced French affairs of state. 9. *Orange:* William III, king of England, with whom Louis was at war. 24. *Marly:* where Louis had a secluded chateau. 25. *Boufflers:* Louis's most illustrious general. 28. *Te
Deum:* the hymn beginning *Te Deum laudamus* ("O God, we praise
Thee").

JOHN DRYDEN (1631–1700)

To the Memory of Mr. Oldham

Farewell, too little and too lately known,
Whom I began to think and call my own;
For sure our souls were near allied, and thine
Cast in the same poetic mold with mine.
One common note on either lyre did strike,   5
And knaves and fools we both abhorred alike.
To the same goal did both our studies drive:
The last set out the soonest did arrive.
Thus Nisus fell upon the slippery place,
While his young friend performed and won the race.   10
O early ripe! to thy abundant store
What could advancing age have added more?
It might (what Nature never gives the young)
Have taught the numbers° of thy native tongue.   *meters*
But satire needs not those, and wit will shine   15
Through the harsh cadence of a rugged line.
A noble error, and but seldom made,
When poets are by too much force betrayed.
Thy gen'rous fruits, though gathered ere their prime,
Still showed a quickness; and maturing time   20
But mellows what we write to the dull sweets of rhyme.
Once more, hail, and farewell! farewell, thou young
But ah! too short, Marcellus of our tongue!
Thy brows with ivy and with laurels bound;
But fate and gloomy night encompass thee around.   25

To the Memory of Mr. Oldham. John Oldham, poet best remembered for his *Satires upon the Jesuits,* had died at thirty. 9–10. *Nisus, his young friend:* these two close friends, as Virgil tells us in the *Aeneid,* ran a race for the prize of an olive crown. 23. *Marcellus:* Had he not died in his twentieth year, he would have succeeded the Roman emperor Augustus. Dryden's line 25 echoes the *Aeneid* (VI, 866), in which Marcellus is seen walking under the black cloud of his impending doom.

T. S. ELIOT (1888–1965)

The Love Song of J. Alfred Prufrock

S'io credessi che mia risposta fosse
a persona che mai tornasse al mondo,
questa fiamma staria senza più scosse.
Ma per ciò che giammai di questo fondo
non tornò vivo alcun, s'i'odo il vero,
senza tema d'infamia ti rispondo.

Let us go then, you and I,
When the evening is spread out against the sky
Like a patient etherized upon a table;
Let us go, through certain half-deserted streets,
The muttering retreats
Of restless nights in one-night cheap hotels
And sawdust restaurants with oyster-shells:
Streets that follow like a tedious argument
Of insidious intent
To lead you to an overwhelming question . . .
Oh, do not ask, "What is it?"
Let us go and make our visit.

In the room the women come and go
Talking of Michelangelo.

The yellow fog that rubs its back upon the window-panes,
The yellow smoke that rubs its muzzle on the window-panes,
Licked its tongue into the corners of the evening,
Lingered upon the pools that stand in drains,
Let fall upon its back the soot that falls from chimneys,
Slipped by the terrace, made a sudden leap,
And seeing that it was a soft October night,
Curled once about the house, and fell asleep.

And indeed there will be time
For the yellow smoke the slides along the street
Rubbing its back upon the window-panes;
There will be time, there will be time
To prepare a face to meet the faces that you meet;
There will be time to murder and create,
And time for all the works and days of hands
That lift and drop a question on your plate;
Time for you and time for me,
And time yet for a hundred indecisions,
And for a hundred visions and revisions,
Before the taking of a toast and tea.

In the room the women come and go
Talking of Michelangelo.

And indeed there will be time
To wonder, "Do I dare?" and, "Do I dare?"
Time to turn back and descend the stair,
With a bald spot in the middle of my hair —
(They will say: "How his hair is growing thin!")
My morning coat, my collar mounting firmly to the chin,
My necktie rich and modest, but asserted by a simple pin —

(They will say: "But how his arms and legs are thin!")
Do I dare   45
Disturb the universe?
In a minute there is time
For decisions and revisions which a minute will reverse.

For I have known them all already, known them all —
Have known the evenings, mornings, afternoons,   50
I have measured out my life with coffee spoons;
I know the voices dying with a dying fall
Beneath the music from a farther room.
      So how should I presume?

And I have known the eyes already, known them all —   55
The eyes that fix you in a formulated phrase,
And when I am formulated, sprawling on a pin,
When I am pinned and wriggling on the wall,
Then how should I begin
To spit out all the butt-ends of my days and ways?   60
      And how should I presume?

And I have known the arms already, known them all —
Arms that are braceleted and white and bare
(But in the lamplight, downed with light brown hair!)
Is it perfume from a dress   65
That makes me so digress?
Arms that lie along a table, or wrap about a shawl.
      And should I then presume?
      And how should I begin?

          .   .   .   .   .

Shall I say, I have gone at dusk through narrow streets   70
And watched the smoke that rises from the pipes
Of lonely men in shirt-sleeves, leaning out of windows? . . .

I should have been a pair of ragged claws
Scuttling across the floors of silent seas.

          .   .   .   .   .

And the afternoon, the evening, sleeps so peacefully!   75
Smoothed by long fingers,
Asleep . . . tired . . . or it malingers,
Stretched on the floor, here beside you and me.
Should I, after tea and cakes and ices,
Have the strength to force the moment to its crisis?   80
But though I have wept and fasted, wept and prayed,
Though I have seen my head (grown slightly bald) brought in
      upon a platter,
I am no prophet — and here's no great matter;

304

I have seen the moment of my greatness flicker,
And I have seen the eternal Footman hold my coat, and snicker, 85
And in short, I was afraid.

And would it have been worth it, after all,
After the cups, the marmalade, the tea,
Among the porcelain, among some talk of you and me,
Would it have been worth while, 90
To have bitten off the matter with a smile,
To have squeezed the universe into a ball
To roll it toward some overwhelming question,
To say: "I am Lazarus, come from the dead,
Come back to tell you all, I shall tell you all" — 95
If one, settling a pillow by her head,
    Should say: "That is not what I meant at all.
    That is not it, at all."

And would it have been worth it, after all,
Would it have been worth while, 100
After the sunsets and the dooryards and the sprinkled streets,
After the novels, after the teacups, after the skirts that trail
    along the floor —
And this, and so much more? —
It is impossible to say just what I mean!
But as if a magic lantern threw the nerves in patterns on a
    screen: 105
Would it have been worth while
If one, settling a pillow or throwing off a shawl,
And turning toward the window, should say:
    "That is not it at all,
    That is not what I meant, at all." 110

          .   .   .   .   .

No! I am not Prince Hamlet, nor was meant to be;
Am an attendant lord, one that will do
To swell a progress, start a scene or two,
Advise the prince; no doubt, an easy tool,
Deferential, glad to be of use, 115
Politic, cautious, and meticulous;
Full of high sentence, but a bit obtuse;
At times, indeed, almost ridiculous —
Almost, at times, the Fool.

I grow old . . . I grow old . . . 120
I shall wear the bottoms of my trousers rolled.

Shall I part my hair behind? Do I dare to eat a peach?
I shall wear white flannel trousers, and walk upon the beach.
I have heard the mermaids singing, each to each.

I do not think that they will sing to me.   125

I have seen them riding seaward on the waves
Combing the white hair of the waves blown back
When the wind blows the water white and black.

We have lingered in the chambers of the sea
By sea-girls wreathed with seaweed red and brown   130
Till human voices wake us, and we drown.

The Love Song of J. Alfred Prufrock. The epigraph, from Dante's *Inferno*, is the speech of one dead and damned, who thinks that his hearer also is going to remain in Hell. Count Guido da Montefeltro, whose sin has been to give false counsel after a corrupt prelate had offered him prior absolution and whose punishment is to be wrapped in a constantly burning flame, offers to tell Dante his story: "If I thought my reply were to someone who could ever return to the world, this flame would waver no more. But since, I'm told, nobody ever escapes from this pit, I'll tell you without fear of ill fame." 29. *works and days*: title of a poem by Hesiod (eighth century B.C.), depicting his life as a hard-working Greek farmer and exhorting his brother to be like him. 82. *head . . . platter*: like that of John the Baptist, prophet and praiser of chastity, whom King Herod beheaded at the demand of Herodias, his unlawfully wedded wife (see Mark 6:17–28). 92–93. *squeezed . . . To roll it*: an echo from Marvell's "To His Coy Mistress," lines 41–42 (see p. 327). 94. *Lazarus*: probably the Lazarus whom Christ called forth from the tomb (John 11:1–44), but possibly the beggar seen in Heaven by the rich man in Hell (Luke 16:19–25).

WILLIAM EMPSON (b. 1906)

Legal Fiction

Law makes long spokes of the short stakes of men.
Your well fenced out real estate of mind
No high flat of the nomad citizen
Looks over, or train leaves behind.

Your rights extend under and above your claim   5
Without bound; you own land in Heaven and Hell;
Your part of earth's surface and mass the same,
Of all cosmos' volume, and all stars as well.

Your rights reach down where all owners meet, in Hell's
Pointed exclusive conclave, at earth's center   10
(Your spun farm's root still on that axis dwells);
And up, through galaxies, a growing sector.

You are nomad yet; the lighthouse beam you own
Flashes, like Lucifer, through the firmament.
Earth's axis varies; your dark central cone   15
Wavers, a candle's shadow, at the end.

306

KENNETH FEARING (1902–1961)

Dirge

1-2-3 was the number he played but today the number came
    3-2-1;
Bought his Carbide at 30 and it went to 29; had the favorite
    at Bowie but the track was slow —

O executive type, would you like to drive a floating-power,
    knee-action, silk-upholstered six? Wed a Hollywood star?
    Shoot the course in 58? Draw to the ace, king, jack?
O fellow with a will who won't take no, watch out for three
    cigarettes on the same, single match; O democratic voter
    born in August under Mars, beware of liquidated rails —

Denouement to denouement, he took a personal pride in the   5
    certain, certain way he lived his own, private life,
But nevertheless, they shut off his gas; nevertheless, the bank
    foreclosed; nevertheless, the landlord called; neverthe-
    less, the radio broke,

And twelve o'clock arrived just once too often,
Just the same he wore one gray tweed suit, bought one straw
    hat, drank one straight Scotch, walked one short step,
    took one long look, drew one deep breath,
Just one too many,

And wow he died as wow he lived,   10
Going whop to the office and blooie home to sleep and biff
    got married and bam had children and oof got fired,
Zowie did he live and zowie did he die,

With who the hell are you at the corner of his casket, and
    where the hell're we going on the right-hand silver knob,
    and who the hell cares walking second from the end with
    an American Beauty wreath from why the hell not,

Very much missed by the circulation staff of the New York
    Evening Post; deeply mourned by the B.M.T.
Wham, Mr. Roosevelt; pow, Sears Roebuck; awk, big dipper;   15
    bop, summer rain;
Bong, Mr., bong, Mr., bong, Mr., bong.

Dirge. 2. *Carbide:* the Union Carbon & Carbide Co. 14. *B.M.T.*: Brooklyn-
Manhattan Transit, a New York subway line.

ROBERT FROST (1874–1963)

Design

> I found a dimpled spider, fat and white,
> On a white heal-all, holding up a moth
> Like a white piece of rigid satin cloth —
> Assorted characters of death and blight
> Mixed ready to begin the morning right, 5
> Like the ingredients of a witches' broth —
> A snow-drop spider, a flower like a froth,
> And dead wings carried like a paper kite.
>
> What had that flower to do with being white,
> The wayside blue and innocent heal-all? 10
> What brought the kindred spider to that height,
> Then steered the white moth thither in the night?
> What but design of darkness to appall? —
> If design govern in a thing so small.

Provide, Provide

> The witch that came (the withered hag)
> To wash the steps with pail and rag,
> Was once the beauty Abishag,
>
> The picture pride of Hollywood.
> Too many fall from great and good 5
> For you to doubt the likelihood.
>
> Die early and avoid the fate.
> Or if predestined to die late,
> Make up your mind to die in state.
>
> Make the whole stock exchange your own! 10
> If need be occupy a throne,
> Where nobody can call *you* crone.
>
> Some have relied on what they knew;
> Others on simply being true.
> What worked for them might work for you. 15
>
> No memory of having starred
> Atones for later disregard,
> Or keeps the end from being hard.
>
> Better to go down dignified
> With boughten friendship at your side 20
> Than none at all. Provide, provide!

308

ROBERT FROST (1874–1963)

Stopping by Woods on a Snowy Evening

Whose woods these are I think I know.
His house is in the village though;
He will not see me stopping here
To watch his woods fill up with snow.

My little horse must think it queer   5
To stop without a farmhouse near
Between the woods and frozen lake
The darkest evening of the year.

He gives his harness bells a shake
To ask if there is some mistake.   10
The only other sound's the sweep
Of easy wind and downy flake.

The woods are lovely, dark and deep,
But I have promises to keep,
And miles to go before I sleep,   15
And miles to go before I sleep.

The Draft Horse

With a lantern that wouldn't burn
In too frail a buggy we drove
Behind too heavy a horse
Through a pitch-dark limitless grove.

And a man came out of the trees   5
And took our horse by the head
And reaching back to his ribs
Deliberately stabbed him dead.

The ponderous beast went down
With a crack of a broken shaft.   10
And the night drew through the trees
In one long invidious draft.

The most unquestioning pair
That ever accepted fate
And the least disposed to ascribe   15
Any more than we had to to hate,

We assumed that the man himself
Or someone he had to obey
Wanted us to get down
And walk the rest of the way.   20

THOM GUNN (b. 1929)

On the Move

"Man, you gotta Go."

The blue jay scuffling in the bushes follows
Some hidden purpose, and the gust of birds
That spurts across the field, the wheeling swallows,
Have nested in the trees and undergrowth.
Seeking their instinct, or their poise, or both,   5
One moves with an uncertain violence
Under the dust thrown by a baffled sense
Or the dull thunder of approximate words.

On motorcycles, up the road, they come:
Small, black, as flies hanging in heat, the Boys,   10
Until the distance throws them forth, their hum
Bulges to thunder held by calf and thigh.
In goggles, donned impersonality,
In gleaming jackets trophied with the dust,
They strap in doubt — by hiding it, robust —   15
And almost hear a meaning in their noise.

Exact conclusion of their hardiness
Has no shape yet, but from known whereabouts
They ride, direction where the tires press.
They scare a flight of birds across the field: 20
Much that is natural, to the will must yield.
Men manufacture both machine and soul,
And use what they imperfectly control
To dare a future from the taken routes.

It is a part solution, after all.   25
One is not necessarily discord
On earth; or damned because, half animal,
One lacks direct instinct, because one wakes
Afloat on movement that divides and breaks.
One joins the movement in a valueless world,   30
Choosing it, till, both hurler and the hurled,
One moves as well, always toward, toward.

A minute holds them, who have come to go:
The self-defined, astride the created will
They burst away; the towns they travel through   35
Are home for neither bird nor holiness,
For birds and saints complete their purposes.
At worst, one is in motion; and at best,
Reaching no absolute, in which to rest,
One is always nearer by not keeping still.   40

310

THOMAS HARDY (1840–1928)

Channel Firing

That night your great guns, unawares,
Shook all our coffins as we lay,
And broke the chancel window-squares,
We thought it was the Judgment-day

And sat upright. While drearisome   5
Arose the howl of wakened hounds:
The mouse let fall the altar-crumb,
The worms drew back into the mounds,

The glebe cow drooled. Till God called, "No;
It's gunnery practice out at sea   10
Just as before you went below;
The world is as it used to be:

"All nations striving strong to make
Red war yet redder. Mad as hatters
They do no more for Christés sake   15
Than you who are helpless in such matters.

"That this is not the judgment-hour
For some of them's a blessed thing,
For if it were they'd have to scour
Hell's floor for so much threatening . . .   20

"Ha, ha. It will be warmer when
I blow the trumpet (if indeed
I ever do; for you are men,
And rest eternal sorely need)."

So down we lay again. "I wonder,   25
Will the world ever saner be,"
Said one, "than when He sent us under
In our indifferent century!"

And many a skeleton shook his head.
"Instead of preaching forty year,"   30
My neighbor Parson Thirdly said,
"I wish I had stuck to pipes and beer."

Again the guns disturbed the hour,
Roaring their readiness to avenge,
As far inland as Stourton Tower,   35
And Camelot, and starlit Stonehenge.

Channel Firing. 9. *glebe*: land belonging to the church, used for grazing.
35. *Stourton Tower*: a fictional medieval landmark, Hardy's invention. 36.
Camelot: where King Arthur held court; *Stonehenge*: circle of huge
stones thought to be the ruins of a prehistoric place of worship.

THOMAS HARDY (1840–1928)

The Convergence of the Twain

(Lines on the loss of the "Titanic")

I

In a solitude of the sea
Deep from human vanity,
And the Pride of Life that planned her, stilly couches she.

II

Steel chambers, late the pyres
Of her salamandrine fires,   5
Cold currents thrid°, and turn to rhythmic tidal lyres.   *thread*

III

Over the mirrors meant
To glass the opulent
The sea-worm crawls — grotesque, slimed, dumb, indifferent.

IV

Jewels in joy designed   10
To ravish the sensuous mind
Lie lightless, all their sparkles bleared and black and blind.

V

Dim moon-eyed fishes near
Gaze at the gilded gear
And query: "What does this vaingloriousness down here?"   15

VI

Well: while was fashioning
This creature of cleaving wing,
The Immanent Will that stirs and urges everything

VII

Prepared a sinister mate
For her — so gaily great —   20
A Shape of Ice, for the time far and dissociate.

VIII

And as the smart ship grew
In stature, grace, and hue,
In shadowy silent distance grew the Iceberg too.

312

Alien they seemed to be: 25
No mortal eye could see
The intimate welding of their later history,

Or sign that they were bent
By paths coincident
On being anon twin halves of one august event. 30

Till the Spinner of the Years
Said "Now!" And each one hears,
And consummation comes, and jars two hemispheres.

The Convergence of the Twain. The luxury liner *Titanic*, supposedly unsinkable, went down in 1912 when she struck an iceberg on her first Atlantic voyage. 5. *salamandrine*: like the salamander, a lizard that supposedly thrives in fires; or like a spirit of the same name that inhabits fire (according to alchemists).

THOMAS HARDY (1840–1928)

During Wind and Rain

They sing their dearest songs —
He, she, all of them — yea,
Treble and tenor and bass,
   And one to play;
With the candles mooning each face. . . . 5
   Ah, no; the years O!
How the sick leaves reel down in throngs!

They clear the creeping moss —
Elders and juniors — aye,
Making the pathways neat 10
   And the garden gay;
And they build a shady seat. . . .
   Ah, no; the years, the years;
See, the white storm-birds wing across!

They are blithely breakfasting all — 15
Men and maidens — yea,
Under the summer tree,

With a glimpse of the bay,
While pet fowl come to the knee. . . .
    Ah, no; the years O!
And the rotten rose is ript from the wall.

They change to a high new house,
He, she, all of them — aye,
Clocks and carpets and chairs
    On the lawn all day,
And brightest things that are theirs. . . .
    Ah, no; the years, the years;
Down their carved names the rain-drop plows.

GEORGE HERBERT (1593–1633)

Love

Love bade me welcome; yet my soul drew back,
    Guilty of dust and sin.
But quick-eyed Love, observing me grow slack
    From my first entrance in,
Drew nearer to me, sweetly questioning
    If I lacked anything.

"A guest," I answered, "worthy to be here";
    Love said, "You shall be he."
"I, the unkind, ungrateful? Ah, my dear,
    I cannot look on Thee."
Love took my hand, and smiling did reply,
    "Who made the eyes but I?"

"Truth, Lord, but I have marred them; let my shame
    Go where it doth deserve."
"And know you not," says Love, "who bore the blame?"
    "My dear, then I will serve."
"You must sit down," says Love, "and taste My meat."
    So I did sit and eat.

ROBERT HERRICK (1591–1674)

To the Virgins, to Make Much of Time

Gather ye rose-buds while ye may,
    Old Time is still a-flying;
And this same flower that smiles today,
    Tomorrow will be dying.

The glorious lamp of heaven, the sun,   5
    The higher he's a-getting,
The sooner will his race be run,
    And nearer he's to setting.

That age is best which is the first,
    When youth and blood are warmer;   10
But being spent, the worse, and worst
    Times still succeed the former.

Then be not coy, but use your time,
    And while ye may, go marry;
For having lost but once your prime,   15
    You may for ever tarry.

GERARD MANLEY HOPKINS (1844–1889)

Pied Beauty

Glory be to God for dappled things —
    For skies of couple-color as a brinded° cow;   *streaked*
        For rose-moles all in stipple upon trout that swim;
Fresh-firecoal chestnut-falls; finches' wings;
    Landscape plotted and pieced — fold, fallow, and plow;   5
        And áll trádes, their gear and tackle and trim°.   *equipment*
All things counter, original, spare, strange;
    Whatever is fickle, freckled (who knows how?)
        With swift, slow; sweet, sour; adazzle, dim;
He fathers-forth whose beauty is past change: 10
        Praise him.

GERARD MANLEY HOPKINS (1844–1889)

The Windhover

To Christ our Lord

I caught this morning morning's minion, kingdom of day-
　　light's dauphin, dapple-dawn-drawn Falcon, in his riding
　Of the rolling level underneath him steady air, and
　　striding
High there, how he rung upon the rein of a wimpling wing
In his ecstasy! then off, off forth on swing,
　As a skate's heel sweeps smooth on a bow-bend: the hurl　　5
　　and gliding
　Rebuffed the big wind. My heart in hiding
Stirred for a bird, — the achieve of, the mastery of the thing!

Brute beauty and valor and act, oh, air, pride, plume, here
　Buckle! AND the fire that breaks from thee then, a billion
Times told lovelier, more dangerous, O my chevalier!　　　10

　No wonder of it: shéer plód makes plow down sillion°　　*furrow*
Shine, and blue-bleak embers, ah my dear,
　Fall, gall themselves, and gash gold-vermilion.

The Windhover. A windhover is a kestrel, or small falcon, so called because it can hover upon the wind. 3. *rung . . . wing:* A horse is "rung
upon the rein" when its trainer holds the end of a long rein and has the
horse circle him. The possible meanings of *wimpling* include (1) curv-
ing; (2) pleated, arranged in many little folds one on top of another;
(3) rippling or undulating like the surface of a flowing stream.

A. E. HOUSMAN (1859–1936)

To an Athlete Dying Young

The time you won your town the race
We chaired you through the market-place;
Man and boy stood cheering by,
And home we brought you shoulder-high.

Today, the road all runners come,　　　　　　　　　　5
Shoulder-high we bring you home,
And set you at your threshold down,
Townsman of a stiller town.

Smart lad, to slip betimes away
From fields where glory does not stay,　　　　　　　　10
And early though the laurel grows
It withers quicker than the rose.

316

Eyes the shady night has shut
Cannot see the record cut,
And silence sounds no worse than cheers   15
After earth has stopped the ears.

Now you will not swell the rout
Of lads that wore their honors out,
Runners whom renown outran
And the name died before the man.   20

So set, before its echoes fade,
The fleet foot on the sill of shade,
And hold to the low lintel up
The still-defended challenge-cup.

And round that early-laureled head   25
Will flock to gaze the strengthless dead,
And find unwithered on its curls
The garland briefer than a girl's.

A. E. HOUSMAN (1859–1936)

'Terence, this is stupid stuff'

"Terence, this is stupid stuff:
You eat your victuals fast enough;
There can't be much amiss, 'tis clear,
To see the rate you drink your beer.
But oh, good Lord, the verse you make,   5
It gives a chap the belly-ache.
The cow, the old cow, she is dead;
It sleeps well, the horned head:
We poor lads, 'tis our turn now
To hear such tunes as killed the cow.   10
Pretty friendship 'tis to rhyme
Your friends to death before their time
Moping melancholy mad:
Come, pipe a tune to dance to, lad."

Why, if 'tis dancing you would be,   15
There's brisker pipes than poetry.
Say, for what were hop-yards meant,
Or why was Burton built on Trent?
Oh many a peer of England brews
Livelier liquor than the Muse,   20
And malt does more than Milton can
To justify God's ways to man.

Ale, man, ale's the stuff to drink
For fellows whom it hurts to think:
Look into the pewter pot
To see the world as the world's not.
And faith, 'tis pleasant till 'tis past:
The mischief is that 'twill not last.
Oh I have been to Ludlow fair
And left my necktie God knows where,
And carried half-way home, or near,
Pints and quarts of Ludlow beer:
Then the world seemed none so bad,
And I myself a sterling lad;
And down in lovely muck I've lain,
Happy till I woke again.
Then I saw the morning sky:
Heigho, the tale was all a lie;
The world, it was the old world yet,
I was I, my things were wet,
And nothing now remained to do
But begin the game anew.

    Therefore, since the world has still
Much good, but much less good than ill,
And while the sun and moon endure
Luck's a chance, but trouble's sure,
I'd face it as a wise man would,
And train for ill and not for good.
'Tis true, the stuff I bring for sale
Is not so brisk a brew as ale:
Out of a stem that scored the hand
I wrung it in a weary land.
But take it: if the smack is sour,
The better for the embittered hour;
It should do good to heart and head
When your soul is in my soul's stead;
And I will friend you, if I may,
In the dark and cloudy day.

    There was a king reigned in the East:
There, when kings will sit to feast,
They get their fill before they think
With poisoned meat and poisoned drink.
He gathered all that springs to birth
From the many-venomed earth;
First a little, thence to more,
He sampled all her killing store;

318

And easy, smiling, seasoned sound,
Sate the king when healths went round.
They put arsenic in his meat
And stared aghast to watch him eat;   70
They poured strychnine in his cup
And shook to see him drink it up:
They shook, they stared as white's their shirt:
Them it was their poison hurt.
— I tell the tale that I heard told.   75
Mithridates, he died old.

'Terence, this is stupid stuff.' 1. *Terence:* As a name for himself, Housman takes that of a Roman poet, author of satiric comedies. 18. *why was
Burton built on Trent?* The answer is: in order to use the river's water in
the town's brewing industry.

RANDALL JARRELL (1914–1965)

The Death of the Ball Turret Gunner

From my mother's sleep I fell into the State
And I hunched in its belly till my wet fur froze.
Six miles from earth, loosed from its dream of life,
I woke to black flak and the nightmare fighters.
When I died they washed me out of the turret with a hose.

The Death of the Ball Turret Gunner. This poem is from a collection
published in 1945. Mr. Jarrell has written: "A ball turret was a plexiglass
sphere set into the belly of a B-17 or B-24, and inhabited by two .50
caliber machine-guns and one man, a short small man. When this gunner
tracked with his machine-guns a fighter attacking his bomber from below,
he revolved with the turret; hunched upside-down in his little sphere, he
looked like the fetus in the womb. The fighters which attacked him were
armed with cannon firing explosive shells. The hose was a steam hose."

ROBINSON JEFFERS (1887–1962)

The Eye

The Atlantic is a stormy moat, and the Mediterranean,
The blue pool in the old garden,
More than five thousand years has drunk sacrifice
Of ships and blood and shines in the sun; but here the
    Pacific:
The ships, planes, wars are perfectly irrelevant.   5
Neither our present blood-feud with the brave dwarfs
Nor any future world-quarrel of westering
And eastering man, the bloody migrations, greed of power,
    battle-falcons,
Are a mote of dust in the great scale-pan.
Here from this mountain shore, headland beyond stormy   10
    headland plunging like dolphins through the gray sea-
    smoke
Into pale sea, look west at the hill of water: it is half the
    planet: this dome, this half-globe, this bulging
Eyeball of water, arched over to Asia,
Australia and white Antarctica: those are the eyelids that
    never close; this is the staring unsleeping
Eye of the earth, and what it watches is not our wars.

The Eye. Jeffers first published this poem in 1944.

BEN JONSON (1573?–1637)

To Celia

Drink to me only with thine eyes,
    And I will pledge with mine;
Or leave a kiss but in the cup,
    And I'll not ask for wine.
The thirst that from the soul doth rise   5
    Doth ask a drink divine;
But might I of Jove's nectar sup,
    I would not change for thine.

I sent thee late a rosy wreath,
    Not so much honoring thee   10
As giving it a hope that there
    It could not withered be.
But thou thereon didst only breathe,
    And sent'st it back to me;
Since when it grows, and smells, I swear,   15
    Not of itself but thee.

JOHN KEATS (1795–1821)

Ode on a Grecian Urn

Thou still unravished bride of quietness,
  Thou foster-child of silence and slow time,
Sylvan historian, who canst thus express
  A flowery tale more sweetly than our rhyme:
What leaf-fringed legend haunts about thy shape   5
  Of deities or mortals, or of both,
     In Tempe or the dales of Arcady?
  What men or gods are these? What maidens loth?
What mad pursuit? What struggle to escape?
     What pipes and timbrels? What wild ecstasy?   10

Heard melodies are sweet, but those unheard
  Are sweeter; therefore, ye soft pipes, play on;
Not to the sensual° ear, but, more endeared,   *physical*
  Pipe to the spirit ditties of no tone:
Fair youth, beneath the trees, thou canst not leave   15
  Thy song, nor ever can those trees be bare;
     Bold Lover, never, never canst thou kiss,
Though winning near the goal — yet, do not grieve;
  She cannot fade, though thou hast not thy bliss,
     For ever wilt thou love, and she be fair!   20

Ah, happy, happy boughs! that cannot shed
  Your leaves, nor ever bid the Spring adieu;
And, happy melodist, unwearièd,
  For ever piping songs for ever new;
More happy love! more happy, happy love!   25
  For ever warm and still to be enjoyed,
     For ever panting, and for ever young;
All breathing human passion far above,
  That leaves a heart high-sorrowful and cloyed,
     A burning forehead, and a parching tongue.   30

Who are these coming to the sacrifice?
  To what green altar, O mysterious priest,
Lead'st thou that heifer lowing at the skies,
  And all her silken flanks with garlands drest?
What little town by river or sea shore,   35
  Or mountain-built with peaceful citadel,
     Is emptied of this folk, this pious morn?
And, little town, thy streets for evermore
  Will silent be; and not a soul to tell
     Why thou art desolate, can e'er return.   40

O Attic shape! Fair attitude! with brede°   *design*
  Of marble men and maidens overwrought,
With forest branches and the trodden weed;
  Thou, silent form, dost tease us out of thought
As doth Eternity: Cold Pastoral!   45
  When old age shall this generation waste,
    Thou shalt remain, in midst of other woe
  Than ours, a friend to man, to whom thou say'st,
Beauty is truth, truth beauty, — that is all
  Ye know on earth, and all ye need to know.   50

Ode on a Grecian Urn. 7. *Tempe, dales of Arcady:* valleys in Greece. 41.
Attic: Athenian, possessing a classical simplicity and grace. 49–50: If
Keats had put the urn's words in quotation marks, critics might have
been spared much ink. Does the urn say just "beauty is truth, truth
beauty," or does its statement take in the whole of the last two lines?

PHILIP LARKIN (b. 1922)

Church Going

Once I am sure there's nothing going on
I step inside, letting the door thud shut.
Another church: matting, seats, and stone,
And little books; sprawlings of flowers, cut
For Sunday, brownish now; some brass and stuff   5
Up at the holy end; the small neat organ;
And a tense, musty, unignorable silence,
Brewed God knows how long. Hatless, I take off
My cycle-clips in awkward reverence,

Move forward, run my hand around the font.   10
From where I stand, the roof looks almost new —
Cleaned, or restored? Someone would know: I don't.
Mounting the lectern, I peruse a few
Hectoring large-scale verses, and pronounce
"Here endeth" much more loudly than I'd meant.   15
The echoes snigger briefly. Back at the door
I sign the book, donate an Irish sixpence,
Reflect the place was not worth stopping for.

Yet stop I did: in fact I often do,
And always end much at a loss like this,   20
Wondering what to look for; wondering, too,
When churches fall completely out of use
What we shall turn them into, if we shall keep
A few cathedrals chronically on show,

Their parchment, plate, and pyx in locked cases,   25
And let the rest rent-free to rain and sheep.
Shall we avoid them as unlucky places?

Or, after dark, will dubious women come
To make their children touch a particular stone;
Pick simples for a cancer; or on some   30
Advised night see walking a dead one?
Power of some sort or other will go on
In games, in riddles, seemingly at random;
But superstition, like belief, must die,
And what remains when disbelief has gone?   35
Grass, weedy pavement, brambles, buttress, sky,

A shape less recognizable each week,
A purpose more obscure. I wonder who
Will be the last, the very last, to seek
This place for what it was; one of the crew   40
That tap and jot and know what rood-lofts were?
Some ruin-bibber, randy for antique,
Or Christmas-addict, counting on a whiff
Of gown-and-bands and organ-pipes and myrrh?
Or will he be my representative,   45

Bored, uninformed, knowing the ghostly silt
Dispersed, yet tending to this cross of ground
Through suburb scrub because it held unspilt
So long and equably what since is found
Only in separation — marriage, and birth,   50
And death, and thoughts of these — for whom was built
This special shell? For, though I've no idea
What this accoutred frowsty° barn is worth,   *musty*
It pleases me to stand in silence here;

A serious house on serious earth it is,   55
In whose blent air all our compulsions meet,
Are recognized, and robed as destinies.
And that much never can be obsolete,
Since someone will forever be surprising
A hunger in himself to be more serious,   60
And gravitating with it to this ground,
Which, he once heard, was proper to grow wise in,
If only that so many dead lie round.

ROBERT LOWELL (b. 1917)

Skunk Hour

(*For Elizabeth Bishop*)

Nautilus Island's hermit
heiress still lives through winter in her Spartan cottage;
her sheep still graze above the sea.
Her son's a bishop. Her farmer
is first selectman in our village;   5
she's in her dotage.

Thirsting for
the hierarchic privacy
of Queen Victoria's century,
she buys up all   10
the eyesores facing her shore,
and lets them fall.

The season's ill —
we've lost our summer millionaire,
who seemed to leap from an L. L. Bean   15
catalogue. His nine-knot yawl
was auctioned off to lobstermen.
A red fox stain covers Blue Hill.

And now our fairy
decorator brightens his shop for fall;   20
his fishnet's filled with orange cork,
orange, his cobbler's bench and awl;
there is no money in his work,
he'd rather marry.

One dark night,   25
my Tudor Ford climbed the hill's skull;
I watched for love-cars. Lights turned down,
they lay together, hull to hull,
where the graveyard shelves on the town. . . .
My mind's not right.   30

A car radio bleats,
"Love, O careless Love. . . ." I hear
my ill-spirit sob in each blood cell,
as if my hand were at its throat. . . .
I myself am hell;   35
nobody's here —

324

only skunks, that search
in the moonlight for a bite to eat.
They march on their soles up Main Street:
white stripes, moonstruck eyes' red fire   40
under the chalk-dry and spar spire
of the Trinitarian Church.

I stand on top
of our back steps and breathe the rich air —
a mother skunk with her column of kittens swills the   45
    garbage pail.
She jabs her wedge-head in a cup
of sour cream, drops her ostrich tail,
and will not scare.

CHRISTOPHER MARLOWE (1564–1593)

The Passionate Shepherd to His Love

Come live with me and be my love,
And we will all the pleasures prove
That valleys, groves, hills, and fields,
Woods, or steepy mountain yields.

And we will sit upon the rocks,   5
Seeing the shepherds feed their flocks
By shallow rivers, to whose falls
Melodious birds sing madrigals.

And I will make thee beds of roses
And a thousand fragrant posies,   10
A cap of flowers and a kirtle°   skirt
Embroidered all with leaves of myrtle;

A gown made of the finest wool
Which from our pretty lambs we pull;
Fair-linèd slippers for the cold,   15
With buckles of the purest gold;

A belt of straw and ivy buds,
With coral clasps and amber studs.
And if these pleasures may thee move,
Come live with me and be my love.   20

The shepherds' swains shall dance and sing
For thy delight each May morning.
If these delights thy mind may move,
Then live with me and be my love.

JOHN MARSTON (1575?–1634)

To Everlasting Oblivion

Thou mighty gulf, insatiate cormorant,
Deride me not, though I seem petulant
To fall into thy chops. Let others pray
Forever their fair poems flourish may;
But as for me, hungry Oblivion,   5
Devour me quick, accept my orison,
    My earnest prayers, which do impórtune thee
    With gloomy shade of thy still empery,
    To veil both me and my rude poesy.

Far worthier lines in silence of thy state   10
Do sleep securely, free from love or hate,
From which this, living, ne'er can be exempt,
But whilst it breathes will hate and fury tempt.
Then close his eyes with thy all-dimming hand,
Which not right glorious actions can withstand.   15
Peace, hateful tongues, I now in silence pace;
Unless some hound do wake me from my place,
    I with this sharp, yet well-meant poesy,
    Will sleep secure, right free from injury
    Of cankered hate or rankest villainy.   20

ANDREW MARVELL (1621–1678)

To His Coy Mistress

Had we but world enough, and time,
This coyness°, lady, were no crime.   *modesty, reluctance*
We would sit down and think which way
To walk, and pass our long love's day.
Thou by the Indian Ganges' side   5
Should'st rubies find; I by the tide
Of Humber would complain°. I would   *sing sad songs*
Love you ten years before the Flood,   *like a courtly lover's*
And you should, if you please, refuse
Till the conversion of the Jews.   10
My vegetable° love should grow   *vegetative,*
Vaster than empires, and more slow.   *flourishing*
An hundred years should go to praise
Thine eyes, and on thy forehead gaze,
Two hundred to adore each breast,   15
But thirty thousand to the rest.

326

An age at least to every part,
And the last age should show your heart.
For, lady, you deserve this state,
Nor would I love at lower rate.   20
    But at my back I always hear
Time's winged chariot hurrying near;
And yonder all before us lie
Deserts of vast eternity.
Thy beauty shall no more be found,   25
Nor in thy marble vault shall sound
My echoing song; then worms shall try
That long preserved virginity,
And your quaint honor turn to dust,
And into ashes all my lust.   30
The grave's a fine and private place,
But none, I think, do there embrace.
    Now therefore, while the youthful hue
Sits on thy skin like morning dew,
And while thy willing soul transpires   35
At every pore with instant° fires,   *eager*
Now let us sport us while we may;
And now, like am'rous birds of prey,
Rather at once our time devour,
Than languish in his slow-chapped power,   40
Let us roll all our strength, and all
Our sweetness, up into one ball;
And tear our pleasures with rough strife
Thorough° the iron gates of life.   *through*
Thus, though we cannot make our sun   45
Stand still, yet we will make him run.

To His Coy Mistress. 7. *Humber:* a river that flows by Marvell's town of
Hull (on the side of the world opposite from the Ganges). 10. *conversion
of the Jews:* An event that, according to St. John the Divine, is to take
place just before the end of the world.

HERMAN MELVILLE (1819–1891)

The Berg

(A DREAM)

I saw a ship of martial build
(Her standards set, her brave apparel on)
Directed as by madness mere
Against a stolid iceberg steer,
Nor budge it, though the infatuate ship went down.   5
The impact made huge ice-cubes fall
Sullen, in tons that crashed the deck;
But that one avalanche was all —
No other movement save the foundering wreck.

Along the spurs of ridges pale,   10
Not any slenderest shaft and frail,
A prism over glass-green gorges lone,
Toppled; or lace of traceries fine,
Nor pendant drops in grot or mine
Were jarred, when the stunned ship went down.   15
Nor sole the gulls in cloud that wheeled
Circling one snow-flanked peak afar,
But nearer fowl the floes that skimmed
And crystal beaches, felt no jar.
No thrill transmitted stirred the lock   20
Of jack-straw needle-ice at base;
Towers undermined by waves — the block
Atilt impending — kept their place.
Seals, dozing sleek on sliddery ledges
Slipped never, when by loftier edges   25
Through very inertia overthrown,
The impetuous ship in bafflement went down.

Hard Berg (methought), so cold, so vast,
With mortal damps self-overcast;
Exhaling still thy dankish breath —   30
Adrift dissolving, bound for death;
Though lumpish thou, a lumbering one —
A lumbering lubbard loitering slow,
Impingers rue thee and go down,
Sounding thy precipice below,   35
Nor stir the slimy slug that sprawls
Along thy dead indifference of walls.

The Berg. 21. *jack-straw needle-ice:* In the children's game of jack-straws, players try to extricate one wire or straw from a heap without knocking down the rest. 24. *sliddery:* a word Melville apparently coined.

328

GEORGE MEREDITH (1828–1909)

Lucifer in Starlight

On a starred night Prince Lucifer uprose.
    Tired of his dark dominion, swung the fiend
    Above the rolling ball in cloud part screened,
Where sinners hugged their specter of repose.
Poor prey to his hot fit of pride were those.   5
    And now upon his western wing he leaned,
    Now his huge bulk o'er Afric's sands careened,
Now the black planet shadowed Arctic snows.
Soaring through wider zones that pricked his scars
    With memory of the old revolt from Awe,   10
He reached a middle height, and at the stars,
Which are the brain of heaven, he looked, and sank.
Around the ancient track marched, rank on rank,
    The army of unalterable law.

JOHN MILTON (1608–1674)

'Methought I saw my late espousèd saint'

Methought I saw my late espousèd saint
    Brought to me like Alcestis from the grave,
    Whom Jove's great son to her glad husband gave,
    Rescued from death by force though pale and faint.
Mine, as whom washt from spot of childbed taint,   5
    Purification in the old Law did save,
    And such as yet once more I trust to have
    Full sight of her in Heaven without restraint,
Came vested all in white, pure as her mind:
    Her face was veiled; yet, to my fancied sight,   10
    Love, sweetness, goodness in her person shined
So clear, as in no face with more delight.
    But oh, as to embrace me she inclined,
    I waked, she fled, and day brought back my night.

'Methought I saw my late espousèd saint.' Milton had been totally blind since 1652; in 1656 he had married his second wife, whose face he probably had never seen, and who had died four months after the birth of a child. (It is possible that the reference is to Milton's first wife, who had died in childbirth and whom he had married before his loss of sight.) 2. Like Alcestis: in myth, Admetus' queen, who took her husband's place among the dead. 3. Jove's great son: Hercules, who brought Alcestis back from Hades. 6. old Law: Hebrew law decreed that a woman after giving birth must undergo a ritual of purification (see Leviticus 12). 10. veiled: as was Alcestis on her return. Still under the influence of the god of the dead, she was warned not to speak to her husband until the third morning.

JOHN MILTON (1608–1674)

'When I consider how my light is spent'

When I consider how my light is spent,
    Ere half my days in this dark world and wide,
    And that one talent which is death to hide
Lodged with me useless, though my soul more bent
To serve therewith my Maker, and present   5
    My true account, lest He returning chide;
    "Doth God exact day-labor, light denied?"
I fondly° ask. But Patience, to prevent   *foolishly*
That murmur, soon replies, "God doth not need
    Either man's work or His own gifts. Who best   10
Bear His mild yoke, they serve Him best. His state
Is kingly: thousands at His bidding speed,
    And post o'er land and ocean without rest;
    They also serve who only stand and wait."

'When I consider how my light is spent.' 1–2. *my light is spent/Ere half my days:* Milton's blindness had become total in 1652. 3. *that one talent:* For Christ's parable of the talents (measures of money), see Matthew 25:14–30.

MARIANNE MOORE (b. 1887)

A Grave

Man looking into the sea,
taking the view from those who have as much right to it as
    you have to yourself,
it is human nature to stand in the middle of a thing,
but you cannot stand in the middle of this;
the sea has nothing to give but a well excavated grave.   5
The firs stand in a procession, each with an emerald turkey-
    foot at the top,
reserved as their contours, saying nothing;
repression, however, is not the most obvious characteristic of
    the sea;
the sea is a collector, quick to return a rapacious look.
There are others besides you who have worn that look —   10
whose expression is no longer a protest; the fish no longer
    investigate them
for their bones have not lasted:
men lower nets, unconscious of the fact that they are
    desecrating a grave,

and row quickly away — the blades of the oars
moving together like the feet of water-spiders as if there 15
were no such thing as death.
The wrinkles progress among themselves in a phalanx —
beautiful under networks of foam,
and fade breathlessly while the sea rustles in and out of the
seaweed;
the birds swim through the air at top speed, emitting
catcalls as heretofore —
the tortoise-shell scourges about the feet of the cliffs, in
motion beneath them;
and the ocean, under the pulsation of lighthouses and noise 20
of bell-buoys,
advances as usual, looking as if it were not that ocean in
which dropped things are bound to sink —
in which if they turn and twist, it is neither with volition
nor consciousness.

THOMAS NASHE (1567–1601)

'Adieu, farewell, earth's bliss!'

Adieu, farewell, earth's bliss!
This world uncertain is;
Fond are life's lustful joys,
Death proves them all but toys,
None from his darts can fly; 5
I am sick, I must die:
　　Lord, have mercy on us!

Rich men, trust not in wealth,
Gold cannot buy you health;
Physic himself must fade; 10
All things to end are made.
The plague full swift goes by;
I am sick, I must die:
　　Lord, have mercy on us!

Beauty is but a flower 15
Which wrinkles will devour;
Brightness falls from the air,
Queens have died young and fair,
Dust hath closed Helen's eye.
I am sick, I must die: 20
　　Lord, have mercy on us!

331

Strength stoops unto the grave,
Worms feed on Hector brave,
Swords may not fight with fate;
Earth still holds ope her gate.   25
Come! come! the bells do cry.
I am sick, I must die:
      Lord, have mercy on us!

Wit with his wantonness
Tasteth death's bitterness;   30
Hell's executioner
Hath no ears for to hear
What vain art can reply.
I am sick, I must die:
      Lord, have mercy on us!   35

Haste, therefore, each degree,
To welcome destiny.
Heaven is our heritage,
Earth but a player's stage;
Mount we unto the sky.   40
I am sick, I must die:
      Lord, have mercy on us!

'Adieu, farewell, earth's bliss.' A song sung during the ravages of a plague,
in Nashe's play *Summer's Last Will and Testament*.

HOWARD NEMEROV (b. 1920)

The Goose Fish

On the long shore, lit by the moon
To show them properly alone,
Two lovers suddenly embraced
So that their shadows were as one.
The ordinary night was graced   5
For them by the swift tide of blood
That silently they took at flood,
And for a little time they prized
      Themselves emparadised.

Then, as if shaken by stage-fright   10
Beneath the hard moon's bony light,
They stood together on the sand
Embarrassed in each other's sight
But still conspiring hand in hand,
Until they saw, there underfoot,   15
As though the world had found them out,
The goose fish turning up, though dead,
      His hugely grinning head.

332

There in the china light he lay,
Most ancient and corrupt and grey.   20
They hesitated at his smile,
Wondering what it seemed to say
To lovers who a little while
Before had thought to understand,
By violence upon the sand,   25
The only way that could be known
    To make a world their own.

It was a wide and moony grin
Together peaceful and obscene;
They knew not what he would express,   30
So finished a comedian
He might mean failure or success,
But took it for an emblem of
Their sudden, new and guilty love
To be observed by, when they kissed,   35
    That rigid optimist.

So he became their patriarch,
Dreadfully mild in the half-dark.
His throat that the sand seemed to choke,
His picket teeth, these left their mark   40
But never did explain the joke
That so amused him, lying there
While the moon went down to disappear
Along the still and tilted track
    That bears the zodiac.   45

EZRA POUND (b. 1885)

The River-Merchant's Wife: a Letter

While my hair was still cut straight across my forehead
I played about the front gate, pulling flowers.
You came by on bamboo stilts, playing horse,
You walked about my seat, playing with blue plums.
And we went on living in the village of Chokan: 5
Two small people, without dislike or suspicion.

At fourteen I married My Lord you.
I never laughed, being bashful.
Lowering my head, I looked at the wall.
Called to, a thousand times, I never looked back.   10

At fifteen I stopped scowling,
I desired my dust to be mingled with yours
Forever and forever and forever.
Why should I climb the lookout?

At sixteen you departed,   15
You went into far Ku-to-yen, by the river of swirling eddies,
And you have been gone five months.
The monkeys make sorrowful noise overhead.

You dragged your feet when you went out.
By the gate now, the moss is grown, the different mosses,   20
Too deep to clear them away!
The leaves fall early this autumn, in wind.
The paired butterflies are already yellow with August
Over the grass in the West garden;
They hurt me. I grow older.   25
If you are coming down through the narrows of the river Kiang,
Please let me know beforehand,
And I will come out to meet you
    As far as Cho-fu-sa.

The River-Merchant's Wife: a Letter. A free translation from the Chinese poet Li Po (eighth century).

JOHN CROWE RANSOM (b. 1888)

Bells for John Whiteside's Daughter

There was such speed in her little body,
And such lightness in her footfall,
It is no wonder her brown study
Astonishes us all.

Her wars were bruited in our high window.   5
We looked among orchard trees and beyond,
Where she took arms against her shadow,
Or harried unto the pond

The lazy geese, like a snow cloud
Dripping their snow on the green grass,   10
Tricking and stopping, sleepy and proud,
Who cried in goose, Alas,

For the tireless heart within the little
Lady with rod that made them rise
From their noon apple-dreams, and scuttle   15
Goose-fashion under the skies!

But now go the bells, and we are ready;
In one house we are sternly stopped
To say we are vexed at her brown study,
Lying so primly propped.   20

334

HENRY REED (b. 1914)

Naming of Parts

Today we have naming of parts. Yesterday,
We had daily cleaning. And tomorrow morning,
We shall have what to do after firing. But today,
Today we have naming of parts. Japonica
Glistens like coral in all of the neighboring gardens, 5
      And today we have naming of parts.

This is the lower sling swivel. And this
Is the upper sling swivel, whose use you will see,
When you are given your slings. And this is the piling swivel,
Which in your case you have not got. The branches 10
Hold in the gardens their silent, eloquent gestures,
      Which in our case we have not got.

This is the safety-catch, which is always released
With an easy flick of the thumb. And please do not let me
See anyone using his finger. You can do it quite easy 15
If you have any strength in your thumb. The blossoms
Are fragile and motionless, never letting anyone see
      Any of them using their finger.

And this you can see is the bolt. The purpose of this
Is to open the breech, as you see. We can slide it 20
Rapidly backwards and forwards: we call this
Easing the spring. And rapidly backwards and forwards
The early bees are assaulting and fumbling the flowers:
      They call it easing the Spring.

They call it easing the Spring: it is perfectly easy 25
If you have any strength in your thumb: like the bolt,
And the breech, and the cocking-piece, and the point of
   balance,
Which in our case we have not got; and the almond-blossom
Silent in all of the gardens and the bees going backwards and
   forwards,
      For today we have naming of parts. 30

EDWIN ARLINGTON ROBINSON (1869–1935)

Richard Cory

Whenever Richard Cory went down town,
We people on the pavement looked at him:
He was a gentleman from sole to crown,
Clean favored, and imperially slim.

And he was always quietly arrayed,   5
And he was always human when he talked;
But still he fluttered pulses when he said,
"Good-morning," and he glittered when he walked.

And he was rich — yes, richer than a king —
And admirably schooled in every grace: 10
In fine°, we thought that he was everything   *in short*
To make us wish that we were in his place.

So on we worked, and waited for the light,
And went without the meat, and cursed the bread;
And Richard Cory, one calm summer night,   15
Went home and put a bullet through his head.

Mr. Flood's Party

Old Eben Flood, climbing alone one night
Over the hill between the town below
And the forsaken upland hermitage
That held as much as he should ever know
On earth again of home, paused warily.   5
The road was his with not a native near;
And Eben, having leisure, said aloud,
For no man else in Tilbury Town to hear:

"Well, Mr. Flood, we have the harvest moon
Again, and we may not have many more;   10
The bird is on the wing, the poet says,
And you and I have said it here before.
Drink to the bird." He raised up to the light
The jug that he had gone so far to fill,
And answered huskily: "Well, Mr. Flood,   15
Since you propose it, I believe I will."

Alone, as if enduring to the end
A valiant armor of scarred hopes outworn,
He stood there in the middle of the road
Like Roland's ghost winding° a silent horn.   *blowing* 20
Below him, in the town among the trees,

Where friends of other days had honored him,
A phantom salutation of the dead
Rang thinly till old Eben's eyes were dim.

Then, as a mother lays her sleeping child   25
Down tenderly, fearing it may awake,
He set the jug down slowly at his feet
With trembling care, knowing that most things break;
And only when assured that on firm earth
It stood, as the uncertain lives of men   30
Assuredly did not, he paced away,
And with his hand extended paused again:

"Well, Mr. Flood, we have not met like this
In a long time; and many a change has come
To both of us, I fear, since last it was   35
We had a drop together. Welcome home!"
Convivially returning with himself,
Again he raised the jug up to the light;
And with an acquiescent quaver said:
"Well, Mr. Flood, if you insist, I might.   40

"Only a very little, Mr. Flood —
For auld lang syne. No more, sir; that will do."
So, for the time, apparently it did,
And Eben evidently thought so too;
For soon amid the silver loneliness   45
Of night he lifted up his voice and sang,
Secure, with only two moons listening,
Until the whole harmonious landscape rang —

"For auld lang syne." The weary throat gave out,
The last word wavered; and the song being done,   50
He raised again the jug regretfully
And shook his head, and was again alone.
There was not much that was ahead of him,
And there was nothing in the town below —
Where strangers would have shut the many doors   55
That many friends had opened long ago.

Mr. Flood's Party. 11. *the poet:* Omar Khayyám, Persian poet, a praiser of wine, whose *Rubáiyát,* translated by Edward FitzGerald, included the lines:

> Come, fill the Cup, and in the fire of Spring
> Your Winter-garment of Repentance fling:
>   The Bird of Time has but a little way
>   To flutter and the Bird is on the Wing.

20. *Roland's ghost . . . horn:* In the battle of Roncesvalles (eighth century), Roland fought to his death, refusing to sound his horn for help until all hope was gone.

THEODORE ROETHKE (1908–1963)

Dolor

     I have known the inexorable sadness of pencils,
     Neat in their boxes, dolor of pad and paper-weight,
     All the misery of manilla folders and mucilage,
     Desolation in immaculate public places,
     Lonely reception room, lavatory, switchboard,   5
     The unalterable pathos of basin and pitcher,
     Ritual of multigraph, paper-clip, comma,
     Endless duplication of lives and objects.
     And I have seen dust from the walls of institutions,
     Finer than flour, alive, more dangerous than silica,   10
     Sift, almost invisible, through long afternoons of tedium,
     Dropping a fine film on nails and delicate eyebrows,
     Glazing the pale hair, the duplicate gray standard faces.

DANTE GABRIEL ROSSETTI (1828–1882)

The Woodspurge

     The wind flapped loose, the wind was still,
     Shaken out dead from tree and hill;
     I had walked on at the wind's will —
     I sat now, for the wind was still.

     Between my knees my forehead was —   5
     My lips, drawn in, said not Alas!
     My hair was over in the grass,
     My naked ears heard the day pass.

     My eyes, wide open, had the run
     Of some ten weeds to fix upon;   10
     Among those few out of the sun,
     The woodspurge flowered, three cups in one.

     From perfect grief there need not be
     Wisdom or even memory;
     One thing then learnt remains to me —   15
     The woodspurge has a cup of three.

CARL SANDBURG (b. 1878)

A *Fence*

Now the stone house on the lake front is finished and the
    workmen are beginning the fence.
The palings are made of iron bars with steel points that can
    stab the life out of any man who falls on them.
As a fence, it is a masterpiece, and will shut off the rabble
    and all vagabonds and hungry men and all wandering
    children looking for a place to play.
Passing through the bars and over the steel points will go
    nothing except Death and the Rain and To-morrow.

WILLIAM SHAKESPEARE (1564–1616)

Spring

When daisies pied and violets blue
    And lady-smocks all silver-white
And cuckoo-buds° of yellow hue   *buttercups*
    Do paint the meadows with delight,
The cuckoo then, on every tree,   5
Mocks married men; for thus sings he,
                    "Cuckoo,
Cuckoo, cuckoo!" — O word of fear,
Unpleasing to a married ear!

When shepherds pipe on oaten straws,   10
    And merry larks are ploughmen's clocks,
When turtles tread°, and rocks, and daws,   *turtledoves*
    And maidens bleach their summer smocks,   *mate*
The cuckoo then, on every tree,
Mocks married men; for thus sings he,   15
                    "Cuckoo,
Cuckoo, cuckoo!" — O word of fear,
Unpleasing to a married ear!

Spring. The songs of "Spring" and "Winter" conclude the play *Love's
Labors Lost.* 2. *lady-smocks:* also named cuckooflowers. 8. O *word of
fear:* because it sounds like the word *cuckold.*

WILLIAM SHAKESPEARE (1564–1616)

Winter

When icicles hang by the wall,
  And Dick the shepherd blows his nail,
And Tom bears logs into the hall,
  And milk comes frozen home in pail,
When blood is nipped and ways° be foul,   *roads*   5
  Then nightly sings the staring owl:
    "Tu-whit, tu-who!"
      A merry note,
While greasy Joan doth keel° the pot.   *cool (as by*
                              skimming or stirring)

When all aloud the wind doth blow,   10
  And coughing drowns the parson's saw°,   *old saw,*
And birds sit brooding in the snow,   *platitude*
  And Marian's nose looks red and raw,
When roasted crabs° hiss in the bowl,   *crab apples*
  Then nightly sings the staring owl: 15
    "Tu-whit, tu-who!"
      A merry note,
While greasy Joan doth keel the pot.

'That time of year thou mayst in me behold'

That time of year thou mayst in me behold
When yellow leaves, or none, or few, do hang
Upon those boughs which shake against the cold,
Bare ruined choirs where late the sweet birds sang.
In me thou see'st the twilight of such day   5
As after sunset fadeth in the west,
Which by-and-by black night doth take away,
Death's second self that seals up all in rest.
In me thou see'st the glowing of such fire
That on the ashes of his youth doth lie,   10
As the deathbed whereon it must expire,
Consumed with that which it was nourished by.
  This thou perceiv'st, which makes thy love
    more strong,
  To love that well which thou must leave ere long.

WILLIAM SHAKESPEARE (1564–1616)

'Let me not to the marriage of true minds'

Let me not to the marriage of true minds
Admit impediments. Love is not love
Which alters when it alteration finds,
Or bends with the remover° to remove.   *the inconstant*
O, no! it is an ever-fixèd mark   *lover*   5
That looks on tempests and is never shaken;
It is the star to every wand'ring bark,
Whose worth's unknown, although his height be taken.
Love's not Time's fool, though rosy lips and cheeks
Within his bending sickle's compass come;   10
Love alters not with his brief hours and weeks,
But bears it out even to the edge of doom.
   If this be error and upon me proved,
   I never writ, nor no man ever loved.

'Let me not to the marriage of true minds.' 2. *impediments*: any reasons
not to seal the marriage contract. In the Church of England, among these
might be *inconstancy* and *change of circumstance* (e.g., the sudden loss
of one's fortune).

'Poor soul, the center of my sinful earth'

Poor soul, the center of my sinful earth,
[. . .] these rebel powers that thee array,
Why dost thou pine within and suffer dearth,
Painting thy outward walls so costly gay?
Why so large cost, having so short a lease,   5
Dost thou upon thy fading mansion spend?
Shall worms, inheritors of this excess,
Eat up thy charge? Is this thy body's end?
Then, soul, live thou upon thy servant's loss,
And let that pine to aggravate° thy store;   *increase*   10
Buy terms divine in selling hours of dross;
Within be fed, without be rich no more:
   So shalt thou feed on Death, that feeds on men,
   And Death once dead, there's no more dying then.

'Poor soul, the center of my sinful earth.' The *Sonnets'* first printer made
Shakespeare repeat himself in the second line: "My sinful earth these
rebel powers that thee array." Subsequent editors have offered many
guesses to fill in the missing two syllables: *Thrall to, Blind to, Fooled by,
Starved by, Sieged by, Pressed by, Gilt with, Leagued with, Rebuke,* etc.

WILLIAM SHAKESPEARE (1564–1616)

'Fear no more the heat o' th' sun'

GUIDERIUS: Fear no more the heat o' th' sun
        Nor the furious winter's rages;
    Thou thy worldly task hast done,
        Home art gone, and ta'en thy wages.
    Golden lads and girls all must,
    As chimney-sweepers, come to dust.   5

ARVIRAGUS: Fear no more the frown o' th' great,
        Thou art past the tyrant's stroke;
    Care no more to clothe and eat,
        To thee the reed is as the oak.   10
    The scepter°, learning, physic°, must   *law; science*
    All follow this and come to dust.   *of medicine*

GUIDERIUS: Fear no more the lightning flash,
ARVIRAGUS: Nor the all-dreaded thunder-stone°;   *thunderbolt*
GUIDERIUS: Fear not slander, censure rash,
ARVIRAGUS: Thou hast finished joy and moan.   15
BOTH: All lovers young, all lovers must
    Consign to thee° and come to dust.   *join their*

GUIDERIUS: No exorciser harm thee!   *signatures to yours*
ARVIRAGUS: Nor no witchcraft charm thee!
GUIDERIUS: Ghost unlaid forbear thee!   20
ARVIRAGUS: Nothing ill come near thee!
BOTH: Quiet consummation have,
    And renownèd be thy grave!

'Fear no more the heat o' th' sun.' Lyrics in Shakespeare's plays generally are sung; in *Cymbeline* (Act IV, scene 2), this one is spoken. While the princess Imogen, disguised as a boy, lies in a deep sleep, her brothers, who do not recognize her, believe her dead and recite these lines over her.

KARL SHAPIRO (b. 1913)

The Dirty Word

The dirty word hops in the cage of the mind like the Pondi-
cherry vulture, stomping with its heavy left claw on the sweet
meat of the brain and tearing it with its vicious beak, ripping
and chopping the flesh. Terrified, the small boy bears the big
bird of the dirty word into the house, and grunting, puffing,   5
carries it up the stairs to his own room in the skull. Bits of
black feather cling to his clothes and his hair as he locks the
staring creature in the dark closet.

All day the small boy returns to the closet to examine and
feed the bird, to caress and kick the bird, that now snaps and   10
flaps its wings savagely whenever the door is opened. How the
boy trembles and delights at the sight of the white excrement
of the bird! How the bird leaps and rushes against the walls
of the skull, trying to escape from the zoo of the vocabulary!
How wildly snaps the sweet meat of the brain in its rage.   15

And the bird outlives the man, being freed at the man's
death-funeral by a word from the rabbi.

(But I one morning went upstairs and opened the door and
entered the closet and found in the cage of my mind the great
bird dead. Softly I wept it and softly removed it and softly   20
buried the body of the bird in the hollyhock garden of the
house I lived in twenty years before. And out of the worn
black feathers of the wing have I made these pens to write
these elegies, for I have outlived the bird, and I have murdered it in my early manhood.)   25

PERCY BYSSHE SHELLEY (1792–1822)

Ode to the West Wind

I

O wild West Wind, thou breath of Autumn's being,
Thou, from whose unseen presence the leaves dead
Are driven, like ghosts from an enchanter fleeing,

Yellow, and black, and pale, and hectic red,
Pestilence-stricken multitudes: O thou,   5
Who chariotest to their dark wintry bed

The wingèd seeds, where they lie cold and low,
Each like a corpse within its grave, until
Thine azure sister of the spring shall blow

Her clarion o'er the dreaming earth, and fill   10
(Driving sweet buds like flocks to feed in air)
With living hues and odors plain and hill:

Wild Spirit, which art moving everywhere;
Destroyer and preserver; hear, O, hear!

II

Thou on whose stream, 'mid the steep sky's commotion,   15
Loose clouds like earth's decaying leaves are shed,
Shook from the tangled boughs of Heaven and Ocean,

Angels of rain and lightning: there are spread
On the blue surface of thine airy surge,
Like the bright hair uplifted from the head 20

Of some fierce Maenad, even from the dim verge
Of the horizon to the zenith's height,
The locks of the approaching storm. Thou dirge

Of the dying year, to which this closing night
Will be the dome of a vast sepulcher, 25
Vaulted with all thy congregated might

Of vapors, from whose solid atmosphere
Black rain, and fire, and hail will burst: O, hear!

III

Thou who didst waken from his summer dreams
The blue Mediterranean, where he lay,
Lulled by the coil of his crystalline streams, 30

Beside a pumice isle in Baiae's bay,
And saw in sleep old palaces and towers
Quivering within the wave's intenser day,

All overgrown with azure moss, and flowers 35
So sweet, the sense faints picturing them! Thou
For whose path the Atlantic's level powers

Cleave themselves into chasms, while far below
The sea-blooms and the oozy woods which wear
The sapless foliage of the ocean, know 40

Thy voice, and suddenly grow gray with fear,
And tremble and despoil themselves: O, hear!

IV

If I were a dead leaf thou mightest bear;
If I were a swift cloud to fly with thee;
A wave to pant beneath thy power, and share 45

The impulse of thy strength, only less free
Than thou, O uncontrollable! If even
I were as in my boyhood, and could be

The comrade of thy wanderings over heaven,
As then, when to outstrip thy skiey speed 50
Scarce seemed a vision; I would ne'er have striven

As thus with thee in prayer in my sore need.

Oh! lift me as a wave, a leaf, a cloud!
I fall upon the thorns of life! I bleed!

A heavy weight of hours has chained and bowed   55
One too like thee: tameless, and swift, and proud.

V

Make me thy lyre, even as the forest is:
What if my leaves are falling like its own!
The tumult of thy mighty harmonies

Will take from both a deep, autumnal tone,   60
Sweet though in sadness. Be thou, spirit fierce,
My spirit! Be thou me, impetuous one!

Drive my dead thoughts over the universe
Like withered leaves, to quicken a new birth!
And, by the incantation of this verse,   65

Scatter, as from an unextinguished hearth
Ashes and sparks, my words among mankind!
Be through my lips to unawakened earth

The trumpet of a prophecy! O wind,
If Winter comes, can Spring be far behind?   70

Ode to the West Wind. 21. *Maenad:* in ancient Greece, a woman of the
cult of the god Dionysus, who now and again would show her devotion by
dancing herself into a frenzy.

SIR PHILIP SIDNEY (1554–1586)

'With how sad steps, O Moon, thou climb'st the skies!'

With how sad steps, O Moon, thou climb'st the skies!
    How silently, and with how wan a face!
    What! may it be that even in heavenly place
    That busy archer his sharp arrows tries?
Sure, if that long-with-love-acquainted eyes   5
    Can judge of love, thou feel'st a lover's case.
    I read it in thy looks; thy languished grace
    To me, that feel the like, thy state descries.
Then, even of fellowship, O Moon, tell me:
    Is constant love deemed there but want of wit?   10
    Are beauties there as proud as here they be?
Do they above love to be loved, and yet
    Those lovers scorn whom that love doth possess?
    Do they call virtue there ungratefulness?

CHRISTOPHER SMART (1722–1771)

'For I will consider my Cat Jeoffry'

For I will consider my Cat Jeoffry.

For he is the servant of the Living God, duly and daily serving him.

For at the first glance of the glory of God in the East he worships in his way.

For is this done by wreathing his body seven times round with elegant quickness.

For then he leaps up to catch the musk°, which is the blessing of God upon his prayer.   *catnip*   5

For he rolls upon prank to work it in.

For having done duty and received blessing he begins to consider himself.

For this he performs in ten degrees.

For first he looks upon his fore-paws to see if they are clean.

For secondly he kicks up behind to clear away there.   10

For thirdly he works it upon stretch° with the fore-paws extended.   *he works his muscles, stretching*

For fourthly he sharpens his paws by wood.

For fifthly he washes himself.

For sixthly he rolls upon wash.

For seventhly he fleas himself, that he may not be inter-   15
rupted upon the beat°.   *upon his patrol*

For eighthly he rubs himself against a post.

For ninthly he looks up for his instructions.

For tenthly he goes in quest of food.

For having considered God and himself he will consider his neighbor.

For if he meets another cat he will kiss her in kindness.   20

For when he takes his prey he plays with it to give it a chance.

For one mouse in seven escapes by his dallying.

For when his day's work is done his business more properly begins.

For he keeps the Lord's watch in the night against the Adversary.

For he counteracts the powers of darkness by his electrical   25
skin and glaring eyes.

For he counteracts the Devil, who is death, by brisking about the life.

For in his morning orisons he loves the sun and the sun loves him.

For he is of the tribe of Tiger.

For the Cherub Cat is a term of the Angel Tiger.

346

For he has the subtlety and hissing of a serpent, which 30
    in goodness he suppresses.

For he will not do destruction if he is well-fed, neither
    will he spit without provocation.

For he purrs in thankfulness when God tells him he's a
    good Cat.

For he is an instrument for the children to learn benevolence
    upon.

For every house is incomplete without him, and a blessing
    is lacking in the spirit.

For the Lord commanded Moses concerning the cats at 35
    the departure of the Children of Israel from Egypt.

For every family had one cat at least in the bag.

For the English Cats are the best in Europe.

For he is the cleanest in the use of his fore-paws of any
    quadruped.

For the dexterity of his defence is an instance of the love
    of God to him exceedingly.

For he is the quickest to his mark of any creature. 40

For he is tenacious of his point.

For he is a mixture of gravity and waggery.

For he knows that God is his Savior.

For there is nothing sweeter than his peace when at rest.

For there is nothing brisker than his life when in motion. 45

For he is of the Lord's poor, and so indeed is he called by
    benevolence perpetually — Poor Jeoffry! poor Jeoffry!
    the rat has bit thy throat.

For I bless the name of the Lord Jesus that Jeoffrey is
    better.

For the divine spirit comes about his body to sustain it in
    complete cat.

For his tongue is exceeding pure so that it has in purity
    what it wants in music.

For he is docile and can learn certain things. 50

For he can sit up with gravity which is patience upon
    approbation.

For he can fetch and carry, which is patience in employ-
    ment.

For he can jump over a stick which is patience upon proof
    positive.

For he can spraggle upon waggle at the word of command.

For he can jump from an eminence into his master's bosom. 55

For he can catch the cork and toss it again.

For he is hated by the hypocrite and miser.

For the former is afraid of detection.

For the latter refuses the charge.

347

For he camels his back to bear the first notion of business.   60
For he is good to think on, if a man would express himself
  neatly.
For he made a great figure in Egypt for his signal services.
For he killed the Icneumon-rat, very pernicious by land.
For his ears are so acute that they sting again.
For from this proceeds the passing quickness of his attention.   65
For by stroking of him I have found out electricity.
For I perceived God's light about him both wax and fire.
For the electrical fire is the spiritual substance which God
  sends from heaven to sustain the bodies both of man
  and beast.
For God has blessed him in the variety of his movements.
For, though he cannot fly, he is an excellent clamberer.   70
For his motions upon the face of the earth are more than
  any other quadruped.
For he can tread to all the measures upon the music.
For he can swim for life.
For he can creep.

'For I will consider my Cat Jeoffry.' This is a self-contained extract from
Smart's long poem *Jubilate Agno* ("Rejoice in the Lamb"), written
during his confinement for insanity. 35. *For the Lord commanded Moses
concerning the cats:* No such command is mentioned in Scripture. 54.
spraggle upon wraggle: W. F. Stead, in his edition of Smart's poem, suggests that this means Jeoffry will sprawl when his master waggles a finger
or a stick. 59. *the charge:* perhaps the cost of feeding a cat.

WILLIAM JAY SMITH (b. 1918)

American Primitive

Look at him there in his stovepipe hat,
His high-top shoes, and his handsome collar;
Only my Daddy could look like that,
And I love my Daddy like he loves his Dollar.

The screen door bangs, and it sounds so funny —   5
There he is in a shower of gold;
His pockets are stuffed with folding money,
His lips are blue, and his hands feel cold.

He hangs in the hall by his black cravat,
The ladies faint, and the children holler: 10
Only my Daddy could look like that,
And I love my Daddy like he loves his Dollar.

W. D. SNODGRASS (b. 1926)

The Operation

From stainless steel basins of water
They brought warm cloths and they washed me,
From spun aluminum bowls, cold Zephiran sponges, fuming;
Gripped in the dead yellow glove, a bright straight razor
Inched on my stomach, down my groin,   5
Paring the brown hair off. They left me
White as a child, not frightened. I was not
Ashamed. They clothed me, then,
In the thin, loose, light, white garments,
The delicate sandals of poor Pierrot,   10
A schoolgirl first offering her sacrament.

I was drifting, inexorably, on toward sleep.
In skullcaps, masked, in blue-green gowns, attendants
Towed my cart, afloat in its white cloths,
The body with its tributary poisons borne   15
Down corridors of the diseased, thronging:
The scrofulous faces, contagious grim boys,
The huddled families, weeping, a staring woman
Arched to her gnarled stick, — a child was somewhere
Screaming, screaming — then, blind silence, the elevator rising   20
To the arena, humming, vast with lights; blank hero,
Shackled and spellbound, to enact my deed.

Into flowers, into women, I have awakened.
Too weak to think of strength, I have thought all day,
Or dozed among standing friends. I lie in night, now,   25
A small mound under linen like the drifted snow.
Only by nurses visited, in radiance, saying, Rest.
Opposite, ranked office windows glare; headlamps, below,
Trace out our highways; their cargoes under dark tarpaulins,
Trucks climb, thundering, and sirens may   30
Wail for the fugitive. It is very still. In my brandy bowl
Of sweet peas at the window, the crystal world
Is inverted, slow and gay.

The Operation. 3. *Zephiran:* like Zephirus, Greek personification of the west wind: gentle, cool and soothing. 10. *Pierrot:* traditional clown in French pantomime, white-faced, wearing loose pantaloons.

WALLACE STEVENS (1879–1955)

Peter Quince at the Clavier

I

Just as my fingers on these keys
Make music, so the selfsame sounds
On my spirit make a music, too.

Music is feeling, then, not sound;
And thus it is that what I feel,   5
Here in this room, desiring you,

Thinking of your blue-shadowed silk,
Is music. It is like the strain
Waked in the elders by Susanna.

Of a green evening, clear and warm,   10
She bathed in her still garden, while
The red-eyed elders watching, felt

The basses of their beings throb
In witching chords, and their thin blood
Pulse pizzicati of Hosanna.   15

II

In the green water, clear and warm,
Susanna lay.
She searched
The touch of springs,
And found   20
Concealed imaginings.
She sighed,
For so much melody.

Upon the bank, she stood
In the cool   25
Of spent emotions.
She felt, among the leaves,
The dew
Of old devotions.

She walked upon the grass,   30
Still quavering.
The winds were like her maids,
On timid feet,
Fetching her woven scarves,
Yet wavering.   35

350

A breath upon her hand
Muted the night.
She turned —
A cymbal crashed,
And roaring horns.   40

                          III

Soon, with a noise like tambourines,
Came her attendant Byzantines.

They wondered why Susanna cried
Against the elders by her side;

And as they whispered, the refrain   45
Was like a willow swept by rain.

Anon, their lamps' uplifted flame
Revealed Susanna and her shame.

And then, the simpering Byzantines
Fled, with a noise like tambourines.   50

                          IV

Beauty is momentary in the mind —
The fitful tracing of a portal;
But in the flesh it is immortal.

The body dies; the body's beauty lives.
So evenings die, in their green going, .   55
A wave, interminably flowing.
So gardens die, their meek breath scenting
The cowl of winter, done repenting.
So maidens die, to the auroral
Celebration of a maiden's choral.   60

Susanna's music touched the bawdy strings
Of those white elders; but, escaping,
Left only Death's ironic scraping.
Now, in its immortality, it plays
On the clear viol of her memory,   65
And makes a constant sacrament of praise.

Peter Quince at the Clavier. In Shakespeare's *Midsummer Night's Dream*, Peter Quince is a clownish carpenter who stages a mock-tragic play. In *The History of Susanna* in the Apocrypha, two lustful elders who covet Susanna, a virtuous married woman, hide in her garden, spy on her as she bathes, then threaten to make false accusations against her unless she submits to them. When she refuses, they cry out, and her servants come running. All ends well when the prophet Daniel cross-examines the elders and proves them liars. 15. *pizzicati:* thin notes made by plucking a stringed instrument. 42. *Byzantines:* Susanna's maidservants.

WALLACE STEVENS (1879–1955)

The Emperor of Ice-Cream

Call the roller of big cigars,
The muscular one, and bid him whip
In kitchen cups concupiscent curds.
Let the wenches dawdle in such dress
As they are used to wear, and let the boys   5
Bring flowers in last month's newspapers.
Let be be finale of seem.
The only emperor is the emperor of ice-cream.

Take from the dresser of deal,
Lacking the three glass knobs, that sheet   10
On which she embroidered fantails once
And spread it so as to cover her face.
If her horny feet protrude, they come
To show how cold she is, and dumb.
Let the lamp affix its beam.   15
The only emperor is the emperor of ice-cream.

The Emperor of Ice-Cream. 9. *deal:* fir or pine wood used to make cheap
furniture.

JONATHAN SWIFT (1667–1745)

The Day of Judgment

Once, with a whirl of thought oppressed,
I sunk from reverie to rest.
An horrid vision seized my head,
I saw the graves give up their dead!
Jove, armed with terrors, burst the skies,   5
And thunder roars, and lightning flies!
Confused, amazed, its fate unknown,
The world stands trembling at his throne!
While each pale sinner hangs his head,
Jove, nodding, shook the heavens, and said: 10
"Offending race of human kind,
By nature, custom, learning, blind;
You who, through frailty, slipped aside;
And you who never fell — through pride;
And you by differing churches shammed,   15
Who come to see each other damned

352

(So some folks told you, but they knew
No more of Jove's designs than you);
The world's mad business now is o'er,
And I resent these pranks no more.   20
I to such blockheads set my wit!
I damn such fools! — Go, go, you're *bit°*."   outwitted,
                                                       defeated (*slang*)

ALFRED, LORD TENNYSON (1809–1892)

Ulysses

It little profits that an idle king,
By this still hearth, among these barren crags,
Matched with an agèd wife, I mete and dole
Unequal laws unto a savage race
That hoard, and sleep, and feed, and know not me.   5
I cannot rest from travel; I will drink
Life to the lees. All times I have enjoyed
Greatly, have suffered greatly, both with those
That loved me, and alone; on shore, and when
Through scudding drifts the rainy Hyades   10
Vexed the dim sea. I am become a name;
For always roaming with a hungry heart
Much have I seen and known — cities of men
And manners, climates, councils, governments,
Myself not least, but honored of them all —   15
And drunk delight of battle with my peers,
Far on the ringing plains of windy Troy.
I am a part of all that I have met;
Yet all experience is an arch wherethrough
Gleams that untraveled world whose margin fades   20
Forever and forever when I move.
How dull it is to pause, to make an end,
To rust unburnished, not to shine in use!
As though to breathe were life! Life piled on life
Were all too little, and of one to me   25
Little remains; but every hour is saved
From that eternal silence, something more,
A bringer of new things; and vile it were
For some three suns to store and hoard myself,
And this grey spirit yearning in desire   30
To follow knowledge like a sinking star,
Beyond the utmost bound of human thought.

This is my son, mine own Telemachus,
To whom I leave the scepter and the isle —
Well-loved of me, discerning to fulfill   35
This labor, by slow prudence to make mild
A rugged people, and through soft degrees
Subdue them to the useful and the good.
Most blameless is he, centered in the sphere
Of common duties, decent not to fail   40
In offices of tenderness, and pay
Meet adoration to my household gods,
When I am gone. He works his work, I mine.
There lies the port; the vessel puffs her sail;
There gloom the dark, broad seas. My mariners,   45
Souls that have toiled, and wrought, and thought with me —
That ever with a frolic welcome took
The thunder and the sunshine, and opposed
Free hearts, free foreheads — you and I are old;
Old age hath yet his honor and his toil.   50
Death closes all; but something ere the end,
Some work of noble note, may yet be done,
Not unbecoming men that strove with Gods.
The lights begin to twinkle from the rocks;
The long day wanes; the slow moon climbs; the deep   55
Moans round with many voices. Come, my friends,
'Tis not too late to seek a newer world.
Push off, and sitting well in order smite
The sounding furrows; for my purpose holds
To sail beyond the sunset, and the baths   60
Of all the western stars, until I die.
It may be that the gulfs will wash us down;
It may be we shall touch the Happy Isles,
And see the great Achilles, whom we knew.
Though much is taken, much abides; and though   65
We are not now that strength which in old days
Moved earth and heaven, that which we are, we are —
One equal temper of heroic hearts,
Made weak by time and fate, but strong in will
To strive, to seek, to find, and not to yield.   70

Ulysses. 10. *Hyades:* daughters of Atlas, who were transformed into a group of stars. Their rising with the sun was thought to be a sign of rain. 63. *Happy Isles:* Elysium, a paradise believed to be attainable by sailing west.

DYLAN THOMAS (1914–1953)

After the Funeral

(*In memory of Ann Jones*)

After the funeral, mule praises, brays,
Windshake of sailshaped ears, muffle-toed tap
Tap happily of one peg in the thick
Grave's foot, blinds down the lids, the teeth in black,
The spittled eyes, the salt ponds in the sleeves,   5
Morning smack of the spade that wakes up sleep,
Shakes a desolate boy who slits his throat
In the dark of the coffin and sheds dry leaves,
That breaks one bone to light with a judgment clout,
After the feast of tear-stuffed time and thistles   10
In a room with a stuffed fox and a stale fern,
I stand, for this memorial's sake, alone
In the snivelling hours with dead, humped Ann
Whose hooded, fountain heart once fell in puddles
Round the parched worlds of Wales and drowned each sun   15
(Though this for her is a monstrous image blindly
Magnified out of praise; her death was a still drop;
She would not have me sinking in the holy
Flood of her heart's fame; she would lie dumb and deep
And need no druid of her broken body).   20
But I, Ann's bard on a raised hearth, call all
The seas to service that her wood-tongued virtue
Babble like a bellbuoy over the hymning heads,
Bow down the walls of the ferned and foxy woods
That her love sing and swing through a brown chapel,   25
Bless her bent spirit with four, crossing birds.
Her flesh was meek as milk, but this skyward statue
With the wild breast and blessed and giant skull
Is carved from her in a room with a wet window
In a fiercely mourning house in a crooked year.   30
I know her scrubbed and sour humble hands
Lie with religion in their cramp, her threadbare
Whisper in a damp word, her wits drilled hollow,
Her fist of a face died clenched on a round pain;
And sculptured Ann is seventy years of stone.   35
These cloud-sopped, marble hands, this monumental
Argument of the hewn voice, gesture and psalm
Storm me forever over her grave until
The stuffed lung of the fox twitch and cry Love
And the strutting fern lay seeds on the black sill.   40

HENRY VAUGHAN (1622–1695)

The Retreat

Happy those early days when I
Shined in my angel-infancy!
Before I understood this place
Appointed for my second race,
Or taught my soul to fancy aught   5
But a white celestial thought;
When yet I had not walked above
A mile or two from my first love,
And looking back at that short space,
Could see a glimpse of his bright face;   10
When on some gilded cloud or flower
My gazing soul would dwell an hour,
And in those weaker glories spy
Some shadows of eternity;
Before I taught my tongue to wound   15
My conscience with a sinful sound,
Or had the black art to dispense
A sev'ral sin to ev'ry sense;
But felt through all this fleshly dress
Bright shoots of everlastingness.   20
  Oh, how I long to travel back
And tread again that ancient track! —
That I might once more reach that plain
Where first I left my glorious train,
From whence th' enlightened spirit sees   25
That shady city of palm trees.
But, ah, my soul with too much stay
Is drunk, and staggers in the way.
Some men a forward motion love,
But I by backward steps would move,   30
And when this dust falls to the urn,
In that state I came, return.

EDMUND WALLER (1606–1687)

'Go, lovely rose'

Go, lovely rose,
Tell her that wastes her time and me
  That now she knows,
When I resemble her to thee,
How sweet and fair she seems to be.   5

356

Tell her that's young
And shuns to have her graces spied
    That hadst thou sprung
In deserts where no men abide,
Thou must have uncommended died.   10

    Small is the worth
Of beauty from the light retired;
    Bid her come forth,
Suffer herself to be desired,
And not blush so to be admired.   15

Then die, that she
The common fate of all things rare
    May read in thee:
How small a part of time they share
That are so wondrous sweet and fair!   20

WALT WHITMAN (1819–1892)

When Lilacs Last in the Dooryard Bloom'd

1

When lilacs last in the dooryard bloom'd,
And the great star early droop'd in the western sky in the
    night,
I mourn'd, and yet shall mourn with ever-returning spring.

Ever-returning spring, trinity sure to me you bring,
Lilac blooming perennial and drooping star in the west,   5
And thought of him I love.

2

O powerful western fallen star!
O shades of night — O moody, tearful night!
O great star disappear'd — O the black murk that hides the
    star!
O cruel hands that hold me powerless — O helpless soul of   10
    me!
O harsh surrounding cloud that will not free my soul.

3

In the dooryard fronting an old farm-house near the
    whitewash'd palings,
Stands the lilac-bush tall-growing with heart-shaped leaves of
    rich green,

With many a pointed blossom rising delicate, with the
    perfume strong I love,
With every leaf a miracle — and from this bush in the   15
    dooryard,
With delicate-color'd blossoms and heart-shaped leaves of
    rich green,
A sprig with its flower I break.

4

In the swamp in secluded recesses,
A shy and hidden bird is warbling a song.

Solitary the thrush,   20
The hermit withdrawn to himself, avoiding the settlements,
Sings by himself a song.

Song of the bleeding throat,
Death's outlet song of life, (for well dear brother I know,
If thou wast not granted to sing thou would'st surely die.)   25

5

Over the breast of the spring, the land, amid cities,
Amid lanes and through old woods, where lately the violets
    peep'd from the ground, spotting the gray debris,
Amid the grass in the fields each side of the lanes, passing
    the endless grass,
Passing the yellow-spear'd wheat, every grain from its shroud
    in the dark-brown fields uprisen,
Passing the apple-tree blows of white and pink in the   30
    orchards,
Carrying a corpse to where it shall rest in the grave,
Night and day journeys a coffin.

6

Coffin that passes through lanes and streets,
Through day and night with the great cloud darkening the
    land,
With the pomp of the inloop'd flags with the cities draped   35
    in black,
With the show of the States themselves as of crape-veil'd
    women standing,
With processions long and winding and the flambeaus of
    the night,
With the countless torches lit, with the silent sea of faces
    and the unbared heads,

358

With the waiting depot, the arriving coffin, and the somber
    faces,
With dirges through the night, with the thousand voices   40
    rising strong and solemn,
With all the mournful voices of the dirges pour'd around
    the coffin,
The dim-lit churches and the shuddering organs — where
    amid these you journey,
With the tolling tolling bells' perpetual clang,
Here, coffin that slowly passes,
I give you my sprig of lilac.   45

7

(Nor for you, for one alone,
Blossoms and branches green to coffins all I bring,
For fresh as the morning, thus would I chant a song for you
    O sane and sacred death.

All over bouquets of roses,
O death, I cover you over with roses and early lilies,   50
But mostly and now the lilac that blooms the first,
Copious I break, I break the sprigs from the bushes,
With loaded arms I come, pouring for you,
For you and the coffins all of you O death.)

8

O western orb sailing the heaven,   55
Now I know what you must have meant as a month since I
    walk'd,
As I walk'd in silence the transparent shadowy night,
As I saw you had something to tell as you bent to me night
    after night,
As you droop'd from the sky low down as if to my side,
    (while the other stars all look'd on,)
As we wander'd together the solemn night, (for something   60
    I know not what kept me from sleep,)
As the night advanced, and I saw on the rim of the west
    how full you were of woe,
As I stood on the rising ground in the breeze in the cool
    transparent night,
As I watch'd where you pass'd and was lost in the nether-
    ward black of the night,
As my soul in its trouble dissatisfied sank, as where you sad
    orb,
Concluded, dropt in the night, and was gone.   65

359

9

Sing on there in the swamp,
O singer bashful and tender, I hear your notes, I hear your
  call,
I hear, I come presently, I understand you,
But a moment I linger, for the lustrous star has detain'd me,
The star my departing comrade holds and detains me.   70

10

O how shall I warble myself for the dead one there I loved?
And how shall I deck my song for the large sweet soul that
  has gone?
And what shall my perfume be for the grave of him I love?

Sea-winds blown from east and west,
Blown from the Eastern sea and blown from the Western   75
  sea, till there on the prairies meeting,
These and with these and the breath of my chant,
I'll perfume the grave of him I love.

11

O what shall I hang on the chamber walls?
And what shall the pictures be that I hang on the walls,
To adorn the burial-house of him I love?   80

Pictures of growing spring and farms and homes,
With the Fourth-month eve at sundown, and the gray
  smoke lucid and bright,
With floods of the yellow gold of the gorgeous, indolent,
  sinking sun, burning, expanding the air,
With the fresh sweet herbage under foot, and the pale green
  leaves of the trees prolific,
In the distance the flowing glaze, the breast of the river,   85
  with a wind-dapple here and there,
With ranging hills on the banks, with many a line against
  the sky, and shadows,
And the city at hand with dwellings so dense, and stacks of
  chimneys,
And all the scenes of life and the workshops, and the
  workmen homeward returning.

12

Lo, body and soul — this land,
My own Manhattan with spires, and the sparkling and   90
  hurrying tides, and the ships,

The varied and ample land, the South and the North in the
light, Ohio's shores and flashing Missouri,
And ever the far-spreading prairies cover'd with grass and
corn.

Lo, the most excellent sun so calm and haughty,
The violet and purple morn with just-felt breezes,
The gentle soft-born measureless light,   95
The miracle spreading bathing all, the fulfill'd noon,
The coming eve delicious, the welcome night and the stars,
Over my cities shining all, enveloping man and land.

13

Sing on, sing on you gray-brown bird,
Sing from the swamps, the recesses, pour your chant from   100
the bushes,
Limitless out of the dusk, out of the cedars and pines.

Sing on dearest brother, warble your reedy song,
Loud human song, with voice of uttermost woe.

O liquid and free and tender!
O wild and loose to my soul — O wondrous singer!   105
You only I hear — yet the star holds me, (but will soon
depart,)
Yet the lilac with mastering odor holds me.

14

Now while I sat in the day and look'd forth,
In the close of the day with its light and the fields of spring,
and the farmers preparing their crops,
In the large unconscious scenery of my land with its   110
lakes and forests,
In the heavenly aerial beauty, (after the perturb'd winds and
the storms,)
Under the arching heavens of the afternoon swift passing,
and the voices of children and women,
The many-moving sea-tides, and I saw the ships how they
sail'd,
And the summer approaching with richness, and the fields
all busy with labor,
And the infinite separate houses, how they all went on,   115
each with its meals and minutia of daily usages,
And the streets how their throbbings throbb'd, and the
cities pent — lo, then and there,

361

Falling upon them all and among them all, enveloping me
    with the rest,
Appear'd the cloud, appear'd the long black trail,
And I knew death, its thought, and the sacred knowledge of
    death.

Then with the knowledge of death as walking one side   120
    of me,
And the thought of death close-walking the other side of me,
And I in the middle as with companions, and as holding the
    hands of companions,
I fled forth to the hiding receiving night that talks not,
Down to the shores of the water, the path by the swamp
    in the dimness,
To the solemn shadowy cedars and ghostly pines so still.   125

And the singer so shy to the rest receiv'd me,
The gray-brown bird I know receiv'd us comrades three,
And he sang the carol of death, and a verse for him I love.

From deep secluded recesses,
From the fragrant cedars and the ghostly pines so still,   130
Came the carol of the bird.

And the charm of the carol rapt me,
As I held as if by their hands my comrades in the night,
And the voice of my spirit tallied the song of the bird.

Come lovely and soothing death,   135
Undulate round the world, serenely arriving, arriving,
In the day, in the night, to all, to each,
Sooner or later delicate death.

Prais'd be the fathomless universe,
For life and joy, and for objects and knowledge curious,   140
And for love, sweet love — but praise! praise! praise!
For the sure-enwinding arms of cool-enfolding death.

Dark mother always gliding near with soft feet,
Have none chanted for thee a chant of fullest welcome?
Then I chant it for thee, I glorify thee above all,   145
I bring thee a song that when thou must indeed come,
    come unfalteringly.

Approach strong deliveress,
When it is so, when thou hast taken them I joyously sing
    the dead,
Lost in the loving floating ocean of thee,
Laved in the flood of thy bliss O death.   150

From me to thee glad serenades,
Dances for thee I propose saluting thee, adornments and
feastings for thee,
And the sights of the open landscape and the high-spread
sky are fitting,
And life and the fields, and the huge and thoughtful night.

The night in silence under many a star,   155
The ocean shore and the husky whispering wave whose voice
I know,
And the soul turning to thee O vast and well-veil'd death,
And the body gratefully nestling close to thee.

Over the tree-tops I float thee a song,
Over the rising and sinking waves, over the myriad fields   160
and the prairies wide,
Over the dense-pack'd cities all and the teeming wharves
and ways,
I float this carol with joy, with joy to thee O death.

15

To the tally of my soul,
Loud and strong kept up the gray-brown bird,
With pure deliberate notes spreading filling the night.   165

Loud in the pines and cedars dim,
Clear in the freshness moist and the swamp-perfume,
And I with my comrades there in the night.

While my sight that was bound in my eyes unclosed,
As to long panoramas of visions.   170

And I saw askant the armies,
I saw as in noiseless dreams hundreds of battle-flags,
Borne through the smoke of the battles and pierc'd with
missiles I saw them,
And carried hither and yon through the smoke, and torn and
bloody,
And at last but a few shreds left on the staffs, (and all in   175
silence,)
And the staffs all splinter'd and broken.

I saw battle-corpses, myriads of them,
And the white skeletons of young men, I saw them,
I saw the debris and debris of all the slain soldiers of the war,
But I saw they were not as was thought,   180
They themselves were fully at rest, they suffer'd not,

363

The living remain'd and suffer'd, the mother suffer'd,
And the wife and the child and the musing comrade suffer'd,
And the armies that remain'd suffer'd.

16

Passing the visions, passing the night,   185
Passing, unloosing the hold of my comrades' hands,
Passing the song of the hermit bird and the tallying song of
    my soul,
Victorious song, death's outlet song, yet varying ever-altering
    song,
As low and wailing, yet clear the notes, rising and falling,
    flooding the night,
Sadly sinking and fainting, as warning and warning, and yet   190
    again bursting with joy,
Covering the earth and filling the spread of the heaven,
As that powerful psalm in the night I heard from recesses,
Passing, I leave thee lilac with heart-shaped leaves,
I leave thee there in the door-yard, blooming, returning with
    spring.

I cease from my song for thee,   195
From my gaze on thee in the west, fronting the west,
    communing with thee,
O comrade lustrous with silver face in the night.

Yet each to keep and all, retrievements out of the night,
The song, the wondrous chant of the gray-brown bird,
And the tallying chant, the echo arous'd in my soul,   200
With the lustrous and drooping star with the countenance
    full of woe,
With the holders holding my hand nearing the call of the
    bird,
Comrades mine and I in the midst, and their memory ever
    to keep, for the dead I loved so well,
For the sweetest, wisest soul of all my days and lands — and
    this for his dear sake,
Lilac and star and bird twined with the chant of my soul,   205
There in the fragrant pines and the cedars dusk and dim.

When Lilacs Last in the Dooryard Bloom'd. On April 21, 1865, a funeral
train bearing the body of Abraham Lincoln left Washington and proceeded slowly, with stops in cities along the way, to Lincoln's home in
Springfield, Illinois, where he was buried.

WALT WHITMAN (1819–1892)

The City Dead-House

By the city dead-house by the gate,
As idly sauntering wending my way from the clangor,
I curious pause, for lo, an outcast form, a poor dead
    prostitute brought,
Her corpse they deposit unclaim'd, it lies on the damp brick
    pavement,
The divine woman, her body, I see the body, I look on it   5
    alone,
That house once full of passion and beauty, all else I notice
    not,
Nor stillness so cold, nor running water from faucet, nor
    odors morbific impress me,
But the house alone — that wondrous house — that delicate
    fair house — that ruin!
That immortal house more than all the rows of dwellings
    ever built!
Or white-domed capitol with majestic figure surmounted,   10
    or all the old high-spired cathedrals,
That little house alone more than them all — poor,
    desperate house!
Fair, fearful wreck — tenement of a soul — itself a soul,
Unclaim'd, avoided house — take one breath from my
    tremulous lips,
Take one tear dropt aside as I go for thought of you,
Dead house of love — house of madness and sin, crumbled,   15
    crush'd,
House of life, erewhile talking and laughing — but ah, poor
    house, dead even then,
Months, years, an echoing, garnish'd house — but dead,
    dead, dead.

OSCAR WILDE (1856–1900)

The Harlot's House

We caught the tread of dancing feet,
We loitered down the moonlit street,
And stopped beneath the harlot's house.

Inside, above the din and fray,
We heard the loud musicians play   5
The "Treues Liebes Herz" of Strauss.

Like strange mechanical grotesques,
Making fantastic arabesques,
The shadows raced across the blind.

We watched the ghostly dancers spin   10
To sound of horn and violin,
Like black leaves wheeling in the wind.

Like wire-pulled automatons,
Slim silhouetted skeletons
Went sidling through the slow quadrille.   15

They took each other by the hand,
And danced a stately saraband;
Their laughter echoed thin and shrill.

Sometimes a clockwork puppet pressed
A phantom lover to her breast,   20
Sometimes they seemed to try to sing.

Sometimes a horrible marionette
Came out, and smoked its cigarette
Upon the steps like a live thing.

Then, turning to my love, I said,   25
"The dead are dancing with the dead,
The dust is whirling with the dust."

But she — she heard the violin,
And left my side, and entered in:
Love passed into the house of lust.   30

Then suddenly the tune went false,
The dancers wearied of the waltz,
The shadows ceased to wheel and whirl.

And down the long and silent street,
The dawn, with silver-sandaled feet,   35
Crept like a frightened girl.

The Harlot's House. 6. *"Treues Liebes Herz"*: "True Love's Heart," a
waltz.

366

YVOR WINTERS (b. 1900)

At the San Francisco Airport

To my daughter, 1954

This is the terminal: the light
Gives perfect vision, false and hard;
The metal glitters, deep and bright.
Great planes are waiting in the yard —
They are already in the night.   5

And you are here beside me, small,
Contained and fragile, and intent
On things that I but half recall —
Yet going whither you are bent.
I am the past, and that is all.   10

But you and I in part are one:
The frightened brain, the nervous will,
The knowledge of what must be done,
The passion to acquire the skill
To face that which you dare not shun.   15

The rain of matter upon sense
Destroys me momently. The score:
There comes what will come. The expense
Is what one thought, and something more —
One's being and intelligence.   20

This is the terminal, the break.
Beyond this point, on lines of air,
You take the way that you must take;
And I remain in light and stare —
In light, and nothing else, awake.   25

WILLIAM WORDSWORTH (1770–1850)

A Slumber Did My Spirit Seal

A slumber did my spirit seal;
   I had no human fears —
She seemed a thing that could not feel
   The touch of earthly years.

No motion has she now, no force;   5
   She neither hears nor sees;
Rolled round in earth's diurnal course,
   With rocks, and stones, and trees.

WILLIAM WORDSWORTH (1770–1850)

Ode: Intimations of Immortality
from Recollections of Early Childhood

> *The Child is father of the Man;*
> *And I could wish my days to be*
> *Bound each to each by natural piety.*

I

There was a time when meadow, grove, and stream,
The earth, and every common sight,
    To me did seem
    Apparelled in celestial light,
The glory and the freshness of a dream.   5
It is not now as it hath been of yore; —
    Turn wheresoe'er I may,
    By night or day,
The things which I have seen I now can see no more.

II

    The Rainbow comes and goes,   10
    And lovely is the Rose,
    The Moon doth with delight
Look round her when the heavens are bare,
    Waters on a starry night
    Are beautiful and fair;   15
    The sunshine is a glorious birth;
    But yet I know, where'er I go,
That there hath passed away a glory from the earth.

III

Now, while the birds thus sing a joyous song,
    And while the young lambs bound   20
    As to the tabor's sound,
To me alone there came a thought of grief:
A timely utterance gave that thought relief,
    And I again am strong:
The cataracts blow their trumpets from the steep;   25
No more shall grief of mine the season wrong;
I hear the Echoes through the mountains throng,
The Winds come to me from the fields of sleep,
    And all the earth is gay;
      Land and sea   30
    Give themselves up to jollity,
      And with the heart of May
Doth every Beast keep holiday; —

Thou Child of Joy,
Shout round me, let me hear thy shouts, thou happy   35
    Shepherd-boy!

IV

Ye blessèd Creatures, I have heard the call
  Ye to each other make; I see
The heavens laugh with you in your jubilee;
    My heart is at your festival,
    My head hath its coronal,   40
The fullness of your bliss, I feel — I feel it all.
    Oh evil day! if I were sullen
    While Earth herself is adorning,
      This sweet May-morning,
    And the Children are culling   45
      On every side,
    In a thousand valleys far and wide,
    Fresh flowers; while the sun shines warm,
And the Babe leaps up on his Mother's arm: —
    I hear, I hear, with joy I hear!   50
    — But there's a Tree, of many, one,
A single Field which I have looked upon,
Both of them speak of something that is gone:
    The Pansy at my feet
    Doth the same tale repeat: 55
Whither is fled the visionary gleam?
Where is it now, the glory and the dream?

V

Our birth is but a sleep and a forgetting:
The Soul that rises with us, our life's Star,
    Hath had elsewhere its setting,   60
      And cometh from afar:
    Not in entire forgetfulness,
    And not in utter nakedness,
But trailing clouds of glory do we come
    From God, who is our home: 65
Heaven lies about us in our infancy!
Shades of the prison-house begin to close
    Upon the growing Boy,
But he beholds the light, and whence it flows,
    He sees it in his joy;   70
The Youth, who daily farther from the east
    Must travel, still is Nature's Priest,
    And by the vision splendid
    Is on his way attended;
At length the Man perceives it die away,   75
And fade into the light of common day.

VI

Earth fills her lap with pleasures of her own;
Yearnings she hath in her own natural kind,
And, even with something of a Mother's mind,
    And no unworthy aim,   80
    The homely Nurse doth all she can
To make her Foster-child, her inmate Man,
Forget the glories he hath known,
And that imperial palace whence he came.

Behold the Child among his new-born blisses,   85
A six years' darling of a pigmy size!
See, where 'mid work of his own hand he lies,
Fretted by sallies of his mother's kisses,
With light upon him from his father's eyes!
See, at his feet, some little plan or chart,   90
Some fragment from his dream of human life,
Shaped by himself with newly-learnèd art;
    A wedding or a festival,
    A mourning or a funeral;
        And this hath now his heart,   95
    And unto this he frames his song:
        Then will he fit his tongue
To dialogues of business, love, or strife;
    But it will not be long
    Ere this be thrown aside,   100
    And with new joy and pride
The little Actor cons another part;
Filling from time to time his "humorous stage"
With all the Persons, down to palsied Age,
That Life brings with her in her equipage;   105
    As if his whole vocation
    Were endless imitation.

Thou, whose exterior semblance doth belie
    Thy Soul's immensity;
Thou best philosopher, who yet dost keep   110
Thy heritage, thou Eye among the blind,
That, deaf and silent, read'st the eternal deep,
Haunted forever by the eternal Mind, —
    Mighty Prophet! Seer blest!
    On whom those truths do rest,   115
Which we are toiling all our lives to find,
In darkness lost, the darkness of the grave;

Thou, over whom thy Immortality
Broods like the Day, a Master o'er a Slave,
A Presence which is not to be put by;   120
Thou little Child, yet glorious in the might
Of heaven-born freedom on thy being's height,
Why with such earnest pains dost thou provoke
The years to bring the inevitable yoke,
Thus blindly with thy blessedness at strife?   125
Full soon thy Soul shall have her earthly freight,
And custom lie upon thee with a weight,
Heavy as frost, and deep almost as life!

                            IX

        O joy! that in our embers
        Is something that doth live,   130
        That nature yet remembers
        What was so fugitive!
The thought of our past years in me doth breed
Perpetual benediction; not indeed
For that which is most worthy to be blest;   135
Delight and liberty, the simple creed
Of Childhood, whether busy or at rest,
With new-fledged hope still fluttering in his breast: —
        Not for these I raise
        The song of thanks and praise: 140
        But for those obstinate questionings
        Of sense and outward things,
        Fallings from us, vanishings;
        Blank misgivings of a Creature
Moving about in worlds not realized,   145
High instincts before which our mortal nature
Did tremble like a guilty Thing surprised:
        But for those first affections,
        Those shadowy recollections,
        Which, be they what they may,   150
Are yet the fountain-light of all our day,
Are yet a master-light of all our seeing;
Uphold us, cherish, and have power to make
Our noisy years seem moments in the being
Of the eternal Silence: truths that wake,   155
        To perish never:
Which neither listlessness, nor mad endeavor,
        Nor Man nor Boy,
Nor all that is at enmity with joy,
Can utterly abolish or destroy!   160
        Hence in a season of calm weather

          Though inland far we be,
      Our Souls have sight of that immortal sea
          Which brought us hither,
          Can in a moment travel thither,   165
      And see the Children sport upon the shore,
      And hear the mighty waters rolling evermore.

                              x

      Then sing, ye Birds, sing, sing a joyous song!
          And let the young Lambs bound
          As to the tabor's sound!   170
      We in thought will join your throng,
          Ye that pipe and ye that play,
          Ye that through your hearts today
          Feel the gladness of the May!
      What though the radiance which was once so bright   175
      Be now forever taken from my sight,
          Though nothing can bring back the hour
      Of splendor in the grass, of glory in the flower;
          We will grieve not, rather find
          Strength in what remains behind;   180
          In the primal sympathy
          Which having been must ever be;
          In the soothing thoughts that spring
          Out of human suffering;
          In the faith that looks through death,   185
      In years that bring the philosophic mind.

                             XI

      And O, ye Fountains, Meadows, Hills, and Groves,
      Forebode not any severing of our loves!
      Yet in my heart of hearts I feel your might;
      I only have relinquished one delight   190
      To live beneath your more habitual sway.
      I love the Brooks which down their channels fret,
      Even more than when I tripped lightly as they;
      The innocent brightness of a new-born Day
          Is lovely yet;   195
      The Clouds that gather round the setting sun
      Do take a sober coloring from an eye
      That hath kept watch o'er man's mortality;
      Another race hath been, and other palms are won.
      Thanks to the human heart by which we live,   200
      Thanks to its tenderness, its joys, and fears,
      To me the meanest flower that blows can give
      Thoughts that do often lie too deep for tears.

WILLIAM WORDSWORTH (1770–1850)

Composed upon Westminster Bridge

Earth has not anything to show more fair:
Dull would he be of soul who could pass by
A sight so touching in its majesty.
This city now doth, like a garment, wear
The beauty of the morning; silent, bare,   5
Ships, towers, domes, theaters, and temples lie
Open unto the fields, and to the sky —
All bright and glittering in the smokeless air.
Never did sun more beautifully steep
In his first splendor valley, rock, or hill;   10
Ne'er saw I, never felt, a calm so deep!
The river glideth at his own sweet will.
Dear God! the very houses seem asleep,
And all that mighty heart is lying still!

SIR THOMAS WYATT (1503?–1542)

'Whoso list to hunt'

Whoso list° to hunt, I know where is an hind,   *likes*
    But as for me, alas, I may no more,
    The vain travail hath wearied me so sore.
    I am of them that farthest come behind;
Yet may I by no means my wearied mind   5
    Draw from the deer, but as she fleeth afore,
    Fainting I follow. I leave off therefore,
    Since in a net I seek to hold the wind.
Who list her hunt, I put him out of doubt,
    As well as I, may spend his time in vain;   10
    And graven with diamonds in letters plain
There is written, her fair neck round about,
    Noli me tangere°, for Caesar's I am,   *Touch me not*
    And wild for to hold, though I seem tame.

'Whoso list to hunt.' 13. *Caesar's:* perhaps a reference to Henry VIII.
Wyatt's sonnet (one theory goes) may be about Henry's second wife
Anne Boleyn.

WILLIAM BUTLER YEATS (1865–1939)

Among School Children

I

I walk through the long schoolroom questioning;
A kind old nun in a white hood replies;
The children learn to cipher and to sing,
To study reading-books and history,
To cut and sew, be neat in everything   5
In the best modern way — the children's eyes
In momentary wonder stare upon
A sixty-year-old smiling public man.

II

I dream of a Ledaean body, bent
Above a sinking fire, a tale that she   10
Told of a harsh reproof, or trivial event
That changed some childish day to tragedy —
Told, and it seemed that our two natures blent
Into a sphere from youthful sympathy,
Or else, to alter Plato's parable,   15
Into the yolk and white of the one shell.

III

And thinking of that fit of grief or rage
I look upon one child or t'other there
And wonder if she stood so at that age —
For even daughters of the swan can share   20
Something of every paddler's heritage —
And had that color upon cheek or hair,
And thereupon my heart is driven wild:
She stands before me as a living child.

IV

Her present image floats into the mind —   25
Did Quattrocento° finger fashion it   *fifteenth century*
Hollow of cheek as though it drank the wind   *Italian artist's*
And took a mess of shadows for its meat?
And I though never of Ledaean kind
Had pretty plumage once — enough of that,   30
Better to smile on all that smile, and show
There is a comfortable kind of old scarecrow.

V

What youthful mother, a shape upon her lap
Honey of generation had betrayed,

374

And that must sleep, shriek, struggle to escape   35
As recollection or the drug decide,
Would think her son, did she but see that shape
With sixty or more winters on its head,
A compensation for the pang of his birth,
Or the uncertainty of his setting forth?   40

VI

Plato thought nature but a spume that plays
Upon a ghostly paradigm° of things;   *pattern*
Solider Aristotle played the taws°   *beat with a strap*
Upon the bottom of a king of kings;
World-famous golden-thighed Pythagoras   45
Fingered upon a fiddle-stick or strings
What a star sang and careless Muses heard:
Old clothes upon old sticks to scare a bird.

VII

Both nuns and mothers worship images,
But those the candles light are not as those   50
That animate a mother's reveries,
But keep a marble or a bronze repose.
And yet they too break hearts — O Presences
That passion, piety or affection knows,
And that all heavenly glory symbolize —   55
O self-born mockers of man's enterprise;

VIII

Labor is blossoming or dancing where
The body is not bruised to pleasure soul,
Nor beauty born out of its own despair,
Nor blear-eyed wisdom out of midnight oil.   60
O chestnut tree, great rooted blossomer,
Are you the leaf, the blossom or the bole?
O body swayed to music, O brightening glance,
How can we know the dancer from the dance?

Among School Children. 8. *public man:* Yeats at the time was an Irish
senator. 9. *Ledaean body:* See "Leda and the Swan," p. 205. Perhaps
Maud Gonne, whom Yeats for years had loved hopelessly. 15. *Plato's
parable:* A speaker in Plato's *Symposium* suggests that the sexes may have
been created when a single being was cut in two (like a hard-boiled egg),
the halves becoming woman and man. 44. *king of kings:* Alexander the
Great. Aristotle was his schoolmaster. 45. *golden-thighed Pythagoras:*
Greek philosopher who taught that the stars and planets, circling in harmonious orbits, make musical sounds. According to legend, he was so
handsome that when undressing he had been seen to have a thigh of
gold.

375

WILLIAM BUTLER YEATS (1865–1939)

Long-Legged Fly

That civilization may not sink,
Its great battle lost,
Quiet the dog, tether the pony
To a distant post;
Our master Caesar is in the tent   5
Where the maps are spread,
His eyes fixed upon nothing,
A hand under his head.
Like a long-legged fly upon the stream
His mind moves upon silence.   10

That the topless towers be burnt
And men recall that face,
Move most gently if move you must
In this lonely place.
She thinks, part woman, three parts a child,   15
That nobody looks; her feet
Practice a tinker shuffle
Picked up on a street.
Like a long-legged fly upon the stream
Her mind moves upon silence.   20

That girls at puberty may find
The first Adam in their thought,
Shut the door of the Pope's chapel,
Keep those children out.
There on that scaffolding reclines   25
Michael Angelo.
With no more sound than the mice make
His hand moves to and fro.
Like a long-legged fly upon the stream
His mind moves upon silence.   30

Long-Legged Fly. This "fly" is the fresh-water insect also known as the
water strider. 11. *topless towers:* of Troy, burned by the Greeks. Yeats
echoes the description of Helen of Troy (whose abduction started the
war) given in Christopher Marlowe's play *The Tragical History of Dr.
Faustus:* "Was this the face that launched a thousand ships,/And burnt
the topless towers of Ilium?" 23. *the Pope's chapel:* Michaelangelo had
to lie on his back while painting upon the ceiling of the Sistine Chapel his
frescoes showing the creation, fall, and final judgment of man.

WILLIAM BUTLER YEATS (1865–1939)

Crazy Jane Talks with the Bishop

I met the Bishop on the road
And much said he and I.
"Those breasts are flat and fallen now,
Those veins must soon be dry;
Live in a heavenly mansion,   5
Not in some foul sty."

"Fair and foul are near of kin,
And fair needs foul," I cried.
"My friends are gone, but that's a truth
Nor° grave nor bed denied,   *neither*   10
Learned in bodily lowliness
And in the heart's pride.

"A woman can be proud and stiff
When on love intent;
But Love has pitched his mansion in   15
The place of excrement;
For nothing can be sole or whole
That has not been rent."

The Magi

Now as at all times I can see in the mind's eye,
In their stiff, painted clothes, the pale unsatisfied ones
Appear and disappear in the blue depth of the sky
With all their ancient faces like rain-beaten stones,
And all their helms of silver hovering side by side,   5
And all their eyes still fixed, hoping to find once more,
Being by Calvary's turbulence unsatisfied,
The uncontrollable mystery on the bestial floor.

INDEX OF AUTHORS, TITLES, AND FIRST LINES

Names of authors of poems appear in CAPITALS; titles of poems, in *italics*. When the title and the opening words of a poem are the same, the poem is indexed only by its first line. A further discussion of a poem is indicated by an italic page number.

379

380

383

or

```
or or o r or
ro ro roro
or or oror
ro ro roro
orororor
```

INDEX OF TERMS

393